of trial, committed to embodying God's vision and enduring life's crises with courage and integrity.

Bruce G. Epperly, Ph.D.
Pastor, Lecturer, and author of *Finding God in Suffering: A Journey with Job* and many other books

Short of providing an introduction to the New Testament, Weiss draws attention to it from an apocalyptic perspective, pointing out the dynamics of a timeless appeal. Elegantly written and replete with original insights, each chapter constitutes a gateway into the next, underscoring the enduring relevance of the biblical books linked by a common theme. Readers will soon discover that the end of the scroll is but its beginning, or that of another inspired by it.

Abraham Terian, Th.D.
Emeritus Professor of Armenian Patristics
St. Nersess Armenian Seminary

Praise for *The End of the Scroll*

Herold Weiss' *The End of the Scroll* offers non-specialists a highly readable and impeccably researched study of biblical apocalyptic literature. Drawing on a lifetime of scholarly immersion in biblical literature, Weiss traces the history of apocalyptic thought, its rise in ancient Israel and its endurance over centuries among Jews and Christians of antiquity. Biblical writers recycled the counsel of their predecessors by refashioning the old to meet the new in response to tragic human conditions in their own time. Weiss's account of these ancient reinterpretations moves through the biblical books from Israelite prophets to the Book of Revelation, rewarding the reader again and again with illuminating insights. He also provides a very helpful analysis of the use of biblical apocalyptic texts by subsequent generations, from scholars in Renaissance Rome to twenty-first century evangelical interpretations of the signs of the times. In almost every case, these later interpreters have misunderstood the intent of biblical apocalyptic thinking by assuming that its purpose was to predict the future. The ancient apocalypticists, Weiss argues, were not invested in predictions. They described their hopes for God's future in order to encourage the faithful in the present, not to foster obsession with timetables. Weiss invites his readers to recover this original intent of the biblical apocalyptic imagination by using their own imaginations to encourage faithful living in the present. Any student of biblical literature who is interested in the historical development of apocalyptic and its interpretation will be richly rewarded by this book.

Charles H. Cosgrove, Ph.D.
Professor of Early Christian Literature
Garrett Evangelical Theological Seminary

For the pastor who wants to bring clarity to the confusion that accompanies the hysteria promoted by those who act as harbingers of the "Last Days," this book will come as a welcome relief. Dr.

Weiss puts apocalyptic in its historical context, not as a map to the future, but as a call to faithfulness for its audience during their times of distress. Weiss also traces the many failures of attempting to bring the apocalyptic messages into the present. In the process, the books of the Old and New Testaments will no longer be useful for "end of days" fodder. Apocalyptic then becomes a friend of today by encouraging faithful living now after the manner of the sages of old.

Rev. Steven F. Kindle, Faith on the Edge Podcast
Retired United Church of Christ Pastor

Herold Weiss is a steady and insightful guide into the sometimes puzzling world of Jewish and Christian apocalyptic literature. He is remarkable in his ability to make complex ideas accessible, to explain how texts work, and to show both how and why the tradition develops and changes over time. Given the importance of apocalyptic thinking in the development of the Christian tradition and its enduring influence, this book ought to be required reading.

Rubén R. Dupertuis, Ph.D.
Associate Professor of Religion and Chair
Department of Religion, Trinity University

Herold Weiss' End of the Scroll is a tour de force of biblical and extra-canonical scholarship on the apocalypse. I found Weiss' text lively and captivating in its depth and relevance to our current national and global crises. This book is solid scholarship and yet accessible to educated laypersons as well as to pastors and academics. While primarily focusing on scripture, Weiss also connects the apocalyptic literature of scripture with the current popular interest in apocalyptic and end times theology. Weiss reminds us that apocalyptic imagery involves much more than charting the end of the world, but summons persons to live faithfully amid the challenges of their time. Apocalyptic inspires us to trust God's future in times

THE END OF THE SCROLL:

BIBLICAL APOCALYPTIC TRAJECTORIES

HEROLD WEISS

Energion Publications
Gonzalez, Florida
2020

Copyright © 2020 Herold Weiss

Unless otherwise noted, all Scripture quotations are from the Revised Standard Version of the Bible, copyright 1952 [2nd edition, 1971] by the Division of Christian Education of the National Council of the Churches of Christ in the United States of America. Used by permission. All rights reserved.

ISBN: 978-1-63199-494-4
eISBN: 978-1-63199-495-1
Library of Congress Control Number: 2020938891

Energion Publications
PO Box 841
Gonzalez, FL 32560

https://energion.com
pubs@energion.com

Dedicated

to

The many excellent students

it has been my privilege to teach

in institutions of higher learning

Table of Contents

	Preface	vii
	Introduction to Apocalyptic Literature	1
1	The Dawn of Biblical Apocalypticism	31
2	Daniel	69
3	The Letters of Paul	99
4	To the Hebrews	133
5	The Synoptic Gospels	161
6	The Gospel of Mark	167
7	The Gospel of Matthew	195
8	The Gospel of Luke	219
9	To the Thessalonians II	239
10	Revelation	251
11	First Peter, Jude, and Second Peter	291
12	The End of the Scroll	323

Preface

In our culture, one of the best ways to understand things is by searching for their origin, or by establishing the function of each of its parts. In this book I follow these paths in search of the purpose that informed the writers and the editors of biblical apocalyptic texts. Anyone reading these texts soon finds out that many of the things they say have been unconfirmed by history. It is also well known that they have been used to lead people to do things that had tragic outcomes. These facts are so well known that they need no demonstration. My purpose in writing this book is to investigate their origin and to establish why in the face of the outcomes just mentioned they were kept for posterity by their first readers. Surely, they considered them worthy of preservation. As biblical documents, they have played a significant role in the history of Christianity, but throughout this time many Christians have been embarrassed by their presence in the canon, and have dismissed them as irrelevant, if not bizarre. My objective has been to clarify their contribution to Christian living.

Some expositors of biblical texts think that their task is to show how everything in Scripture fits together in a harmonious whole. To do this, however, they do not actually take the whole Bible into account. They select texts from different biblical books to construct a doctrine that fits their ideological presuppositions. The texts used to construct their idiosyncratic doctrinal edifices are selected according to their whims and placed according to blueprints found in their imaginations. They leave most of the blocks in the biblical quarry as eyesores on the ground with lots of debris spread about. To pretend that such constructions represent what the Bible teaches is to sell a forgery. The basic premise for the building of such structures is the claim that the Bible is its own interpreter. It allows them to hide their controlling role as architects. They say that when a text is difficult to understand it must be understood in terms of another biblical text that is clear. The characterization of a text as difficult or clear, however, is determined by whether or not they fit with what these interpreters wish to teach. This methodology ensures that what is presented as what the Bible teaches is what fits the ideology of a particular interpreter.

As a student of the Bible, I consider it essential to pay attention to what each author of the books that compose it had to say. All of them had a relevant message for their contemporaries. If an author of the Bible corrects, contradicts, elaborates or applies what a previous author of the Bible said, that is evidence of his humanity, his integrity, and his desire to effectively address a new situation. If these sorts of things are in evidence within a single biblical book, that is evidence that the editors of the text we now possess put together in the text oral traditions of different prophets. My aim has been to understand what the edited texts now in the Bible said to their first readers. I seek answers to these questions: Why were these apocalyptic written texts kept by their intended audiences? Was it because they provided them with a chronology of the future? Was it because what they predicted came to pass?

Why is it that the one thing these apocalyptic trajectories have in common is a Final Judgment?

Those who claim that God wrote or dictated the Bible usually don't take at face value what each one of the texts now in the Bible actually says. Their method, as I explained above, allows them to choose texts and make them say what they see fit. I read the books of the Bible to discover how the biblical ancestors of my faith in the Creator God expressed their faith in terms of their historical circumstances. Their inspiration did not provide them with information, but with the necessity to proclaim the Word that the world in which humans live is God's world, and life in it is a gift of God. Thus, in the various biblical books, God reveals himself as the Living God who is the source of life, even as biblical authors affirm this within the limits of their own cultural horizons.

I have written this book, in part, to demonstrate that when reading the Bible as the depository of God's Word in the twenty-first century it is not only necessary to have faith in God; it is also necessary to be a citizen of one's own culture and society, just as the authors and editors of the books in the Bible were. One cannot be a fully integrated person and ignore what modern sciences, and the technologies they have made possible, say about the universe and the inner lives of human beings. To affirm that we live in God's world while ignoring what the study of history, literature, psychology and all modern sciences have contributed to our understanding of ourselves and the universe in which we live only makes whatever one may say totally irrelevant. Just as biblical authors, writing between the tenth century B.C.E. and the second century C.E., were fully alive to their culture and society, so too those of us who believe in God must be alive to our culture and society if we intend to say something significant in the twenty-first century. It is with this end in mind that I have written this book.

This means that I have not read the apocalyptic texts found in the Bible with an apocalyptic hermeneutic because, as I argue in this book, my contemporaries no longer live in the symbolic universe in which the authors of these texts lived. Their hermeneutic was based on two presuppositions: 1) the prophets did not write for their contemporaries. They wrote for those living at the time of the end, and 2) we are living at the time of the end. I agree with the authors of apocalyptic texts in that they wrote for the benefit of their own contemporaries. But the authors of the writings they recycle for that purpose also wrote for their contemporaries. Since this is the case, I have examined their texts in their most likely chronological sequence. This becomes necessary because biblical apocalyptic authors and editors used the writings of their predecessors as a foundation on which to build their message for their own contemporaries.

In the writing of this book I have benefited from the generous help of friends and family. As it has been the case for over twenty-five years, my colleague at Saint Mary's College and good friend, Terence Martin, has read and commented on every one of the chapters of this book. Our lunches, in which we go over what one of us has been writing, have been a steady source of delight and enlightenment over the years, especially lately when both of us are enjoying retirement. Another former colleague and long-standing friend, Edward W. H. Vick, has also given me generous and wise suggestions for the improvement of early drafts. I am also indebted to Christopher Eyre, of Energion Publications, for the professional editing of my manuscript. The dedication expresses my belief that in university classrooms the one who learns the most is the teacher.

Introduction to Apocalyptic Literature

The apocalyptic literature of the Bible has been seen as both the most important element within it, to be given singular attention as the key to a successful Christian life, or as a source of embarrassment that is better ignored. These opposing attitudes toward apocalypticism within Christianity have been a constant feature of its history. It would be possible to write a history of Christianity with the contrasting views of the value of apocalyptic literature as its organizing principle. My purpose in this book is to take a serious look at the apocalyptic texts found in the Bible in order to establish why they were written and what they were concerned with at the time of writing. I will pursue this objective by asking: 1) for whom were they written? 2) What is the issue they are concerned with? And 3) within which symbolic universe does their message make sense? My task is to reconstruct as much as possible their historical context. The ancient Hebrews, the post-exilic Jews and the early Christians went through traumatic experiences of national defeat, exile, denials of national independence and significant changes in the cultural and religious milieu in which they lived. It was within these circumstances that the authors of these texts wrote. All these factors need to be taken into account before one can make any sense of these texts in the twenty-first century.

The Bible contains full blown apocalyptic books, like Daniel and Revelation, books that contain apocalyptic chapters which don't fit comfortably within them, and books that while belonging to a different category work up themes that eventually became characteristic of the apocalyptic perspective. Since the biblical apocalyptic perspective developed as a descendant of the prophetic tradition in Israel, in this book I will first establish the nature of the prophetic tradition. Then I will explore how the apocalyptic perspective developed within the prophetic and other traditions. After that, I will analyze the major apocalyptic texts in the Bible. Finally, I will draw some conclusions and make some practical suggestions as to the relevance of the apocalyptic perspective in the twenty-first century. For full disclosure, I am using the labels "prophetic" and "apocalyptic" as heuristic devices that help in the analysis of these texts. No author of one of these books understood himself as an apocalyptic author. These labels are modern tools of analysis with which to contrast and compare different points of view. Characteristics of one or the other of these labels may be found in books classified in the other group.

THE FUNCTION OF PROPHECY IN ISRAEL

The apocalyptic authors of the Old Testament were descendants of the prophets. Both aimed at quite similar objectives. It is a misunderstanding, however, to think that their basic objective was to forecast the future. The prophets' primary interest was to interpret the present, call for a change of direction in the lives of the people of Israel and advise them on what needed to be done at the moment. That they are known as prophets does not say that they foretold what would happen in the future, but that they spoke on behalf of another. The word "prophet" is composed of two Greek words: *pro* and *phemi*. The preposition pro may mean either "to anticipate" or "to take the place of." Thus, in English we have the word prophylactic (to anticipate an infection), propensity (to anticipate liking) and proscribe (to anticipate writing). We also have the word proselyte (an alien who is in), prosthesis (taking the place of a missing part), and protestant (one who testifies against, or for another). Phemi means "to say," "to affirm." The prophets spoke for another, for the Lord. Doing this, they were not "fore-telling," but "telling for," standing for, in place of the Lord. Through them the Lord was telling the Israelites how he viewed their present course of action, describing what the future held if they continued in their present course, and advising them to change course.

This definition of a prophet was still in use in early Christian times. The apostle Paul points out that different members of the church have been given different gifts and identifies "prophecy" among them (1 Cor. 12:10). He also gives a list of the roles God has established for the proper functioning of the church. He lists "prophets" after "apostles" and before "teachers" (1 Cor. 12:28). As Paul describes them, the prophets were the ones who spoke a "Word of the Lord." We would call them "preachers." In antiquity, the Word of the Lord was understood to be oral, even after its later compilation in books by editors. With some significant differences demanded by the circumstances, the apocalyptic writers did the same three things the prophets had been doing. It is in this discrete sense that the apocalypticists are to be thought of as descendants of the prophets. They also were analyzing the present and concerned to recommend a course of action.

In the process of analyzing what was taking place from the divine perspective, the prophets revealed a God who is not primarily attached to natural phenomena in their yearly cycles, but a God who has been actively involved in bringing the people out of a troubled past is taking notice of what they are doing in the present and has control over their future. The prophets examined the life of the people in its historical setting. According to them, Yahveh is the Lord who has been guiding the people of Israel as they have advanced toward their present unparalleled and unexpected prosperity. Human affairs are not bound to the natural cyclical return to the beginning. Human activity is significant when it does something new, something different. Human beings do not promote well-being and prosperity by faithfully celebrating feasts that keep them attuned with the turning of the seasons and promote the reception of the bounties of nature. The prophets insisted that shalom, health, well-being, prosperity, peace, was a gift of Yahveh, the Lord of time. They released time from the circle of yearly repetitions and cast it on a time-line that came from the past and reached forward to an open future. This gave the present significance not because of its correspondence with a primordial divine action or a particular natural phenomenon that demanded the performance of a specified ritual, but because it gave human beings the opportunity to collaborate with God in the formulation of the future. In Israel, feasts which had been celebrations of transitions in the course of natural events, under their new cosmology became celebrations that had to do with particular historical events.

The prophets admonished the people to remember how God had blessed them in their past history, and that they had entered into a covenant agreement with Yahveh. This made it necessary to live according to *chesed*, covenant loyalty. Having entered into a covenant with Yahveh, the people were now Yahveh's bride. The understanding that their connection to their God was not in nature, but in the way in which they lived in obedience to covenant stipulations set the Israelites in a peculiar trajectory. Rather than depending on the performance of religious rituals for security and prosperity, they were to depend on Yahveh' guidance for security and prosperity. This required a particular way of living at all times, not just at festival time. God's demands have primarily to do with life in society. God's retributive justice is applied in reference to one's relationships with others and one's commitment to God. Since God had elected Abraham and his descendants as his people, they were now Yahveh's bride. Any deviation from their commitment to their husband was denounced by the prophets as harlotry. To their chagrin, the prophets found pervasive evidence of Israel's deviations from its covenant commitments. Therefore, God aimed to punish Israel severely. If the people continued in their present course of action, God's judgment would be their historical downfall. On the other hand, if they turned away from their evil ways and became loyal to the God of the covenant, God would reward them with security and prosperity.

THE ORIGINS OF PROPHECY

The prophets whose writings we possess were not the only ones giving advice to the people. In Israel there were sorcerers, diviners, augurs, soothsayers, necromancers and witches. The Old Testament contains repeated warnings against consulting them or paying attention to their pronouncements. There were also "seers" who were also called "men of the spirit," and later came to be called "prophets" (1 Sam. 9:10). When Saul encountered a group of them he was also empowered by the spirit, which gave rise to the saying "Is Saul also among the prophets?" (1 Sam. 10:12). In time, the old schools of the prophets produced professional prophets who were attached to the temple and were servants of the king. They spoke what the king wanted to hear. By contrast, the prophets whose oracles are now found in the Bible were for the most part the ones who stood against those in power who were abusing the weak among them: the widow, the orphan, the day laborer, the poor.

In the canon of the Hebrew Bible one section is designated as the Former Prophets and another as the Latter Prophets. What according to this nomenclature is designated as the Former Prophets are books that we consider narratives (1 and 2 Samuel, 1 and 2 Kings). The Latter Prophets section of the Hebrew canon contains the books which have collections of the sayings of prophets, which we call now the prophetic books. The first of the "former prophets" in Israel is Samuel who was also a judge. He marks the transition from the leadership of the judges, who were endowed by the spirit to become military leaders charged to deliver the people from the oppression of neighboring chieftains, and the kings, who gave the people security with a standing army and royal prestige. This was a major shift in the history of Israel, and left scars that brought about the future division of the nation under two competing kingdoms. It was the transition from charismatic to institutional leadership. The endowment of the Spirit on the judges had been for the accomplishment of a specific task. Once the task had been accomplished, judges returned to their normal life. That is, their spiritual endowment had been temporary.

The establishment of a king, with hereditary rights of succession, institutionalized the power of the Spirit; its flow was thought to have been restricted to official channels. There are two contradictory narratives about Samuel's participation in the establishment of the monarchy, evidence of the controversy that characterized its establishment. The institutionalization of the Spirit was strongly resisted by many. According to one account, the people asked for a king because they did not wish to have one of the sons of Samuel as their judge. Faced by this request, God advised Samuel to comply, and identified Saul as the one to be anointed king (1 Sam. 8-11). In this account, God is behind the introduction of kingship, and Samuel, the prophet, is following God's directive when he anoints the first king. According to the other narrative, the people asked for a king because they were being threatened by Nahash, the king of the Ammonites. God was displeased by this request, and Samuel felt duty-bound to warn the people of the consequences of their request. Loyalty to a king would become a competitor to their obedience to God (1 Sam. 12). According to this account, the people did not trust God's ability to provide protection from foreign attacks, and God took their request for a king as an offense against him. Obviously, not everyone in Israel was happy with the crowning of what proved to be despotic kings. These stories also reflect on the role of the prophet. According to one, he is a loyal servant of the king who is a servant of God. According to the other, the prophet stands in opposition to the king who has been enthroned as a reluctant concession on the part of God.

THE PROPHETS AS ADVISERS OR ACCUSERS OF THOSE IN POWER

The prophets we know for their activities in the narratives of the books of Samuel and Kings were concerned with matters having to do with kingship, dynastic stability, foreign policy and military activity. Elisha, in particular, exemplifies these roles. Nathan was a prophet attached to the royal household who gave David the message that, while Yahveh did not wish him to build the house of God in Jerusalem, Yahveh would establish his "house" (dynasty) forever (2 Sam. 7:14-29). This promise was the foundation of all future expectation of a Messiah, the One Anointed by the Lord. Nathan also determined the dynastic line and made sure that Solomon, rather than Adonijah, became the successor to King David (1 Kg. 1:5-53). It is somewhat of a surprise to read that Nathan also charged King David with the murder of Uriah, Bathsheba's husband, and told David what would be God's punishment for his crime (2 Sam. 12:1-25). This story, however, ends by telling that on account of this intervention God loved Nathan and changed his name to Jedidiah. It is somewhat difficult to see how Nathan was both a promoter of the Davidic dynasty and an accuser of King David. Maybe the Nathan who provided the divine stamp on the Davidic dynasty is not the same as the person who charged David with a crime and came to be known as Jedidiah. Elijah the Tishbite, who stood against King Ahab and his worship of Baal, acted like Jedidiah (1 Kg. 17:1; 18:1-19). So also did Huldah, the wife of Shallum. She confirmed the judgment of God against Judah. Because of King Josiah's repentance before God, however, she declared that God would postpone the downfall of Jerusalem until another king came to power (2 Kg. 22:14-20, 2 Chr. 34:22-28).

The prophets whose oracles were preserved in books were protestants who testified for the Lord against those in power. They stood against wayward kings, hired prophets, corrupt priests and greedy nobles. Amos was the first of these prophets, or Latter Prophets according to the Hebrew canon. He stood in defiance to the authority of Amaziah, the priest of the temple at Bethel and the king he served. At the time of Jeroboam II (786-746 B.C.E.), the kingdom of Israel was enjoying its largest territorial expansion and great economic prosperity (Am. 7:10-17). Being a shepherd from Tekoa, in the southern kingdom of Judah, Amos had the temerity to prophesy against Jeroboam at the royal sanctuary at Bethel, the northern competitor to the temple in Jerusalem. His message exposed the injustices done by the prosperous and flamboyant princes who thought themselves blessed because of their generosity with the sacrifices of bulls and heifers at the temple. Amos pointed out to them that their ritual displays at the altar did not cover up their abuses of the poor, their greed and their trust in their own piety. Being descendants of Jacob, they considered themselves the elect of Yahveh who were destined to even greater prosperity. They had the idea, its origin is obscure, that on the Day of the Lord, when God would personally enter history, they would be able to celebrate with much rejoicing as they would achieve the pinnacle of national glory and untold fame. Amos announced to them, to the contrary, that on account of their way of life, their expectations were totally unfounded. He told them, *"Woe to you who desire the day of the Lord! It is darkness, and not light; as if a man fled from a lion, and a bear met him; or went into the house and leaned with his hand against the wall, and a serpent bit him. Is not the day of the Lord darkness, and not light, and gloom with no brightness in it?"* (Am. 5:18-20). Amos' aim was not to prognosticate the future. It was to call for a change of behavior that would cause their dark future not to be. The constant advice of the prophetic messages in the tradition of Amos was *shub*, turn, return, change course, repent. Amos' message was quite negative because God's ways were not being followed. His intention, however, was to cause them to change their unjust ways so that they could continue to live in the land in security and peace.

Hosea, who prophesied in the northern kingdom a few years later, also gave a negative appraisal of the way in which the Israelites were living. After charging the people with harlotry (Hos. 4:13-15) and other sins, Hosea announced, *"The days of punishment have come, the days of recompense have come; Israel shall know it.... They have deeply corrupted themselves as in the days of Gibeah; he will remember their iniquity, he will punish their sins"* (Hos. 9:7-9). His description of God's punishments is disturbing, "Samaria shall bear her guilt, because she has rebelled against her God; they shall fall by the sword, their little ones shall be dashed in pieces, and their pregnant women ripped open" (Hos. 13:16). If life in Samaria, the capital of the northern kingdom of Israel, continued in its present course, Hosea predicted a future that today rings as one devised by a sadistic torturer. He, however, balanced his indictments with calls to repentance, *"Return, O Israel, to the Lord your God, for you have stumbled because of your iniquity. Take with you words and return to the Lord, say to him, 'Take away all iniquity'.... They shall return and dwell beneath my shadow, they shall flourish as a garden; they shall blossom as the vine, their fragrance shall be like the wine of Lebanon"* (Hos. 14:1-2, 7). Hosea reports God saying *"I will heal their faithlessness; I will love them freely"* (Hos. 14:4); *"How can I give you up, O Ephraim! How can I hand you over, O Israel! ... My heart recoils within me, my compassion grows warm and tender. I will not execute my fierce anger"* (Hos. 11:8-9). The contrast between the two possible futures could not be more pronounced: the sadist killer against the romantic lover. The early prophets aimed at causing the people to take seriously the present and live according to their commitments to Yahveh. For them, the future was still open. God could change his mind and not execute the dire judgments their present conduct called for. While Amos is unique in his concentration on the coming doom that will punish a sinful people, all the other prophets, starting with Hosea, balance their announcements of doom with demonstrations of God's loving commitment to his people.

PROPHETIC ADJUSTMENTS TO NEW CIRCUMSTANCES

The prophets active in the southern kingdom of Judah just prior to the destruction of Jerusalem and afterwards during the Exile in Babylon, Isaiah, Jeremiah and Ezekiel (630-570 B.C.E.), found the situation untenable and lamented the extreme corruption taking place at the palace and the temple. They could do no other but announce the downfall of the city and the temple due to the total disregard for the God of the covenant. Their idolatry had no bounds. Yahveh is a jealous God of justice, and retributive justice would take its course.

Jeremiah and Ezekiel, however, realized that the retributive justice of God needed to be adjusted to a new understanding of the self. They recognized that the traditional understanding of the self as a member of a family, or tribe, does not make sense to those who saw themselves as individual persons. The notion that the exiles were suffering on account of the sins of ancestors who had been idol-worshipers in Jerusalem was no longer reasonable. Both Jeremiah and Ezekiel refer to a proverb that was used to justify suffering as punishment for sins committed by ancestors. It said, *"The fathers have eaten sour grapes and the children's teeth are set on edge"* (Jer. 31:29; Ez. 18:2). According to these prophets, justice does not operate this way any longer. They proclaimed instead, *"the soul that sins shall die"* (Ez. 18:4) or *"each man who eats sour grapes, his teeth shall be set on edge"* (Jer. 31:30). The individualization of responsibility for one's actions was a major shift in the Israelite understanding of justice.

Until then it was perfectly reasonable to punish a whole clan for the crime of one of its members. The story of the conquest of Jericho, tells that Achan *"took some of the devoted things; and the anger of the Lord burned against the people of Israel"* (Jos. 7:1). The story ends with the resolution of the problem created by the fateful deed. *"And Joshua and all Israel with him took Achan the son of Zerah, and the silver and the mantle and the bar of gold, and his sons and daughters, and his oxen and asses and sheep and his tent, and all that he had; and they brought them up to the Valley of Achor. And Joshua said, 'Why did you bring trouble on us? The Lord brings trouble on you today.' And all Israel stoned him with stones; they burned them with fire, and stoned them with stones. And they raised over him a great heap of stones that remains to this day; then the Lord turned from his burning anger"* (Jos. 7:24-26). At that time it apparently seemed quite reasonable for God to be angry with all the people of Israel and cause their defeat at Ai as punishment for the transgression of one man. To solve the problem that had affected all the people of

Israel, the people did not execute just Achan, but Achan, his sons and his daughters. Besides, all his possessions were burned. That God's justice works on the basis of tribal identity is in evidence throughout the history of Israel up to the Exile. What Jeremiah and Ezekiel proclaimed was that the way in which God's justice had been working in the past was no longer to be. From now on, punishment would only affect the guilty perpetrator.

Among the features that contributed to the dawn of an apocalyptic perspective during and following the Exile, this shift in the identification of a person from one who is a member of a tribe to one who is a single individual is crucial. This is the transition from corporate to individual identity. Jeremiah and Ezekiel proclaimed this new vision of how Yahveh's justice works to disallow the excuse being given by the exiles who blamed their fathers rather than themselves for their sufferings in Exile. The prophets told them that because they did not turn away from the evil ways of their fathers they were responsible for their own suffering. This transition, of course, reflects a new understanding of the value of an individual. It became logical to understand that God's justice works on the basis of individual responsibility because of the influence of the Greek philosophers who established a new vision of the person. In Greece, it had brought about the rejection of autocrats and the establishment of the right of each individual citizen to vote for the election of rulers. In Israel, where history had become the arena of God's activity, the arrival of individual identity brought about a new understanding of God's justice.

The basic theological proposition supporting the reaffirmation of the Law in Deuteronomy is that God is the God of retributive justice. The book contains three discourses given by Moses at the gates of the Promised Land interpreting God's words at Sinai. By the time Deuteronomy was written and "found" at the temple (2 Kg. 22:3-8) to become the basis for the reforms of King Josiah (621 B.C.E.), Moses was considered the greatest of the prophets on the basis of his having been the One who spoke for God. It was written as Moses' "testament;" as a warning to the future which they would face after his imminent death. In the book, Moses functions in a new role. He interprets the word the Lord had given in the past, rather than proclaiming a new word for the present. *"If you obey the voice of the Lord your God, being careful to do all his commandments which I command you this day, the Lord your God will set you high above all the nations of the earth. And all these blessings shall come upon you and overtake you, if you obey the voice of the Lord your God ... Blessed shall you be in the city, and blessed shall you be in the field ... The Lord will establish you as a people holy to himself ... And the Lord will make you abound in prosperity ... And the Lord will make you the head, and not the tail; and you shall tend upwards only, and not downward .... But if you will not obey the voice of the Lord your God or be careful to do all his commandments and his statutes which I command you this day, then all these curses shall come upon you and overtake you. Cursed shall you be in the city, and cursed shall you be in the field ... Cursed shall be the fruit of your body, and the fruit of your ground ... Cursed shall you be when you come in, and cursed shall you be when you go out. The Lord will send upon you curses, confusion, and frustrations in all that you undertake to do until you are destroyed and perish quickly .... And as the Lord took delight in doing you good and multiplying you, so the Lord will take delight in bringing ruin upon you and destroying you .... "* (Dt. 28:1-68). This very explicit advice to obey the Lord, and the even greater detailing of the consequences of disobedience, sets up retributive justice as the Lord's way of dealing with the people of Israel. But when personal individual experience proved that this type of justice was not working, it brought about a major theological crisis. It became necessary to justify the ways of an Almighty God, something quite unnecessary when the present sufferings were understood to be caused by the sins of ancestors.

The end of the Exile did not mean the restoration of the Kingdom of Judah. Most of the descendants of the Hebrews who had been exiled to Babylon had become established in their new home and decided to stay in Mesopotamia. In Palestine there were remnants of the people who had been defeated by the Assyrians

The End of the Scroll

in 722 B.C.E., now known as Samaritans, or people of Samaria. The Jews who decided to settle in Judah were now subjects of the Persian satrap of the region. They did not establish an independent kingdom. Under these circumstances, prophecy could not fulfill its traditional role as the Word of the Lord defending the weak against the abuses of the powerful, or as the adviser of kings in matters of diplomacy and war. Under Persian rule the priests and a new class, the scribes, came to positions of prominence, as demonstrated by Ezra and Nehemiah. Kings and princes were no longer in power over the people.

Also to be noticed is that the compilation of the Pentateuch, beginning just before and during the Exile, gave the people "the Scriptures." At the same time, the oracles of the prophets were being compiled into books by anonymous editors. Guidance as to how to live under conditions different from the ones in which they had lived before the destruction of Jerusalem and its temple was to be gained by the study and interpretation of "the Torah" (That which has been said and taught authoritatively). The scribes who interpreted the Scriptures took the place of the prophets who spoke the Word of the Lord. The shift from an oral Word of the Lord to a written word that needs interpretation for its reapplication was another major shift in the religious life of the Israelites. The Pentateuch became the Scriptures studied and interpreted by the scribes. Traditional prophecy was now preserved in books; therefore, it came to an end. Besides, the construction of a new temple in Jerusalem (520–515 B.C.E.) gave the priests a new base of operations. A high priest, rather than a king, was the local leader of the people. The Jewish governor was a servant of the Persian satrap. Expectations for a full restoration of life under a royal figure enjoying all the blessings that God had promised them, therefore, were ever-present. These expectations, however, were not being fulfilled. Nathan's promise that a descendant of David would be seated on a throne in Jerusalem forever (2 Sam. 7:11, 16), or Moses' promise of a prophet *"like me"* (Dt. 18:15), were spelled out in different versions of the role of the Messiah, the Lord's Anointed. It became the task of scribes to formulate how the promises of the Scripture would come to pass, and to tell the people how to obey the will of God while living under circumstances quite different from the ones in which their ancestors had lived both as sojourners in the desert and as farmers or merchants dependent on the military protection of judges or kings. The written law envisioned circumstances that no longer existed.

The expansion of Greek culture after Persia took its armies into Europe and later Alexander the Great took his to Mesopotamia and India brought with it a new cosmopolitan class with broader horizons. The exile of the Jews in Babylon had put them in touch with another vibrant culture and its religious manifestations. There they had learned the views of Zoroaster. Among them, his dualistic understanding of the human predicament as life in the midst of cosmic forces of good and evil. Traditional stories of creation had told how the gods who created the present world had to conquer evil gods. In other words, a chaotic situation under the rule of evil powers had to be dismantled before cosmos could be established. In the case of the *Enuma Elish,* the Babylonian creation myth, Marduk had defeated Tiamat, the Deep Sea, and used her body to build the cosmos. The armies of the defeated god or goddess, however, may still be about enticing human beings to do evil. This means that human beings live subject to external forces which try to control their behavior.

This is something unknown to the prophets of Israel. According to them, evil impulses acting in the heart of human beings are somewhat of a puzzle. Human beings have the power to decide whether to obey God or to worship idols. Even though the Psalms, for example, admit the existence of the council of the gods, and Yahveh is exalted above all the other members of the council of the gods, the Psalms, Proverbs, and the prophets do not know of supernatural beings who are engaged in causing human beings to disobey God, or to worship Baal, Astarte, Ammon or Tammuz. Jeremiah, the most introspective of the prophets, wonders about the fact that human beings lack *chesed,* covenant loyalty. Loyalty to their God should be natural in them, but it is not. He asked, *"Can the Ethiopian change his skin or the leopard his spots?"* The answer, of course, is no. If it were possible for them to do it, *"then also you can do good who are accustomed to do evil"* (Jer. 13:23). For Jeremiah, evil is a problem that resides inside human beings. It causes them to develop bad habits. Observing what is true in the case of migratory birds, Jeremiah laments that what is true with other animals in the natural world is not true with human beings. *"Even the stork in the heavens knows her times; and the turtledove, swallow, and crane keep the time of their coming; but my people know not the ordinance of the Lord"* (Jer. 8:7). A mechanism that works in birds and keeps them on course does not work in men and women who constantly deviate from their commitments. Jeremiah makes this point again with another rhetorical question and a metaphor also taken from nature, *"Do the mountain waters run dry, the cold flowing streams? But my people have forgotten me"* (Jer. 18:14-15). Mountain snows keep melting into streams year-round; they never run dry. This time, what is not the case in nature is the case among God's people. That people forget their God is a puzzle, especially after each individual has sole responsibility for his/her actions. For the prophets, the Israelites' forgetfulness, lack of loyalty, rebellion against God are a puzzle. Such behaviors do not make sense. They do not envision evil supernatural forces at work causing human beings to be disloyal to the covenant with their God.

CONTRASTS BETWEEN PROPHETIC AND APOCALYPTIC TEXTS

Several factors came together to give rise to the apocalyptic perspective. Like prophecy, it was not a peculiar phenomenon to the Israelites, or the Jews. Apocalyptic literature is known from all the surrounding nations in antiquity, and most students of apocalyptic texts are concerned with the exploration of their features in different cultural situations. These studies come to different conclusions as to the distinctive features all apocalypses have in common.

Among the most prominent are an emphasis on a final judgment, the revival of the language of creation stories and a predetermined understanding of history. The classification of apocalyptic and prophetic texts according to characteristics has been difficult; therefore, my use of characteristics in order to contrast apocalyptic and prophetic texts is purely heuristic.

As stated already, the apocalypticists were the descendants of the prophets, but they faced a problem which the prophets did not encounter. That Yahveh is a God of justice who rewards the righteous and punishes the wicked was an observable truism for the prophets who worked within a corporate personality understanding of identity. The apocalypticists had to find a way to affirm God's retributive justice within the new understanding of the self as an individual person. To affirm that an almighty God deals with his creatures according to retributive justice became problematic when it was disproved by personal experience. Confronted with the suffering of a righteous person, it became difficult to argue that God is both almighty and just. It was primarily to solve this theological problem that apocalypticism arose among the Jews. Biblical apocalyptic literature, the only one with which I am concerned, differs in several significant ways from the prophetic literature of Israel because due to changes in their historical existence and direct contacts with other more developed societies made it necessary to give an account for the suffering of the righteous. The prophets working within a symbolic universe with a corporate understanding of human identity could assume that God's retributive justice is at work.

Since in our civilization we are conditioned to think that the best way to understand something is to describe its historical development, some time ago it became almost axiomatic to see apocalyptic texts as the answers to unfulfilled prophecies. That is, Hebrew eschatology evolved this way because, as noticed above, the expectations of the re-establishment of the Davidic dynasty after the exile were not fulfilled. This linear explanation of the rise of apocalyptic texts overlooks the tensions existing between different traditions running within the people of Israel. Cultic, royal/military and wisdom traditions did not come to a satisfactory synthesis either before or after the exile. Different prophets had different allegiances and described different scenarios. As said above, they actually desired that their announcements of the coming doom would not actually take place.

The apocalyptic authors were dealing with a new, different situation because God's judgment of his people had taken place at the Exile. Their agenda was to interpret the present for people who were in Exile, or were ruled by foreigners while living in their land. They were not addressing a people who enjoyed political and military stability and prosperity by abusing the weak among them. It was not that the prophecies of the prophets were unfulfilled, but that the present conditions were totally different from the ones in which their fathers lived. Thus, while the prophets pleaded for a change of course so that the coming punishment could be avoided, and the future could be the establishment of a restructured, purified present, the authors of apocalypses foretold a future that would break into the present and destroy it. For them, the future could not be a continuation of the present, not even a purified one. The difference in their perceptions of the future was caused by their different evaluations of the nature of history. Both the prophets and the authors of apocalypses had a negative view of the present. The prophets thought that the present could be salvaged because they understood that the future was open. If the people repented, God could change his mind. If they experienced suffering, it had been caused by the sins of their fathers. The apocalypticists could not see a happy future coming out of a chaotic present; conceived as chaotic especially from the perspective of individual identity. According to them, the present had no future because their suffering made no sense.

Like the prophets, the apocalypticists understood the connection between human beings and their God to be in history, but unlike the prophets the apocalypticists understood that the future was predetermined rather than open. According to the prophets, the Israelites needed to reconsider their course of action. If they continued as they were going, the future was bleak, but if they changed course and turned to the Lord, God was more than willing, in fact he was anxious, to relent from his anger and "love them deeply." Thus the prophets admonished the people to repent. If they did so, God knew how to forgive and forget. Their sins will be buried in the depths of the sea.

By contrast, the apocalypticists understood that history is predetermined. God had set things up "from before the foundation of the world." History has been running along as it was meant to be and the future is just as firmly set as the past was. There is nothing that men and women can do to change what the future brings. The apocalypticists plead for patience and endurance, rather than repentance. What "the chosen" now need is perseverance in their faithfulness and obedience to God. The apocalypticists do not advise repentance because their message is for the elect ones, those who are suffering unjustly. The course of history is firmly set; therefore, their advice to them is to persevere with patient endurance until God enters history on their behalf, as he has determined already before the foundation of the world to do at the appointed time.

Another significant difference between the prophets and the apocalypticists is their views on the origin of the human predicament and its full implications. The prophets considered the Exodus the formative period in the history of Israel. God had chosen them, taken them out of Egypt and made them a people at Sinai. There he had revealed himself to them and made a covenant with them, thus reaffirming all previous demonstrations of his loving care for them. How did the people respond to God's multiple manifestations of his love for them? They rebelled. At the Sinai desert they worshiped the golden calf. Their rebellion against Yahveh at Sinai was for the prophets the paradigmatic sin that marked the existence of Israel as a rebellious, stiff-necked people. When they asked Aaron to make them *"gods who shall go before us,"* they established themselves in a continuous rebellion against Yahveh (Ex. 32:1-9; see Ez. 20:13). For them, idolatry is the sin that defines the conduct of the people. The prophets know nothing about the sin of Adam and Eve. Evil in the human heart is somewhat of a puzzle, but its presence among the Israelites is evident in their rebellion against the God who made them a nation and entered into a covenant relation with them at Sinai.

The shift to the consideration of the sin of Adam and Eve as the primordial sin becomes explicit within the biblical canon, for the first time, in the letters of the apostle Paul. With the shift from Sinai to the Garden of Eden the nature and the consequences of the primordial sin also become different. It is not just a sin that marks the Israelites as a rebellious people, but one that brings about the enslavement under the power of sin not only of all humanity, but of the whole creation. Paul is the one who tells us that Satan is the ruler of this world, intent on deceiving and taking advantage of the weak in faith (2 Cor. 2:11; 4:4). Jeremiah wondered how it could be that the mechanism that keeps migratory birds healthy by following the laws for their wellbeing the mechanism that makes for obedience to God's designs is not functioning in human beings. Paul, on the other hand, took for granted that humans lived under the power of cosmic forces of evil that kept them bound to sin and used the power of the Law to kill them. He did not wonder about the reasons for their evil ways. He knew that Adam had opened the door and Satan had entered God's world and taken control of it (Rom. 5:12-14). The difference between Jeremiah and Paul can only be understood when one realizes the emergence of the concept of The Fall as a cosmic tragedy that brought about a world no longer under Yahveh's direct control. Satan and his angels are thought to be free agents in this "fallen" world (2 Cor. 4:4). What was a puzzle to Jeremiah was not a puzzle for Paul.

The shift from the sin of Israel at Sinai to the sin of Adam and Eve at the Garden as the paradigmatic sin also brought about a shift from a historical to a cosmic, mythological, setting to the human drama. To elaborate on the concept of the Fall as a cosmic transition from the sovereignty of God to Satanic free range over the world, the apocalypticists borrowed from the ancient creation myths of

Canaan and Mesopotamia that told of a war between the powers of Good and Evil. There is a trace of them in the story of Genesis one. It begins referring to the "formless" and the "void," and points out that the "Wind/Spirit" of God was moving over (suppressing or incubating?) a restless "sea" that was engulfed in primordial darkness (Gen. 1:2). Are the formless and the void, and the wind and the sea, two theogonic pairs? Theogonic pairs are the standard constituents of the divine pantheon in creation stories. In all apocalyptic literature the sea (Tiamat) is the place from which evil forces come forth. Of course, Genesis one is a theological breakthrough. It is a concerted attempt to avoid stories of creation with their pantheons. There is no battle between the sea and the wind, between the creative Word and the formless and the void, or between darkness and light, as in the *Enuma Elish*. Elohim, the god of creation, is a transcendent god who never gets involved with the material world he is bringing into existence out of the void, the sea and the darkness. This is not a narrative. It is a structured polemic, with repeated formulas, against polytheistic creation myths that narrated cosmic battles and established a natural connection between the creation and the world of the gods. It starts with the creation of a day and ends with the sanctification of a Day. The structure is designed to give the Sabbath a cosmic footing in creation itself. This is a much stronger footing than the historical one, as a sign of freedom from slavery, given to it in the earlier version of the Ten Commandments found in Deuteronomy. In the process it confirms the process of secularization that had begun with the worship of Yahveh as the god of history, and the denial of divinity to the forces of nature. By conceiving the predicament of humanity under the cosmic power of sin to involve the whole of creation, apocalypticism reached back to stories of creation and their cosmologies. In the process it also gave to God's activity universal, cosmic range, something that Jeremiah anticipated when he compared God's commitment to his covenant with Israel with his commitment to the stability of the cosmic order in nature (Jer. 31:35-36).

The prophets' concerted efforts to disassociate worship from any natural phenomena transferred the significance of the yearly festivals from seasonal events in nature to episodes in the history of Israel. It reached its goal at the Exile. Throughout the course of Israel's dwelling in the promised land, the worship of fertility gods and goddesses was alive and well among the Israelites. The Former and the Latter Prophets never tire of condemning the fertility rites taking place at the groves and the high places throughout the land. From the Exile on, the Israelites became monotheists, and Yahveh was enthroned as the only God. All others were not gods but idols. Loyalty to Yahveh, was essential not only because of the historical relationship the Israelites had with Yahveh, but also because he is the universal only true God.

This had not been so earlier, as evidenced in the story of Ruth. When Ruth and Orpah, Naomi's daughters-in-law, inform her that they wish to go with her on her return to Judah, Naomi tells them that they must remain with their families in Moab and worship their family's gods. Orpah takes the advice and goes back to her family and its gods. Ruth, however, insists that she will go to Judah and worship Naomi's god (Ru. 1:15-16). The story presupposes that it is perfectly proper for people to worship the gods of their families in their land. Once in the promised land most Israelites naturally became worshipers of the gods of their new land at the groves and the high places. Altars to them were found in the court of the Jerusalem temple.

The prophetic battle against the worship of other gods and the explicit denial of the existence of other Gods, one of the main purposes of the post-exilic chapters in *Isaiah*, was severely compromised by the apocalyptic introduction of Satan and his angels as cosmic forces that influence human actions. The notion of The Fall was necessary in order to account for the suffering of the just, those who were loyal to Yahveh. To admit that God is no longer the god who rules over history and dispenses rewards and punishments was unthinkable. The way out of the dilemma was to admit that at the moment God is not in total direct control of what goes on in the world, but it is not the case that women and men have free will allowing them to develop evil habits. The problem is not a historical problem that affects only human beings. The problem is that the whole of creation has fallen under the power of the forces of evil, personified by the Devil, Beelzebul or Satan and his angels. The introduction of Satan as the one who controls, or at least is a free agent in, the fallen creation, and thus brought with him sin and death into the world, shifted the extent of the predicament from that of the Israelites living in their land to that of the whole of humanity living under cosmic evil forces. In fact, sin is not just a Jewish problem connected to the Law given at Sinai. It is the problem of all humanity connected with a creation fallen under Satan and his evil forces.

This cosmic problem requires a cosmic solution. For the prophets, the problem had been a historical problem that was to be solved historically. On the Day of the Lord God would intervene and set up Jerusalem as the capital of the world and all the kings of the world would come to learn the Law and wisdom from Yahveh at Jerusalem (Mic. 4:1-4; Is. 2:1-4). For the apocalypticists, the prophetic solution was no longer tenable. The problem was beyond repair within the present fallen creation. It required the termination of a fallen creation and its history. The evil in the world had become so pervasive that it could not be fixed within the present structure of things.

To have a world in which God's intentions when he created the world could be operational, God needed to destroy the world that is now controlled by evil forces and create a new world to take its place. This is the doctrine of the Two Ages: reality consists of This Age and The Age to Come. The suffering of the just is possible now because retributive justice may not be operative in this present evil Age. This means that it is possible for righteous people to suffer in the fallen creation. God's justice, however, will be fully operative in the Age to Come. Then, both those whose ways are evil and those whose ways are just will receive the recompense they deserve. In spite of all the evidence to the contrary at the moment, ultimately, behind the scenes, God is in control of the universe. Even if in This Age the wicked prosper and the righteous suffer, in The Age to Come things will be set right. To know this is wisdom, but for most it is a mystery. This mystery, however, has been revealed to a chosen few. The prophets envisioned "the restoration of the fortunes of Israel" in the promised land within the historical continuum. The apocalypticists envisioned the functioning of God's retributive justice in The Age to Come, after the end of history.

The divine revelation of the mystery which the apocalyptic texts convey takes place in one of two ways. According to one of them, as the author was praying and wondering about the incongruity of believing that he lives in God's world when so many terrible things are going on all around him, an angel of God comes down from heaven and reveals to him God's understanding of what is going on and how God will take care of things. He is assured by the angel that God's ultimate purpose is going to be accomplished. According to the alternative way, the author was taken up to heaven and brought before the presence of God. There he is informed of what is going on by witnessing the actions of different angels. In either case, the context for the apocalyptic resolution of the human predicament of the righteous sufferer, while described in earthly, historical activities, is in reality being determined by divine activities that contribute to the accomplishment of God's righteous purposes for Creation. By placing himself in the heavenly realm before the throne of God (Rev. 4:1), or by receiving a message by an angel sent from the throne of God (Dan. 8:15-20), the apocalyptic visionary escapes the nationalistic perspective of the prophets. He may still envision Jerusalem as the umbilical cord of the universe and the Torah as central, but the dwellers of the New Jerusalem are the chosen ones from every nation. This means that the apocalyptic perspective has no attachments to political of national identities. Its only attachment is to the God of creation. The prophets, by contrast, were attached to the God of Israel's history.

Another major cosmological shift took place in the period following the Exile. It contributed to the way in which the apocalyptic imagination described the future bliss of the elect. It involved the conception of the human person in the world. It is natural to conceive one's home as the place where one was born. Throughout one's life one remains attached to one's birthplace. Humans are normally permanently attached emotionally to their place of origin; finding themselves in any other place they feel "away from home." In that situation, their underlying desire is to "return." The notion of one's home can be understood not only in personal terms, but also in terms of humanity at large. According to the traditional Hebrew understanding of human origins, God had made them from dust of the earth and the earth was their home. On the earth, God had designated the land where he directed Abraham on his journey out of Mesopotamia, and in which he became a sojourner, as the land where his descendants would dwell and become a great nation. For the Hebrews the possession of the land, and dwelling in the Promised Land had become a major element of their self-awareness as a people. As noticed earlier, they understood that their future with God after the restoration of their fortunes would continue to be in their earthly home.

With the opening of travel, commerce and political connections between the Mediterranean and the Indian cultures, the notion of the human soul as an immortal, eternal living thing that had become entrapped in a physical body became widespread in the West and it convinced women and men that the earth was not their real home. Their essential being, their immortal soul, was "at home" only in heaven, the soul's place of origin. This shift to heaven as the true home of human beings created the pervasive desire to return home to heaven. Salvation ceased to be identified with health and prosperity on earth and became attached to the ability to escape the earth and return home to heaven. This gave rise to multiple esoteric, ascetic religious ways to achieve salvation through knowledge of the path on which the soul could make the journey back to heaven. It became the main agenda of the Mystery Cults that invaded the Roman Empire from the East, where they had been originally fertility cults. In a way, the notion that human beings were eternal souls who had become entrapped in a body of flesh was another version of the notion of The Fall. According to it, The Fall consists of the entrapment of the immortal soul in a mortal body. Unlike the prophetic visions of a blessed future on this earth, the apocalyptic conceptions of salvation envision the future in either an earthly or a heavenly new home. The choice seems to be influenced by whether the apocalyptic author is still strongly conditioned by his Jewish roots, or is somewhat more open to the Hellenistic cultural milieu.

Symbolic Apocalyptic Language

Finally, I would like to consider the most immediately evident difference between prophecy and apocalypticism: its appropriation of the language of creation myths and of ancient iconography. Many factors seem to have been involved in the development of apocalyptic discourse. To come to terms with them, it may help to start with a consideration of the risks involved in the use of words. Words are the indispensable means for communication, but words may also be the barriers to communication. In verbal communication three factors are involved: the speaker (writer), the hearer (reader) and the reality being symbolized by words. Modern philosophy has been particularly interested in the connotative and the denotative aspects of words. As a result, it has been affirmed that what is said but is "beyond proof" is meaningless. This reduction of meaningful speech to what can be demonstrated functions well in systematic scientific discourse that works through logic and appeals to reason, constricting the role of the imagination. It says that a human person may express ideas, desires, feelings, regrets, aspirations, etc., but since they cannot be confirmed with the objectivity required of scientific discourse, they are ultimately disconnected from reality. Discourse about what the imagination conceives, be it artistic, literary or religious, however, cannot be demoted to the fantasies of childhood that have no connection with reality. When what the imagination conceives is expressed by an intelligent adult it does not reveal immature flights to unreality. It has to do with what is as real as anything that can be proven in time and space. Attempts to give meaning to such discourse by transposing it to verifiable prose do not improve communication of what the discourse is about. To represent something symbolically does not imply that the speaker is in doubt about the reality or the validity of what he is saying. The use of symbols is concomitant to the use of words; it does not reflect the desire to impress aesthetically, or to lack confidence about the content of the discourse. The prophets not only used symbolic language, but also symbolic actions. By their performances they were not trying to magically bring about the future. They were trying to make as plain as they could what they understood to be the will of God. It was the most effective way for them to communicate the divine involvement with the present.

The authors of apocalypses conceived the crisis of their present as more dire than that faced by the prophets. It involved not just the unjust conduct of Israel's princes, priests and kings. It involved the whole of creation. This crisis could not be solved by using intermediaries: locust, drought, hunger, foreign armies, etc. This crisis required the direct intervention of the Omnipotent God. The only way to depict the personal impingement of God in the material and historical order in which people lived was the radical way in which God had brought about creation, as was being said by their time, "out of nothing," thus increasing the power of the God who does not use water or soil to create, as said in the creation stories of Genesis. The adoption of the language of creation myths, however, was not just an easy revival of traditional language. It was a very conscious use of mythological symbols to give conceptual clarification to the existential confusion of life in the present.

The symbols used by the authors of apocalypses were indeed traditional. They found them in the ancient myths of creation and in earlier books of the Old Testament, and they were easily understood by their contemporaries. Modern attempts by some interpreters to distinguish between what is to be taken literally and what is to be taken symbolically would have been inconceivable to the original readers of these books. They lived in the symbolic world of the imagination. There were no canons telling them that they were to tell about the past as it actually happened, or to prognosticate about the future as it would actually happen. Historical writing as an academic discipline committed to tell it "as it actually happened," as von Ranke in the nineteenth century taught historians to be their duty, did not exist back then. Before von Ranke everyone who wrote about the past, including all ancient Greek and Latin "historians," told about the past with a heuristic agenda. The prophets looked at the past to understand the present and offer moral advice. From the past they learned about the times when the Israelites had rebelled against their God and about the many demonstrations of God's covenant loyalty to his people. Thus, they contrasted the people's loyalty to their covenant with God by describing God's loyalty as a "Rock," and the people's loyalty as "the morning dew." It evaporates as soon as the sun heats up the atmosphere. They hoped, however, that the people would turn away, repent from their past and the future they envisioned would actually not happen.

The apocalypticists looked at the past to counterbalance the blessed future that will put an end to the past that got the people into their unacceptable present. After the exile, the *Endzeit wird Urzeit* pattern is standard in apocalypses. The future "end time" is to become like "primeval time." The future is described in terms of the pastoral simplicity, agricultural abundance and creature harmony that obtained in Eden. The final judgment is described with parallels with Noah's times. According to the first Greek thinkers, all matter is made of four basic elements: air, water, earth and fire. Two of them are characterized as being essential to the flourishing and the destruction of life: water and fire. While God destroyed the world of Noah with water, his future destruction of the fallen world will be with fire. It is not surprising that the authors of apocalypses found the appropriate language with which to depict the future that would displace the present in the language of the ancient stories that told how chaos was displaced by cosmos and the flood put an end to a world engulfed in wickedness.

The apocalypticists used a range of symbols: white bulls for the patriarchs of Israel, fallen stars for the sons of God that descended to earth to marry women, wild animals for the gentiles, blind sheep for the Jews, composite, monstrous beasts for nations, and their horns for their kings, etc. If today these symbols seem distractions it is because we may fail to perceive the agendas informing these apocalyptic accounts. It is also probable that sometimes the symbols were understood only by those belonging to a particular apocalyptic tradition. In any case, to use them now to extract "revelations" about the historical future is to abuse them.

The function of the apocalyptic texts was to give the members of a community a secure self-understanding at a time when the present brought about confusing distortions of accepted theological notions. When the present does not make sense, and does not provide significant prospects for the future, persons in an individualistic society feel insecure in a confusing existential situation, their very being finds itself anchored in a void. The present becomes oppressive. At such times, the attention of people is not directed to a phenomenological explanation of what is happening, but to a basis for ontological certitude. The function of apocalyptic texts is to provide needed ontological certitude in the present and prescribe a course of action. For this, the symbolic language that enriches the imagination is the most effective means of communication.

I conclude this introduction by summarizing that on the basis of the doctrines of The Fall and of The Two Ages, apocalypticism developed all kinds of scenarios in order to affirm God's sovereignty and God's justice in circumstances that required significant modifications of the prophetic tradition. These scenarios often depict how what is going on in heaven directly affects the conditions on earth as God demonstrates his ultimate control over his creation. Their intention, however, is not to foretell what will happen. They are designed to tell confused believers who cannot make sense of their present in a fallen world to persevere with patience so as to receive their just reward at the end. They affirm that while in This Age they are experiencing tribulations, in The Age to Come they will enjoy eternal life. The apocalyptic message is: patient endurance and faithfulness to Yahveh will be rewarded. In the following chapters I will elaborate on how the transitions described above appear in the late prophets and how the apocalyptic texts in the Bible express the message that while at the moment God's justice is not quite evident it will be quite evident at the End. Those faithful to God will see their hopes fully realized. The expression of this basic message, however, does not always fit all the features singled out for contrasts between prophetic and apocalyptic. They may appear heavily nuanced at times. This is the case because the characteristics of prophecy and apocalyptic texts outlined here, as already said, basically serve heuristic purposes to facilitate understanding and further investigation.

The Dawn of Biblical Apocalypticism

The transition from a prophetic to an apocalyptic perspective did not take place in a short period due to exceptional circumstances. The apocalyptic point of view came about in the course of centuries with no central authority guiding its course. It has been suggested that the fact that *First Enoch* is a compilation of several documents, that began to be put together toward the end of the second century B.C.E. and ended toward the end of the first century C.E., argues for the existence of an apocalyptic movement during those centuries, and this is a possibility. A convincing delineation of such a movement, however, has not yet been made, and if it were to be recognized it would not, by itself, mean that its influence was extensive. The apocalyptic imagination does not work according to rules and consistent outlines. Most probably, several apocalyptic traditions developed during the last centuries B.C.E. This means that there were different apocalyptic traditions tracing their own trajectories. During the ministry of Jesus and his disciples, apocalyptic perspectives were being held by different Jewish groups, each with its own characteristics. The apocalypticism of the Pharisees was not that of the Covenanters of Qumran, and both were quite different from that of the Zealots. In the New Testament, apocalyptic descriptions also have their own variations; quite often they do not agree with each other. Their differences, most likely, are due to choice of sources used by their authors and the situation with which they were concerned. Needless to say, each author endeavored to give a message that was relevant to the contemporary experience of his audience.

While still clearly within the standard prophetic tradition, Ezekiel and Zechariah, whose ministries took place during the exile and the re-settlement in the land, already begin to deal with themes that became central to the apocalyptic perspective. The same can be said of the non-canonical Book of the Watchers, which has been identified in the first 36 chapters of *First Enoch*. It is dated to the end of the third century B.C.E., that is, prior to the writing of *Daniel*. Even though when the Jews settled on the canon of Scripture, in the second century C.E., *First Enoch* was not included in the canon, it was a very widely read and appreciated book, as its having been translated from Hebrew to Aramaic, Greek and Ethiopic amply testifies. Besides, *First Peter, Second Peter*, and *Jude* demonstrate that the early Christians valued *First Enoch* as an authoritative book written, according to the author of *Jude*, by a patriarch who lived before the Flood. In this chapter I will explore *Ezekiel, Zechariah* and "The Book of the Watchers" in *First Enoch* to show how an apocalyptic perspective was developed from the sixth to the third centuries B.C.E. The period after the exile was a time of significant new developments in the religious experience of the Jews. My aim in this chapter is to discern how important shifts in perspective took place and how, even though these writings are prophetic in nature, they begin to explore themes that were not given attention by the prophets but became very important to the authors of apocalypses. These texts demonstrate the emergence of apocalyptic solutions to the human predicament.

Ezekiel

Among the canonical prophetic books, *Ezekiel* more than any other dates some of its oracles. In the book the oracles are not arranged chronologically. Three of them are out of order. The inaugural oracle (Ez. 1:2) is dated in 593 B.C.E., and the latest one (Ez. 29:17) in 571 B.C.E. The oracles dated between those two, however, cannot be used to date those undated. The evidence indicates that some of the oracles must have been spoken during *Ezekiel's* ministry in Jerusalem prior to the beginning of the Exile in 605 B.C.E., and certainly before the capture and removal to Babylon of King Jehoiachin in 597 B.C.E. The turning point in *Ezekiel's* ministry is the destruction of Jerusalem in 586 B.C.E.

In connection to his initial call, he reports that the Spirit closed his mouth and made him dumb (Ez. 3:25-26). Later he was informed that when a messenger brought the news of the fall of Jerusalem his dumbness would go away (Ez. 24:27). When one who escaped from the city as it was being taken by the Babylonians came to him with the news of its destruction, he reports that he recovered the ability to speak (Ez. 33:21-22). How it was possible for him to communicate the word of the Lord to the people by the river Chebar in Mesopotamia if he had been dumb for several years is not explained.

While the dating of the oracles in reference to dramatic historical events gives significant clues for their interpretation, the evident editorial work done by compilers and editors make their interpretation uncertain at times. Evidence of these activities, among others, is that the Hebrew version of Ezekiel available to us (Massoretic Text, IX C.E.) is longer and more repetitious than the much earlier Greek version (Septuagint, II B.C.E.). The fragments of Ezekiel found among the Dead Sea Scrolls (I B.C.E.) are closer to the Septuagint than to the Massoretic Text, suggesting the existence of variations in the text as it was transcribed through the centuries. It would appear that Ezekiel had a group of followers who collected his oracles and probably added some that took into account later developments among the exiles. These collections were then placed one after the other in the book now in the canon, thus explaining repetitions and inconsistencies.

Characteristic of the ministry of Ezekiel are his many strange prophetic performances. On account of their bizarre nature some commentators consider them to be literary devices. Taking them as live occurrences, other commentators think they show that Ezekiel must have been psychologically imbalanced. Besides the dumbness already referred to, he says that he had to lie down for 390 days on his left side (Ez. 4:5), apparently in public view. Once completed this number of days, he was to lay down on his right side for 40 days (Ez. 4:6). Then, he was told to eat bread cooked with human excrement (Ez. 4:9-12). When he refused because doing it would defile him, he was allowed to cook the bread with cow's dung (Ez. 4:15). He was also told to cut his hair and his beard and cast a third of the hair to the wind, one third to the fire and one third just scattered about. On another occasion, he was to go out of the city during the day and during the night carrying the luggage of an exile. He was not, however, to go through one of the city gates. He was to make a hole in the wall and go out through it (Ez. 12:4-5). Obviously, this could only take place before his exile, and the task would have taken herculean effort. To cap it all, when his wife died, he was told not to mourn her death (Ez. 24:15-18). Faced by this most inexplicable behavior, the people asked him, *"Will you not tell us what these things mean for us, that you are acting thus?"* (Ez. 24:19). Thus, readers are informed that these were prophetic performances that called for their interpretation.

Besides distinguishing himself by his bizarre prophetic performances, Ezekiel also stands out for his penchant for proverbs (Ez. 12:22; 16:44; 18:2), riddles and allegories (Ez. 17:2; 24:3). Due to this aspect of his ministry, the people had an easy time dismissing his oracles, saying *"Is he not a maker of allegories?"* (Ez. 20:49). The book provides ample evidence that Ezekiel was endowed with amazing language skills, as his poems unmistakably demonstrate. Ezekiel's performances, proverbs, riddles and allegories required wisdom for their interpretation. Thus his ministry is not just the communication of a word of the Lord. His mission is also to interpret both his allegories and his performances for the people. This represents a significant first step in the transition from the role of a prophet as one speaking for another to the role of interpreter of imaginative language.

As a prophet in the tradition of the Hebrew prophets, Ezekiel is concerned to establish the sovereignty and justice of God. Announcing that the patience of God has been exhausted and the end of Judah's national life is imminent (Ez. 7:2, 6, 10, 12, 19), Ezekiel advises repentance and the abandonment of their present course of action (Ez. 14:6; 18:30-32; 33:11). He gives long, detailed descriptions of how the people have departed from the statues and the commandments of God (Ez. 8:10-18; 22:6-12). His characterization is of a people in rebellion (3:9, 26; 5:6; 12:2, 9; 20:13, 21). To enable Ezekiel to deal with the rebellious people, God promises to make his *"face hard against their faces ... like adamant harder than flint have I made your forehead"* (Ez. 3:8-9). This hardening would allow him to withstand the predictable animosity of his audience. On account of the prevalent sinfulness of the people, God has been going about trying to find a man but, like Diogenes in Athens, he found none (Ez. 22:30). The commandments, which were intended to give the people life, are not being followed (Ez. 20:11, 13, 21). The people's rebellion, therefore, justifies the punishment God will inflict, or in fact has inflicted, on them (Ez. 14:23; 18:5). The people must recognize that what is happening to them is due to God's direct involvement in history. They are the cause of God's punishments (Ez. 14:23). In this, Ezekiel is in the tradition of the prophets who analyzed the present and announced God's punishment, hoping that knowledge of the consequences would bring about a change of course, repentance. The difference with his prophesying is that being in exile in Babylon, God's punishment is already taking place. His message, therefore, does not include the possibility that the expected future may not happen. This is a significant shift toward a deterministic understanding of history. God insists, *"I will do it; I will not go back; I will not spare; I will not repent"* (Ez. 24:14). What God has determined for the future will take place; he does not change his mind. God's current punishment of his people was already set in God's designs. Therefore, rather than to announce possible future punishments, Ezekiel justifies God's current punishment. A different historical moment calls for a different explanation of what God is doing.

The transition from a corporate, or a tribal identity to an individual one makes it necessary for Ezekiel to give detailed descriptions of how a person is held accountable for his conduct. Contrary to what happened at Ai, where Israel suffered a defeat on account of the greed of Achan, if *"a land sins against me,"* God tells Ezekiel, *"even if Noah, Daniel and Job were in it, they would deliver but their own lives by their righteousness; ... they would deliver neither sons nor daughters; they alone would be delivered, but the land would be desolate"* (Ez. 14:14-16). No amount of previous covenant-keeping will save from punishment those who abandon the ways of the Lord. On the other hand, a person who has been in rebellion against God but who turns and follows the way of the Lord will be saved from punishments (Ez. 14:12-20). Like Jeremiah, he quotes the proverb declaring that the sins of the fathers will be visited on their children, only to declare that this proverb no longer applies. Unlike Jeremiah, he goes to some lengths elaborating on how this new situation affects real life (Ez. 18:5-29).

On the basis of the tensions between the former understanding of corporate identity and the new understanding of personal identity, the people are complaining that *"the way of the Lord is not just"* (Ez. 18:25, 29; 33:17-20). Ezekiel is very much concerned to disprove this accusation. Besides, the Exile of the people of Israel to Babylon is being interpreted by all the neighboring nations as a demonstration of the weakness of their God. Ezekiel, therefore, considers his main responsibility to both prove to the people in exile that their punishment is amply deserved, and to the surrounding nations that the God of Israel is not weak. In his defense of God's power and justice, Ezekiel gives extreme demonstrations of God's anger, fury and wrath. God's sovereignty rules not only over Israel but also over all neighboring nations. Connected to this apologetic interest is a pervasive historical determinism. Everything that happens is the direct result of God's personal control of events according to his eternal will.

One of the most objectionable demonstrations of the idolatry prevalent among the Jerusalemites was the offerings of their sons and daughters in sacrifices to foreign gods (Ez. 16:20; 20:31; 23:37). This, of course, was one of the obvious reasons why they are being punished by God. Ezekiel knows well, since he is also a priest and very much in favor of cultic rituals, that among the commandments there is one asking for the sacrifice of the first-born to Yahveh (Ex. 22:29; Num. 3:13). Apparently, Ezekiel thinks that the reason why the people were sacrificing sons to Moloch (Lev. 18:21), and women were wailing to Tammuz (Ez. 8:14), was that they were performing these sacrifices in the same way in which they had been doing them to Yahveh. There is no lack of evidence that in Babylon the Jews had adopted syncretistic practices. From this, Ezekiel comes to the conclusion that the law requiring the sacrifice of babies to Yahveh was one of his "bad laws" (Ez. 20:25-26). He then explains the reason for these bad laws. God had given these laws to bring about their misapplications once the people rebelled against him. Thus their sacrifices of the firstborn to foreign gods were also foreordained by God's total control over history. This shift to a radical determinism running the course of history, which even prevents God from repenting of a previous decision, is certainly a step toward the apocalyptic world view. As an aside, it may be noted that Jeremiah also witnessed the sacrifices of firstborns. His reaction was to deny that God had ever given a law asking for them; such a law had not even ever entered his mind (Jer. 7:31). The evidence, however, supports Ezekiel's acknowledgment of its existence.

Another move toward the apocalyptic perspective is the way in which in Ezekiel the prophet introduces himself as one under *"the hand of the Lord"* in the *"land of the Chaldeans by the river Chebar"* (Ez. 1:3). Rather than to receive a "word of the Lord," the priest Ezekiel sees a stormy wind with great brightness and fire. In its midst he sees "the likeness" of four living creatures with human forms that sparkled like burnished bronze. They had four faces, four wings, straight legs and feet like the sole of a calf's foot. Under their wings on all four sides they had human hands. They were able to fly in all directions without turning, always straight forward in relation to one of their faces. One face was that of a man, another that of a lion, yet another that of an ox and the last one that of an eagle. From the center of the four creatures, fire and lightning flashed out. Looking further, Ezekiel sees a large wheel in which there were four wheels, each being within a wheel. The spirit of the four living creatures was in the wheels, which allowed them to move in every direction, sideways, backwards and forward, upward and downward (Ez. 1:4-21). Above the living creatures there was "the likeness" of a firmament, and over it "the likeness" of a throne like sapphire, and seated upon the throne "the likeness" of a human being. This being was engulfed upwards and downwards in the brightness of gleaming bronze and fire, much like the rainbow that shines on a rainy day. Such was "the likeness" of the glory of the Lord (Ez. 1:22-28).

This is a fantastic vision of the glory (throne) of God. From the throne, Ezekiel receives his commission to become *"a watchman for the house of Israel"* (3:17; 33:7), and to produce a scroll containing *"lamentation and mourning and woe"* (Ez. 2:10). When told to eat the scroll, he discovers that it is sweet as honey (Ez. 3:3-4). Scrolls with descriptions of what is to come shortly became a common feature of apocalyptic texts. Their origin and their content, however, varies in these texts. Later on, in a section that repeats some of the details of the original vision by the river Chebar, readers learn that the Spirit took Ezekiel on a tour of the temple in Jerusalem by lifting him and setting him up in space between heaven and earth (Ez. 8:3). Taking the visionary to the heavenly realm in a tour of either heavenly or earthly realities (Ez. 8:3 -10:22) became a standard feature of apocalyptic literature.

As already said, Ezekiel is concerned to demonstrate that what both the exiles and the neighbors of Israel are saying is not true. Specifically contradicting their charges, Ezekiel insists that the God of Israel is all-powerful and that his ways are just. He supports his contention by giving detailed descriptions of God's anger, fury, wrath and jealousy in accord with retributive justice (Ez. 5:13-

17; 36:5-6). These attributes will be displayed both against the rebellious people who complain that God's ways are not just, and against the nations who dismiss him as a weak god. As a result of his exhibitions of anger, fury, wrath and jealousy, both his people and the peoples of the surrounding nations *"shall know I am the Lord"* (Ez. 6:7, 14;12:20; 13:23; 14:23; 16:62; 17:21; 20:12, 16, 38, 42; 21:4; 24:24; 29:21; 32:15; 33:29; 36:23; 37:14). This claim is the leitmotiv of the book. At the moment, the Lord is being dishonored. His name, however, will be vindicated. After the God who has absolute control of history has punished not only Israel, but also Ammon (Ez. 25:2), Edom (Ez. 25:12; 35:2), Philistia (Ez. 25:15), Tyre (Ez. 26:2), Sidon (Ez. 28:22) and Egypt (Ez. 29:3) no one will be accusing the God of Israel of being weak and unjust. Both the broad descriptions of God's anger and its international reach anticipate apocalyptic expressions of delight with the demonstrations of God's wrath. Special punishments are to fall upon the Pharaoh of Egypt by the hand of the Babylonians who, God explains, *"work for me"* (Ez. 29:20). Apparently, God's special anger toward Egypt is due to Israel's tendency to doubt God's ability to provide security, and to rely on Egypt for it. This flames up God's jealousy; therefore, he will take care that this never happens again (Ez. 29:16). Also to be understood is that God will punish all the surrounding nations not only to avenge their enmity toward Israel, but for his own sake (Ez. 20:9, 14; 36:22, 32). Both in Israel and among the nations, people are saying that God is weak and unjust; he has been dishonored. When the people see the full display of God's anger, fury and wrath, and understand his jealousy for his good name, then God would have vindicated himself before all peoples (Ez. 36:23; 39:25, 27). The vindication of God's power and justice is the main agenda item in *Ezekiel*. Any hope for a future of bliss depends on God's vindication. Centuries later, in the book of *Revelation*, this is described as God's vengeance.

The most intensive display of God's power takes place in his dealings with Gog of the land of Magog, located to the north and associated with Meshesk and Tubal (Ez. 38:2). It is difficult to identify these names with certainty. They seem to have been taken from the list of nations in Genesis 10. The army of Gog consists of soldiers coming from the four quadrants of the earth: Gomer (north), Put (Ethiopia, south), Cush (Tarshish, west) and Persia (east) (Ez. 38:5-6). This enormous army from "the uttermost parts of the north" will descend *"against the land that is restored from war, the land where people who were gathered from many nations upon the mountains of Israel, which had been a continual waste,"* but where now those living in it *"dwell securely"* (Ez. 38:8). The description of the exiles living again securely in the mountains of Israel, and the explanation that God is using Gog by putting hooks into his jaws in order to bring him out against the restored people of God, anticipate future apocalyptic scenarios. Gog seems to be an all-encompassing surrogate for the forces of evil, coming from "the north," that will try to prevent the full vindication of the God of Israel. Subjugating him by putting hooks in his mouth (Ez. 38:4), as well as the references to God gaining control over the surrounding nations by catching them with his net (Ez. 12:13; 17:20; 19:8) reflect the mythological story of Marduk catching Kingu and Tiamat in the *Enuma Elish*. In *Job*, God draws out Leviathan from the sea with a fishhook (Job 41:1) This language indicates that Gog is being compared to Leviathan, the dragon of the sea where the forces of evil are gestated (Is. 27:1). The use of mythological language for the descriptions of evil and how God will deal with it became standard in apocalyptic texts. In this also *Ezekiel* is a forerunner. The mythological scene portrays the future destruction of all evil once Israel is back to its land and is no longer prey to the nations (Ez. 34:28), thus bringing about the total vindication of the God of Israel (Ez. 36:23; 39:27). It is important to note that Gog of the land of Magog is described doing what God is causing him to do. He is neither an independent agent nor the surrogate of a supernatural being who has rebelled against God. Satan is not a protagonist in Ezekiel's symbolic universe.

Being shown the harsh ways in which God punishes rebellious Israel, Ezekiel asks God in horror, *"Ah Lord God! Wilt thou make a full end of the remnant of Israel?"* (Ez. 11:13). The implicit answer is "No." Throughout the book, God repeatedly announces that he will "restore the fortunes" of Israel. He will gather them from among the peoples and give them back their land (Ez. 11:17; 16:55; 28:25; 36:24; 37:12, 25; 16:53; 39:25). In poetic language God gives a vivid description of how he will make the land flourish again, when all *"the cities shall be inhabited and the waste places rebuilt."* His people *"will soon come home."* God *"will do more good to them than ever before"* (Ez. 36:8-11).

While restoring their fortunes, God promises to *"give them one heart, and put a new spirit within them ... that they may walk in my statutes and keep my ordinances and obey them; and they shall be my people, and I will be their God"* (Ez. 11:19-20). The placing of a new spirit and the giving of one heart, which are referred to on three other occasions (Ez. 18:31; 36:26-28; 37:12), are essential to the successful restoration of Israel in her land. The one heart is to be understood in terms of the Hebrew way of expressing doubt or indecision as having two hearts, the heart being the organ of the will. It was in this context also that in one of his beatitudes Jesus spoke of having a pure heart, that is a will not confused by contrary tendencies. This condition will facilitate Israel's perfect obedience back home in their land.

For Ezekiel, those who live in a restored Jerusalem will not be all those who are now scattered among the nations. There will be a judgment that separates those who will enter the land from those who, although they have been taken out of Babylon, will not enter the land. *"I will purge out the rebels from among you, and those who transgress against me; I will bring them out of the land where they sojourn, but they shall not enter the land of Israel"* (Ez. 20:38). The notion of individual identity serves to separate individuals from within the body of God's people. In the vision where Ezekiel is taken on a tour of Jerusalem and shown the many ways in which the people have abandoned their God and carry out abominations, Ezekiel sees one dressed in white linen being instructed to *"go through the city, through Jerusalem, and put a mark upon the foreheads of the men who sigh and groan over all the abominations that are committed in it. And to the others he said in my hearing, 'Pass through the city after him, and smite; your eye shall not spare, and you shall show no pity; slay old men outright, young men and maidens, little children and women, but touch no one upon whom is the mark. And begin at my sanctuary'"* (Ez. 9:4-6). This total destruction of not only those who are sinning by robbing, lending with usury, taking bribes, disrespecting their elders, failing to keep the Sabbath, sacrificing children to Moloch, weeping for Tammuz and worshiping the sun (Ez. 8:5-16), but also those who are indifferent to what others are doing, including the priest at the sanctuary, reveals a God who is determined to assert his power and re-establish his reputation by demonstrating that retributive justice works. *Ezekiel's* apologetic agenda became the agenda of all biblical apocalypses which double down and describe a God whose justice includes sadistic vengeance.

In connection with the description of the destruction of those who have not been marked on their foreheads because they were not lamenting the abominations done by their neighbors, Ezekiel is told that God gave his people *"my [his] Sabbaths, as a sign between me and them, that they might know that I the Lord sanctify them"* (Ez. 20; 12). As a sign, or a marker of being God's property, the Sabbath receives singular attention, and its profanation provokes God's extreme jealousy (Ez. 20:13, 21; 22:8, 26; 23:38). Apparently, Ezekiel already realized that, due to the extent of human rebellion against God, it was impossible for human beings to sanctify any thing. Thus, he gives Sabbath observance a different function. It is not a commandment requiring "to sanctify" the Sabbath in recognition of human creaturehood (Ex. 20:8), or the celebration of the Israelites' freedom from slavery in Egypt (Deut. 5:12). It is a mark on those who have been sanctified by God. The notion that the elect will be distinguished by a seal, or a mark, became standard with the apocalyptic understanding that not all those who are called are chosen.

The vision of the valley of the dry bones, no doubt, is one of the preeminent features of *Ezekiel*. It may be related to the com-

The End of the Scroll

plaint of the exiles who say *"Our bones are dried up, and our hope is lost; we are clean cut off"* (Ez. 37:11). It may also have a connection to the story of the Moabite man who was buried in the grave of the prophet Elisha, and *"as soon as the man touched the bones of Elisha, he revived, and stood on his feet"* (2 Kings 13:21). The vision of the valley of the dry bones (Ez. 37) does not serve to announce the resurrection of the dead but the restoration of the exiles to their land. It also makes the point that those who will return to the land are not only the remnant of those exiled in Babylon, but also of those who had been dispersed by the Assyrians when they conquered the northern kingdom with its capital in Samaria. This is an emphasis of the whole of *Ezekiel*. It was announced by Ezekiel's lying on his left side for 390 days to represent the 390 years of punishment assigned to the house of Israel, as distinct from the 40 years assigned to the house of Judah (Ez. 4:5-6). Besides the inclusion of the kingdom of Israel, the vision of the valley of the dry bones suggests that *Ezekiel* is concerned with how God's justice applies to previous generations.

That both of the kingdoms that resulted from the partition of the kingdom of David after the death of Solomon will experience a restoration of their fortunes is also described by the allegory of the two sisters, Oholah (she who has a tent) and Oholibah (my tent is in her). The reader is told that Oholah is Samaria, and Oholibah Jerusalem (Ez. 23:4). Both of them will be restored in their land. That the restoration will include not just the northern kingdom of Israel but also the southern lands that belonged to David's original kingdom is told by another metaphor involving three sisters. Ezekiel identifies Samaria to the North and Sodom to the South as the sisters of Jerusalem. Their mother was a Hittite and their father an Amorite, and they are the personification of the proverb, "Like mother, like daughter." Among the daughters, Jerusalem is the one whose harlotry is the worst. Normally men go out looking for a harlot who gets paid. Jerusalem has been going out looking for lovers and paying them (Ez. 16:44-47). The inclusion of Sodom among the daughters extends the land to be restored to the southern borders of the kingdom of David. The restoration of Israel is to be complete; it will include all three daughters of the ancient Hebrew stock (Ez. 16:53-55). God's promise is, *"I will deal with you as you have done, who have despised the oath in breaking the covenant, yet I will remember my covenant with you in the days of your youth, and I will establish with you an everlasting covenant"* (Ez. 16:59-60). The everlasting covenant to be established when the fortunes of all Israel are restored, unlike the covenant which the Israelites broke, is also described as a *"covenant of peace"* (Ez. 34:25; 37:26), because upon their return to their land they will no longer be *"a prey to the nations, nor shall the beasts of the land devour them; they shall dwell securely, and none shall make them afraid"* (Ez. 34:28). That the beasts of the land will not devour them anticipates apocalyptic depictions of primordial evil as beasts coming out of the sea.

Such will be the situation after God defeated Gog and sent him down to Sheol to join the prince of Tyre, who has already been condemned to be *"no more for ever"* (Ez. 28:3, 9, 19). Gog and the other nations he has gathered to come against a restored Israel will suffer a resounding defeat. Then God will invite all *"the birds of every sort and all the beasts of the field"* to come to the great feast that he has prepared, telling them, *"eat the flesh of the mighty, and drink the blood of the princes of the earth, ... at the sacrificial feast which I am preparing for you"* Ez. 39:18-20). Cleansing the land by burying the dead left from the great demonstration of God's power and justice will take seven months (Ez. 39:12). If bones are still found in the land after that, they will be properly buried. Restored Israel will dwell in a land that is not only enjoying peace and prosperity but is also ceremonially clean, fully cleansed from all ritual pollution.

This description of Israel as a nation ruled by a descendant of David in a pure land after a horrendous battle that ends with the total triumph of God is the harbinger of the apocalyptic descriptions that later were adopted, with significant modifications, by the author of *Revelation*. The oracles having to do with the situation of exile conclude with a reaffirmation of the agenda that informs the book. *"The house of Israel shall know that I am the Lord their God, from that day forward"* (because my ways are just!). *"And the nations shall know that the house of Israel went into captivity for their iniquity, because they dealt so treacherously with me that I hid my face from them"* (not because I am weak!). *"Now I will restore the fortunes of Jacob, and have mercy upon the whole house of Israel; I will be jealous for my holy name ... when I have brought them back from the peoples and gathered them from their enemies' lands, and through them have vindicated my holiness in the sight of many nations"* (Ez. 39:23-27). Ezekiel ends naming the city that is now the capital of a restored Israel: *"The name of the city henceforth shall be, The Lord is there"* (Ez. 48:35). In this way, Ezekiel's apology for the exile and for the sovereignty and justice of God has been demonstrated. God will be vindicated. Ezekiel proclaims an all-powerful God quite capable to vindicate his good name. Whether his God is also just was, apparently, not thought demonstrated by all his readers.

In *Ezekiel* the Israelites are suffering at the hand of God as a just punishment for their sins. It is not the case that they are suffering for the sins of their fathers, as it was previously said, nor is it on account of evil forces that persecute them because of their desire to adhere faithfully to the statutes and commandments of the Lord, as will become the case in the future. In this universe, God is in complete control and the course of history is totally determined so that even the abominations that the Israelites have been practicing, on account of which they are being punished, are due to their rebellious nature and the bad laws that God gave them knowing of their coming rebellion against him. The restoration of the Israelites in their land does not involve the termination of history or the destruction of the present creation. Once the forces of Gog have been defeated and the burial of all those killed has been completed, after birds and wild animals feasted on their carcasses, the land will be purified and the river of life will flow from the throne of the temple in Jerusalem and give life to the waters of the Dead Sea (Ez. 47:8-9). The restoration does not bring about a new heaven and a new earth, but a renewed earth. This demonstrates that the two basic doctrines of biblical apocalyptic theodicy are absent in Ezekiel. It ignores the doctrine of The Fall and the doctrine of The Two Ages. The way in which Ezekiel describes the abominable conditions pervading in the world and the vindication of God's power and justice, however, provided the tools with which the apocalypticists elaborated these two distinctive doctrines. Besides, his detailed descriptions of what God will do to demonstrate his power and justice anticipate the apocalyptic descriptions of how God will bring about shortly a world in which justice and peace are the norm and the sea, the fountain of evil and death, has been eliminated.

In reference to God's vindication, Ezekiel accuses the people of Israel and the neighboring nations of defaming him by declaring him unjust and weak. His vindication depends on a demonstration of his power and his ability to keep covenant with his people. To accomplish this, Ezekiel looks forward to the restoration of Israel in her land, where she will live securely in an eternal covenant of peace because God will destroy all those who used to prey on her. To explain the absolute sovereignty and justice of God, Ezekiel makes God responsible for the existence of both good and evil in his world. He has given bad laws (Ez. 20:25-26), and in his anger for the abominations being done in Jerusalem, he "will cut off from you both righteous and wicked" (Ez. 21:4).

The flowering of apocalypticism was an effort to solve the problem left unsolved by Ezekiel. God's vindication as sovereign and just is not quite being achieved while declaring that present evil also comes from God. God cannot be worshiped if he is conceived as the source of both good and evil, as one who punishes equally the righteous and the wicked. The cause of evil in the world must have a source other than God, even if to achieve his purpose God at times uses evil. Apocalypticism's doctrine of The Fall was the tool with which it attempted to deal with this problem.

The End of the Scroll

ZECHARIAH

The prophet Zechariah gives dates that place his activity between the years 520 and 518 B.C.E., that is after the end of the exile in 537 B.C.E. He was an optimistic prophet who, like Haggai, belonged to the cultic establishment at the time when those who had returned to Jerusalem were involved in reconstituting a viable community of worshipers of Yahveh. Most scholars agree that in its present form the book consists of two separate documents. The first, chapters 1-8, contains Zechariah's oracles encouraging the people to rebuild the temple of Jerusalem at a time when messianic expectations were high. Chapters 9-14 is a later document with eschatological reinterpretations of messianic themes after the conquests of Alexander the Great made Greece a player in the international horizon of the Fertile Crescent in the second half of the IV century B.C.E. (Zech. 9:13). The prophecies of Haggai, Zechariah's contemporary, see the political upheavals taking place after the death of Cambyses in July of 522 B.C.E. as propitious for the establishment of an independent nation ruled by a descendant of David, Zerubbabel, the current governor of Jerusalem under Persian rule (Hag. 2:6-9, 20, 23). At that time there were revolts in Babylon led by royals who called themselves Nebuchadrezzar III and IV. It was only in his second year that Darius was able to restore order within his domains. Zechariah's first oracle is dated to the eighth month of Darius' second year (Zech. 1:1).

The chapters that undoubtedly come from Zechariah deal with the ups and downs of the expectations for a full restoration of the fortunes of Israel with a descendant of David on the throne of Jerusalem. Chapters 1 to 6 contain seven visions, one of them in need of some rearrangement due to the intervention of later hands. The first one (Zech 1:7-17), seems to reflect on the disappointment felt when the revolts of the Babylonians against their Persian rulers did not succeed, thus taking away the possibility of an independent Jerusalem free from Persian control. In a night vision Zechariah sees a man riding a red horse and other riders on four horses of different colors. An angel then provides an interpretation of what is going on. It would seem that this angel is the man sitting on the red horse, but that is not explicit. The riders of the four horses have been patrolling the earth, and they come back to report that *"all the earth remains at rest."* Hearing this the angel takes it to be bad news because it means that the Persians have squelched the Babylonian rebellion and that Jeremiah's prophecy that God's punishment would last seventy years, or Ezekiel's prophecy that it would last forty, were not going to be fulfilled. The angel appeals to God, *"O Lord of hosts, how long wilt thou have no mercy on Jerusalem and the cities of Judah?"* God, who is in control of all political changes, reassures the angel that he has *"returned to Jerusalem with compassion; my house shall be built in it."* While political independence has become less likely, the assurance that worship of Yahveh at the Jerusalem temple is to be reinstated seems to have satisfied Zechariah. The distinction between political arrangements and worship arrangements became a feature of future apocalyptic discourse; true worship is the basic requirement for the elect, as Revelation would later demonstrate.

The second vision (Zech. 1:18-21) announces that the four "horns" that had scattered Judah, Israel and Jerusalem will be terrified and cast down by four "smiths" being sent for that purpose. The most likely interpretation is that the Babylonian revolts against the Persians have been defeated, thus the nations that had scattered the Israelites out of Judah and Israel, Assyria and Babylon, are now no longer "raising their heads." That the forces of evil are not gaining power again and favorable conditions will prevail is essential to the continuation of fidelity to the God of Israel. And fidelity to God under problematic conditions, of course, is the main preoccupation of apocalyptic texts.

The third vision (Zech. 2:1-13) sees a man with a measuring line ready to establish the breadth and the length of Jerusalem. When the angel who has been talking with Zechariah comes forward, another angel intercepts him and tells him to prevent the man from measuring Jerusalem. God' plan for Jerusalem is that it be inhabited as if it were a village, without walls. *"I will be to her a*

The End of the Scroll

wall of fire round about, says the Lord, and I will be the glory within her." Of course, if the inhabitants were to begin rebuilding the wall, that would have been interpreted by the Persians as an act of rebellion that called for immediate military intervention. Now is not the time for the people of Jerusalem to provoke the Persians by sending the wrong signal. On the other hand, the Jews who are still living in Babylon should get out before the Persians come to Babylon with reprisals for the uprisings of Nebuchadnezzar III and IV. They should come to Jerusalem because God is back in her and many nations *"shall join themselves to the Lord."* This vision reaffirms the need to trust God for security in this world. Seeking security by means of alliances or defensive walls is a denial of trust in the power of God to do what he has promised. That would become a most important characteristic of the biblical apocalypses. They do not urge those suffering oppression under foreign powers to rebel with the force of arms.

The fourth vision is somewhat dismembered (Zech. 3, 4, 6:9-15). It announces the coming of the Messiah, The Branch, identified as Zerubbabel. He has laid the foundation of the temple and he will be the one who completes it. The vision also includes a crown made with silver and gold brought from Babylon by recently arrived Jews. The crown, it would seem, was to be placed on the head of Zerubbabel, the Branch. With the passage of time, however, the messianic expectations centered on Zerubbabel faded, and his name disappears from the records. The crown, therefore, is said to be for Joshua, the High Priest. This vision does not begin with a dialogue with an angel. Rather, Zechariah is shown Joshua dressed in filthy garments with an angel by his side. Satan is also standing by to accuse him. Joshua's filthy garments indicate that he must have had a dubious past in Babylon where syncretistic practices, referred to in *Jeremiah, Ezekiel* and post-exilic *Isaiah*, were adopted by the exiles. These, apparently, render Joshua ineligible for the High Priesthood, and Satan is there to point this out. Joshua's filthy rugs, however, are taken off and he is dressed in rich apparel and a turban. Then he is charged to *"rule my house and have charge of my courts."* This arrangement conforms to the Persian predilection for rule through the mediation of priests, rather than civil servants.

Central to this vision, which occupies the core of a series of seven, there is *"a lamp stand of gold, with a bowl on its top, and seven lamps on it, with seven lips on each of the lamps. Next to it are two olive trees, one on the right of the bowl and the other on its left."* When Zechariah asks the angel for the interpretation of the vision, the angel responds with words addressed to Zerubbabel, *"Not by might, nor by power, but by my Spirit, says the Lord of hosts"* (Zech. 4:6). In other words, the establishment of the descendant of David on the throne would take place by peaceful means, not by an armed uprising against the Persians. Jerusalem is not going to have a protecting wall and a warrior Messiah. As already said, the hopes placed on Zerubbabel did not last, and the vision clearly sets up the lamp stand as a symbol of the temple and the two olive trees as the dual leadership of a religious High Priest and a civil governor, not an independent king. The difficulties in the present text apparently were caused by the need to take Zerubbabel out of the picture when the expectations of his messianic role proved unfounded. Thus, while Zechariah tries to keep alive faith in the power of God to restore the fortunes of Israel, it has to water down the expectations for a messiah. The need to face up to the disappointment with Zerubbabel brought about a revision of the expectations for a military and political messiah. Instead, Jews came to expect a priestly messiah, as later apocalyptic texts from Qumran reveal.

The fifth vision (Zech. 5:1-4) is of a flying scroll with the dimensions of the vestibule of the temple. The scroll contains a curse upon those who steal and those who swear falsely. Their houses will be consumed, *"both timber and stone."* Obviously, the curse is upon the ones who stayed in the land of Israel during the exile and took possession of real estate left empty by the exiles. They, apparently, had not only stolen the properties but also perjured themselves claiming ownership after the exile. The prophet has something quite specific to say to them: God will destroy their stolen houses. The punishment imposed gives the clue as to the situation being addressed. This anticipates later apocalyptic descriptions of specific punishments for specific offenders.

The sixth vision (Zech. 5:5-11) has a barrel being carried around. The angel lifts the cover of the barrel and identifies a woman in it as "Wickedness." Then he puts down the barrel with the cover against the ground, making it impossible for wickedness to get out. Two women with wings like the wings of storks lifted the barrel to the sky. When Zechariah asks the angel where they are taking it, he is told that the barrel is being taken to the land of Shinar, where it will be placed on its base. The vision describes the elimination of the remnants of the worship of the fertility goddess of the Canaanites which was, of course, still quite prevalent in the land after the exile. This wickedness would be done in a foreign land, not any more in Jerusalem. Thus, while in *Zechariah* we do not read about a new heaven and a new earth free from the pollutions that permeate the fallen creation, like in *Ezekiel* we do read of the purification of a polluted land of Israel. Cleansing from pollution is a primary concern in a culture centered on a temple, and apocalypticism reinstated an attachment to the Temple, the place where the unity of the universe is displayed. In *Revelation* the throne is found in the temple. The two are the central symbols of apocalyptic texts.

The final vision (Zech. 6:1-8) is of four chariots driven by four horses of different colors (red, black, white and dappled gray) which come from between two bronze mountains and take off in the direction of the four winds of heaven. They are to "patrol the earth," like the four riders of the first vision. The vision ends with the angel telling Zechariah, *"Behold, those who go toward the north country have set my Spirit at rest in the north country."* From the perspective of all the prophets, all the enemies of Jerusalem come from the north. Since the north is being carefully patrolled, God is at rest. In this way the seventh vision comes full circle to a land at rest, carefully patrolled by God's agents. The agenda of all seven visions is to affirm that the world is under God's total control.

The chapters that come from Zechariah end with the report of a matter that was causing confusion among the people who had returned from the exile. Chapter 7 tells of a delegation from Bethel that came to Jerusalem with a question to the priests at the temple: Were they to observe the fast of the fifth month? The answer given by Zechariah is a word of the Lord which does not refer to the question. It gives a lengthy list of what the Lord expects from his people. It would seem that the answer is that rather than being concerned with fasting they should be concerned with kindness, mercy, non-oppression of others, etc. This answer is in agreement with the prophetic tradition that prioritizes upholding justice and peace rather than cultic performances. In the process, it shifts attention from the past to the future. Actually, since God is going to *"be their God in faithfulness and in righteousness,"* from now on *"the fast of the fourth month, and the fast of the fifth, and the fast of the seventh, and the fast of the tenth shall be to the house of Judah seasons of joy and gladness, and cheerful feasts; therefore love truth and peace"* (Zech. 8:19). The future will not consist of fasts but of celebrations. The only explanation for the question having been raised by the delegation from Bethel, it would seem, is that they thought that on account of their syncretistic practices during the exile in Babylon they were now in no condition to observe the fast commemorating the destruction of the temple in 587 B.C.E. The answer, rather than to place attention to the destruction of the temple, calls attention to the restoration of the fortunes of Israel, something which apocalyptic texts will consider essential.

In the tradition of the prophets, Zechariah reviews what is going on at the time and pleads with the people to repent and live according to the ways the Lord expects from them. Yet, significantly, he does what no other prophet had done before. At the very introduction, God instructs Zechariah, *"The Lord was very angry with your fathers, . . . Therefore say to them, 'Thus says the Lord of hosts: Return to me, says the Lord of hosts, and I will return to you, says the Lord of hosts. Be not like your fathers, to whom the former prophets cried out, Thus says the Lord of hosts, Return from your evil ways and from your evil deeds.' But they did not hear or heed me, says the Lord. 'Your fathers, where are they? And the prophets, do they live for ever? But my words and my statutes, which I commanded my servants the prophets, did they not overtake your fathers?'"* (Zech. 1:2-6). Zechariah is calling attention to the past as a source of valuable lessons. Their fathers did not follow God's advice to repent, and the punishments God described to them in advance came to pass. In this way he places himself in the tradition of the *"former prophets"* (Zech. 7:7, 12), and applies their oracles to his own day. Many of his images are taken from them, suggesting that he sees himself as the interpreter of previous prophetic sayings. He refers to the seventy years of Jeremiah (Zech. 1:12; Jer. 25:11; 29:10), the smiths (Is. 54:16-17), the measuring line (Ez. 42:20), the north country (Jer. 1:13-16; Ez. 38:6), the Branch (Jer. 22:5; 33:15), the wall of fire (Is. 4:5) and probably the horsemen with news of Babylon's defeat (Is. 21:9). Thus, Zechariah is the forerunner of a characteristic of the authors of apocalypses who saw themselves as the eschatological interpreters of the "former prophets."

Another innovation found in *Zechariah* is the way in which angels functions in his oracles. In *Micah* and in *Isaiah* one reads of supernatural beings who speak to each other or with the seer. It is only in *Zechariah* that the angel becomes the interpreter of what the prophet is seeing. This means that the role of the prophet has been changed. Rather than being the one who receives the Word of the Lord, or is inspired to speak for the Lord, the prophet has become the interpreter of previous words of the Lord, or the messenger of the interpretation of visions provided by an angel. One needs to note that the Hebrew word for angel, *mal'ak*, also means messenger, and in time also came to mean prophet. In *Zechariah* the angel also functions as intercessor (Zech. 1:12) and the giver of oracles (Zech. 1:14-17; 2:4-5).

As I said at the beginning of this section, chapters 9 to 14 of *Zechariah* come from a different, later source. They are actually two booklets of a collection of three anonymous announcements that are titled "oracles" (*massa'*). The third one is now known as the book of *Malachi* (from *mal'ak*), that is to say "my messenger," on account of the expression, *"Behold, I send my messenger"* (Mal. 3:1). The first two oracles now found in *Zechariah* (Zech. 9:1-11:17 and 12:1-14:21) are also eschatological oracles of "the messenger" who had been identified before as a prophet. These two are similar to the third *massa'* which was published independently as Malachi.

Like Ezekiel, Zechariah envisions the restoration of the land in peace and prosperity to take place in Judah and the surrounding regions, especially toward the South. God's promise is, *"I will return to Zion, and will dwell in the midst of Jerusalem."* Like Ezekiel, Zechariah gives to Jerusalem a new name, actually two different ones: *"The faithful city," "The mountain of the Lord of hosts,"* or *"The holy mountain"* (Zech. 8:3), rather than *"The Lord is there"* (Ez. 48:35). Then the Lord promises that *"old men and old women shall again sit in the streets of Jerusalem, each with staff in hand for very age. And the streets of the city shall be full of boys and girls playing in its streets .... For there shall be a sowing of peace; the vine shall yield its fruit, and the ground shall give its increase, and the heavens shall give their dew"* (Zech. 8:4-5, 12). Also in agreement with Ezekiel, Zechariah understands that God is the source of both good and evil. God says, *"As I purposed to do evil to you, when your fathers provoked me to wrath, and I did not relent, says the Lord of hosts, so again have I purposed in these days to do good to Jerusalem and to the house of Judah; fear not"* (Zech. 8:14-15). Unlike the future apocalypticists, Zechariah does not attribute to Satan and his cohorts the power to bring about the suffering experienced by God's people. As in *Job*, here Satan is known as the accuser at the heavenly court, not as the one who operates freely in a fallen world. It is clear that Zechariah introduces changes to the prophetic perspective in reference to its view of inspiration and its view of God as the Lord of history. These changes became prominent in apocalyptic texts, but *Zechariah* is not yet an apocalyptic book. In the tradition of the prophets, Zechariah shows a God who is zealous and punishes discrete sins in specific ways, and he envisions the future of Israel still in nationalistic terms. He does not envision the people's historical experience as the result of a cosmic Fall, and the future he describes is still a historical one in a purified land.

THE BOOK OF THE WATCHERS

The Ethiopic Book of Enoch, also identified as *First Enoch*, was first brought to the attention of modern biblical scholarship when it was published at the beginning of the nineteenth century. Later, fragments of the book were found in a Greek version, which was the basis for the Ethiopic version. Copies in Aramaic have also become available. Among the discoveries made in the caves near the ruins of Kirbeth Qumran by the Dead Sea, fragments of the book were found in Hebrew. These fragments have been most diligently studied because they are in the book's original language. The full text of *First Enoch* in our possession, however, is found only in Ethiopic. After two centuries of intense study by biblical scholars, it is agreed that *First Enoch* is not one book, but a collection of five independent books, which are themselves editorial compilations of different earlier texts. The five separate compositions have been identified as follows: The *Book of the Watchers* (chaps. 1-36), The Parables [or Similitudes] (chaps. 37-71), The Book of the Luminaries [or The Astronomical Book] (chaps. 72-82), The Book of Dreams (chaps. 83-90), and The Epistle of Enoch (chaps. 91-108).

The discovery of fragments of *First Enoch* at Qumran in the 1950s greatly strengthen the dating of its two earliest documents before the Maccabean revolt in 167-164 B.C.E. These are the Book of the Luminaries and the *Book of the Watchers*. The first is primarily concerned to defend the authority of a 360-day yearly calendar against various others being used by Jews at the time. This was very important because the proper celebration of the festivals and the keeping of the Sabbath depended on following the "correct" calendar. Thus, The Book of the Luminaries serves purposes similar to those of the book of *Jubilees*, which comes from about the same time. The establishment of the right calendar became necessary after Hellenistic culture and greater travel opportunities gave the

Jews access to the lifestyles of other societies with more accurate calendars.

The *Book of the Watchers*, is of special interest to the theme of my book on account of two reasons. One is that it predates the book of *Daniel*, which was published at the time of the Maccabean revolt (167-164 B.C.E.). Thus, it contributes to our understanding of the transition from prophetic to apocalyptic literature, even if it did not become part of the Jewish canon of Scripture at the Council of Jamnia in the second century C.E. The second reason is that it was extremely popular and considered authoritative by Jews and early Christians before their respective canons were established. That it was considered Scripture by early Christians is evident by the adoption of some of its peculiar features by the authors of *First Peter, Second Peter, Jude* and *Revelation*. The author of *Jude* specifically identifies Enoch, the seventh from Adam, as the author of the book, thus taking at face value the pseudonym used by the author to establish his authority. Jude says that Enoch prophesied that the false teachers among the early Christians were going to be *"wandering stars ... for whom the nether gloom of darkness has been reserved for ever"* (Jude 14). *First Peter* says that when Christ was crucified he was *"put to death in the flesh but made alive in the spirit, in which he went to preach to the spirits in prison who formerly did not obey, when God's patience waited in the days of Noah during the building of the ark"* (1 Pet. 3:18-20). *Second Peter* exemplifies God's willingness to punish rebels, among others, by the fact that he *"did not spare the angels when they sinned, but cast them into hell, and committed them to pits of nether gloom to be kept until the judgment"* (2 Pet. 2:4). *Revelation* reports that the martyred saints' clamor for revenge from under the altar, and issues a blessing on those who keep the words of its prophecy (Rev. 6:10; 22:7). That angels who sinned and were cast down from heaven are prisoners kept in gloomy, dark pits waiting for their final judgments, and that the dead clamor for God to hear their plea are prominent features of the *Book of the Watchers*. The use of the *Book of the Watchers* by these authors tells us that early Christians recognized it as authoritative.

As demonstrated earlier, it is possible to reconstruct with some confidence the historical circumstances that inform the prophetic oracles. Ezekiel had to deal with fellow Israelites in exile who thought their condition revealed an unjust God, and had to answer charges made by Israel's neighbors that their God was weak. Zechariah had to deal with people who had to accept the leadership of a High Priest with a dubious reputation once their hopes for the restoration of the Davidic monarchy had become unrealizable. The hopes they had placed on Zerubbabel faded as their hero disappeared from the historical record. Rather than a kingdom ruled by a descendant of David, the people had to build the temple and be led by a High Priest. As will become evident in the next chapter, the editors of the book of *Daniel* had to deal with people who were tempted to adopt the lifestyle and the worship of a more cosmopolitan Greek culture and encourage those with a firm allegiance to the Law of Moses and their ancestral customs to remain faithful when facing severe punishments and even death. In contrast to these books, the author of The *Book of the Watchers* does not seem to be addressing a specific historical situation. His message does not seem to be linked to particular circumstances. He is concerned with an intellectual problem: Why do people act in ways that God does not approve? This had been a problem already faced by the prophets. This problem was to become the central concern of the authors of apocalypses. What causes people to rebel against God? Why do righteous people suffer without cause? To the apocalypticists these became big problems due to their belief that all human activity is determined by God. Facing these problems, Ezekiel taught that God is the source of both good and evil. But that solution was not accepted by all. Then, how is the presence of evil in God's world to be accounted for? If God is not the source of evil, where does evil come from? This is the problem being addressed by the author of The *Book of the Watchers*. It is a problem especially for those who hold that God is in control of this world. As such, it is a problem that transcends specific circumstances.

To deal with this problem, the author of *The Book of the Watchers*, the first 36 chapters of *First Enoch*, resorts to accounts of the beginnings of human life. He is aware of the story of Adam and Eve's disobedience. It brought about the opening of their eyes to realize their nakedness, and resulted in their expulsion from the garden of Eden. No canonical book of the Old Testament, besides Genesis, contains a reference to the sin of the first human pair in the garden of Eden. All the prophets consider the worship of the golden calf at Sinai the paradigmatic sin that stamped Israel as a rebellious people. Beside the sin of the first pair in the Garden, the author of *The Book of the Watchers* also knows that Noah was told ahead of time to prepare for the survival of his family and be saved from the coming destruction, and that Enoch is the father of Methuselah, who is the father of Lamech, who is the father of Noah. More than anything else, he knows that *"when men began to multiply on the face of the ground, and daughters were born to them, the sons of God saw that the daughters of men were fair; and they took to wife such of them as they chose"* (Gen. 6:1-2). The *Book of the Watchers* is an expansion of this text in Genesis. Thus, the author does not claim to have received a Word of the Lord. Rather, as noticed already in *Zechariah*, guided by an angel, he delivers an interpretation of a previous word of the Lord. He calls "watchers" the angels who watched the daughters of men and desired them. His reaching back to ancestral pre-historic narratives is a most significant move in the direction later taken by apocalyptic authors.

The book opens with the blessings Enoch has for the elect and righteous who *"will be living in the day of tribulation."* His use of Enoch as a pseudonym and the projection of his message to a time of trouble in the future anticipate practices that became common among the apocalypticists. The author, identifying himself as Enoch, is not writing for Enoch's contemporaries, of course. He is writing *"not for this generation, but for a remote one which is to come"* (1 En. 1:1-2). In this way the author, while writing for the benefit of his contemporaries, accommodates his appeal to the authority of an antediluvian patriarch who was in heaven. The opening announces that *"the eternal God will tread upon the earth, (even) on Mount Sinai ... and all shall be smitten with fear, and the Watchers shall quake."* God will be coming with *"ten thousands of His holy ones to execute judgment upon all"* (1 En. 1:4-9). Without any introductory remarks, divine judgment is the center of attention. Then, the author shifts gears and follows the example of Jeremiah, wondering why while in nature everything acts according to the laws established to be followed by them, human beings do not follow theirs. The luminaries, the seasons, the sea, the rivers, they do not deviate from their appointed roles; among them, *"according as God has ordained so it is done, ... but you – you have not been steadfast, nor done the commandments of the Lord"* (1 En. 2:1-4). Therefore, at the judgment there shall be a curse for the sinners, but for the righteous *"there shall be forgiveness of sins, and every mercy and peace and forbearance: there shall be salvation unto them, a goodly light"* (1 En. 3:6). This is the introduction that sets up the agenda: at the judgment the cause of evil shall be revealed and retributive justice will be applied.

The rest of the book explores the way in which evil entered the world, and how God, who still has full control of his creation, has already made arrangements to deal with those who do evil. As a consequence, at the news of a judgment the Watchers trembled. The Watchers are the sons of God, the angels, who lusted after the daughters of men. The entrance of evil into the world, however, is told by two contrasting stories. According to one version, Semjaza, who was the leader of the angels, convinces 200 angels to join him and have children with daughters of men. They are aware, of course, that the plan carries a penalty. Still, they come down to earth and take women for wives, knowing that by doing it they were defiling themselves. To their wives they taught *"charms and enchantments, and the cutting of roots, and made them acquainted with plants. And they became pregnant, and they bare great giants, whose height was three thousand ells"* (1 En. 7:1-2). The description would indicate the introduction of magical healing arts by plants, roots and charms. The giants, for their part, soon consumed all the resources available and, when they could no longer find food for themselves, they devoured mankind. Not satisfied, they began to sin against birds, and beasts, and reptiles, and fish, and to devour one another, and drink the blood. *"Then the earth laid accusation against the lawless ones"* (1 En. 7:3-6). That the earth accuses the wrongs being done on it reflects the story of Abel's blood calling for justice from the ground on which it fell (Gen. 4:10).

According to the other version of the appearance of evil, Azazel *"taught men to make swords, and knives, and shields, and breastplates, and made known to them the metals (of the earth) and the art of working with them, and bracelets, and ornaments, and the use of antimony, and the beautifying of the eyelids, and all kinds of costly and all coloring tinctures. And there arose much godlessness, and they committed fornication, and they were led astray, and became corrupt in all their ways"* (En. 8:1-2). In this account, the problem was the introduction of the tools for making women more beautiful and the tools for the warfare that resulted from men desiring them. One cannot avoid remembering Helen and the Trojan War. In this way, the *Book of the Watchers* assigns the origin of evil among human beings to angels who defiled themselves with the daughters of men, something alluded to in the story of the flood in Genesis. Now God has to deal with angels who have defiled themselves, and humans who have acquired arts that cause them to sin. The move in this direction sets up a theme that became a major concern of apocalyptic writings.

The last thing one should require of mythical stories is that they be consistent. Thus in the remainder of the The *Book of the Watchers* one finds inconsistencies, but that should not be surprising. Since the Watchers under the leadership of Semjaza have killed all human beings, Michael, Uriel, Rafael and Gabriel in heaven hear the cry of the souls of the dead saying, *"Bring our cause before the Most High"* (1 En. 9:3). To bring up the cause of the dead, these good angels address God with a list of titles reminiscent of those used by the Greek successors of Alexander the Great: *"Lord of lords, God of gods, King of kings (and God of the ages), the throne of thy glory (stands) unto all the generations of the ages, and Thy name holy and glorious and blessed unto all the ages."* This manner of address reveals a new universal, imperial understanding of God. The complaint of the souls of the dead is that Azazel has *"revealed the eternal secrets which were (preserved) in heaven, which men were striving to learn."* And Semjaza and his associates *"have gone to the daughters of men upon the earth, and have slept with the women, and have defiled themselves, and have revealed to them all kinds of sins. And the women have borne giants, and the whole earth has thereby been filled with blood and unrighteousness"* (1 En. 9:6-9).

In response to the complaint of the dead, God sends Gabriel to *"proceed against the bastards so that the sons of the Watchers will kill each other in battle;"* as a result, their hope to have eternal life [five hundred years] will not come to pass. God then sends Uriel to the son of Lamech with a message for Noah that the end is approaching with a deluge that will destroy the earth. He is to hide himself and save himself and his seed for all future generations. God also sends Rafael to bind Azazel and cast him into an opening in the desert and to cover the hole with big rocks. There he will be kept until the judgment, when he will be cast into the fire (this prefigures the fortunes of the dragon in the book of *Revelation*). Rafael is also told to heal the earth from the corruption brought about by the secrets revealed by Azazel, so that all sins are ascribed to him. Finally, God sends Michael to bind Semjaza and his associates. *"Let them see their sons killing themselves. Then take them to the valleys of the earth for seventy generations till the day of their judgment. Then they shall be led off to the abyss of fire, the torment and prison where they shall be for ever. Any others who are condemned shall join them there so that all the spirits of the reprobate and the children of the Watchers are destroyed."* Michael then is to destroy all wrong from the earth and let righteousness and truth flourish again in it with truth and joy for evermore (1 En. 10 – 11). It became popular in apocalyptic books to follow the lead of *First Enoch* and have the wicked taken to a place to wait until the time comes for them to be thrown into the fire, and to extend the geography of the earth to mythological locations that are appropriate for the eternal punishment of the wicked.

This section of the book describes the punishment God has already established for the Watchers who brought about sin to earth. This, however, is their first "judgment." Together with all mankind, they will also have to stand at the final judgment. The time between the two judgments is said to last seventy generations, that is the time between the life of Enoch and the writing of the *Book of the Watchers*. The seventy years of exile referred to by Jeremiah had caused Zechariah to wonder about its fulfillment. In the post-exilic chapters of *Isaiah* and in *Ezra*, about 444 B.C.E., Cyrus, the Persian, is identified as the Lord's anointed who will finally restore the fortunes of Israel, after the non-establishment of the Davidic dynasty with Zerubbabel. In the *Book of the Watchers*, the messianic establishment of justice and peace must wait seventy generations, rather than years. It is not quite clear, however, when their counting starts. Evidently, messianic expectations have had many revivals with the passage of time, even to our own days. The ways in which they are related in time to previous events varies according to different agendas. Still, in all of them the judgment or judgments occupy central stage.

Chapters 12 to 16 have Enoch in conversation with the Watchers who ask him to plead their cause to the Most High so that they may return to heaven. Enoch takes up their cause and pleads with God on their behalf, but God rejects their appeals. In the process, one reads that the Giants are now evil spirits (1 En. 15:8) who cause havoc among men and women until the time when the Watchers will face their final judgment (1 En. 16:1). While mediating on their behalf, Enoch is informed that though when they were in heaven the Watchers had learned many secrets, they actually learned only "worthless ones" (1 En. 16:2). Thus, their indiscretions on earth did not cause a major upheaval in heaven. Still, what they taught human beings had been the cause of much wickedness; therefore, they will not have peace until the judgment.

In chapters 17 to 36, Enoch is given a guided tour of the universe. The tour starts in the West where fire receives the sun as it sets down and the mouths of the rivers and the waters of the deep are found. Also there he is shown the foundations and the cornerstone of the earth. Beyond is a place with no firmament and no earth or water beneath. An angel informs Enoch that this is the prison of the stars that disobeyed God and are waiting till their consummation at the judgment after 10,000 years. The spirits of the children born of the cohabitation of Watchers and women are not there. They are defiling mankind in different ways (1 En. 17 – 19; 21:5). At the center of a great mountain range with seven mountains, Enoch sees the highest mountain which, Michael informs him, is the throne of *"the Holy Great One, the Lord of Glory, the Eternal King."* There is found the *"fragrant tree no mortal is permitted to touch till the great judgment.... It shall be given to the righteous and holy. Its fruit shall be for food to the elect: it shall be transplanted to the holy place, to the temple of the Lord, the Eternal King"* (1 En. 25:3-5). That the tree whose fruit could not be eaten is being kept for future transplantation after the judgment stresses the need for obedience now, and provides a model for John in *Revelation*. Following East from the middle of the earth, Enoch is shown valleys where the accursed are gathered for judgment in the presence of the righteous (1 En. 27:1). Further East he is shown mountains covered with wonderful aromatic trees: frankincense, myrrh, almond, nard, cinnamon, pepper, etc. Finally he arrives, east of the Persian and Indian oceans, to the garden of righteousness with fragrant trees and the tree of Wisdom. Its height is that of a fir, its leaves those of a carob and its fruit is like the clusters of the fruit of the vine with a strong aroma. Rafael now informs Enoch that this is the tree *"of which thy father old (in years) and thy aged mother, who were before thee, have eaten, and they learned wisdom and their eyes were opened, and they knew that they were naked and they were driven out of the garden"* (En. 32:6). By bringing up the expulsion of the first pair from the garden of Eden, and the reference to the tree that was not to be touched, the *Book of the Watchers* reaches back to the beginning, further back than the rebellion at Sinai, as the time when sin entered the world. Thus, the book reveals the origin of evil in the world, and informs the readers that the preservation of the tree for future transplanting is a sign that the original purpose of creation will be accomplished.

From there, Enoch was taken to the ends of the earth where he saw great beasts and birds, all different from each other. To the East he saw where the heavens rest and the portals of heaven open. Through those portals the stars enter the heavens on their journeys West. Going North from there he saw other portals of heaven. From one of them comes the North Wind with cold, rain and snow. From the other two enter violence and affliction. After the tour of the whole universe, the *Book of the Watchers* ends with Enoch blessing *"the Lord of Glory who has brought great and glorious wonders, to show the greatness of his work to the angels and to spirits and to men, that they might praise his work and all his creation ... and bless him for ever"* (En. 36:4). The book had begun with Enoch's blessings, and records his blessing of God throughout (1 En. 1:1; 11:1; 12:3; 22:14; 36:4). As demonstrated, the book is concerned to convince the reader that, even though angels who defiled themselves with women and brought into the world giants whose spirits cause men and women to sin, this is still God's world. He has full control over his creation, and his original purpose for creation will be accomplished. The angels who defiled themselves and taught charms and arts to men are already in prison waiting for the final judgment which will eventually take care of all sinners. Then God will restore the world so that peace and joy will endure in it forever. Thus, while making a more extensive use of mythological descriptions, the *Book of the Watchers* follows the course established by *Ezekiel* and *Zechariah*. Its author gives to his contemporaries an explanation for the origin of evil and provides a vision of God's dealing with it.

It is to be noticed that, while The *Book of the Watchers* is aware of the sin of the first couple and of their expulsion from the Garden of Eden, it does not see their disobedience as the cosmic Fall of all creation. Still, its reference to the sin of the first couple is a move in the direction that gave place to the concept of the Fall. The entrance of sin in the human world is thought to have been brought about by the angels who defiled themselves with women and introduced warfare and medical charms and potions. They are the ones who brought into the world fornication, defilement and debauchery. Besides, the book marks a significant shift in Hebraic anthropology, one that facilitated the emergence of apocalypticism. As pointed out above, the prophets Jeremiah and Ezekiel brought about a shift from a corporate to an individual identity. The *Book of the Watchers* introduced a new understanding of the dead as capable of pleading for justice. This opened a new path to eschatological scenarios.

The books of the Old Testament reveal that among the ancient Israelites there were two contrasting conceptions of the dead. On the one hand, there was the view that when a person dies the body that is placed in a grave is still somewhat alive. The nails and the hair are still growing, and the bones remain articulated. In very dry climates, they may stay that way for an indefinite length of time. At the time, the Israelites held a psycho-physical understanding of the person. They did not distinguish between material and ethereal or psychic aspects of an individual. They had no abstract nouns in their vocabulary. This means that they did not conceive the notions of mind, will, idea, etc. They located psychic functions in physical organs. The hand indicates intentions; the arm, strength; the bowels, emotions; the heart, will power. The Hebrew word translated "soul" does not refer to an independent, abstract, essential aspect of a person, but to the whole person as alive, active; in fact it is best translated as "person" or "being." One of the creation stories says that God breathed into the nostrils of a clay form and it became a *"living person, or being"* (Gen. 2:7). When a person, or being, dies, for the Hebrews the "soul" dies (Gen. 37:21; Dt. 19:6; Jer. 40:14-15). Moreover, the word for "spirit" which also means "wind," refers to the moving forces within, the feelings, the ideas, the character of the whole person. Thus, according to one point of view found in the Old Testament, when a person is placed in the grave, it goes into the pit and joins the *rephaim*, the shades. They are negative replicas of living persons who have the remnants of life still in the body. They are a very weak form of life. In this understanding of human beings, life and death are not opposites. They are related to each other within a continuum of different degrees of vitality. While in the realm of the living, persons experience reductions of vitality when they are sick, suffering or under great distress. These experiences are understood to be drawing the person to the gates of Sheol, the place where the *rephaim*, the shades, are found. Thus, while living on the face of the earth, persons may be already feeling that Sheol is taking vital power away from them. The basic characteristic of the shades in Sheol is that they are weak.

The other view of the dead in the Old Testament sees death as the opposite of life. The living exist; the dead do not exist. They are extinct. Death brings about the extraction of life from the body. It is the emptying of life, the dissolution of the person. Of the suffering servant it is said that he *"poured out his soul [being] to death"* (Is. 53:12). Dying in childbirth, Rachel called the newborn Benoni *"as her soul [being] was departing"* (Gen. 35:18). When a woman of Tekoa is coached by Joab to convince King David that he should admit back Absalom into the family, she gives the iconic metaphor for death according to this view. The woman says to David, *"We must all die, we are like water spilt on the ground, which cannot be gathered up again"* (2 Sam. 14:14). According to this view, the dead are in Abaddon (destruction, Job 28:22; Ps. 15:11; 27:20), Dumah (silence, Ps. 115:17). Pleading with God to relent from the unjust treatment he is inflicting on an innocent man, Job says, *"Are not the days of my life few? Let me alone, that I may find a little comfort before I go whence I shall not return, to the land of gloom and deep darkness, the land of gloom and chaos, where light is as darkness"* (Job 10:20-22). In *Job* the dead are in total annihilation. Job reminds God, *"now I shall die on the earth; Thou will seek me, but I shall not be"* (Job 7:21). Under distress, the Psalmist pleads, *"Look away from me, that I may know gladness, before I depart and be no more"* (Ps. 39:13).

The author of the *Book of the Watchers* is aware of the biblical language describing the pit as a place of chaos and "darkness with no light in it." But he is also living in a time when Hellenistic culture has made significant inroads in the Fertile Crescent. Among its many contributions, the Greeks fostered the cross-fertilization of cultural features between Greece and India. Among these was the distinction between the body of the dead and their souls and spirits. Our author describes the Watchers, or the giants, as dead and says that their souls ask Enoch to intercede on their behalf before God. He also sees that the spirits of the dead children of the Watchers are causing women and men to sin. This, of course, reveals the influence of the notions of the soul as an independent, living entity. The language of the defiled angels as spirits in prison, found in *First* and *Second Peter* clearly comes from The *Book of the Watchers* and the Hellenic understanding of life after death. To be noticed also is that those in this prison are not just there, as the *rephaim* in Sheol are described in *Ezekiel* and *Isaiah*. They are suffering punishments while waiting for the judgment that will exterminate them.

The *Book of the Watchers* provides a topography of the underworld, a place not found within the three levels of the biblical world constituted by the heavens above, the earth beneath and the waters under the earth. In the different places surveyed by Enoch the souls seems to be quite alive. This view of death informs the story of the rich man and Lazarus in the gospel According to Luke. That story says that the rich man died and was buried; *"and in Hades, being in torment, he lifted up his eyes and saw Abraham far off and Lazarus in his bosom."* He then pleaded for Abraham to send Lazarus with some water to mitigate the anguish in which he found himself (Lk. 16:19-24). In *Revelation*, when the Lamb opens the fifth seal, John the Prophet sees *"the souls of those who had been slain for the word of God and for the witness they had borne."* They cried out to God asking how much longer they are going to have to wait for the judgment that will avenge their blood (Rev. 6:9-10). These scenarios could only be conceived after the notion of an independent living soul entered the apocalyptic imagination in the *Book of the*

Watchers. Besides, Enoch's tour of the universe in this book provided a proto-apocalyptic model for future descriptions of journeys to the frontiers of the heavens. The tour of the universe serves to prove that God is in complete control of what takes place in the world and that, even if the spirits of the Giants are bringing havoc among women and men at the moment, those who introduced evil in the world are now in prison and all evil doers, together with the Watchers and the Giants, will be annihilated at the final judgment. The righteous are thereby assured that they will be receiving their reward. Certainty that God is in control is what gives hope.

This survey of *Ezekiel, Zechariah* and the *Book of the Watchers* in *First Enoch* reveals how different themes and concepts, both of the nature and identity of human beings and of the origin and agents of evil in God's world, mark the transition from prophetic to apocalyptic biblical literature. While still working within the prophetic understanding of the God of history, these texts move in different directions as they address different historical circumstances. The widening of the horizon within which the Jews lived and the necessity to keep their faith in the promises of God forced them to seek new means for the expression of their faith. In this way these books provided the colors used by the authors of apocalypses with which to paint a relevant picture of the God of creation. The books here reviewed, however, did not quite reach the apocalyptic worldview of God and his world. They reveal that, as the Jews experienced life in a world full of confusing forces that brought about doubts and sometimes despair, they sought new ways to express their faith in the power and justice of the God they worshiped. In the process, they came up with a new conception of the world in which they lived.

Daniel

The prophet Ezekiel refers to Daniel as a most righteous and wise man. He was known as a paragon of righteousness who, if God were to punish Israel for her sins, though he was quite righteous would not be able to save any other member of his family. He would be able to save only himself. This illustration is used by Ezekiel to establish the significance of the change from a corporate, tribal to an individual, personal identity (Ez. 14:14). This legendary ancient worthy, listed by Ezekiel in the company of legendary Noah and Job, was not only remembered for his righteousness but also for his wisdom. Thus, in his taunt of the King of Tyre, Ezekiel sarcastically quotes the king claiming to be "wiser than Daniel" (Ez. 28:3). Other ancient texts from the neighboring nations also know a Dnil, or Danel, who is remembered for his extraordinary wisdom, particularly texts from the XIV century B.C.E. found at Ugarit. Whether the author of *Daniel* is telling stories that had come to him about a Daniel who went to Babylon as an exile from Judea, or is giving the legendary Daniel a more recent Babylonian setting, cannot be determined.

What is clear is that the court tales describe Daniel as a man with *"learning and skill in all letters and wisdom ... and understanding in all visions and dreams"* (Dan. 1:17). King Nebuchadnezzar appointed him *"chief of the magicians, because I know that the spirit of the holy gods is in you and that no mystery is difficult for you"* (Dan. 4:9, 18). King Belshazzar's wife tells him that Daniel is *"a man in whom is the spirit of the holy gods"* and *"light and understanding and wisdom, like the wisdom of the gods, are found in him,"* and that

"King Nebuchadnezzar, your father, made him chief of the magicians, enchanters, Chaldeans, and astrologers, because an excellent spirit, knowledge, and understanding to interpret dreams, explain riddles, and solve problems were found in this Daniel" (Dan. 5:11-12). In line with these characterizations, the ultimate accolade is given by the angel sent to give Daniel an explanation for the delay of Jeremiah's prophecy that after seventy years Israel's fortunes would be restored (Dan. 9:2). He tells Daniel, *"O Daniel, I have come out to give you wisdom and understanding ... to tell it to you, for you are greatly beloved"* (Dan. 9:23). That he is "greatly beloved" by God is repeated twice by the angel (Dan. 10:11, 19). Then, when presidents and satraps, out of envy, seek for a legitimate accusation against him *"they could find no ground for complaint or any fault, because he was faithful, and no error or fault was found in him"* (Dan. 6:4). They, therefore, set up a trap as a means to accuse him of disloyalty to the king and send him to the den of lions. When Darius, after having anxiously spent the night unable to sleep, in the early morning calls on Daniel in the lion's den, he answers, *"My God sent his angel to shut the lion's mouths, and they have not hurt me, because I was found blameless before him, and also before you, O king"* (Dan. 6:22). These descriptions and this claim would be considered gratuitously self-serving in the writings of any author. They can only be taken for what they are when one understands that they were made by another person who is trying to establish his own credentials through Daniel's reputation. All indications point out that *Daniel* was written pseudonymously.

Like in other pseudonymous texts, e.g. *First Enoch, Baruch* and *Ezra*, in *Daniel* are found also the usual devices used by authors impersonating a famous ancestor. Prominent among them is the accounting of past history as prediction, that is *vaticinia ex eventu*. In every case the accuracy of their "predictions" comes to an end at the time when the author is writing. Whenever the author writes about events in his actual future the descriptions are nebulous, and in many cases prove not to be what actually happened. Another characteristic is the need for the visionary to seal the vision because it does not concern his own times. It has to do with what will happen much later, at the time of the end, that is, at the time when the actual author is writing. Thus, the interpreting angel tells Daniel, "Seal up the vision, for it pertains to many days hence" (Dan. 8:26), or that the vision tells *"what will befall your people in the latter days"* (Dan. 10:14). The author, of course, thinks that those days have arrived. "Predicting" ominous events of the recent past, the angel warns Daniel, *"the end is not yet at the time appointed"* (Dan. 11:27). This means that the author is writing about a present that is just short of the time of the end for the benefit of his contemporaries. Thus, the past history presented as what Daniel "predicted" would happen between his time in Babylon, around 580-537 B.C.E., and the author's actual time in Jerusalem, around 167-164 B.C.E., serves to guarantee the authority of the information that the author presents as the solution to the crisis being experienced by his contemporaries.

Another device in common use is to have the ancient worthy confess that when he received the vision, or the angel's interpretation of it, he was troubled and confused. In the case of Daniel, after the angel had interpreted the vision for him, he confessed, *"I, Daniel, was overcome and lay sick for some days, then I rose and went about the king's business; but I was appalled by the vision and did not understand it"* (Dan. 8:27). After the angel *"swore by him who lives for ever"* that the holy people would be persecuted only *"for a time, two times and half a time"* and then Michael would arise to put an end to their suffering and reward them with resurrection, Daniel says, *"I heard, but I did not understand"* (Dan. 12:8). In another occasion, he says, *"As for me, Daniel, my thoughts greatly alarmed me, and my color changed; but I kept the matter in my mind"* (Dan. 7:28). In other words, full understanding of the vision will be possible at the time of the end, that is to say the author's time. Both the sealing of the vision, and the lack of its understanding when received *"by Daniel in Babylon,"* only serves to explain why the "prediction" was not known until now, the author's time.

Further evidence that the book offers *vaticinia ex eventu* is the designation of the dreams or visions as mysteries (Dan. 2:19, 22, 27, 29, 47). As pointed out earlier, the way this word was meant in antiquity is not the way in which it is used in modern times. In antiquity a mystery was discrete information not available to the public at large. It was, in fact, not available on the basis of human abilities to discover things or solve problems. It was, however, within reach of human comprehension. It was information that was privately revealed to the elect few who had been judged worthy by God. Access to a mystery was gained by contact with those who already possessed it. In other words, a mystery was esoteric knowledge. It is because knowledge of a mystery depends on its having been revealed by a divine agent, that we now describe a text that makes use of this device as an *apocalypse,* and this literary genre as apocalypticism. This is a Greek word composed of *apo*, out of, and *kalupto,* to cover, to hide. What has been revealed has been taken out of hiding, what covered it has been removed. The author of an apocalypse has a revelation of divine origin for his contemporaries. To give his revelation ultimate validity, he introduces it with confirming authority by "predicting" events that have already taken place.

Also to be considered in terms of the formal characteristics of the book, is the language and identity of the pseudonymous author. *Daniel* contains two kinds of materials. One section consists of stories about Daniel and his companions in the courts of pagan kings, told by an anonymous narrator in the third person (chapters 1 – 6). Another contains visions which Daniel relates in the first person (chapters 7 – 12). Besides, the book was written in two languages: 1:1 – 2:4a, and 8 – 12 in Hebrew, and 2:4b – 7:28 in Aramaic; but the languages do not match the division of the material according to their contents. Besides, the Greek translation of *Daniel* in the Septuagint has a prayer of Azariah (Abednego) and the Song of the Three Young Men added to chapter 3. The stories of Susana and of Bel and the Dragon, not found in the Hebrew canon of Scripture, also appear as separate units in the Septuagint. These additions to the Hebrew-Aramaic contents suggest that the text was edited putting together separate pieces, a process that continued for some time and gave rise to different recensions of the text. That the compilation of existing materials in different languages was done by editors is also suggested by the presence of different visions with idiosyncratic details dealing with the same historical period. Most likely, by this means the editors indicated that by itself one telling of a vision does not exhaust the message being conveyed. Even multiple allegorical versions of an event may not quite capture its significance. Thus, the publication of different versions of apocalyptic visions was not intended to give information. The visions were meant to spark the imagination, and to awake desires that would bring about specific behaviors. The different descriptions of the same event open up horizons for understanding. This characteristic of the text has allowed readers of *Daniel* in later times to favor a particular version of the story in order to concoct scenarios that fit their own historical circumstances and thus identify their own time as the time of the end.

It is generally agreed that the "author" of *Daniel* were scribes in Jerusalem who edited preexisting materials. Their handling of the text also gave the text thematic unity. Their work, however, also makes it difficult to take at face value the details of the court tales. Besides the length of time involved, covering the reigns of Nebuchadnezzar, Belshazzar, Darius the Mede and Cyrus, there are no historical records of a Darius the Mede. The Persian Darius who succeeded Cyrus was not from Media. Fundamentalists who have attempted to find Darius the Mede in the historical record have relied on anachronistic arguments from silence that prove nothing. Accounts of past events in antiquity were not primarily concerned to establish what had actually taken place. They tell the past with a specific agenda in mind, with either moral or political implications. *Daniel* is no exception. This text is not a historical but a theological work.

Reading Daniel Theologically

The court tales

While Jerusalem scribes, obviously, had significant historical records covering events from the Exile to the Maccabean War, the book's agenda is what determines the twists in the story. Already in the third century C.E., Porphyry noticed that while the author "predicted" the course of events from the time of the Exile to the time of Antiochus IV Epiphanes, with recognizable historical correspondences, he could not do so beyond that time. Modern scholarship has found Porphyry's observation valid and has determined, on the basis of it and other factors, that the book was written at the time of the Maccabean War, 167-64 B.C.E. Recognizing this fact helps to understand why the book was published in two languages. Facing the trials brought about by Antiochus' suppression of Jewish customs and religion, and his imposition of Greek culture and religion, the author thought appropriate to adapt the court tales from the Babylonian exile, available in Aramaic oral traditions, as models of what faithful Jews were expected to do under the present circumstances.

By means of editorial devices the author/editors adapted the traditional tales and used them to offer advice to the readers of their apocalyptic visions. The *vaticinia ex eventu* were written using information found in their chronicles. Chapters 4 and 5 present parallel stories of pagan kings who exalted themselves. Nebuchadnezzar is depicted in a dream as a tree *"whose top reached to heaven, and was visible to the ends of the whole earth ... the beasts of the field found shade under it, and the birds of the air dwelt in its branches, and all flesh was fed from it"* (Dan. 4:11-12). That all humanity could be fed from one tree is, to say the least, an exaggeration serving a purpose. Sometime later Nebuchadnezzar bragged, *"Is not this great Babylon, which I have built by my mighty power as a royal residence and for the glory of my majesty?"* (Dan. 4:30). Apparently, he had not taken seriously what Daniel had told him as the meaning of his dream of the giant tree, *"the Most High rules the kingdom of men, and gives it to whom he will"* (Dan. 4:25).

Belshazzar, for his part, took the vessels of silver and gold which had been carried to Babylon as booty after the destruction of Jerusalem and its temple and used them so that *"the king and his lords, his wives and his concubines might drink from them … They drank wine, and praised the gods of gold and silver, bronze, iron, wood and stone"* (Dan. 5:2, 4). They used sacred objects for profane drunkenness and idolatry. In these stories, a dream or a mysterious writing on the wall needs to be interpreted, and only Daniel, with the help of his God, is able to reveal the meaning of the dream or what was written on a wall by a non-human hand. The judgment of God on the hubris of these two kings took place swiftly. Nebuchadnezzar was reduced to live like a beasts of the field, while the words of his boast *"were still in the king's mouth"* (Dan. 4:31). The other story tells that *"that very night Belshazzar the Chaldean king was slain"* (Dan. 5:30). Both stories have something important to say to the readers of *Daniel* about the author's contemporary king, who is profaning "the temple and fortress, and [is taking] away the continual burnt offering. And [is setting] up the abomination that makes desolate" (Dan. 11:31): The hubris of Antiochus will bring upon him also a swift divine judgment. In fact *Daniel* predicts that Antiochus *"shall come to his end, with none to help him"* (Dan. 11:45). This actual prediction did not take place swiftly, however.

The stories in chapters 3 and 6 constitute another couplet. Both tell about Jews who disobeyed a royal decree, were punished by being placed where it is impossible to survive, but came out of those places having suffered no harm. On account of this marvelous demonstration of God's power to rescue from places where no other god could possibly rescue anyone, those who had accused the Jews before the king are placed into those places, and the efficacy of their power to end human life is amply demonstrated. In chapter 3, envious of the fact that Nebuchadnezzar had appointed Shadrach, Meshach and Abednego over the affairs of the province of Babylon, *"certain Chaldeans came forward and maliciously accused the Jews*" of not paying heed to the king. They said, *"they do not serve your gods or worship the golden image which you have set up"* (Dan. 3:8, 12). Confronted by the king and asked whether the accusation was true, the three declared their confidence that their God would deliver them. They actually go further and affirm that if their God should decide not to deliver them, they would rather be martyrs than serve the gods of the king, or worship the image he has set up (Dan. 3:13-16). This, obviously, provides direct instructions to those facing martyrdom at the hands of Antiochus. Nebuchadnezzar's challenge, *"who is the god that will deliver you out of my hands?"* (Dan. 3:15), is answered by no other than himself confessing, *"Blessed be the God of Shadrach, Meshach, and Abedenego, who has sent his angel and delivered his servants, who trusted in him, and set at naught the king's command, and yielded up their bodies rather than serve and worship any god except their own God"* (Dan. 3:28). It is difficult to imagine that King Nebuchadnezzar blessed the God of the Jews because three of them had set at naught his decree. Every word in this confession is addressed to those facing a serious threat to their allegiance to the God of Israel in Maccabean times. The story demonstrates that God keeps his promise to deliver those willing to face martyrdom.

The same is true of the story of *"all the presidents of the kingdom, the prefects and the satraps, the counselors and the governors"* who were envious of the king's desire to set Daniel over the whole kingdom, and asked Darius the Mede to decree that *"whoever makes petition to any god or man for thirty days, except to you, O king, shall be cast into the den of lions"* (Dan. 6:7). Unlike Nebuchadnezzar, who takes seriously the charge of those anonymous Chaldeans, Darius realizes that he has fallen into a trap set up by envious courtiers. He knows that once he has issued a decree *"according to the law of the Medes and the Persians, which cannot be revoked"* (Dan. 6:8), he should let events run their course. Still, he seeks for a way to avoid the application of the law, but fails. Once Daniel is in the lions' den, the king spends a restless night and in the morning is anxious to find out what happened to Daniel. When he comes to the den,

The End of the Scroll

Daniel tells him that the lions had not hurt him, and when he was out of the den it was determined that *"no kind of hurt was found in him, because he had trusted in his God"* (Dan. 6:22-23). Again, this was a direct message to the author's contemporaries who faced martyrdom. Unlike Nebuchadnezzar who pronounced a blessing, Darius the Mede *"wrote to all the peoples, nations, and languages that dwell in all the earth: 'Peace be multiplied to you. I made a decree, that in all my royal dominion men tremble and fear before the God of Daniel, for he is the living God, enduring for ever; his kingdom shall never be destroyed, and his dominion shall be to the end"* (Dan. 6:25-26). Obviously, apocalyptic writers never pass by an opportunity to stress that foreign kings recognize the absolute power of their God. After all, for them the issue is whether God is all-powerful and just. To have foreign kings recognize the power of the God of the Israelites was one of the two items in the agenda of *Ezekiel*.

While the first pair of stories in chapters 3 and 6 inculcate the power of God to protect his chosen ones from death, the second pair in chapters 4 and 5 demonstrate that proud kings who pretend to have more power than any god are brought down by the Almighty God of the Jews. The third pair of stories are found chiastically in chapters 2 and 7, which adopt the very well known ancient pattern of the four kingdoms. In its traditional form the four are: Assyria, Media, Persia and Macedonia. They are found in Hesiod's *Works and Days,* 106-201. The Greek poet argued that mankind, which had a glorious past, now finds itself in a descending slope, and represents it with metals of declining value: gold, silver, bronze and iron. While the presentation by the same metals in chapter 2 comes from the West, the schema of four kingdoms, or four historical stages, including Assyrians and Medes, appears to have originated in the East because the Assyrians and the Medes never had a foothold in the West. Most likely, Herodotus, who also uses the schema, learned it during his travels in the East. The author of *Daniel* introduced Babylon as a replacement for Assyria, and invented Darius the Mede to flesh out the rule of Media. Thus the series of Nebuchadnezzar, Belshazzar, Darius the Mede and Cyrus, though not historically correct, restates the schema of the four kingdoms found in chapter 2. To be noticed, also is that chapter 7 reverts back to the reign of Belshazzar, thus two kings represent Babylon. The four kingdoms sequence is then retaken with Darius the Mede in chapter 8 and Cyrus the Persian in chapter 10, where reference is made to the divinely appointed rise of Greece after Persia (Dan. 10:20).

In both chapter 2 and chapter 7 the four kingdoms appear and disappear together. This is the clue to their function in the book. Since the audience surely had some notions of the past history of the Jews under Babylonian, Median, Persian and Hellenistic rule, the listing of the four kingdoms is not intended to tell them what they do not know, but to let them know that God is in charge of the affairs of nations. The court tales emphasize that not only pagan kings but all "the living" must learn that the God of Daniel, Hananiah, Mishael and Azariah (named as Belteshazzar, Shadrach, Meshach and Abednego by the Babylonians) *"rules the kingdom of men, and gives it to whom he will, and sets over it the lowliest of men"* (Dan. 4:17). This most certainly means that those suffering persecution and death at the hands of Antiochus must understand that their historical circumstances are also controlled by the Most High, and their deliverance is certain to come just as swiftly as the punishment of proud kings had come in the past. Of the future of Antiochus IV, Epiphanes, Daniel predicts, *"the king shall do according to his will; he shall exalt himself and magnify himself above every god, and shall speak astonishing things against the God of gods. He shall prosper until the indignation is accomplished; for what is determined shall be done"* (Dan. 11:36). Thus, *Daniel* follows the tradition established already by *Ezekiel* and *Zechariah*. The course of history has already been determined, the only wise course of action in this world is to persevere with patient endurance until the (also predetermined) time of the end arrives. Then those who have remained faithful to God's purpose will be delivered from their sufferings.

The apocalyptic visions

Chapter 7 serves as a link between the court tales and the visions by its use of the schema of the four kingdoms, but its agenda is to set up the stage for the fourth beast. In the vision, Daniel says, *"I desired to know the truth concerning the fourth beast, which was different from all the rest, exceedingly terrible, with its teeth of iron and claws of bronze; and which devoured and broke in pieces, and stamped the residue with its feet; and concerning the ten horns that were on its head, and the other horn which came up and before which three of them fell, the horn which had eyes and a mouth that spoke great things, and which seemed greater than its fellows"* (Dan. 7:19-20). At the telling of the vision, the speech of the rising greater horn, Daniel says, *"I looked then because of the sound of the great words which the horn was speaking. And as I looked, the beast was slain, and its body destroyed and given over to be burned with fire. As for the rest of the beasts, their dominion was taken away, but their lives were prolonged for a season and a time"* (Dan. 7:11-12). When the interpreting angel answers Daniel's desire to know about the fourth beast, he interprets the speech of the greater horn, saying, *"He shall speak words against the Most High, and shall wear out the saints of the Most High, and shall think to change the times and the law; and they shall be given into his hand for a time, two times, and a half time. But the court shall sit in judgment, and his dominion shall be taken away, to be consumed and destroyed to the end"* (Dan. 7:25-26).

With these descriptions, *Daniel* presents some details of the fourth beast, the one that is of particular interest to the intended audience. The four beasts, as already noticed, are Babylon, Media, Persia and Greece/Macedonia. Naturally, the contemporaries of the author are interested in the present, the time of the Hellenistic rule of the Near East. After the conquest of Alexander the Great and his early death at Babylon in 313 B.C.E., the lands he had conquered were contested by his generals and after some time four of them succeeded in securing territories of their own. Two of those were of particular significance to the Jews now living in Judea. Seleucus, who secured his throne in Syria, and Ptolemy, who established himself in Egypt. Eventually the Seleucid Antiochus III expanded his dominions further East and tried to also extend them South into Egypt and North into Asia Minor. In response, the Ptolemies resisted the invasions of the Seleucid kings and tried to push the frontier between the two kindgoms as far North as possible in the narrow corridor between the Mediterranean Sea and the desert just East of the Jordan valley. As a consequence, for many years Judea saw the armies of the Seleucids and the Ptolemies going over their territory back and forth. These military operations are described in cryptic details in chapter 11 as campaigns of the king of the North and the king of the South who trample over the "glorious land" (Dan. 8:9; 11:16, 41) and "the glorious holy mountain" (Dan. 11:45). Eventually, attempts to conquer Egypt were stopped by "ships of Kittim" who came to prevent further expansions by the Seleucids (Dan. 11:30). The reference is to the intervention by the Romans, who depended on their purchase of grains from Egypt, and were also beginning to expand into Asia Minor after their victory at Magnesia in 190 B.C.E. They prevented the expansion of the dominions of the Seleucids of Syria.

As a result, Antiochus IV decided on the consolidation of his dominions by means of a unifying culture, including its religious aspects. These developments, apparently, were accepted gladly by local peoples, including many Jews, because Hellenism, after all, was a more advanced culture. In Jerusalem, while cultural features gained wide acceptance, the official enforcement of Hellenistic religion brought about a major confrontation because it interfered with Jewish religious observances. The introduction of the Hellenistic calendar was rejected because according to it the Jewish feasts would be celebrated on the wrong days. The tensions created by the imposition of the Hellenistic solar calendar are described in The Astronomical Book (chapters 72-82 of *First Enoch)* and the book of *Jubilees.* To abandon living according to the Mosaic Law and adopt a Hellenistic lifestyle was quite acceptable to many, but was rejected by the very pious. These disruptions of the Jewish way of life are described as the horn's *thinking* to change the times and the law (Dan. 7:25). In other words, what Antiochus IV decreed did not change anything. It was only in his mind that things changed, not in reality. As far as the faithful Jews were concerned, their traditional calendar and the requirement to observe all the statutes of the Mosaic law were still fully in force (Dan. 9:10-13).

Chapter 11 describes Antiochus IV's takeover of the Jerusalem temple to use it for the worship of Zeus. *"Forces from him shall appear and profane the temple and fortress, and shall take away the continual burnt offering. And they shall set up the abomination that makes desolate"* (Dan. 11:31). The ultimate insult to the Most High God of the Jews was the stoppage of the continual burnt offering and the setting up of sacrifices to Zeus, the abomination that makes desolate. The continual burnt offering was the offering of a lamb every morning and every evening for the unconscious sins of all the people. Having committed a specified sin, a Jew was required to go to the temple and offer a sacrifice to expiate for it. Sins committed unintentionally, of which one may not even be aware, were covered by the perpetual burnt offering. Their discontinuation created a major disruption in the temple's effective maintenance of the people's connection with God. Besides this interference, Antiochus IV decreed that the altar of the temple be used to offer white pigs as sacrifices to Zeus. In Greek religion, Zeus did not particularly like lambs; he liked best a white pig, an animal classified as impure in Torah. This usage of the altar, of course, was the ultimate abomination, a total desecration of the temple that rendered the walled city of Jerusalem impure. According to *Daniel*, this was to take place for three and a half years, *"time, two times and half a time"* (Dan. 7:25; 12:7, compare with 4:16 for the identification of a "time" as a year). This period, with a little discrepancy most likely due to our lack of knowledge of the calendar used to count the years, is also given as 1,290 days (Dan. 12:11). It did take place between the years 167 and 164 B.C.E. In December of 164, after Judas Maccabeus had taken back Jerusalem, the purification of the altar and re-consecration of the temple was carried out with much solemnity and devotion. The remembrance of that event takes place to this day at the Feast of Hannukah. After saying that the cessation of the burnt offering and the abomination that makes desolate would last 1,290 days, the author announces a blessing: *"Blessed is he who waits and comes to the thousand three hundred and thirty five days"* (Dan. 12:12). Exactly what took place at that time it has not been possible to determine. It may have to do with the re-dedication of the temple sometime after the taking back of Jerusalem by Judas. The book ends with this blessing, which most likely was added by someone after the successful Maccabean war.

What did not take place at that time was the total destruction of the Seleucid dominion, and the survival of Babylon, Media and Persia without dominion as predicted in *Daniel*. It announced that *"at the time of the end the king of the south [Egypt] shall attack him [Antiochus IV]; but the king of the north shall rush upon him like a whirlwind ... And he shall become ruler of the treasures of Egypt; and the Lybians and the Ethiopians shall follow in his train ... and he shall pitch his palatial tents between the sea and the glorious holy mountain; yet he shall come to his end, with none to help him"* (Dan. 11:40-45). The different visions going over the same events and announcing different outcomes, demonstrate that the book was put together from materials by different hands written at different moments of these traumatic times.

The activities of Median, Persian and Seleucid kings who had control over Jerusalem and "the glorious land" are described with purposely indefinite characterizations. The reference to the four kingdoms in one of the court tales uses metals in a descending order of value. Beasts with features reminiscent of sphinxes, griffins or centaurs, but also incongruous elements from other animals, are identified by an angel as Media, Persia and Greece (Dan. 8:20-21), there are repeated references to *"kings shall arise"* and *"another shall arise"* (Dan. 7:24), or *"a king of bold countenance ... shall arise"* (Dan. 8:23). These references are at times difficult to identify with any certainty. After an explicit reference to a *"fourth king of Persia"*

The End of the Scroll

who stirs up *"all against the kingdom of Greece,"* however, the account tells that *"a mighty king shall arise, who shall rule with great dominion and do according to his will. And when he has arisen, his kingdom shall be broken and divided toward the four winds of heaven, but not to his posterity"* (Dan. 11:2-4). Even twenty two centuries later, it is quite possible for us to identify the references to the Medic wars and the career of Alexander the Great. This preliminary sketch of the entrance of Greece sets up the extended account of the struggles between *"the king of the north"* and *"the king of the south"* (Dan. 11:7-45), which obviously describe several rulers of the Seleucid and the Ptolemaic dynasties which were the beneficiaries of the *"broken and divided"* dominions of Alexander the Great which were not ruled by *"his posterity."* Also identifiable is the reference to *"ships from Kittim"* (Dan. 11:30), the Roman control of shipping in the Mediterranean, after having taken care of the pirates that controlled the Southern coast of Asia Minor. In between the descriptions of the campaigns of the Syrian and Egyptian rulers who trampled over Palestine in their struggles against each other, there is a reference to *"a commander"* who *"shall put an end to his insolence"* (the king of the north's; Dan. 11:18), and to "the prince of the covenant" (Dan. 11:22). Readers are also told that *"the king shall do according to his will"* (Dan. 11:36). All these fuzzy references, obviously, were easily deciphered by those with knowledge of the recent past in the affairs of Jerusalem and its powerful neighbors. The common feature in the accounts is that they come again and again to the time when the continual burnt offering is stopped and the abomination that makes desolate is installed in its place (Dan. 8:11; 9:27; 11:31). According to the editors of *Daniel*, when this takes place the time for Jeremiah's prophecy about the desolation of Jerusalem, about which Daniel prays intensely (Dan. 9:18), has finally arrived.

WHAT ABOUT JEREMIAH'S PROPHESY?

Chapter 9 considers a matter that had been a source of discomfort to the Jews who returned to Judea at the end of the exile. Jeremiah had prophesied that seventy years would pass before the end of the desolation of Jerusalem at the hands of Nebuchadnezzar (Jer. 25:11-12). Exactly when these years would begin is not quite clear. The taking of Jerusalem and the sending of captives to Mesopotamia took place in 605 B.C.E. The Jewish king was taken captive to Babylon in 597 B.C.E., and the total destruction of the temple and Jerusalem took place in 586 B.C.E. If by the "desolation" of Jerusalem is meant the destruction of the city and the temple, then the return of the Jews from captivity took place before seventy years had passed, in 536 B.C.E. As noticed in my analysis of the message of Zechariah, at the time of the rebuilding of the temple, beginning in 520 B.C.E. people were also concerned with the fulfillment of Jeremiah's prophecy. Of course, they were expecting the "restoration of the fortunes of Israel," and this caused great expectation of the Messiah, the descendant of David who was the anointed of the Lord. He would bring about the restoration not just of the temple but also of the nation as an independent kingdom. This had not happened, as expected, under the leadership of Zerubbabel (Zech. 4:9-10).

A revival of Messianic expectation had taken place also at the time of Ezra and Nehemiah, around 445 B.C.E., when the expectations that had Zerubbabel in mind had faded and new ones were placed on Cyrus, the Persian king. In a post-exilic passage of *Isaiah* a prophet announces, *"Thus says the Lord, your Redeemer, who formed you from the womb: I am the Lord who made all things ... who says of Jerusalem, 'She shall be inhabited,' and of the cities of Judah, 'They shall be built' ... who says of Cyrus, 'He is my shepherd, and he shall fulfill all my purpose ... Thus says the Lord to his anointed, to Cyrus ... I will go before you ... For the sake of my servant Jacob, and Israel my chosen, I call you by your name ... that men may know ... that there is none beside me; I am the Lord, and there is no other"* (Is.

The End of the Scroll

44:24 – 45:6). The messianic expectations centered on Cyrus also proved evanescent. Jerusalem continued to be ruled by Persian satraps. The expectation of a Messiah that would restore the fortunes of Israel, whether placed on Zerubbabel, a descendant of David, or on an unlikely pagan king of Persia, Cyrus, proved unfounded. Instead of living in a restored kingdom ruled by the Messiah, the editors of *Daniel* and their fellow Jews found themselves prevented from worshiping Yahveh in Jerusalem and being martyred because they were refusing to worship Zeus. Where is the God who claims that beside him there is no other god? Where is the fulfillment of Jeremiah's prophecy that after seventy years the desolation of Jerusalem would end?

To allay the concerns about the disconfirmation of Jeremiah's prophecy, *Daniel* offers a re-interpretation. The seventy years are not seventy years. Actually, *"seventy weeks of years are decreed concerning your people and your holy city, to finish the transgression, to put an end to sin, and to atone for iniquity, to bring in everlasting righteousness, to seal both vision and prophet, and to anoint a most holy place"* (Dan. 9:24). This revision of Jeremiah's prophecy specifies that the prophecy was concerned with the punishment for Israel's sins and their atonement, but it explicitly changes the length of this punishment from seventy to four hundred and ninety years. This time period runs *"from the going forth of the word to restore and build Jerusalem"* (Dan. 9:25) *"until the decreed end is poured out on the desolator"* (Dan. 9:27). The desolator, of course, is Antiochus IV. It is not clear how the editors of *Daniel* came to the understanding that between the end of the Exile and the Maccabean War there were four hundred and ninety years, seventy weeks of years. Neither can it be determined on what basis did they count *"two thousand and three hundred evenings and mornings"* as the duration of *"the vision concerning the continual burnt offering, the transgression that makes desolate, the giving over of the sanctuary and host to be trampled underfoot ... before the sanctuary is restored to its rightful state"* (Dan. 8:13-14). The restoration of the sanctuary, or course, is a reference to the dedication of the temple after the Maccabean War.

That number of days is just short of six years and 4 months. On the other hand, if the reference to "evenings and mornings" is to the morning and evening burnt offerings taking place twice a day, the time would be reduced to about three and a half years. These numbers certainly prove that the editors who put together the book of *Daniel* worked with different sources and had archives at their disposal. Most likely, then, they were scribes. It is because they were confident of the accuracy of their sources that they repeatedly affirm that what they are writing is true (Dan. 8:26; 10:1; 11:1). It has been a characteristic of apocalyptic visionaries to claim to have access to the predetermined plan of God concerning "the future" because they know *"what is inscribed in the book of truth"* (Dan. 10:21). Their basic premise is that they know exactly when the appointed "time of the end" is to be Thus they can say that when something happened *"the end is yet to be at the time appointed,"* that is, this recent event does not mark the time of the end. On the other hand, they can also say that *"at the time appointed"* (Dan. 10:29) such and such will happen, or that something will not happen *"until the decreed end is poured out on the desolator."*

This established a pattern for future apocalyptic interpreters of Scripture to have as their basic premise that everything in Scripture was written for "the time of the end," and that they are living at "the time of the end." This hermeneutical method was at work, for example, when the Covenanters of Qumran interpreted *Habakkuk*, a non-apocalyptic book, with this apocalyptic hermeneutic. A few years later, however, after the debacles produced by the revolts against Rome in 70 and 135 C.E., the Jews rejected all apocalyptic interpretations of history. When Rabbinic Judaism established its canon of Scripture, the book of *Daniel* had a hard time becoming part of it. Unfortunately, at different times throughout the history of Christianity there has been a succession of apocalyptic enthusiasts who have taken biblical texts and read them as apocalyptic "predictions" of their own "time of the end," which proved not to have been.

The End of the Scroll

PRINCES, WATCHERS AND HOLY ONES

Like in *First Enoch*, in *Daniel* the activities of powerful, haughty kings is not only against the armies of earthly opponents, but their battles are being fought also in heavenly realms. The interpretation given by the angel to the vision of the four terrible beasts coming out of the sea ends affirming that *"the saints of the Most High shall receive the kingdom, and possess the kingdom for ever, for ever and ever"* (Dan 7:18). The Hebrew word *kad'dishah* translated "saints" is usually translated "holy ones," as is the case in *First Enoch*, where they are unmistakably angels. In the account of the vision, however, the kingdom is received by "one like a son of man." He, therefore, must have some close relationship to the holy ones, that is, to the angels. In *Daniel* one reads that *"a watcher, a holy one, came down from heaven"* and that a sentence was given *"by the decree of the watchers, the decision by the word of the holy ones"* (Dan. 4:13, 17). The identification of holy ones as watchers leaves no doubt that, as is the case in *First Enoch*, the holy ones or watchers are angels. In other words, the affairs of human beings on earth are being represented as the affairs of heavenly, holy beings. The descriptions of Antiochus IV in chapters 10 – 12 say that *"he shall exalt himself and magnify himself above every god, and shall speak astonishing things against the God of gods"* (Dan. 11:36). In a corresponding vision the little horn *"grew great, even to the host of heaven; and some of the host of the stars it cast down to the ground, and trampled upon them. It magnified itself, even up to the Prince of the host"* (Dan. 8:10), also described as *"the Prince of princes"* (Dan. 8:25). There can be no doubt that the conflict against the "Prince of the host," or "of princes," in which Antiochus IV, who "magnifies himself above every god" is involved, is being conceptualized and represented as a battle between supernatural beings. In *Daniel* kings are human beings, but princes are leading angels. The *"prince of Persia"* (Dan. 10:20), for example, is the angel charged with the affairs of Persia, not its king. That in a battle stars are cast down to earth means that it is taking place in heavenly places as well as on earth, and angelic beings are being defeated. The supernatural stage of the struggle is made explicit when Michael, *"one of the chief princes"* (Dan. 10:13), *"your prince"* (Dan. 10:21), or *"the great prince who has charge of your people"* (Dan. 12:1) is fighting with the *"the prince of the kingdom of Persia"* (Dan. 10:13) and *"the Prince of Greece"* (Dan. 10:20). These princes are all angels. Repeatedly, angels are identified as having *"the appearance of a man"* (Dan. 8:15; 10:18), having *"a man's voice"* (Dan. 8:16) and being able to touch humans (Dan. 10:10, 18). At times, they are described as *"man"* (Dan. 10:5; 12:6-7). Besides Michael, described as the angel in charge of the Jews, *"the man Gabriel"* (Dan 9:21), whom Daniel had already seen before, is an angelic being involved in communicating the meaning of a vision. It may be recalled that in *Ezekiel* the one sitting on the throne has *"the likeness as it were of a human being"* (Ez. 1:26). In the apocalyptic universe, the earthly and the heavenly realms are mutually permeable.

All these descriptions demonstrate that what takes place on earth is not determined by human beings. The human and the divine worlds are linked together. Divine interventions in the human world are not interruptions of the "laws of nature" but evidence of God's control over creation. This is frequently the case in ancient Eastern texts. In the New Testament, it is explicit in the song of the angelic host who sang to the shepherds, *"Glory to God in the highest and on earth; peace among men with whom he is pleased"* (Lk. 2:14), and the petition *"...thy will be done on earth as it is in heaven,"* in the Lord's Prayer (Mt. 6:10). In traditional thought the heavenly and the earthly realms are intimately related; ritual acts are enactments, or repetitions of primordial divine acts. Human observance of rest on the Sabbath is in keeping with what God did at creation week, and as such keeps creation stable. In apocalyptic texts, the activities of angels describe earthly realities. So, in *Daniel* the angelic *"holy ones"* receive the kingdom, but *"the kingdom and the dominion and the greatness of the kingdom under the whole heaven shall be given to the people of the saints [holy ones] of the Most High"* (Dan. 7:27). Now, the people of the saints certainly are earthly human beings who are led by angelic ones. As said in the introduction, apocalyptic thought conceives things in terms of heavenly realities that determine earthly realities.

THE ANCIENT OF DAYS AND THE ONE LIKE A SON OF MAN

Apocalyptic thought is primarily concerned with a judgment that establishes God's power and justice. In *Daniel*, the judgment takes place in a heavenly court, not on earthly battle fields. Rather than to present the judgment, as in *Ezekiel* or *First Enoch*, as severe, harsh punishments on those who do evil on earth, *Daniel* presents the judgment in a heavenly court scene, and its protagonists are fashioned in traditional mythic terms. The description is succinct, *"As I looked, thrones were placed and one that was ancient of days took his seat; … the court sat in judgment, and the books were opened"* (Dan. 7:9-10). *"I saw in the night vision, and behold, with the clouds of heaven there came one like a son of man, and he came to the Ancient of Days and was presented before him. And to him was given dominion and glory and kingdom"* (Dan. 7:13-14). In this way the activities of the little horn that grew greater than all the other horns, spoke *"words against the Most High"* and thought *"to change the times and the law"* (Dan. 7:25) come to an end. This double description of the setting for the Judgment reflects the use of sources about the events leading to the desecration of the temple by the editors. In a parallel vision, the little horn is said to be a King of the North who is to *"profane the temple and fortress," "take away the continual burnt offering," "set up the abomination that makes desolate"* and *"seduce with flattery those who violate the covenant"* [collaborators with Antiochus] (Dan. 11:31). The "Ancient of Days" and the "One Like a Son of Man" are, undoubtedly, heavenly figures. One is the judge and the other the plaintiff who receives the benefits of the judgment taking place at the throne where the books had been opened. Thus, the dominion that was being exercised by the King of the North [the little horn] was taken away from him and given to one like a son of man without any violence involved. The desolation of Jerusalem, which according to Jeremiah would last seventy years (Jer. 25:11), according to Ezekiel would last 40 years (Eze. 4:6) and according to Daniel's interpreting angel would last 70 weeks of years (Dan. 9:24), would end when the One Like a Son of Man receives dominion and glory and kingdom (Dan. 7:14). This kingdom, however, is also given to *"the saints of the Most High"* (Dan 7:18, 22), that is the angels, and to *"the people of the saints of the Most High"* (Dan. 7:27), that is righteous human beings. In this roundabout way the righteous people of God are being assured that the human agent of the primordial powers of evil causing their suffering will be defeated, and the dominion over the affairs of men on earth exercised by kings (horns) energized by primordial evil (beasts coming out of the deep sea) will be given to them by the Ancient of Days "at the time appointed." *Daniel* was written to affirm that *"God is righteous in all the works he has done"* (Dan. 9:14). This is its positive theological message.

Biblical authors were quite familiar with mythological motifs and traditions. Mythic conflicts as a reference to creation in which Rahab, Leviathan, Behemoth, the fleeting or the twisting serpent and the dragon of the sea are the main protagonists are found in *Isaiah* (27:1; 51:9-10), *Job* (Job 26:7-13; 40:15-34) and *Psalms* (74:13-14). The creation story of Gen. 1:1 – 2:4a, begins stating that *"darkness was upon the face of the deep; and the wind (Spirit) of God was moving over the face of the waters."* This description of the chaos that existed before creation has its roots in familiar mythological stories. Of course, one of the great theological breakthroughs of the Old Testament is the way in which its story of creation in Genesis 1 overcomes the mythological world by depicting God as totally absent from the world he is creating. The only link between God and his world is the creating Word. The story fleshes out the insight preserved in a Psalm, *"By the word of the Lord were the heavens made, and all their host by the breath of his mouth"* (Ps. 33:6). The Danielic vision in chapter 7 starts saying, *"the four winds of heaven were stirring up the great sea. And four great beasts came up out of the *sea*" (Dan. 7:2). This immediately places the vision in a primordial cosmic context. In the interpretation of the vision, the beasts are identified as four kings that will arise, and the fourth is further identified as a kingdom. This does not limit the vision to just an earthly reality. The beasts turn out to be terrifying, indomitable monsters that have emerged out of the deep sea as manifestations of maleficent forces of chaos. The symbolism of the "great sea" as the locus of evil cannot be overlooked. The vision has to do with evil forces manifesting themselves in the human world. In this way *Daniel* does not see the presence of evil as a puzzle, like in *Jeremiah*, or as having been brought about by watchers who desired the daughters of men, as in *First Enoch*. Here evil has a primordial, cosmic origin, and it manifests itself in human beings who pretend to be stronger than God and cause death to those who wish to remain faithful to God's will as found in the Law of Moses. God is righteous in all he does, however. He will take away the dominion and the power of these primordial evil forces and give it to the people of the saints of the Most High.

The scene of the monstrous beasts emerging from the sea, and the struggles between the horns of the fourth beast, does not culminate in battles between armies on earth, as in *Ezekiel* (Ezek. 38-39). The chaotic situation presented by the dominion of the beasts and their horns is interrupted by a majestic scene in heaven. Judgment is set up as the Ancient of Days appears and the books are opened. This depiction of God is not found anywhere else in the Bible. It can only be understood as an adaptation of the figure of El, as depicted in the XIV century B.C.E. texts from Ugarit. In them El is called the *abu shanima*, "father of years." In the Old Testament, as is well known, God is called both *Yahveh* and *El*, or *Elohim*, the plural form of *El*. In English Bibles, *El* or *Elohim* is translated as "God," and *Yahveh* as "Lord." Thus the Hebrew expression *Yahveh Elohim* is translated "the Lord God." The Ancient of Days in *Daniel* is another way of referring to *El*, or its plural of majesty *Elohim*.

The other protagonist in the majestic divine judgment scene is introduced saying, *"with the clouds of heaven there came one like a son of man, and he came to the Ancient of Days*" (Dan. 7:13). As noticed already, in *Daniel* angels are said to be men. The Hebrew expression "son of man," like the Hebrew expression "daughters of Jerusalem," are circumlocutions for respectively "man" and "Jerusalem" or "inhabitants of Jerusalem." The "One Like a Son of Man" is, therefore, a man who, as it is said of Michael, Gabriel and other angels, is also a divine being. He is the prototype of angels and men because, as I pointed out above, the dominion and the kingdom that is taken away from the monstrous chaotic beasts and their horns is given to him, to the holy ones of the Most High and to the people of the holy ones of the Most High. The prototype of this divine figure who rides on the clouds is Baal, the god of rain and fertility who is a subordinate to El in the Canaanite pantheon. In *Daniel*, the one like a son of man who rides the clouds of heaven is a divine subordinate of God who takes over the dominion that had been exercised by the personifications of primordial evil. Like Baal, who is a victor over the forces of drought, famine and death, he is an angelic Prince who appears, like all angelic Princes, to have the characteristics of man and brings prosperity and life to earth.

What must be learned from this vision is that the tragedy in which the Jews find themselves as they faced the requirement to offer sacrifices to Zeus is not just a human conflict. The forces of evil that have their origin in the primordial chaos of the "deep" and the "great sea" are the ones causing the sufferings which the people of the saints of the Most High are now experiencing. As a Christian of the late first century C.E. would clarify, *"we are not contending against flesh and blood, but against the principalities, against the powers, against the world rulers of this present darkness, against the spiritual hosts of wickedness in the heavenly places"* (Eph. 6:12). These monsters of darkness that have come out of the deep sea seem to have taken control of what is taking place on earth. *Daniel*'s agenda is to put the situation in its proper context by placing it within its cosmic horizon, and to assure the people of the holy ones of the Most High that God's justice will prevail. His aim is not to foretell

The End of the Scroll

the future but to give assurance in a chaotic present. He is asserting the righteousness of God.

Martyrdom and the Resurrection

Unlike *Ezekiel, Zechariah* and *First Enoch, Daniel* does not describe the resolution to the problem of evil by means of battles fought on earthly battlefields in which God is able to defeat both human and supernatural forces and "restore the fortunes of Judah and Israel" in a purified "glorious land." He sets the vindication of the righteousness of God in a heavenly scene and introduces into the Judeo-Christian theological horizon the notion of the resurrection of the dead. Just as the creation story of Genesis 1 introduced the notion of creation by a Word, thus disengaging creation from mythological battles and material connections between the divine and the human, Daniel introduced the concept of the resurrection of the dead as the solution to the difficulty of explaining God's retributive justice in human terms without recourse to God's anger, fury, wrath and jealousy, in repulsive, cruel scenes as Ezekiel did, or Revelation would do later. The people of the saints of the Most High do not receive an earthly kingdom in which to enjoy peace and prosperity after cosmic battles, as envisioned in Ezekiel and Zechariah. Daniel announces that all the dead *"who sleep in the dust of the earth shall awake, some to everlasting life, and some to shame and everlasting contempt. And those who are wise shall shine like the brightness of the firmament; and those who turn many to righteousness, like the stars for ever and ever"* (Dan. 12:2-3). In this way, Daniel projects the just reward of the righteous sufferers to life as stars, that is angels, out of the darkness of this world. Like the angels they will shine *"like the brightness of the firmament."* Descriptions of the angels regularly picture them shining like bronze and fire. To accomplish this revision of the reward from a nationalistic vision of a restored *"glorious land"* to a heavenly resurrected life as angelic beings, the author of Daniel brings back the mythological descriptions that connect the heavenly and the earthly, which the author of the first creation story in Genesis had tried to eliminate.

Ezekiel saw, in a vision, dry bones scattered on a desert which were articulated into skeletons, covered with flesh and given life. In this way he metaphorically announced that the Jews who were *"dead"* in a Babylonian exile would come to life again when the fortunes of Israel were restored in the *"glorious land"* (Ez. 37:12). Daniel is told that *"those who sleep in the dust of the earth shall awake."* This is the first time that the resurrection of those who are dead is affirmed within the Old Testament. A book written about the same time, or shortly after, also asserts the resurrection of the dead, but expresses it within a different perspective. These two references to the resurrection work with the two different understanding of death found in the Old Testament.

According to one, the dead are *rephaim*, shades, weak negative replicas of the living who reside in the pit, or Sheol. Daniel works with this understanding of death when it refers to those "sleeping" in the dust. Second Maccabees, a text describing events at the time when Daniel was written, has a different understanding of the resurrection. It tells the story of the seven brothers who refused to offer sacrifices to Zeus and, therefore, were facing martyrdom. When the seventh of them was about to be executed, Antiochus IV asked the widowed mother to convince her son to go ahead with the sacrifice so that she wouldn't be left without the support and protection of a man in the house during her old age. Taking advantage of the opportunity to speak to her son, the mother tells him, *"look at the heavens and the earth; consider all that is in them, and realize that God did not create them from what already existed and that a human being comes into existence in the same way. Do not be afraid of this butcher; accept death willingly and prove yourself worthy of your brothers, so that by God's mercy I may receive back both you and them together"* (2 Mac. 7:28-29). The words of the mother of the seven martyrs have become the classic description of the way in which God created the heavens and the earth. He created them ex nihilo, out of nothing. The translation has it as *"did not create them from what already existed."* The stories in Genesis, on the contrary, have different pre-existent matter having been used: one says that God dealt with the primordial water, and the other with the available dust of the ground. This description of the resurrection as God bringing back the seven sons to their mother from nothing, or from what did not already exist, is built on the other view of death found in the Old Testament. According to it, when a person dies it is no more. Rather than to continue to exist as weak replicas of what they were when alive, the dead have ceased to be.

Both affirmations of the resurrection of the dead that entered Judaism at the time of the Maccabees represent the abandonment of the view that the vindication of God's justice and power is to take place in a happy, prosperous and peaceful earthly life at the time of the end. Whether the dead are *rephaim* who come out of their sleep in the dust, or are a new creation out of nothing, those raised will be like the angels in heaven who shine with the brightness of the firmament forever. That those raised will be like angels, is what Jesus told the Sadducees who thought they were going to ridicule belief in the resurrection by asking about the validity of marriage vows in heaven (Mk. 12:25/Mt. 22:30).

According to Daniel, those who will awake from their sleep are destined to two different futures. Not all will become angels shining in heaven; some will rise *"to shame and everlasting contempt"* (Dan. 12:2). This differentiation was already made in the description of Antiochus IV's enforcing the worship of Zeus in Judea. It is said that he *"shall turn action against the holy covenant. He shall turn back and give heed to those who forsake the holy covenant.... He shall seduce with flattery those who violate the covenant; but the people who know their God shall stand firm and take action. And those among the people who are wise shall make many understand, though they shall fall by sword and flame, by captivity and plunder, for some days"* (Dan. 11:30-33). Those raised *"to everlasting life"* are those who stand firm and take action by making others understand what is demanded under the circumstances, but who, by so doing, have fallen by sword and flame. Those who violate the covenant are the ones who go to everlasting contempt. Whether this involves, like in *First Enoch*, an everlasting endurance of pain and torture, is not specified. That all are raised, but not all are going to enjoy life, is an adaptation to a new scenario of what Ezekiel said about the end of the exile: all will come out of Babylon, but not all will enter the glorious land (Ez. 20:38).

The introduction of life after death as the time when God's retributive justice will be effectively evident serves as the solution to the confounding experience of the suffering of the just, obedient, loyal covenant-keeping people of God who face martyrdom. Daniel describes the source of evil in a new context. As I pointed out already, Jeremiah wondered about the presence of evil in God's world. He was quite aware of its existence but was unable to define its source. Zechariah, convinced as he was of God's omnipotence, came to the conclusion that God is the source of both good and evil. This, of course, was problematic to anyone who worshiped God. The editors of Daniel found another place in which to locate the source of evil, now available to them by their use of ancient mythological creation stories. Evil comes out of the primordial waters of the deep, the chaos that the Spirit of God had to control before he would speak the Word that brought about the light that overcame darkness and the separation of the waters by means of a "firmament," or celestial dome.

Martyrdom, of course, is the ultimate price that can be paid for obedience to God. For the forces of evil to bring out this weapon into the struggle is, it would seem, the ultimate evil. The editors of Daniel found a way to provide a silver lining for martyrdom. Given that it does not bring about death because those who are loyal to the covenant with God will be raised to life, it does not have a negative function. It, actually, has a positive one. Those who *"fall by sword and flame, by captivity and plunder, for some days,"* fall to be refined and to be cleansed, to be made white (Dan. 11:33-35). By martyrdom *"they shall purify themselves, and make themselves white, and be refined"* (Dan. 12:10). Their martyrdom is a means to their purification as they are transferred from life as humans to life as angels. In Ezekiel the glorious land needs to be purified after the battle that puts an end to Gog of the land of Magog. All the cadavers left polluting the land have to be buried and, if afterward any bones are still found on the land, they have to be properly taken away. Only then can the people live prosperous and peaceful lives in the land. In Daniel, martyrdom is provided with a silver lining by becoming the purification of those who will receive the kingdom. This understanding of the suffering of the righteous was adopted by several New Testament authors.

Martyrdom is thus made to fit into God's predetermined course of history. The goal pursued by those who bring about the martyrdom of the righteous is not to be achieved. That is what the court tales of Shadrach, Meshach and Abednego in the fiery furnace and of Daniel in the lions' den teach. Those who remain loyal to the covenant enshrined in the Law of Moses are delivered from death by angels who make fire harmless and close the mouths of lions. These stories are part of the message of Daniel to those facing martyrdom under Antiochus IV's dominion over Jerusalem. Ultimately, they may not be rescued by angels from very effective means of death like lions and fire. They can be assured, however, that death itself will have no power over them. Rather than being rescued from death by angels, they will become angels themselves.

My reading of Daniel has revealed a fully apocalyptic text that has found what would become the established cosmology of apocalypticism. The world in which humans live is one in which the primordial forces of evil are in command and cause humans to act in evil ways. This condition is one that obscures the power of God's justice in the world so that its effectiveness is put in doubt. Evil comes out of the chaos that raises itself in the form of kingdoms that assume total control over the lives of their subjects. Since the power of evil controls the world, for God's original purpose in creation to be achieved some traumatic new beginning is necessary. The solution to this problem cannot be achieved in the earthly present world. It will be accomplished when humans at their resurrection are taken out of the earth and given life forever as angels. The Jews who preferred to die rather than to offer sacrifices to Zeus were the first martyrs in human history. They died to remain faithful to a religious commitment. When the suffering of the righteous was not due to living under foreign oppressors, the losing of property, or having been exiled to a foreign land without access to the temple that connects one to God, but has reached the ultimate price, death, God's power and justice can only be affirmed within a different, new vision of reality. This is what theology does, and what apocalyptic authors did by expanding their horizons into the cosmos and finding new ways to express their faith in God while struggling within chaotic circumstances.

THE LETTERS OF PAUL

The New Testament contains thirteen letters which claim to have been written by Paul and one that has traditionally been ascribed to him. With the rise of modern scholarship, the authorship of these letters has been under review, and many biblical scholars think that some of them were not written by him. Today every student of Paul agrees that Paul wrote seven letters now found in the New Testament. They also agree that he wrote at least one, and probably quite a few others, which were lost in antiquity. The seven universally considered to have been written by Paul are: *To the Romans, To the Corinthians I, To the Corinthians II, To the Galatians, To the Philippians, To the Thessalonians I* and *To Philemon*. That Paul wrote the other seven is defended by some scholars and denied by others. Each one of them, of course, is considered separately on its own merits.

Already in the third century, Origen questioned the Pauline authorship of *To the Hebrews*, and at the time of the Renaissance it was much debated. Its having been written by Paul was based on tradition, since it does not claim to have been written by Paul. Today most scholars don't think that Paul wrote it. The evidence against Pauline authorship is overwhelming, both in terms of style and content. In terms of style, its Greek is, together with that of the gospel *According to Luke, Acts of the Apostles,* and *First Peter,* the most stylish in the New Testament, a much more highly literary Greek than that of the letters of Paul. As an exhortation against falling back to the service of Aaronic priests seeking for purification from sin, it has a totally non-Pauline understanding of the death and the resurrection of Christ, and sees things from a Stoic rather than a Platonic cosmology.

After *To the Hebrews,* the letter *To the Ephesians* is probably the one whose Pauline authorship is denied by most scholars. Again, it is a matter of style and content. Both argue for its belonging to the latter part of the first century. The letters of Paul flow like a mountain brook, bubbling and jumping in rapid descent with impromptu detours. By contrast, *To the Ephesians* moves ponderously, slowly, like a river in marshlands, with long sentences and dependent clauses that project the impression of profundity. Its style represents the beginnings of liturgical pomposity. Its content argues for the centrality of the apostolic church as the mediator of access to God's saving grace. Thus, it belongs within the development of an institutional Christianity. Paul, of course, insisted that only the Risen Christ could be the foundation on which a Christian community can be built, but in this letter the church is said to be founded on the apostles. Besides, while Paul sees the *Parousia* prominently in his horizon, *To the Ephesians* does not refer to it even once.

The Pastoral Epistles, *To Timothy I, To Timothy II* and *To Titus,* also belong to the period when Christianity was becoming an ecclesiastical institution with a hierarchical clergy who sought to restrict the flow of the Holy Spirit within ecclesiastical channels. This was an effort to curtail the activities of those spontaneously endowed with empowerment by the Spirit, especially women. In Paul's house churches, women were quite active and fully recognized as apostles by their peers.

To the Thessalonians II is considered by many to have been written by someone other than Paul because it projects the *Parousia* into a distant future. In *To the Thessalonians I,* Paul prepares his readers for an imminent appearance of the Lord, certainly while both he and them will be alive, and urges preparation for its arrival like a thief in the night, unexpectedly. The author of *To the Thessalonians II*, argues against their excitement, thinking that the day of the Lord had arrived, because what needs to happen before it has not yet happened. He identifies a traditional apocalyptic series of events as the Truth they should hold. Besides, while in the first letter Paul speaks to his addressees in familiar terms, portraying himself as both the father who guided them and the mother who nursed them, in the second the author adopts a stern, imposing attitude that demands strict obedience to his commands.

The letter on which the scholarly opinion is most balanced between those in favor and those opposed to Pauline authorship is *To the Colossians*. This letter is an argument against teachers who make Christianity a mystery cult according to which, by means of ascetic practices that follow prescribed rules, initiates can ascend through the heavenly spheres ruled by the "elemental spirits of the world" and participate in worship with angels. Since the "elemental spirits of the world," the powers that rule the spheres between heaven and earth and prevent God's direct control over what goes on in the world, are also referred to by Paul in his letter *To the Galatians*, some scholars see connections that argue for the Pauline authorship of *To the Colossians*. To be taken into account, however, is that in *To the Galatians* Paul argues that Gentiles need not become Jews, as some other Christian apostles have been telling them. In his argument, Paul characterizes the Law of Moses as one of the "elemental spirits of the world" which, therefore, can no longer guide the lives of those who live "in Christ." His argument, however, is consistently based on Torah as the only context for understanding the significance of Christ's death and resurrection. In *To the Colossians*, on the other hand, the author sees the rules for the ascetic life prescribed by false Christian preachers to be the ones related to the "elemental spirits of the world," and he never refers to Torah at all.

More significantly, the author of *To the Colossians* gives to the crucifixion a meaning totally different from the one assigned to it by Paul. According to him, the death of Christ on the cross is the circumcision of the body of the cosmos that was in need of being perfected. This is a Jewish understanding of the significance of circumcision as the perfection of the body. According to this author, those who are baptized are also circumcised and thereby become members of the perfected cosmic body of the Risen Christ. According to him, their perfection through baptism renders unnecessary the ascetic practices recommended by the proponents of an esoteric Christianity. Paul, of course, relativized circumcision; it had ceased to have any significance as the demarcation of the people of God. Besides, he explicitly denies the attainment of perfection while living in the flesh.

After a careful consideration of the arguments presented in favor and against the Pauline authorship of the fourteen letters assigned to Paul, I agree with the scholars who think that Paul wrote the seven letters listed at the beginning of this discussion. They, therefore, will be the only ones I will use as evidence for the study of Paul's apocalyptic symbolic universe. This, of course, says nothing against the authority of the anonymous *To the Hebrews* and the six letters that were written pseudonymously. They, no doubt, are legitimate, inspired letters of the Christian canon which fruitfully contribute to our understanding of how our ancestors in the Faith expressed their faith in God. As already noticed, pseudonymity was a common practice among Jewish groups at the time. Besides, *First Peter, Second Peter, James* and *Jude* are also pseudonymous canonical letters .

PAUL'S APOCALYPTIC SYMBOLIC UNIVERSE

Since the nineteenth century, when the tools of research established by modern methods for literary and historical investigations began to be applied by biblical scholars, there have been quite a few suggestions as to how to characterize and understand the apostle Paul. Friedrich Nietzsche considered Paul an ambitious and cunning authoritarian with delusions of grandeur, a very insecure man due to anxieties caused by guilt from his failure to be obedient to the Law of Moses. According to him, Paul was the main culprit for the subversion of the radiant and brilliant Hellenistic culture of Apollo and Dionysus and the adoption of a masochistic

Christian culture, much to the detriment of Western civilization. Most feminists, assigning to him the authorship of letters which he did not write, judge Paul to have been the one who imposed a chauvinist cultural aberration on Christianity. To deny that Paul is the author of this sentiment, of course, does not deny that in the process of becoming an ecclesiastical organization Christianity officially suppressed the ministry of women. In the Middle Ages, Paul was seen as a Platonist who exposed the evils of the material world, thus devaluing the life of the senses, especially that which has to do with sexuality. He has been understood as an other-worldly idealist, a prototype of the medieval mystics. More recently scholars have been arguing whether Paul was primarily a theologian or an ethicist. Were the concluding ethical remarks in his letters secondary byproducts of his theological teachings, or where his theological initial observations the foundation on which to build the ethical instructions which were his primary concern?

Since the publication of Johan Christiaan Beker's *Paul's Apocalyptic Gospel*, in 1982, most students of Paul have become convinced that he is to be understood as an apocalyptic theologian. This means that his theological discourse and his ethical injunctions are of one piece. As a theologian, he explained the present in terms of what God had done at the death and the resurrection of Christ. He came to understand these events as acts of God within the apocalyptic framework that had structured his life as a Jewish persecutor of Christians. When Christians began to proclaim that the one who had died the most humiliating, ignominious death on a cross was the Messiah, Paul reacted by launching a most passionate campaign against such theological nonsense.

According to Torah, those who die on a cross, die abandoned and cursed by God. When he was confronted by the Risen Christ on the road to Damascus, however, he had to come to terms with the fact that God had done something extraordinary. The one who died on a cross had been raised by God. This meant that the crucifixion of Jesus had not been just the Roman execution of a Jewish seditious pretender to David's throne. In that case, then, what was it that God had done?

The first followers of the Risen Christ came to understand what God had done employing various metaphors. Some saw the crucifixion as a sacrifice, as atonement for the sins of the world. More specifically, they thought of it as the Passover sacrifice that marked the people who would come out of Egypt to the Promise Land. Others saw it as a ransom that brought about redemption from slavery to sin. Others saw it as the death of the suffering servant portrayed in *Isaiah*. Paul understood the Christ Event within the apocalyptic scenario of the doctrines of The Fall and of The Two Ages which by now had incorporated a transitional short period as The Age of Messiah. This meant that at the death and the resurrection of Christ The Day of the Lord had come. That The Day had come was also understood by the author of the gospel *According to John*. But while he saw God's personal involvement in history in totally unapocalyptic terms, as having taken place at the incarnation of the Logos, Paul saw it within the standard apocalyptic framework as the termination of This Age, and the introduction of The Age of Messiah that would culminate with the establishment of The Age to Come.

In Paul's schema, in This Age the world has fallen from direct control by God and finds itself under the rule of Satan, "the god of this world" (2 Cor. 4:4). He is constantly seeking ways "to tempt you through lack of self-control" (1 Cor. 7:5), sends his messengers [angels] "to harass" those living "in the flesh" (2 Cor. 12:7) and he has the power to bring about "the destruction of the flesh" (1 Cor. 5:5). Therefore, human beings should by all means try "to keep Satan from gaining advantage over us; for we are not ignorant of his designs" (2 Cor. 2:11). We know that to carry out his designs "Satan disguises himself as an angel of light" (2 Cor. 11:14). In other words, human existence in This Age is life under the power of Satan and his angels who, taking advantage of the weakness of the flesh, have every one living in sin. Sin, therefore, is not just a sinful act committed by an individual who fails to keep the Law, as was traditionally thought, but the dominant force under which humans live; it permeates the environment in which the whole creation exists and "has been groaning in travail together," and from which it is anxious to be liberated (Rom. 8:22). Under the power of Satan, life in This Age, which Paul designates also as life "in the flesh," is characterized by its "weakness." Even the Law given by Moses came down through the spheres to this fallen world "ordained by angels" (Gal. 3:19) and operates in a distorted way because it was "weakened by the flesh" (Rom. 8:3) as it entered the fallen creation. As a result, it cannot give life to those who live under the dominion of Satan. Thus, even if Moses may have intended it, and the misguided Jews sought to achieve righteousness and life by keeping the Law (Rom 9:30-32; 10:5), God did not give a law that could give righteousness and life (Gal 3:21). Since even the Law of Moses, as an object within the world, is also affected by the weakness that characterizes the fallen world, there is an imminent need for God to regain power over the fallen creation that is now under the control of Satan.

To be noticed is that Paul conceives the Fall as affecting not only human beings but the whole of creation because he locates it in a new historical setting. In the prophetic tradition, sin and salvation were located at what happened at Sinai during the Exodus. There the people rejected the God who had taken them out of Egypt and constructed and worshiped a golden calf. This was an open rejection of Yahveh, and the prophets did not tire to remind the people that at Sinai they marked themselves as a "stiff necked" and rebellious people. At Sinai, of course, God had concluded with them a Covenant which they promised to keep. Their failures in this regard resulted in the punishments God had been imposing on them.

The author of *First Enoch* pushed back the time of The Fall to the time when sons of god came down and took as wives daughters of men. The result was the birth of giants. The Fall had been brought about by angels who disobeyed God, and as a consequence the earth had to be destroyed by the Flood. The Flood, however, did not destroy everything. God arranged for Noah, his family, and samples of every animal species to survive. He informed Noah in advance and gave instructions for the construction of an ark. This narrative from *First Enoch*, based on the story of the flood in *Genesis*, informs the way in which the author of *First Peter* understands the significance of the death and the resurrection of Christ and of baptism (1 Pet. 3:18-21).

The scribes who compiled the book of *Daniel* already realized that the human predicament had gotten much worse. Those who wished to remain faithful to the God of the Covenant now were facing martyrdom. This could only be because evil had been gaining dominance over the world God had created. They located the source of evil in the waters of the primeval deep ocean which God had to control by means of the Spirit that moved over them to bring about the conditions under which God could speak the word and create a day. In *Daniel* the beasts that rise from the sea are the agents of evil that bring about the martyrdom of the faithful. To maintain that God's retributive justice works, under those circumstances, it was necessary to bring in a new way for God to realize his original intentions when he created humanity and set it to live happily in the Garden he had created for them. All human beings will be raised from their graves to receive their just rewards.

Paul gave more specificity to the presence of evil in the world by describing what happened at the Garden of Eden as the Fall of creation under the power of Satan. Then death entered the world *"through sin"* (Rom. 5:12). This allowed him to give to the Fall cosmic significance. The disobedience of one man, Adam, caused "sin" to enter the world, but sin, Paul explains, is not to be understood in the Jewish way as the transgression of a law. Before the giving of the Law at Sinai, there had already been sin in the world. Since death is the result of sin, and all those who lived between Adam and Moses died, it is obvious that they were all sinners even when there was no law (Rom. 5:12-14). In other words, when Adam opened the door and *"sin came into the world,"* the whole creation fell under the power of death, the ultimate enemy of God (1 Cor. 15; 26). The death caused by sin is eschatological.

While the doctrine of the Fall sets up the problem, the doctrine of The Two Ages provides the pattern for understanding what God did in the death of Jesus and the resurrection of Christ to regain full control over a world that had fallen under the control of Satan. Implicitly, in *Daniel* the transition from one age to the other is accomplished by the resurrection of the righteous (Dan. 12:1-2). *Zechariah*, within its limited national horizon, contends that the restoration of the fortunes of Israel would not take place by the force of arms: *"This is the word of the Lord to Zerubbabel: Not by might nor by power, but by my Spirit says the Lord of hosts"* (Zech. 4:6). This was a significant change to the end-time scenarios typical of apocalyptic texts. The mythological battles described in *Ezekiel* and *First Enoch*, with excursion to different locations in the depths of the abyss and the upper regions of the cosmos, are not found in Paul's vision of the future, where the Spirit is now the main player. For Paul, the Age to Come is to be brought about, as *Zechariah* says, *"by my Spirit says the Lord of hosts."*

The function of the battles described in *Ezekiel* and *First Enoch* was to bring about the changes necessary for the termination of the present situation, understood by them as the restoration of the fortunes of Israel. Considering that the present conditions are much worse than previously thought, in the apocalyptic imagination, The Age to Come is not just the restoration of Israel, but a totally new creation. Given the depths of depravity in the present conditions, a transitional period came to be considered necessary to make the preparations needed before The Age to Come could become a reality. Rather than to accomplish the preparation for a future of bliss by terrifying warfare, the task was assigned to The Age of Messiah. In this period, the result of God's work in Jesus Christ would make possible for human beings to live "in the Spirit," and lay the groundwork for the ultimate victory of God over sin and death.

Paul saw that Jesus, a divine being incarnated as a Jew in a woman "when the time had fully come" (Gal 4:4), had been crucified by the fallen heavenly rulers of the world. In this way these forces of evil thought they had defeated God's attempt to bring about his reunion with humanity. In fact, by the death of the divine being who had been incarnated, God had redeemed humanity from its subjection to the power of death, the condition in which the divine being given birth by Mary had been incarnated. This divine act had terminated the absolute dominion of Satan over the fallen world. The power under which all flesh had been living was no longer supreme. The death of Christ was the divine way to gain a foothold in the dominion of the "the elemental spirits of the world." They thought that by killing Jesus they were accomplishing their evil designs, but "none of the rulers of this age understood" the "hidden wisdom of God" which had been revealed to Paul when he met the Risen Christ. This mystery is what Paul was now proclaiming for the benefit of both Jews and Gentiles. If "the rulers of this age" had known the secret wisdom of God, "they would not have crucified the Lord of glory" (1 Cor. 2:6-8).

The rulers of this age, of course, are the rulers, authorities and powers, "the enemies" which Christ has been fighting to bring under subjection since his resurrection (1 Cor. 15:24-28). Following the traditional apocalyptic view, Paul sees the triumph of God over the forces that had taken control of the lives of human beings to be a triumph over celestial enemies, not human beings. He places the responsibility for the death of Jesus neither on the Jews nor the Romans. The real enemies of the will of God are the celestial "elemental spirits" (*stoixeia*) who control the space between heaven and earth and are quite active among humans causing them to sin. The Law of Moses, which had been ordained by these celestial powers, therefore, had been functioning as an instrument of sin to bring about death (Rom. 7:13). By his death on the cross, Christ had stormed the realm of death and liberated humanity from its subjection to sin and death. During the Age of Messiah, he was battling the rulers of the air until he would subject them to the dominion of God. Then God would be again in full control of his creation with everything subjected to him (1 Cor. 15:28).

By the power of the Spirit, without fighting any earthly battle, God raised Christ from the dead. In this way, God is giving life to human beings and, thereby, accomplishing the purpose of Creation. God raised from the dead the divine being who had become incarnate, and appointed the Risen Christ to occupy a higher position in the chain of being than this divine being had occupied before his incarnation (Phil. 2:6-9). At his resurrection, God named him Son of God (Rom. 1:4). For Paul, the solution to the problem of The Fall is not possible within the creation that is under the control of rulers, authorities and powers who by means of the Law of Moses keep God's creation condemned to eschatological death. Paul radicalized the doctrine of the resurrection in the person of the Risen Christ. The Spirit of God that once moved over the waters of the abyss before God said, *"Let there be light"* (Gen. 1:3), had now raised Christ as Son of God and thereby established a New Creation (2 Cor. 4:6; 5:17). This is not the fulfillment of the prophecy of the seventy years of punishment announced by Jeremiah. It is not the means for the restoration of the fortunes of the Jews as an independent nation enjoying the respect and admiration of their neighbors. This is not at all the establishment of a new earthly kingdom that takes the place of the earlier four kingdoms. The resurrection of Christ by the Spirit that had been present at creation is a New Creation of life "in the Spirit," totally different from the creation of Adam which fell under the power of Satan, and has been since then characterized by "the weakness of the flesh." By the resurrection of Christ, God bought about a New Creation. This is already an accomplished fact which has resulted in a totally new realm within which human beings can live. During the Age of Messiah, full life "in the Spirit" is a reality only in the Risen Christ. However, those human beings who by means of baptism join themselves to Christ's death and resurrection also may now live as new creature "in the Spirit," even while they still live "in the flesh."

As said earlier, Paul conceives the celestial authorities and the rulers of *"this present evil age"* (Gal. 1:4) as agents of Satan with evil designs to tempt men and women, taking advantage of the weakness of the flesh in which humans live. They are the ones responsible for the crucifixion. Thus, like all apocalyptic authors, Paul sees the earthly and the celestial spheres as mutually permeable. Unlike other apocalyptic authors, however, Paul does not envision the kings of the world as manifestations of primordial evil. He understands that the kings and governors are agents of God who have received from him authority to punish evildoers according to the laws of the land, and legitimately collect taxes for the proper functioning of government (Rom. 13:1-7). For Paul, the sufferings of life now are not caused by evil human kings but by evil celestial powers. He is not concerned about the coming of a Messiah who will put an end to earthly kingdoms and bring about the kingdom of David established by God's intervention in the affairs of mankind. He does not envision Jesus as the promised Messiah of Israel. For him, the Christ [the Greek equivalent to Messiah] is the One raised from the dead by God. He is the Risen Christ, not a human being in the line of David. Jesus may have been a descendant of David "according to the flesh," but that is not particularly significant. What counts is that he was *"designated Son of God in power according to the Spirit of holiness by his resurrection from the dead, Jesus Christ our Lord"* (Rom. 1:4). The incarnation of a divine being who was given birth by Mary in the fallen world was necessary for the accomplishment of God's redemption of humanity, but of no significance in itself as far as Paul was concerned.

For Paul, the triumph of God in the resurrection of Christ as Son of God, which effectively accomplished the direct intervention of God in the world, is to take place in two stages. The first stage has already taken place in the death and the resurrection of Christ. The final stage is to take place in the resurrection of those who now live by the power of the Spirit as creatures of the New Creation accomplished by God at the resurrection of Christ from the dead. The first intervention was the Day of the Lord, the second will be the *Parousia* of the Lord. This means that while it is now possible for human beings no longer to live "under the Law," or under the power of the rulers of this age, it is not yet possible for them not to live "in the flesh;" therefore, suffering is still part of the human condition because of its weakness. To live "in the flesh" is not sinful; it is to live tempted by the agents of Satan who seek to take advantage of the weakness of the flesh. While living in This Age all human beings, Christians included, unavoidably live "in the flesh." Jesus was born "in the flesh" and lived in it until his crucifixion. Being incarnated "in the flesh" made it possible for Jesus to experience the suffering that ended with death. This means that those who join themselves to Christ's death by baptism will also suffer while living "in the flesh." Joining oneself to Christ in his death and resurrection does not bring about deliverance from suffering. It does bring about, however, deliverance from the condemnation of the Law that imposes eschatological death of its transgressors (Rom. 8:1).

Those who live "in the flesh" and also "in the spirit" must not live "according to the flesh." They must live guided "by the spirit;" they must live "according to the spirit." While living "in the flesh" Christians will suffer, but those who live "according to the flesh" will die condemned by the Law that operates in the flesh (Rom. 8:12-13). On the other hand, those who crucify the "old self" with Christ (at their baptism) no longer live *"enslaved to sin"* and *"shall also live with him. For we know that Christ being raised from the dead will never die again; death no longer has dominion over him"* (Rom. 6:6-9). And those who now live *"in Christ"* shall also live *"with him"* forever in a creation where there is no death.

When the powers, authorities, and rulers of the air have been finally conquered by the Risen Christ and everything has again become subjected to God, *"then comes the end"* (1 Cor. 15:24). Then The Age of Messiah will have ended; The Age to Come will have arrived. The ultimate consequence of the restoration of the dominion of God over the whole universe, not just the restoration of the fortunes of Israel, is that eschatological death, the last enemy, has been annihilated (1 Cor. 1:26). This is the final accomplishment of the triumph of God. For Paul the problem is not a historical national problem but a cosmic universal one. That is why his apocalyptic scenario of God's ultimate triumph over evil is totally different from the ones depicted by apocalypticists who felt that they had to show how God deals with earthly empires, like Gog from the land of Magog, before the end. According to Paul, God has to deal with the principalities, authorities, rulers of the air who by killing Jesus thought they had derailed God's attempt to recover his creation. The resurrection of Christ as the Son of God broke the power of death. Now the Risen Christ could subject all the elemental spirits that were still operating in the spheres. When that had been accomplished, the end of human life "in the flesh" would have arrived.

Paul announces his radical Christian revision of the apocalyptic scenario at the beginning of his letter *To the Romans*. He affirms that the Gospel reveals the justice and the wrath of God (Rom. 1:16). In the typical apocalyptic vision of things, the justice and the wrath of God will be on full display when God finally interrupts the historical course of time. Then the righteous and the wicked will receive their just rewards and, as *Ezekiel* has it, God will display his anger, wrath and fury, by killing all the wicked both on the earth and in the heavens. Paul, as already said, understands the Fall as not limited to the human situation, and sees the human and the divine realms as mutually permeable; thus, he identifies the triumph of God over the power of death and sin with the triumph of God over the principalities, authorities and rulers of the spheres that brought about the death of Jesus. The cross and the resurrection of Jesus Christ, which is the initial battle that leads to the final triumph, has brought about already a clear demonstration of God's power. The Gospel is not information, the conveyer of knowledge about God's designs. As Paul specifically says, the Gospel is *"the power of God;"* in it the justice and the wrath of God are revealed in actions. What follows the definition of the Gospel as power, in Rom. 1:17-3:31, is a long description of how the justice and the wrath of God are revealed by his power. The wrath is revealed in people who continue to live *"according to the flesh"* and descend into deeper and deeper depravity, and the justice is revealed in people who now live empowered by the Spirit. The triumph of God over the eschatological death demanded by the Law that enslaved humanity has already been achieved. What is still in need of being accomplished is the submission of the rulers of the spheres who are still deceiving those who live *"in the flesh"* (1 Cor. 15:24-27). Paul, however, felt no need to describe how Christ is engaging the celestial powers, authorities and rulers of the air in apocalyptic battles that bring about their subjection.

In Paul's scenario, the justice and the wrath of God are in full display already. When Christ has succeeded in subjecting and placing the rulers of the spheres under God's control, the time for the resurrection of the righteous would have arrived. Thus, while he sees that during The Age of Messiah Christians live both "in the flesh" and "in the spirit," there is total discontinuity between This Age and The Age to Come. In that Age all life will only be "in the spirit." This is elucidated by the differentiation between the mortal, corruptible "physical" body in which Christians live "in the flesh" and the immortal, incorruptible "spiritual" body in which they will live fully "in the Spirit" after the resurrection from "biological death," a normal feature of those living in the flesh.

Those living in the fallen world in a "body" that objectifies life "in the flesh" are not by nature sinners; but, because of the weakness of the flesh inescapably sin on account of the superior power of the rulers of the air who are determined to make humans sin. This "body," which Paul characterizes as *"this body of death"* (Rom. 7:24), was created in the beginning, according to the story of creation in Genesis 2:4b – 3:24, a mortal body. In order to live Adam and Eve had to eat the fruit of the tree of life. After they disobeyed the command not to eat of the tree of the knowledge of good and evil, they were expelled from the garden to deny them access to the tree of life. Since they depended on the fruit of this tree to continue living, they eventually died. According to Paul, the body in which humans live in a world where sin *"reigns"* (Rom. 5:12-14) goes into the ground at death and, since it is made *"of dust"* and is by nature *"perishable"* it cannot inherit life. The resurrected body is going to be *"imperishable,"* a *"spirit body"* (1 Cor. 15:50).

The New Creation is not an improved version of the original Creation. Paul elaborates, *"There are celestial bodies and there are terrestrial bodies.... If there is a physical body, there is also a spiritual body. Thus it is written, 'The first man Adam became a living being'; the last Adam became a life-giving spirit... The first man was from the earth, a man of dust; the second man is from heaven.... Just as we have borne the image of the man of dust, we shall also bear the image of the man of heaven"* (1 Cor. 15:40-49). The Risen Christ did not rise from the tomb with the body of Jesus. He was raised by the Spirit with a spirit, imperishable, immortal celestial body. This shall also be the case with those who have lived in bodies of death, "in the flesh," but not "according to the flesh." They shall be raised with spirit, imperishable bodies, bearing the image of the man of heaven. They would have been buried mortal beings with bodies of death, but will be raised immortal beings with spirit bodies. This is a radical intensification of eschatological life. In *Daniel "those who sleep in the dust of the earth shall awake"* ... and *"shine like the brightness of the firmament ... like the stars for ever and ever"* (Dan. 12:2-3). Paul gives to the Danielic announcement a more specific contour by modeling it in terms of the new creation established by the resurrection of Christ. In the process, a significant transition has taken place. The notion that the earth is the human eternal home has been abandoned. The notion that heaven is the true human home has taken its place.

Paul thinks that eschatological life is already a reality in those who live not only "in the flesh" but also "in the spirit" and are, therefore, "guided by the Spirit." Those who live "in Christ" or "in the Spirit," he specifies, are not "under the Law" (Rom. 6:14). This means that those who, through baptism, have died and been raised with Christ, may do things that the Law defines as sin, but the Law has no power to condemn them and subject them to eschatological death (Rom. 8:1). Like Christ who through death and resurrection now lives forever as Son of God, so also those who through baptism are *"united with him in a death like his ... shall certainly be united with him in a resurrection like his"* (Rom. 6:5). The resurrection experienced at baptism is already effective so that those baptized are *"no longer enslaved to sin"* (Rom. 6:6), as defined by the law of sin (Rom. 7:23, 25). This affirmation of the effectiveness of the new life given by the Spirit to those who die with Christ at their baptism, unfortunately, gave rise to misinterpretations of Paul's view of the resurrection.

COUNTERING MISUNDERSTANDINGS OF THE RESURRECTION

Paul's understanding of the death and the resurrection of Christ was too radical for most of his contemporary Jews, and a bit too complicated for his Gentile converts. This forced him to spend a great deal of effort arguing against some of his fellow Christian Jews. They charged that his gospel proclaimed a God who had broken his word to the Jewish people. He also had to argue against some of his Gentile converts who thought that, because they had been raised with Christ at their baptism and, therefore, were no longer "under the Law," as spiritual beings, it was impossible for them to sin.

The author of *To Timothy II*, writing toward the end of the first century, warns against *"Hymenaeus and Philetus, who have swerved from the truth by holding that the resurrection is past already."* He then advises, *"Let everyone who names the name of the Lord depart from iniquity"* (2 Tim. 2:18-19). Holding that they had already experienced resurrection, these Christians thought they were free to indulge in libertine behaviors with their mortal bodies, since what they did with their "body of death" did not affect their life in the spirit. In other words, they absolutized the effectiveness of their baptismal raising with Christ. That some Gentiles understood Paul in this way is already made clear in his own letters. Paul tells the Corinthian converts who claim that *"all things are lawful"* (1 Cor. 10:23) that they had better not use *"this liberty of yours"* (1 Cor.

8:9) to condemn themselves. Paul charges them with idolatry and debauchery. To the Galatians he warns, *"do not use your freedom as an opportunity for the flesh"* (Gal. 5:13). While Paul insists that *"for freedom Christ has set us free"* (Gal 5:1), he consistently warns that freedom from the "elemental spirits of the world," from the cosmic power of sin, from the Law, is not a license for living as one pleases. Whether living "in the flesh" or "in the Spirit" human beings are creatures and, as such, they are under either the authority of evil forces or the authority of God. Either they are *"slaves of sin"* or *"slaves of righteousness"* (Rom. 6:16-18). To think that because one has been baptized one is now raised with Christ and free from the consequences of living "according to the flesh" was a misunderstanding that Paul repeatedly had to deal with.

In his long exposition of the resurrection, Paul is most likely arguing against the notion that the resurrection is fully accomplished in those who have been baptized and still live "in the flesh." He starts the argument by basing it in the earliest Christian confession of faith, which he says, was already embedded in the tradition: *"For I delivered to you as of first importance what I also received,"* in other words, I am the bearer, i.e. the tradent, of a tradition.

"Christ died for our sins, in accordance with the scriptures;

he was buried;

he was raised, in accordance with the scriptures,

and he appeared.

He then gives two traditional lists of witnesses to the Risen Christ. In them, the first two items correspond to each other: Cephas corresponds to James, and the twelve and the apostles also match. The third item receives a significant twist. In the second list, Paul himself takes the place of *"more than five hundred brethren at one time, most of whom are still alive, though some have fallen asleep"* (1 Cor. 15:3-6). The confession consists of two sets: died and buried, raised and appeared, both of which were foretold in the scriptures. It serves to establish that the resurrection of Christ was that of a dead and buried person, and that it had witnesses.

The argument that follows is against those who say "there is no resurrection of the dead" (1 Cor. 15:12). The emphasis falls on the last phrase, "of the dead." The first point is that God raised Christ *from the dead*. If Christ had not died, then God would have had no need to raise him. And if that were the case, those of us who have faith in God and hope for our resurrection *"are of all men most to be pitied"* (1 Cor. 15:12-19). Rejecting this understanding of the situation, Paul explains that the resurrection of Christ was *"the first fruits of those who have fallen asleep."* "Those who belong to Christ" will be raised from the dead *"at his coming,"* that is at *"the end, when he delivers the kingdom to God the Father after destroying every rule and every authority and power. For he must reign until he has put all his enemies under his feet"* (1 Cor. 15:20-25). Then Christ will subject himself, and all those over whom he now reigns, to God, so that *"God may be everything to everyone"* (1 Cor. 15:28). The whole argument concludes affirming that *"the last enemy to be destroyed,"* that is death, will have been destroyed when those who belong to Christ and are now dead are raised at the *Parousia* of the Lord. The destruction of death will be accomplished by the one who had been raised by God as *"the first fruits of those who have fallen asleep."* Thus, the Law's power to condemn to death those who sin is still in effect among those who do not belong to Christ. Its power to kill will be terminated only when mortal beings have put on immortality *"at the last trumpet"* (1 Cor. 15:56). That will be the end not only of biological death but also of eschatological death. Then, the ultimate triumph of God will have been established by the one who was dead and now is bringing into subjection all the forces of evil in heavenly places. In this way Paul disproves the claim of those who practice iniquity because they hold that "the resurrection is past already." They do not belong to Christ, and the Law still has the power to condemn and kill them eschatologically.

It is not clear whether the Thessalonians thought that the resurrection was past already, as it was the case among the Corinthian libertines. That they may have been influenced by this view is suggested by what Paul writes to them before he gives them some details about the *Parousia* and the resurrection. He tells them, *"this is the will of God, your sanctification: that you abstain from immorality."* He then, in general terms describes how each man should *"take a wife for himself in holiness and honor, not in the passion of lust"* and that *"no man transgress, and wrong his brother in this matter ... For God has not called us for uncleanness but in holiness"* (1 Th. 4:3-5). Were they exchanging wives among themselves? His advice does suggest the question, but Paul does not address it.

The following explanation of what to expect at the resurrection is concerned with the unexpected death of some of the believers. Paul had told them that the *Parousia* would come soon and, as he now repeats, that it would *"come like a thief in the night"* (1 Th. 5:2), unexpectedly. It is significant that in connection with this description of the *Parousia* he claims to have a "word of the Lord," and the synoptic gospels report that Jesus said that the coming of the Son of man would be like that of a thief in the night. This is the only time Paul does this, while throughout his proclamation of "the Gospel" he hardly ever refers to traditions about Jesus. The few of them have to do with Jesus' apocalyptic vision.

Since Paul's visit with them, some members of the church at Thessalonica had unexpectedly died. This had left the grieving fellow believers confused. Rather than making a distinction between the resurrection of Christ and the resurrection of those in Christ, as he does in *To the Corinthians I*, in this letter Paul makes a distinction between those who will be dead and those who will be alive at the *Parousia*. *"This we declare to you by the world of the Lord, that we who are alive, who are left until the coming of the Lord, shall not precede those who have fallen asleep .... the dead in Christ will rise first; then we who are alive, who are left, shall be caught up together with them in the clouds to meet the Lord in the air; and so we shall always be with the Lord. Therefore comfort one another with these words"* (1 Th. 4:15-18). Two things stand out in this further detailing of the resurrection of those who are in Christ. One is that at his coming the Lord does not touch ground. Those "in Christ" who are alive will have to wait for those "in Christ" who are dead to be raised first, but together they will meet the Lord "in the air." In this telling the fallen creation is left behind, abandoned in darkness and silence. There is no attempt to purify it, cleanse it or renew it. The other important point is that the emphasis is not cosmic or anthropological. It is Christological. The fulfillment of God's purpose in creation is not achieved by the rehabilitation of Israel in the promised land, or of a full humanity in a cosmic paradise. It is visualized as *"we shall always be with the Lord."* Life and happiness is living with the Lord. The surroundings have no significance whatever. There is no need for scenic backgrounds.

The other major rejection of Paul's radical apocalyptic gospel was made by Christian Jews who complained that, according to his gospel of the New Creation, God is failing to keep his word to the Jews. They based their argument on the Covenant God had made with the people at Sinai, when he gave them the Law and declared them to be the ones he had chosen as his own people. Paul was proclaiming that circumcision was no longer the distinguishing mark of the people of God, that Gentiles need not become circumcised in order to be among the elect people of God. Paul's cosmic apocalyptic doctrine of the New Creation was a radical break with the ties that bound God to the Jews. For him, the problem was not the rebellion of the Jews at Sinai, but the disobedience of Adam at Eden. The problem was universal and the solution had to be universal also.

According to these Christians, Christianity was a Jewish sect, just like the Pharisees, Sadducees, Essenes, Zealots, Disciples of John the Baptist, Covenanters of Qumran, Therapeutai, etc. At that time Judaism was characterized by its diversity. What united all these various groups with distinctive doctrines and practices was their worship at the Jerusalem temple. Most Christians, it would appear from the accounts in *Acts of the Apostles,* also worshiped at the temple while holding that Christ had been raised by God. Paul did not agree with this view and, therefore, was persecuted and vilified by the Christian leaders in Jerusalem who sent apostles to undermine his authority in the churches he had founded. During his lifetime the temple of Jerusalem was still standing and functioning. Paul declared that the community of those who had faith in the God who raised Christ from the dead are the temple of God (1 Cor. 3:16-17). The New Creation also had a new temple, a new *axis mundi*, a new *omphelos* (Greek = navel) as the center for communication and transfers of energy between the human and the divine worlds. In his attempt to establish Paul's significance to the Christian leaders at the end of the first century, the author of *Acts of the Apostles* depicts Paul as one who was intent to celebrate the Jewish feasts at the temple, but that was just an apologetic strategy on his part. Paul himself makes clear that he did not go to Jerusalem to celebrate Pentecost but to deliver the monies he had been collecting in Asia Minor and Europe for the relief of the poor in Jerusalem (Rom. 15:25-26). He did not see the Gospel as a modification or an addendum to Judaism, but as a new beginning.

Like all believers in Christ, Paul explained the meaning of Christ by the authority of scriptures. It was only by reference to Torah that the significance of what God had done in the death and the resurrection of Christ could be understood. But Paul did not see the Covenant made at Sinai as the centerpiece of the relationship between God and Israel. He saw the foundation of life with God in the Promise God gave to Abraham. The difference between a covenant and a promise was essential to him. A covenant requires the keeping of its terms. *"Moses came and told the people all the words of the Lord and all the ordinances, and all the people answered with one voice, and said, 'All the words which the Lord has spoken we will do.'"* After Moses had written all the words of Lord, he *"took the book of the covenant, and read it in the hearing of the people; and they said, 'All that the Lord has spoken we will do, and we will be obedient'"* (Ex. 24:3, 6).

A promise, on the other hand, requires that the one receiving it has faith in the one giving it. In other words, while a covenant demands commitment to an agreement, a promise demands trust in the one promising. This trust, as Paul understands it, is demonstrated by *"the obedience of faith"* (Rom 1:5; 16:26). The difference between "works of law" and the "obedience of faith" is that while one is the human effort to remain in God's good graces by keeping the terms of the Covenant, the other is the result of actualizing one's faith in the One who promised by being "obedient" to "the guidance of the Spirit." Those who are baptized exercise the same faith that Christ exercised when he died trusting in God's righteousness. For Paul, God's righteousness had already been demonstrated when he raised Christ from the dead on account of his faith. The basic apocalyptic agenda is to argue that God is just and powerful, as shown in the previous chapters. Rather than having to predict how God's power and justice will be demonstrated at the final battles against the evil powers that rise up from the primeval chaos of the deep sea, Paul argues that the power and justice of God has already been demonstrated by the raising of Christ, and continues to be demonstrated by those who, like Christ, trust God and *"walk in newness of life"* (Rom. 6:4). Against those who charge that, as a Jew, Paul should be ashamed of preaching a gospel that leaves out the centrality of the Law and the Jews as the Covenant People, Paul affirms, *"For I am not ashamed of the gospel: it is the power of God for salvation to everyone who has faith, to the Jew first and also to the Greek"* (Rom. 1:16). For him, the gospel is not information, an intellectual commodity about the future, or a reaffirmation of God's commitment to the Covenant; it is the manifestation of power to live in the present guided by the Spirit that raised Christ from the dead. The Christian lives believing the Promise his faithful God made to Abraham.

Paul could not ignore the charge that according to his gospel God is being unfaithful to the Jews. Three long chapters of his letter *To the Romans* are devoted to answering this accusation. The answer is framed by the affirmation at the beginning, *"But it is not as though the word of God had failed"* (Rom. 9:6), and by restating his position at the beginning of his final summation, *"I ask, then, has God rejected his people? By no means! ... God has not rejected his people whom he foreknew"* (Rom. 11:1-2). Paul builds his argument on God's absolute freedom to accomplish his will, and a redefinition of the notion of election. After a passionate affirmation of his identification with his Jewish heritage and the recognition of the many ways in which the Jews had been blessed by God in the past (Rom. 9:1-5), Paul disallows that God's election of the Jews in a defining historical moment ties God to the past. Election is not a once-only definitive event; it is a dynamic process in historical times as God chooses the way in which to carry out his predetermined purposes. The argument starts by showing that not all the children of Abraham were elected. Election is based on God's will, not a person's genes. Election takes place according to God's freedom to show mercy on whomever he wills (Rom. 9:6-18).

This basic premise raises the objection that, if that is the case, God should not find fault in those he did not choose to have mercy on, and Paul anticipates it (Rom. 9:19). To answer this objection, Paul does a midrash on Jeremiah's visit to a potter's workshop (Rom. 9:22-24, on Jer. 18:1-11). From the story Paul extracts two points. One is that the potter has control over the clay and can not only decide how to use it, but can also change his mind about it. These observations give Paul room to speculate about the shelf-life of clay vessels, whether made for daily use, and eventually becoming discarded shards, or for display, and thereby becoming heirlooms. Renaming them as vessels of wrath, destined for destruction, and vessels of mercy, destined for glory, Paul rhetorically asks, *"What if God, desiring to show his wrath and to make known his power, has endured with much patience the vessels of wrath made for destruction, in order to make known the riches of his glory for the vessels of mercy, which he has prepared beforehand for glory, even us whom he has called, not from the Jews only but also from the Gentiles?"* (Rom. 9:22-24). His true-to-fact hypothetical question reveals his apocalyptic horizon with the important modification already noticed. God has prepared beforehand all things to achieve his purpose. The power of God is revealed in his wrath and his mercy, as already pointed out at the beginning of the letter; it is not necessary to patiently endure until God decides to use his power and justice in an apocalyptic battle. All along, God's will has been *"to make known the riches of his glory for … us whom he has called, not from the Jews only but also from the Gentiles."* To be noticed is that while Paul at the beginning of his defense identified himself with his *"kinsmen by race"* who had been the recipients of *"the sonship, the glory, the covenants, the giving of the Law, the worship, and the promises"* (Rom. 9:4), he now identifies himself with "us," a group called by God from among both Jews and Gentiles. This tells his opponents that it is still quite possible for Jews like him to be "vessels of mercy", who are destined for glorification.

That Jews are not responding to God's call in Christ does not mean that God has rejected the Jews, but that some Jews are rejecting God's call, while other Jews, he among them, are accepting it. From the Scriptures they should have known that what is required is faith, as Abraham's example demonstrates (Rom. 4:13-24). By pursuing a "righteousness which is based on law," they stumbled on the stone God placed as a stepping stone (Rom. 9:31-33). Paul states his diagnosis of the situation in a pithy, somewhat awkward statement. The Jews are misusing the stone placed by God before them because of their misinterpretation of the role of Christ. God's purpose has been to justify those who have faith. Christ demonstrated what faith is about by the way he faced death. Faith must be placed in God, the one who promised life, and must be modeled on the faith of Abraham and, most significantly, in the faith of Christ facing the cross. Paul writes, *"For Christ is the end of the Law, that everyone who has faith may be justified"*. Both Jews and Gentiles are now being justified with the "righteousness that comes from God" when they, like Abraham and like Christ, believe in God as the giver of life. If not all Jews are being justified, it is not because the word of God to them has failed, but because, *"seeking to establish their own [by keeping the Law], they did not submit to God's righteousness"*

(Rom. 10:3-4). As Paul had written earlier, *"So it depends not upon man's will or exertion, but upon God's mercy"* (Rom. 9:16). Thus, like Ezekiel, Zechariah and Daniel, who before him had been primarily concerned with God's power and justice, Paul also insists that God is righteous and faithful (Rom. 3:3; 1 Cor. 1:9; 10:13; 2 Cor. 1:18; 1 Th. 5:24).

In his defense of the power and faithfulness of God, Paul explains some things in a way that seems contrived, almost following the example of Ezekiel's declaration that God issued bad laws because he knew that the Israelites were going to be rebellious. Besides the illustration of God's ways by observing a potter at work, Paul also uses an illustration from what olive growers did in order to keep the trees in production for a longer period of time. The illustration serves to tell Gentiles who have become new creatures in Christ that they should not feel superior to the Jews whose privileges they are now enjoying. He tells them to *"not become proud, but stand in awe"* (Rom. 11:20) at the way in which God has extended his grace to them.

Today agriculturalists graft fruit trees into stems with roots that are resistant to infections. In antiquity grafting was done in order to keep old olive trees in production. When the branches of the trees began to dry up, they were cut off and young branches were grafted into the old trunk. By doing this, growers avoided having to take the old trees out of the ground, plant new trees and wait a few years before they became productive. So, Jews who did not believe God's promise and sought to become righteous on their own had been cut off, and Gentiles who believe God's Promise have been grafted in so that God's purpose for his people may be fulfilled. In this way the Promise God made to Abraham that all nations would be blessed through his descendants, those who like him believe God, was also being fulfilled. Paul tells his Gentile converts, however, that they should not harbor feelings of superiority because they had become the recipients of the blessings that God had bestowed previously on the Jews. If they were to depart from the "obedience of faith" they would also be cut off. In the meantime they should be quite conscious that they were benefiting from the sap provided to them by the "holy root." Moreover, if the Jews *"do not persist in their unbelief, [they] will be grafted in, for God has the power to graft them in again"* (Rom. 11:15-24). The illustration begins with a reference to the need to make the Jews jealous of the Gentiles who are now taking their place as the beneficiaries of God's mercy (Rom. 11:14), and ends explaining that *"just as you were once disobedient to God but now have received mercy because of their disobedience, so they have now been disobedient in order that by the mercy shown to you they also may receive mercy. For God has consigned all men to disobedience, that he may have mercy upon all"* (Rom. 11:30-32). In his illustration about the freedom and power of the potter who does what he wills with the clay, Paul says that God shows his wrath with the vessels made for destruction (Rom. 9:22). Here he says that God causes different people at different times to be disobedient, which places them under his wrath (Rom. 1:18-32), in order to also have mercy upon all. This is, it must be admitted, a problematic way of explaining God's righteousness working within a pre-determined view of history.

Paul is a well-educated Jew, and as such is well aware that such an explanation is not quite convincing. Having tried by the illustration of what growers do with old olive trees to argue that God had not rejected the Jews, even while incorporating the Gentiles into the chosen people, Paul realizes that he has gone beyond the limits of what can be demonstrated, and he finds refuge in the Wisdom tradition that must have been also part of his good education at the feet of Gamaliel. While affirming that God's election of Israel is irrevocable, he affirms also that those Jews who stumble on the stone intended as a stepping stone cannot attain to God's righteousness by trying to establish their own. Thus, he realizes that to explain God's ways is beyond human reach. *"O the depth of the riches and wisdom and knowledge of God! How unsearchable are his judgments and how inscrutable his ways!"* (Rom. 11:33). God is faithful, indeed, but my best efforts to demonstrate it are not sufficient.

To confess the faithfulness of God is a declaration of faith. As the Wise men had said, God *"has made everything beautiful in its time, also he has put eternity into man's heart, yet so that he cannot find out what God has done from the beginning to the end.... God is in heaven, and you upon earth; therefore let your words be few"* (Ec. 3:11; 5:2). His indebtedness to the Wisdom Tradition not only prevented him from trying to demonstrate God's power and justice by descriptions of his wrath in cosmic battles in the nether regions of the abyss and the outposts of the universe where the winds originate. It also prevented him from claiming to know exactly how God acts in the accomplishment of his will. Paul's intellectual horizon, informed by the Wisdom tradition, put limits to his apocalyptic vision. While undoubtedly working with the apocalyptic schema of the Two Ages in order to understand what God had done in Christ, Paul revised apocalypticism in significant ways by rejecting its mythological cosmic battles and universalizing the nationalistic outlook of previous apocalyptic authors. He did not use history as a way to prove the authenticity of his apocalyptic views. He recognized the wisdom of those who claimed that men do not have total access to God's mind.

THE EVIDENCE OF GOD'S POWER AND JUSTICE

As an apocalypticist, Paul is also sure that there is to be a final judgment. Even though he does not connect explicitly the Judgment to the *Parousia*, it would seem that they are related. His references to the Judgment lack a time frame. He writes that *"we shall all stand before the judgment seat of God"* (Rom. 14:10), but he also describes it as *"the judgment seat of Christ,"* before which all must appear *"so that each may receive good or evil, according to what he has done in the body"* (2 Cor. 5:10). To any Jew who thinks himself to be better than any Gentile, and judges all Gentiles as sinners, Paul asks, *"Do you suppose, O man, that when you judge those who do such things and yet do them yourself, you will escape the judgment of God?"* (Rom. 2:11). That there is going to be a righteous judgment when God, or Christ, sits on the judgment seat and some receive eschatological life and others receive eschatological death is central to the apocalyptic vision. As such, it is part of Paul's apocalyptic scenario, but he does not expand on it. As already noticed, influenced by the Wisdom tradition, he admits, *"How unsearchable are his judgments!"* (Rom. 11:33). Like Daniel, whose vision of the outrageous conduct of the Little Horn did not include the battles that brought his dominion to an end, but left it hanging by the abrupt interruption of the Ancient of Days sitting in judgment and opening the books (Dan. 7:10), Paul also brings in the judgment as the climax to all human affairs. Unlike what is described in *Daniel*, Paul does not give details of the judgment. Just as he does not give details of life in heaven, but is satisfied that it is going to be living forever "with the Lord," the judgment will also have eternal consequences. There is no need for background scenarios.

Paul saw himself living in the final moments of The Age of Messiah. He wrote to the Corinthians, *"the appointed time has grown very short,"* and *"the form of this world is passing away"* (1 Cor. 7:29, 31). His certainty of the Judgment and of the nearness of The Age to Come reveals his apocalyptic world view, but his apocalypticism is radically transformed by his certainty of the resurrection of Christ as the already established foundation of The New Creation. Thus, while he is looking forward to the *Parousia* when the body of flesh will be left behind and fully eschatological life in a spirit body will begin, his theology is built on the fact that God has already revealed his justice by raising Christ from the dead. *Daniel* and *First Enoch* give authority to their predictions of future divine activity that will demonstrate God's power and justice by their presentation of past history as *vaticinia ex eventu*. Paul also gives authority to his affirmation of the soon-to-be *Parousia* by reference to what God has done in the past, but he does not need to use a subterfuge. His hopes for the future are based on his faith in what God had done already recently. The cross and the resurrection are past events that only faith can comprehend. Rather than to present his writing so that his readers think they are reading something written by the seventh from Adam, or a Jew exiled in Babylon, Paul asserts the power of the Spirit that raised Christ from the dead and is now energizing the lives of his readers as new creatures in Christ (Gal. 3:1-3). That the power of the Gospel has transformed their lives proves the reality of the New Creation and confirms that the power and the justice of God are already at work. Their own experience is all the evidence needed to establish God's righteousness. The Jewish apocalypticists predicted a future demonstration of the power and justice of God. Paul affirms that the demonstration has already taken place in the resurrection of Christ and in the life "in the Spirit" enjoyed by believers (Rom. 1:16). The effectiveness of faith is not demonstrated by the ability to take some piece of information seriously, but having become a new type of being by the power of the Spirit that raised Christ from the dead. For Paul, God has already manifested his righteousness in the power of the Gospel that is experienced in the present by those who have faith in the God who gave them the Promise of life.

Unlike Ezekiel, Zechariah and Daniel, Paul does not ask, "How much longer are we going to suffer under the power of evil?" Unlike Daniel, he does not ask God, "What happened to Jeremiah's prophecy of the seventy years of Israel's punishment?" He does not ask his readers to endure with patience until God decides to reveal his power and justice. God's righteousness and wrath is right now being revealed in people (Rom. 1:18-32; 3:21-26). God's decisive intervention in history has already taken place, without any battles with mythical armies and gory descriptions of children and women torn apart by monsters or impaled by giants. Concerning the fate of the wicked who are the recipients of God's wrath, as he "gives them up" while still living on this earth, Paul keeps a thunderous silence.

Supporting the thesis of this book, Paul's apocalypticism is concerned with the present. But, unlike Ezekiel and Daniel who enjoin obedience to the Law of Moses, Paul advises his readers to allow the Holy Spirit to transform their minds to help them ascertain what is the will of God, *"what is good and acceptable and perfect"* (Rom. 12:2). Those whose minds have been made new from above by the Spirit live "in the Spirit," are "guided by the Spirit," and having *"set the mind on the Spirit"* enjoy *"life and peace"* (Rom. 8; 5-9). Peace, the ultimate *desideratum* of all apocalyptic visions, is a reality now among those who live "according to the Spirit." As noticed above, however, while they live "in the flesh" crucified with Christ, they, like Christ when he lived "in the flesh," will still suffer. Therefore, the apocalyptic *Parousia* is a prominent feature in Paul's horizon.

Paul's hope is for a life where *"what is mortal"* has been *"swallowed up by life"* (2 Cor. 5:4). This is not a palliative administered to his converts to help them endure the hardships of economic injustices or cultural authoritarianism within the Roman Empire. He was not, as he charges other apostles of being, a *"false merchant of the word of God"* (2 Cor. 2:17). The hope of sharing in the glory of God, of being changed from the image of the earthly to the image of the heavenly being (1 Cor. 15:49), is not a blind hope that God eventually, after incomprehensible delays, will do something for humanity. The assurance that God's purpose for creation is being realized is based on three things that faith affirms God has already accomplished: in the first place, God created the world (2 Cor. 4:4-6); second, even though the visible, material structure of the present age has not changed, the cross and the resurrection of Christ have accomplished a new creation, and those who have faith in God already live in it (2 Cor. 4:18), and third, those who have faith in what God did in Christ (2 Cor. 5:5), and have already received the Spirit as a down payment, will enjoy their final glorification at the Day of Christ (Phil. 1:19).

Paul encapsulates his theological vision in a pithy statement, *"For in this hope we were saved"* (Rom.8:24). Salvation, eschatological life in the Spirit now and in spirit bodies at "the end," the ultimate goal of God's creation, has been achieved. It is a fact of the past that faith can apprehend. But, it is also a fact that at present believers are saved "in this hope." Faith and hope are bound to exist together. Faith transcends all evidence and therefore sparks hope. Fruitful hope can only be based on faith. If it is based on evidence, as Paul says, it is not hope. He rhetorically asks, *"For who hopes for what he sees?"* (Rom. 8:24). Hope needs faith as its basis, and faith sparks hope as its consequence because faith has God's Promise, not his Covenant, as its basis. Both of them, however, can remain abstract ideas comforting the intellect, lacking relevance. Paul does not conceive faith and hope as twins *in abstracto*. They belong in a trinity that is completed by love. That "we" were saved in this hope is true because love actualizes this hope in the body, not just in the mind, that is in the concreteness of social life, and that is what is going to be looked up at the Judgment (2 Cor. 5:10).

Paul gives full expression to the trinity of faith, hope and love in his hymn to love in *To the Corinthians I*, chapter 13, but that is not the only place in which he shows their ultimate significance in the lives of those who have faith in God. Describing the present, not the past nor the future, he writes, *"Therefore, since we are justified by faith, we have peace with God through our Lord Jesus Christ ... and we rejoice in our hope of sharing the glory of God. More than that we rejoice in our suffering ... because God's love has been poured into our hearts through the Holy Spirit which has been given to us"* (Rom. 5:1-5). Here faith, hope and love are interlocked with peace, God, Christ, joy, suffering and the Holy Spirit. Paul's letters do not have a more pristine statement of his Gospel. It affirms that the peace of those who have faith in the Christ Event is the gift of the justification received from God. Hope is dependent on faith in God. Besides, God does not only justify; he also pours love into human hearts. He does not give it counting the drops. He does not sprinkle it. He does not let it flow stingily. He prodigally pours his love. The statement parallels the trinity of faith, hope and love with the trinity of God who justifies, Christ who gives peace, and the Holy Spirit who is the agent of love. This happens because *"God shows his love for us in that while we were yet sinners, Christ died for us"* (Rom. 5:8). Thus, it is the love of God that provides the object which faith apprehends and God recognizes by justifying sinners. In turn, faith in God sparks hope. Then both of them become manifest by being transposed from the realm of thought into the realm of life by Christians who live as lovers. Thus faith and hope, which may be elements in the mind, become immanent realities in the social life of those who believe in God. This is how the apocalypticism of Paul is fully engaged with the suffering world of the flesh, not by descriptions of God's future exercises of his power to destroy it, but by demonstrations of God's power to give life and peace in the present.

Not to be overlooked in this wonderful intertwining of the trinity of God, Christ and the Spirit, with the trinity of faith, hope and love is the fact that Paul includes "suffering" in this description of the effectiveness of the Gospel to bring about life. This is another instance of the radical revision of the apocalyptic scenario accomplished by Paul. The core of the apocalyptic agenda is to argue that the present suffering of the righteous will come to an end. God's power and justice will eventually prevail. If now the righteous suffer and the wicked prosper, this is not going to be the case much longer. Both the wicked and the righteous will receive their just reward at the Judgment. Paul turns the apocalyptic perspective on its head arguing that the power and the justice of God have been fully displayed in the death and the resurrection of Christ. There the righteous suffered; there the suffering of the righteous was consummated. This means that those who participate in both Christ's death and resurrection in order to receive "a life like his" will inevitably suffer in a death like his. Having been born "in the flesh" to bring life to humanity, Christ suffered. The apocalypticism of Paul is fully engaged with the suffering characteristic to those who live "in the flesh." Christians who live "in the flesh" and "in Christ" will suffer. They should, however, rejoice in their suffering because it confirms their identification with Christ and God's redemptive love. By faith they identify themselves with the righteous one who suffered on a cross, and brings to them eschatological life in the Spirit and hope in an eschatological spirit body. This can only generate joy. Christians who rejoice in suffering, according to Paul, do so because they have already received the down payment of the Spirit that sustains their present life and their hope for the future. It is a total misunderstanding of Paul to see in his "rejoicing in suffering" a masochistic streak in his personality. As Krister Stendhal well argued long ago, one must not read Paul in terms of "the introspective conscience of the West," which originated with Augustine's explorations of the roles of memory.

In the present, Christians do not live exercising patient endurance under suffering, but patiently accepting the reality that they are still living "in the flesh." *"If we hope for what we do not see, we wait for it with patience"* (Rom. 8:25). Paul does not envision, as I have already pointed out, that the realization of what is hoped for will come about when God reveals his wrath, fury, jealousy and vengeance, and puts an end to suffering, as was necessary for Ezekiel. According to Paul, suffering will surely come to an end, just as faith and hope will also come to an end, when the God in whom "we" believe accomplishes what "we" hope for. He writes, *"For now we see in a mirror dimly, but then face to face. Now I know in part; then I shall understand fully, even as I have been fully understood"* (1 Cor. 13:12). When sight and knowledge are perfect, faith and hope have ceased to be. In the meantime, Christians enjoy not only their sufferings but also their life "in Christ" until the Day of Christ.

For Paul, the greatest power in the universe is the power of God's love (Rom. 8:35-39). The power and justice of God will not be revealed in a future confrontation when human and angelic armies will overcome the forces of evil that rise from the great waters of the abyss, finally determining whose world this is. God's power and justice is being revealed now by the pouring of God's love on sinners. As the ultimate agent of God's power and justice, love will continue to flow prodigally forever. Unlike faith and hope, *"love never ends"* (1 Cor. 13:8). Lovers will be forever with the Lord at his coming. The trajectory of Paul's apocalyptic theology does not culminate in gory battles with armies led by a dragon coming out of a bottomless pit, but in the love of God that never ends. This is the core of Paul's radical apocalyptic theology.

To the Hebrews

The author of *To the Hebrews* describes what he has written as an *exhortation*, and appeals to his audience to *"bear with"* it, *"for I have written to you briefly"* (Heb. 13:22). He then ends his writing as if he were writing a letter: *"Greet all your leaders and all the saints. Those who come from Italy send you greetings. Grace be with all of you. Amen"* (Heb. 13:24). His exhortation, it must be noticed, does not open as a letter. He and his addressees remain unidentified throughout his text. The anonymous author begins his text by pointing out that in the past God spoke in many and various ways *"to our fathers;"* but *"in these last days he has spoken to us by a Son"* (Heb. 1:1-2). Thus, rather than to set himself apart from his audience he identifies himself with his readers as a beneficiary of God's speaking to his generation in a special, unique way. In the process he identifies his time as "these last days." In this way, the author sets his agenda on a apocalyptic course.

From the text of the exhortation, one gets a good idea of the intended audience. They are Christians who have *"been enlightened, who have tasted the heavenly gift, and have become partakers of the Holy Spirit, and have tasted the goodness of the word of God and the powers of the age to come"* (Heb. 6:4-5). As a result of these benefits, they have been showing consistently the love of God in their service to the saints (Heb. 6:10). Like the author, they had also *"fled for refuge"* from the fear of death that keeps people in *"lifelong bondage"* (Heb. 6:18; 2:15). As a consequence of their having become partakers of the Holy Spirit, they had *"endured a hard struggle with sufferings, sometimes being publicly exposed to abuse and affliction, and sometimes being partners with those so treated. For [they] had compassion on the prisoners, and ... joyfully accepted the plundering of [their] property"* (Heb. 10:32-34). Some of them, however, had been neglecting to attend the meetings of the community of believers (Heb. 10:25). These descriptions tell that the recipients of the exhortation are Christians who had already experienced both the rewards and the social and economic consequences of their having become followers of the crucified and risen Christ.

The experience of sufferings, no doubt, had been taking its toll, and the author recognizes that on account of it they could become *"weary or fainthearted,"* even though they had not yet had to face martyrdom (Heb. 12:3-4). Their suffering is to be understood in terms of their having become sons of God. He reminds them of the exhortation: *"'For the Lord disciplines him whom he loves, and chastises every son whom he receives.' It is for discipline that you have to endure, God is treating you as sons"* (Heb. 12:6-7). To drive the point home, he explains that those who are not disciplined by their father are not sons but bastards (Heb. 12:8).

It appears, then, that the suffering of those being exhorted not to become weary or fainthearted is not caused by the imposition of worship to idols or traditional accounts of the great tribulations that must take place before the *Parousia*. These Christians have been suffering at the hands of families who have disinherited them and neighbors who abuse them in public. That those who became attached to the movement about Jesus experienced social dislocations is evident in the gospels. Predicting what will happen to the disciples at the time of the end, *According to Mark* says, *"But take heed to yourselves; for they will deliver you up to councils; and you will be beaten in synagogues .... And brother will deliver up brother to death, and the father his child, and children will rise against parents and have them put to death"* (Mk. 13:9, 12). This most likely would have been the case in a Jewish context where traditional family ties and religious identifications were quite strong.

That the exhortation is being given to Jews who are experiencing persecution and abuse from family and neighbors who resent their withdrawal from participation in the Jewish way of life is also indicated by a significant small explanation by the author. Among his final exhortations, he says: *"Do not be led away by diverse and strange teachings,"* and refers to one of them in particular. *"It is well that the heart be strengthened"* (*bebaioushai* = be made stable, unwavering) *"by grace, not by foods which have not benefited their adherents"* (Heb. 13:9). This suggests that their "falling away" from Christianity was also evident by their adoption of food laws which, according to the following elaboration of the matter, had to do with eating the meat of animals who had been sacrificed at the altar of the earthly "tent" (Heb. 13:10-15).

Another aside intended to clarify who are the object of God's concern also throws light on the intended audience. Elaborating on the task accomplished by *"the pioneer of their salvation"* (Heb. 2:10), the author makes clear that the Son *"is concerned ... with the descendants of Abraham,"* not with angels (Heb. 2:16). The explanation is connected to the affirmation that the Son, who was higher than the angels, became for a short time lower than the angels and lived in *"flesh and blood"* to experience death (Heb. 2:14). It would seem that this aside caused the first collectors of Christian scriptures to give to this exhortation the title *To the Hebrews*. That God is concerned with the descendants of Abraham illumines the author's agenda, which is concerned to demonstrate the superiority of the Son's high priesthood by relating it to the laws of the sacrificial system carried out by Aaronic priests. This gives to *To the Hebrews* a particular cultic setting that creates some tension with the universalistic outlook of apocalypticism. But that the author has an apocalyptic mind set, as I will demonstrate, cannot be overlooked.

THE THEOLOGICAL BASIS OF THE EXHORTATION

The identification of its recipients helps in understanding the theme of the exhortation, which examines the problem at hand from different perspectives and has a word of exhortation for each of the different aspects of the situation. The theme is that God's

Son shared in flesh and blood with the children of God to make "purification for sins" (Heb. 1:3). God then *"appointed"* him *"with an oath"* as *"a high priest for ever after the order of Melchizedek"* Heb. 6:20). About this appointment by God, the author says that he has *"much to say which is hard to explain"* (Heb. 5:11). After having stated his premise, the author specifies, *"Now the point in what we are saying is this: we have such a high priest, one who is seated at the right hand of the throne of the Majesty in heaven, a minister in the sanctuary and the true tent which is set up not by man but by the Lord"* (Heb. 8:1-2). The exhortation is based on this premise: "we have a high priest." From this premise the author draws the conclusion as an exhortation; since that is the case, we must with confidence and absolute certainty come to this high priest in order to be purified from sin. But the author does not just spend a great deal of effort to convince his readers to seek the services of the Son as high priest after the order of Melchizedek (Heb. 5:10). He spends an equal amount of effort pointing out why the priesthood established by the Law "after the order of Aaron" has become obsolete (Heb. 7:11; 8:13). In other words, the exhortation is not only that Jesus is *"the apostle and high priest of our confession"* (Heb. 3:1) and that they must "hold firm" this confession without wavering (Heb. 10:23). It is also to prevent them from "falling away," becoming "sluggish," "weary or fainthearted," and seek to have the remission of sins done by the Aaronic system of repeated sacrifices of goats and calves which are unable to "make perfect" those who sin. I surmise that these Christians were seeking purification from sin at the temple not only because they trusted the effectiveness of its sacrifices but also because by doing this they would be avoiding the sufferings inflicted by family and neighbors who disapproved their withdrawal from the Jewish way of life.

Because the author's agenda is not only to affirm the effectiveness of the high priesthood of Christ, but also to specify the limitations of the high priesthood that serves in a temple made with hands, the theological foundations for his exhortation are established by comparing and contrasting the two available orders of priests, the sacrifices being offered by them, the status of the sanctuary in which they function and the divine economy of which they are a part. An exhortation based on this foundation makes sense only when access to the sacrifices offered at the temple in Jerusalem was available.

Even before he comes to the crux of the matter, he compares the ministry of Jesus with that of Moses. Evidently the author refers to the Son, Jesus and Christ without distinctions, and I will just adopt his undifferentiated vocabulary. The first comparison points out the superiority of the Son, the builder of the house, over the house that has been built. Then he distinguishes between Moses, who was faithful as a *servant in* God's house, and Christ, who was faithful as a *Son over* God's house (Heb. 3:1-6). The priests who serve in the house, are appointed by God, but are human beings who need to offer sacrifices for their own sins. Thus, *"in the days of his flesh, Jesus offered up prayers and supplications, with loud cries and tears, to him who was able to save him from death."* Besides, he *"learned obedience through what he suffered; and being made perfect he became the source of eternal salvation to all who obey him, being designated by God a high priest after the order of Melchizedek"* (Heb. 5:1-10). Here the author singles out some correspondences between the two orders of priests, something that may have been explored by Jewish Rabbis who tried to explain how Melchizedek could have been identified as a priest before the establishment of the Levitical priesthood. He points out that both Moses, the one who established the Levitical priesthood, and the Son were faithful, and that both the Levitical priests and the Son were ultimately appointed by God. While the Levitical priests had to offer sacrifices for their own sins, Jesus had to suffer to learn obedience. That is, both were not without needs. In these details the author finds similarities.

Admonishing those who are "falling away" against following strange teachings about food, the author supports his advice by citing another similarity between the order of Aaron and the order of Melchizedek. According to the Law, the flesh of the animals whose blood the high priest takes into the Most Holy place to expiate for the sins of all the year on the Day of Atonement was not supposed to be eaten. It was "burned outside the camp." In the same way, the author claims, *"Jesus also suffered outside the gate in order to sanctify the people through his own blood."* Then he exhorts, *"Therefore, let us go forth to him outside the camp, bearing abuse for him. For here we have no lasting city, but we seek the city which is to come"* (Heb. 13:11-13). The comparison touches on three important considerations. In the first place it was brought in to indicate that the meat of those animals sacrificed on the Day of Atonement was not to be eaten, which serves to stress that those adopting some strange teachings, while they think to be improving their standing before God, are actually acting against the Law of the "old" Covenant by what they eat. In the second place, it points out that the body of Christ suffered outside "the camp," that is outside the gate of the city of Jerusalem, the same place where the bodies of the sacrificed animals were burned. In the third place, unlike those who are abandoning "the hope," they are not concerned with Jerusalem, but with a city which is to come, where their high priest is now making atonement for all those who draw near. To be noticed also is that the author starts his comparison stating, *"We have an altar from which those who serve the tent have no right to eat,"* identifying himself as a Jew, and the eating of the meat of animals that were supposed to be burned outside the camp is something which apparently the adherents of strange teachings are actually doing at the time (Heb. 13:9, 10). This is advice to the author's contemporaries concerning current practices.

After having made a proviso, that what the order of Melchizedek entails is hard to explain, and that he will not burden his readers with the repetition of elementary notions about Christianity which they already know, the author elaborates on the significant differences between the order of Aaron and the order of Melchizedek. He begins by stating that Abraham was blessed by Melchizedek and *"to him Abraham apportioned a tenth part of everything"* he had gained from the battle against the kings who had taken Lot captive. Translating his name, he brings out that Melchizedek is king (*melek*) of righteousness (*zedek*), and from his title one learns that he is king of Salem, peace. Righteousness and peace, of course, are what all the sons of God hope for. Besides, *"he is without father or mother or genealogy, and has neither beginning of days nor end of life, but resembling the Son of God he continues a priest for ever"* (Heb. 7:1-3). This means that the order of Melchizedek is a superior order.

To establish how much greater is the priesthood of Melchizedek than that of the priests of the tribe of Levi, the author admits that these priests are authorized by the Law to receive tithes from their fellow descendants of Abraham. But Abraham paid tithes to a man with no Levitical genealogy, and the Levitical priests were already in Abraham's loins when he paid tithes to, and was blessed by Melchizedek. This only demonstrates the superiority of the priesthood of Melchizedek over all Levitical priests who paid tithes to him and were blessed by him through Abraham. Not to be overlooked was that at the time when Melchizedek blessed Abraham he had already received God's tripartite promise of the land, a multitude of descendants and a role as the source of blessings to all the nations. He was not only the bearer of his descendants in his loins but the bearer of God's Promise as well (Heb. 7:4-10).

Having established the superiority of Melchizedek's priesthood, the author argues for the necessity of a priest belonging to his order. The argument begins with a contrary to fact conditional sentence. *"If perfection had been attainable through the Levitical priesthood (for under it the people received the law), what further need would there have been for another priest to arise after the order of Melchizedek, rather than one named after the order of Aaron?"* (Heb. 7:11). A change from one order to another, when the existing order was established by the Law, means that a different law is now in effect. The Law that established the services at the Sanctuary also established that the priests serving in it were to be of the tribe of Levi, but Jesus, of whom it is said that he would be a priest forever, belonged to the tribe of Judah. Moses in the Law, however, did not appoint priests from the tribe of Judah. Therefore, God's appointment of Jesus, a descendant of Judah, as high priest must have been authorized by a different law.

Besides, the one who had been made perfect through suffering and had been appointed high priest was installed *"by the power of an indestructible life,"* that is the power of the Spirit that gave us the risen Christ. Thus the appointment of Jesus as high priest after the order of Melchizedek means that the Law establishing the priesthood of Levites has been *"set aside because of its weakness and uselessness (for the law made nothing perfect)"* (Heb. 7:11-19). This paragraph establishes the inability of the Law of Moses to make anyone perfect, and perfection is what the high priesthood of Jesus provides to those who come to him for purification from sin. The author of *To the Hebrews* agrees with Paul that the Law has become inoperative. Paul said the same thing in a non-cultic setting arguing that the Law was not given to give life; it could only condemn transgressors (Gal. 3:21; Rom. 4:15; 8:1-2). Paul, however, did not think that perfection was possible while living "in the flesh." Those who live both "in the flesh" and "in Christ" will be perfect only when they receive a spirit body at the *Parousia*. Christians now strive toward perfection, but it is not within their reach (Phil. 3:12). The author of *To the Hebrews*, however, is only concerned with the perfection of the forgiveness provided by the different sacrifices offered by the different priesthoods.

To set up the high priesthood of Jesus on an even stronger foundation, the author contrasts the appointment of priests according to the Law on the basis of genealogy to the appointment of Jesus not only by the power that raised him from the dead but also by an oath of God, something which Levitical priests lacked. He substantiates his claim quoting a Psalm, *"The Lord has sworn and will not change his mind, 'Thou art a priest for ever'"* (Ps. 110:4). Since he was appointed forever by an oath from God, the author deduces that Jesus has become *"the surety of a better covenant"* (Heb. 7:22). Thus while, like Paul, the author considers the Promise to Abraham basic, he now brings in the Covenant set up at Sinai only to declare it obsolete. Under the "old" Covenant, given the mortality of all humans, not one high priest could serve for very long; death prevented their continuation in office. The one high priest appointed by the power of the Spirit who raised Christ from the dead, and who was confirmed by an oath from God as a priest forever, "always lives to make intercession" for those who come to him asking for purification from sin. Unlike a Levitical high priest who had *"to offer sacrifices daily, first for his own sins and then for those of the people, he [the Son] did this once for all when he offered up himself. Indeed, the law appoints men in their weakness as high priests, but the word of the oath, which came later than the law, appoints a Son who has been made perfect for ever"* (Heb. 7:20-28).

Concerning both the Promise and the Covenant, the author brings out that they were established by a divine oath. In the case of the Covenant, the oath serves to establish that the priesthood of the Son is forever. In the case of the Promise, the oath shows the immutability of God's purpose. All those who make an oath appeal to something greater than themselves, but God having nothing greater than himself swore by two things that cannot be proven false. These two things are also immutable, unchangeable: his Promise and his Oath. Since these are unchangeable, the future, in which his promise is to be fulfilled, is also unchangeable (Heb. 6:17-18). This early appeal to what is unchangeable to guarantee the effectiveness of God's word and as his exhortation that the heart (the mind) of his readers must be unwavering to guarantee their hope, are indicators of the author's cosmology and apocalyptic vision.

Having argued for the superiority of the priesthood after the order of Melchizedek, the author sets up to establish the superiority of the sanctuary in which the Son officiates as high priest. He begins recognizing that if Jesus *"were on earth, he would not be a priest at all, since there are priests who offer gifts according to the law."* This recognizes that at the time of writing, the ministry of Jesus and the ministry of Levitical high priests are contemporary. The point of all his argument is that "we have such a high priest, one who is seated at the right hand of the throne of the Majesty in heaven, a minister in the sanctuary and the true tent which is set up not by man but by the Lord." As such, he is the superior choice. The priests on earth "serve a copy and shadow of the heavenly sanctuary." It was built according to the pattern shown to Moses on Mt. Sinai. The sanctuary in which priests offer sacrifices on earth is the central feature of the Covenant established at Sinai and priests who operate under that Covenant still offer sacrifices according to the Law. Through the prophet Jeremiah, however, God told the people that in the future he would establish a "New" Covenant, which would not be like the first one (Jer. 31:31-32). Now, *"if that first covenant had been faultless, there would have been no occasion for a second."* The obvious conclusion from this is, according to the author, that *"in speaking of a new covenant he [God] treats the first as obsolete, and, growing old, is ready to vanish away"* (Heb. 8:1-13).

To be noticed is that declaring the "Old" Covenant obsolete does not declare it void. It is still functional with its imperfections. Jews are still going to a Levitical priest to offer sacrifices and some among the recipients of the author's exhortation are no longer attending the community's worships but falling back to their former Jewish cultic practices. The author does say, however, that as obsolete it is growing old; eventually, the "Old" Covenant will "vanish away." That the sacrifices of the "Old" Covenant are considered effective still is also evident from a *gezera shawa* deployed by the author in the course of his exhortation. This is an argument from minor to major, *de minoris ad maioris*. *"For if the sprinkling of defiled persons with the blood of goats and bulls and with the ashes of a heifer sanctifies for the purification of the flesh,* **how much more** *shall the blood of Christ, who through the Eternal Spirit offered himself without blemish to God, purify your conscience from dead works to serve the living God."* (Heb. 9:13-14, bold added). The logic of the statement depends on the validity of the premise. The argument rests on the effectiveness of the sacrifices offered by priest at the earthly sanctuary to sanctify the flesh. In other words, the "Old" Covenant is effective as far as it goes, within its limitations. To declare something obsolete does not deny its value. It only establishes that something better is now available.

This argument from minor to major establishes the difference between the "Old" and the "New" Covenant: the superiority of the blood of Christ to the blood of goats and bulls, or the ashes of heifers. The difference between the two is that while the blood of Christ makes a sinner perfect the blood of animals could not ever make anyone perfect. The difference is that the cultic practices at the earthly sanctuary operated at the level of the earthly, visible, changeable, temporary realm of the flesh. As such those who offer sacrifices and come to the temple on the Day of Atonement to have their sins removed go home and find that their conscience still condemns them.

Like Paul, the author of *To the Hebrews* makes use of the discovery of the conscience by the Greek moralists. As first used the word says that someone else knows what one thinks nobody knows. The Greek word, *syneidesis*, is a composite of *syn* (= together with) and *oida* (= to know). It says that another knows with you what you had done. As such, the conscience functioned as the accuser of the wrong doer which highlights his guilt. Toward the end of the third century B.C.E., Polybius said that there is *"no witness so fearful nor accuser so terrible as that conscience which dwells in the soul of every man"* (XVIII. Xliii. 13). Paul used the word to affirm that Gentiles know themselves to be sinners. Jews are accused by the Law, and Gentiles are accused by their conscience (Rom. 2:15-16).

The author brings up "the purification of the conscience," something that no one knew about in Old Testament times, as what makes the "New" Covenant better than the first and thereby renders it obsolete. By cleansing not just the flesh but also the conscience, the ministration of Christ as high priest in the heavenly sanctuary makes the sinner perfect, something that a law has never been able to do. Thus, the author proclaims, *"But when Christ had offered for all time a single sacrifice for sin … by a single offering he has perfected for all time those who are sanctified."* As a consequence, *"where there is forgiveness of these [sins], there is no longer any offering for sin"* (Heb. 10:12, 14, 18). According to the author, within the "Old" Covenant arrangement *"gifts and sacrifices are offered which cannot perfect the conscience,"* but *"the blood of Christ ... purifies your conscience from dead works"* (Heb. 9:9, 14). Obviously, the argument is against the perception that one must go to the altar with a gift to be offered by a Levitical priest and thus attain purification from sin, and that this must be done repeatedly. The objectivity of such sacrifices may give some satisfaction but the conscience continues to condemn sinners who need to continue to offer sacrifices as long as they live. For the author, that sinners must offer sacrifices time and time again only proves that their conscience continues to condemn them. That is certainly not the case of those who put their confidence in the sacrifice that Christ offered once for all time as high priest in the true tent. Once his sacrifice became available, there is no longer any need to offer sacrifices for sin. This argument would seem irrelevant if sacrifices for sin were not being offered at the temple when *To the Hebrews* was written.

After the offering of himself to God as a sacrifice for the purification of the conscience of all those who come to him for sanctification, God appointed him high priest by *"the power of an indestructible life."* This places him in the realm of the unchangeable, immutable and eternal. There he is *"a minister in the sanctuary and the true tent which is set up not by man but by the Lord"* (Heb. 7:26; 8:2). The author expands on this stating that *"when Christ appeared as a high priest of the good things that have come, then through the greater and more perfect tent (not made with hands, that is, not of this creation) he entered once for all into the Holy Place ... thus securing an eternal redemption"* (Heb. 9:11-12). With this, the author has set the groundwork for his exhortation.

THE CRUX OF THE MATTER

The exhortation is to *"hold fast the confession of our hope without wavering, for he who promised is faithful"* (Heb. 10:23). This advice is repeated often. The readers must hold firm *"our confidence and pride in our hope"* (Heb. 3:6). The author reminds his audience that *"we share in Christ only if we hold our first confidence firm to the end"* (Heb. 3:14). Said in another way, God swore by that which cannot be changed when he gave the Promise to Abraham so that, "we who have fled for refuge," from the bondage of the fear of death (Heb. 2:15) provided by the accusations of conscience, *"might have strong encouragement to seize the hope set before us. We have this as a sure and steadfast anchor of the soul, a hope that enters into the inner shrine behind the curtain where Jesus has gone as a forerunner on our behalf, having become a high priest for ever"* (Heb. 7:18-20). In the last instance, the exhortation is that rather than to go to the earthly altar to offer the blood of goats and bulls, they should with confidence and perfect assurance, more assurance than that provided by the objectivity of sacrifices that cannot clear the conscience, *"draw near"* to our high priest, so as *"to have no longer any consciousness of sin"* (Heb. 10:2). Unlike the Levitical priests, The Son who was made perfect by God (Heb. 5:9) can *"make perfect those who draw near"* (Heb. 10:1).

In its most concise expressions, the exhortation consists of "hold fast" (3:6, 14; 10:23) and "draw near" (Heb. 4:16; 7:25; 10:22; 11:6; 12:22). But, do not "draw near" to the altar on earth (Heb. 10:1; 12:18). What needs to be held firm *"with audacity and boasting"* is *"our unwavering confession of hope,"* which is *"the anchor of our soul"* (Heb. 6:19). The content of our hope is what faith provides. It makes possible for the "New" Covenant to be based on "better promises" (Heb. 8:6).

The "Old" Covenant guaranteed to those who kept it living on the land that had been promised to Abraham and which Moses surveyed from the top of Mt. Nebo, but into which he never entered. The "New" Covenant guarantees to those who "hold fast" entering "God's *sabbatismos,*" the rest he has been enjoying since he completed the work of creation (Heb. 4:3). In chapter 3 the author shows that, even though God promised the people who left Egypt that they would find rest in the promised land, they failed to enter it on account of their rebellion, or lack of faith. Those who rebelled *"were unable to enter because of their unbelief"* (Heb. 3:19). This observation serves as a warning. The readers should *"take care ...*

lest there be in any of you an evil, unbelieving heart, leading you to fall away from the living God. But exhort one another every day ... that none of you may be hardened by the deceitfulness of sin" (Heb. 3:12-13). For a further lesson to be learned from the exodus generation that left Egypt with the hope of reaching the Promised Land but never entered it, the author quotes a psalm: *"O that today you would hearken to his voice! Harden not your hearts, as at Meribah, as on the day at Massah in the wilderness, when your fathers tested me, and put me to the proof, though they had seen my work. For forty years I loathed that generation and said, 'They are a people who err in heart, and they do not regard my ways.' Therefore I swore in my anger that they should not enter my rest"* (Ps. 95:7-11). From the psalm, the author draws two lessons: first, unbelievers fail to receive the promise, but an oath of God which is unchangeable supports it; and two, when David exhorted his generation not to harden their hearts, and based his exhortation on God's saying that it applied "today," he makes clear that when the Spirit says "today do not harden your heart" the promise to enter God's rest was not limited to the generation that left Egypt. It still stands today. Moreover, the promise to enter no longer refers to the land into which the generation that left Egypt never entered. The promise now is to enter *God's sabbatical rest*, and faith is what allows us to visualize where it is that God rests, the land we hope to enter. This gives the author the basis for his exhortation. Since *"there remains a sabbath rest for the people of God ... Let us, therefore, strive to enter that rest, that no one fall by the same sort of disobedience"* (Heb. 4:9, 11). Rather than having unbelieving hearts, like those of the exodus generation, his readers must *"draw near with a true heart with full assurance of faith"* and *"hold fast the confession of our hope without wavering, for he who has promised is faithful"* (Heb. 10:22-23).

The author of *To the Hebrews* agrees with Paul that faith is known by the conduct it promotes. Its results are visible in the actions of those who have it. For Paul faith takes hold of what God did in the past. As a result, those who believe ask for baptism to participate in the death and the resurrection of Christ. The author of *To the Hebrews* also thinks that faith is demonstrated by actions, so he writes that by their faith *"the men of old received divine approval"* by what they did (Heb. 11:2). He ends his list of those who acted on their faith saying that all of them were *"well attested by their faith"* (Heb. 11:39). The list starts with Abel, who by offering a more acceptable sacrifice than Cain *"received approval as righteous,"* and though he died *"through his faith he is still speaking"* (Heb. 11:4). The reference is to the cry for justice of all those who suffer for doing good. The blood of Abel is still crying to God from the ground asking for justice (Gen. 4:10). Enoch, on account of his faith, *"was taken up so that he should not see death; and he was not found; ... now before he was taken up he was attested as having pleased God"* (Heb. 11:5). *"Noah ... took heed and constructed an ark for the saving of his household; by this he ... became an heir of the righteousness which comes by faith"* (Heb. 11:7). This is surely an echo of Paul.

Paul's two basic texts from Scripture are: *"the righteous shall live by faith"* (Hab. 2:4), and *"he [Abraham] believed the Lord; and he reckoned it to him as righteousness"* (Gen. 15:6). The author of *To the Hebrews* expands on Abraham's faith and gives it a twist to fit his understanding of the relationship between faith and hope. After stating that Abraham "obeyed" when he was told to go to a foreign land, and that he "sojourned" in the land of promise, the author reveals the reason for his having done so. *"He looked forward to the city which has foundations, whose builder and maker is God"* (Heb. 11:8-12). According to Paul, Abraham believed the promise that God had given him, that is, he believed in the God who made him a promise. For the author, Abraham believed because he hoped to live in the place that God had already built, that is, faith allows one to see what one hopes for.

This understanding of faith is also in evidence in how the author narrates Abraham's willingness to sacrifice Isaac, the son of the Promise. *"He considered that God was able to raise men even from the dead"* (Heb. 11:17-19). Abraham, by faith, saw what God would do in the future. This is also evident in the previous summary of the lives of the first patriarchs. *"These all died in faith, not having received the promise, but having seen it and greeted it from afar."* Even though they were looking for a homeland, they were not seeking it as land on earth. *"They desired a better country, that is, a heavenly one. Therefore God is not ashamed to be called their God, for he has prepared for them a city"* (Heb. 11:13-16). In other words, for the author faith is what makes what is not physically visible, visible. It provides content to what is hoped. That is not the way in which Paul understands faith.

After Abraham, the author lists Isaac, Jacob, Joseph, Moses, the people who crossed the Red Sea and their descendants who circled around Jericho for seven days to cause its walls to fall down. About these he gives specific descriptions of what they did by faith. He then decides that it is taking too much time to continue on this vein, so he just lists names: Gideon, Barak, Samson, Jephthah, David, Samuel. He then lists what some did, or was done to them, without identifying individuals. The point, again, is that *"all these, though well attested by faith, did not receive what was promised, since God had foreseen something better for us, that apart from us they should not be made perfect"* (Heb. 11:39-40). The purpose for the whole narration of the exemplars of faith and of the kind of acts faith produces is to argue that perfection, the purification of all consciousness of sin, is the goal achieved only by the blood of him who God had already made perfect. Describing the difference between what priests do every day by taking blood into the "outer tent" and what the high priest does once a year taking blood into "the second [tent]," he explains, *"By this the Holy Spirit indicates that the way into the sanctuary is not yet opened as long as the outer tent is still standing (which is symbolic* [parabole] *for the present age)"* (Heb. 9:8-9). In other words, it is only by faith that we enter behind the veil to be perfected by our high priest. He then describes how the sacrificial system going on currently, that is, during *"the present age,"* which can only cleanse from impurities of the flesh but cannot *"perfect the conscience,"* is to last *"until its complete rectification"*

(Heb. 9:9-10, my translation). That is, when the present age gives way to what is eternal.

Before leaving the consideration of faith as the energizer of specific actions and the provider of access to what is now not visible, I would like to point out that the author singles out two women as exemplars of faith: Sarah and Rahab. Sarah is praised for having had the kind of faith Paul would recognize. *"Even when she had passed the age, ... she considered him faithful who had promised;"* therefore, she *"received power to conceive."* Had it not been for her faith, Abraham would not have had *"descendants as many as the stars of heaven and as the innumerable grains of sand by the seashore"* (Heb. 11:11-12). Rahab, duly identified as *"the harlot," "gave friendly welcome to the spies"* and as a consequence *"did not perish with those who were disobedient"* (Heb. 11:31). Besides these two, among the things that happened to those with faith, he mentions *"women received their dead by resurrection"* (Heb. 11:35). The acknowledgment of these women as having been attested by God for their faith is rather remarkable. It certainly could not have been done toward the end of the first century, when the church began to restrict positions of leadership to men only, and systematically eliminated women as apostles and prophets. Women as leaders of congregations and as legitimate apostles were not unusual at the time of Paul, however. (See my *Meditations on the Letters of Paul*, 189-90).

THE SYMBOLIC UNIVERSE OF *TO THE HEBREWS*

The author of *To the Hebrews* defines faith as *"the assurance of things hoped for, the conviction of things not seen."* He then explains what faith does and how creation took place: *"By faith we understand that the world was created by the word of God, so that what is seen was made out of things which do not appear"* (Heb. 11:1, 3). In his description of the faith of Abraham, we have already noticed that for him faith is related to hope, and the definition makes this explicit. The original Greek says that faith is the *hypostasis* of what is hoped. In the RSV, the version I am using throughout this book, the word *hypostasis* is translated here as "assurance;" it is translated "confidence" in Heb. 3:14, and is translated "nature" in Heb. 1:3. Since confidence and assurance are more or less synonymous, I will detail the last reference. The text reads, *"He [the Son] reflects the glory of God and bears the very stamp of his nature."* A clumsy, literal translation would read, *"who is an effulgence of the glory and an imprint* [charakter] *of his* [God's] *hypostasis."* This definition of the Son and the definition of faith, together with clues that I have been noticing already, tell us that the author is using the word *hypostasis* in the technical way it had acquired among the Stoics.

The Stoics rejected the dualism of the Platonic symbolic universe. According to it, the universe consists of two realms, one is material and the other is ideal. The material world, which is available to the senses, is transitory, always in the process of becoming something else; it exists. Being, on the other hand, belongs to the ideal world. Ideas are real; they are. Reality is immaterial and therefore eternal. Everything in matter appears to be real, but is not. The task of philosophy is to train the mind not to be deceived by appearances and develop ways to get to know what is real by identifying the idea in which a material object participates. In order to gain greater understanding of this universe, Platonism developed the chain of being, according to which things are placed lower or higher on the scale according to the amount of "being" in them. At the bottom are found inanimate rocks and at the top is found God, who is pure Being himself. Human souls are found trapped in a material world, and are eager to escape to the ideal world which is their original home.

The apostle Paul's theology works with a Platonic symbolic universe, according to which there is a sharp contrast between the flesh and the spirit, and the spheres between heaven and earth are populated by principalities, authorities and powers of the air who are more powerful than human beings who are caught in material bodies and live according to the passions of the flesh. Paul was a thoroughly Hellenized Jew who understood Christianity to be a totally new creation, not an improved version of Judaism. He did not base Christianity on a Covenant, but on a Promise. According to him, salvation will become an accomplished reality when those who are raised from their graves leave behind their material bodies and are taken up to be with the Lord in spirit bodies, as we noticed in a previous chapter.

The author of *To the Hebrews* was a Jew who considered Christianity's "New" Covenant to be an improved version that made the old covenant obsolete. He has been more or less unanimously seen by scholars as a Platonist to be compared to Philo of Alexandria, the illustrious Jew contemporary to Jesus and Paul who interpreted the Pentateuch in Platonic terms. I find it more helpful to see the author working with a Stoic symbolic universe. The Stoics rejected the Platonic reduction of the real to the non-material. According to them all that is real is material. God is matter. The author defines God as "a consuming fire" (Heb. 12:29). According to Greek physics, water, earth, air and fire were the four basic elements of all material objects. For the Stoics, the ground of being is an undifferentiated mass of matter. Differentiated objects come out of the ground of being and acquire hypostatic being, incapable of being seen, touched, smelled, heard or tasted by human sensory faculties. In the material world available to the senses of human beings things exist as copies of their primary being in the hypostatic realm. Thus, while phenomenological objects are visible, shakeable, mutable and perishable, hypostatic material objects are invisible and unchangeable. According to the definition of the Son, for him to be the imprint of the *hypostasis* of God, God must be matter that leaves an imprint. And to say that faith is the *hypostasis* of what is hoped for, and the "concreteness" [*pragmaton elegchos*] of what is not visible" (my translation) is to say that faith gives to human beings visibility of what is not visible. It makes the primordial, unmovable, invisible, eternal, hypostatic realm accessible to humans.

The inaccessible hypostatic realm is, of course, superior to the phenomenological realm in which humans live their everyday lives. In order to make the argument about the superiority of the high priesthood of Christ which makes perfect those who draw near to him by the sprinkling of his blood on their hearts, the author points out to his readers that *"you have not come* [drawn near] *to what may be touched, a blazing fire, and darkness, and gloom, and a tempest, and the sound of a trumpet, and a voice whose words made the hearers entreat that no further messages be spoke to them"* (Heb. 12:18-19). Rather, they had come [drawn near] *"to Mount Zion and the city of the living God, the heavenly Jerusalem, and to innumerable angels in festal gatherings, and to the assembly of the first-born who are enrolled in heaven, and to a judge who is God of all, and to the spirits of just men made perfect, and to Jesus the mediator of a new covenant, and to the sprinkled blood that speaks more graciously than the blood of Abel."* (Heb. 12:22-24). This is the realm that faith makes visible and audible to believers, but is inaccessible to human beings without faith. In *To the Hebrews*, this realm does not consist of ideas, or non-material objects, but of beings in differentiated matter. The notion that matter and form are two different things, essential to Platonism, was unknown to the ancient Hebrews. This may explain why the author of *To the Hebrews*, who is clearly very much an heir of the Hebrew mindset, found the cosmology of the Stoics more congenial.

That material reality is divided into two discrete realms, causes the author purposely to rearrange the plan of the sanctuary built by the Israelites in the wilderness. According to the instructions given to Moses, a *"veil shall separate for you the holy place from the most holy. You shall put the mercy seat upon the ark of the testimony in the most holy place"* (Ex. 26:33-34). Both the holy and the most holy place separated by a veil were, according to the instructions, within one tent. Moses was further instructed to *"make an altar to burn incense upon ... and you shall put it before the veil that is by the ark of the testimony"* (Ex. 30:1, 6). This indicates that the altar of incense was in the holy place, while the mercy seat on top of the ark of the Covenant was in the most holy place. According to the author, however, the sanctuary consists of two tents. The holy place is in the "outer tent" and the most holy place, where the high priests enters only once a year, is the "second" (Heb. 9:6-7). In other descriptions of the sanctuary, he says that Moses was instructed *"to erect the tent"* (Heb. 8:7), and that *"a tent was prepared"* (Heb. 9:2). But then he goes on to say that in *"the outer tent"* were found *"the lamp stand and the table and the bread of the Presence, it is called the Holy Place."* He continues, *"Behind the second curtain stood a tent called the Holy of Holies, having the golden altar of incense and the ark of the covenant"* (Heb. 9:3-4). Exactly what he means by saying that the Holy of Holies was a tent that stood behind the second curtain is difficult to determine because it does not conform to the description given in *Exodus*. As noticed, he is inconsistent saying that there were "an outer" and "a second" tent, not agreeing with his description of the sanctuary as "a tent." Doing this rearrangement to "the true tent," however, was not at all out of the ordinary. Prior to the academic concerns of modern universities to reconstruct the past as it actually was, accuracy was not a *desideratum* of those describing things in the past. Writing about the past was driven by propaganda or moral advice.

When the author comes to his exhortation, he writes, *"Therefore, brethren, since we have confidence to enter the sanctuary by the blood of Jesus, by the new and living way which he opened for us through the curtain, that is, through his flesh, and since we have a great priest over the house of God, let us draw near with a true heart in full assurance of faith"* (Heb. 10:19-22). The "living way" is the way opened by the resurrected Son who is now High Priest after the order of Melchizedek. Of course, without the full assurance of faith the "living way" into the heavenly sanctuary is not at all available. The old way, with the blood of dead animals, does not require faith; the blood that is sprinkled for sinners is available to sight, and is unable to make perfect those who enter the earthly sanctuary through it. Those of faith can "enter" behind the curtain that separates the phenomenological from the hypostatic realm to the second tent of the true sanctuary.

That the sanctuary has two tents, and a curtain between them, and that the altar of incense is in the most holy place, the second tent, makes sense only when it is understood that the author changed the arrangement of the sanctuary on account of his Stoic cosmology. In his symbolic universe the immovable things in the hypostatic realm must include the altar of incense, which was where the priests sprinkled the blood of the sacrificial animals being brought by those seeking forgiveness for their sins. On the Day of Atonement all the sins which had been deposited on the altar of incense were then carried into the most holy place and sprinkled on the mercy seat above the ark. The resurrected Son, however, serving as high priest went directly behind the curtain with his blood. He does not need a holy place receiving the blood of repeatable daily sacrifices for his ministration. The author pictures the death and the resurrection of Jesus as his passage through the curtain that separates two tents, that is, the phenomenological and the hypostatic realms. In the process he left his visible flesh behind and became an invisible being to all humans, except those who draw near to him by faith. In the heavenly sanctuary, where the Son is the High Priest there is no need for the holy place. The blood of Jesus' sacrifice outside the gates is sprinkled directly only once on the hearts of those who draw near, and it cleanses them from all consciousness of sin.

In an aside, condemning the practice of those who are teaching diverse and strange things, the author makes the point that while the meat of the regular sacrifices, whose blood is sprinkled on the altar of incense, is eaten by the priests and those who brought the sacrificial animal, the body of the animals whose blood is brought into the sanctuary by the high priest on the Day of Atonement is not eaten but burned "outside the camp." Apparently the proponents of strange teachings were "eating" from their ministry. The author uses this aside to reaffirm his argument. He writes, *"We have an altar from which those who serve the tent have no right to eat."* Then he makes his point: *"So Jesus also suffered outside the gate in order to sanctify the people through his own blood. Therefore, let us go forth to him outside the camp, bearing abuse for him. For here we have no lasting city, but we seek the city which is to come. Through him then let us continually offer up a sacrifice of praise to God"* (Heb. 13:9- 13).

The End of the Scroll

Rather than to go inside the camp, and offer sacrifices whose blood was then taken to the altar of incense in the holy place, Christians must go outside the camp, not to the Jerusalem temple, and offer praises to God for the one who died and left his flesh buried outside the gate of Jerusalem. By faith they can enter the second tent where Jesus has already entered as a pioneer and perfector of their faith (Heb. 12:2), and have their hearts sprinkled by the blood that perfects their conscience. [the RSV has "perfecter"]

THE APOCALYPTIC SETTING

The author of *To the Hebrews* is a contemporary of Paul. As already noticed, however, he has a different way of relating Christianity to Judaism. The author of *Acts of the Apostles* depicts the first disciples of Jesus to be at the temple of Jerusalem carrying on their proclamation of the significance of the life and resurrection of Jesus. This describes the Christian community as another sect of Jews who worship at the temple together with all the other Jewish sects in existence at the time. The author of *Acts* describes how it took a special revelation for Peter to be willing to open up the mission to the Gentiles (Acts 10:14-17), and how when Paul went to Jerusalem to gain recognition for his mission to the Gentiles, the leaders in Jerusalem insisted on keeping some "burdens" as necessary. Gentiles were also to *"abstain from what has been sacrificed to idols and from blood and from what is strangled and from unchastity"* (Acts 15:28-29). In other words, the author of *Acts*, writing toward the end of the first century C.E., depicts early Christianity as still attached to the temple and finding ways to preserve some markers of the Jewish way of life.

The author of *Acts* also does an apologetic job depicting Paul as one eager to go to Jerusalem to celebrate Pentecost, and offer sacrifices to purify himself together with other four men (Acts 2:16; 21:24-26). After reading Paul's own letters, it is impossible to think that he was eager to offer sacrifices at the temple and to demonstrate, against the charges made against him, that he, among the other many Jews who had believed, was also "zealous for the law," and lived "in observance of the law" (Acts 21:20-24). He repeatedly declares that Christians do not live "under the Law" (Rom. 3:19; 6:14-15; 7:4, 6; 9:31; 10:4; 1 Cor. 9:20; Gal. 3:12, 23; 4:5, 21; 5:18). Paul, obviously, understood that Christ, who had been *"born of a woman, under the Law"* had done it *"to redeem those under the Law"* (Gal. 4:4). As one *"living in Christ,"* and not *"under the Law,"* Paul understood that those who live in Christ are *"a new creation, the old has passed away, behold, the new has come"* (2 Cor. 5:17). The Law no longer has the power to condemn them (Rom. 8:1).

The author of the *Acts of the Apostles*, however, leaves no doubt that, for some time, Christians understood themselves as Jews living under the Law. The author of *To the Hebrews* finds himself arguing against those Christians who insist on living under the Law and are seeking purification from sin at the altar in the court of the temple. He does not quite agree with Paul that the old has "passed away." The Law has become obsolete and is growing old, but the sacrifices offered in accordance with it, while unable to purify the conscience, are still able to cleanse from the sins of the flesh. The whole argumentation of the author only makes sense while the altar at the temple is still functioning, before the destruction of Jerusalem in 70 C.E.

Like Paul, the author thinks that he is living *"in these last days"* (Heb. 1:1). He says that Jesus offered himself once for all *"at the end of the age"* (Heb. 9:26). He exhorts that the need to *"hold fast the confession of our hope"* and *"to stir up one another to love and good works"* is now urgent *"all the more as you see the Day drawing near"* (Heb. 10:25). Unlike later Christian authors who felt the need to account for the delay of the *Parousia*, also like Paul the author is among those who are "eagerly waiting" for the second appearance of Christ during their own lifetime (Heb. 9:28). Even though the author does not agree with Paul that now Satan is the god of this world, and that since his resurrection Christ is waging war to subject the powers of the air, like Paul he does not engage in apocalyptic descriptions of the future before the *Parousia*. He envisions Christ *"seated at the right hand of the throne of the Majesty in heaven, a minister in the sanctuary"* (Heb. 8:1-2). He does recognize that, even though the psalmist says, *"Thou hast given him dominion over the works of thy hands; thou hast put all things under his feet"* (Ps. 8:6), in fact *"we do not yet see everything in subjection to him"* (Heb. 2:8). This is the problem that apocalyptic literature is intended to explain. The author refers to the "deceitfulness of sin" (Heb. 3:13), but does not identify Satan, or a surrogate, as the deceiver, as is the case in other apocalyptic texts.

The author does have a unique description of the apocalyptic end, one in accordance with his Stoic cosmology. He does not give descriptions of a purified land where the Garden of Eden will be re-installed, or of a new heaven and a new earth where peace and justice will obtain and tears and death will be no more. Rather than to envision the future in terms of something new, he envisions the future as something that has been there in the hypostatic realm forever. He describes his vision of the Day by contrasting it to the establishment of the "Old" Covenant at Sinai. The Day of the Lord is to be an improvement to what the men of old experienced at Mount Sinai. At Sinai there was *"a blazing fire, and darkness and gloom, and a tempest, and the sound of a trumpet, and a voice whose words made the hearers entreat that no more messages be spoken.... His voice then shook the earth"* (Heb. 12:18-19, 26).

Now, the author says, we have an altar in which to *"offer up a sacrifice of praise to God."* We draw near to a high priest who *"is able for all time to save those who draw near to God through him, since he always lives to make intercession for them"* (Heb. 7:25). Therefore, we do not draw near to Mount Sinai. We *"draw near to Mount Zion and to the city of the living God."* At Mount Sinai, God's *"voice then shook the earth, but now he has promised, 'Yet once more I will shake not only the earth but also the heaven'"* (Heb. 12:26). This is what God has promised, a "better promise," one which promises something much better than rest in the land between the Jordan river and the Mediterranean Sea (Heb. 8:6). The author then elaborates on the phrase "Yet once more." It indicates that God once shook the earth at Mt. Sinai, but he is going to shake it once more, and this time with much greater consequences. This time the shaking will result in *"the removal of what has been made, in order that what cannot be shaken may remain. Therefore, let us be grateful for receiving a kingdom that cannot be shaken, and thus offer God acceptable worship, with reverence and awe"* (Heb. 12:27-28). This is what needs to be done because God is not only fire that consumes those who fall away after having *"tasted the goodness of the word of God and the gifts of the age to come"* (Heb. 12:29; 6:5, 8). He is also the judge of all (Heb. 12:23), and the one who *"rewards those who seek him"* (Heb. 11:6). The author's claim that at the judgment God requires perfection, sets up the argument that the only way to achieve it is by means of the purification of conscience carried out in the hypostatic rather than the earthly realm. Thus, the apocalyptic solution to the human condition in sin is framed within a Stoic cosmology in which what has been in place since before the existence of a phenomenological creation will become the human home of those who are eagerly waiting for the second coming of Jesus (Heb. 9:29). There they will inherit *"a kingdom that cannot be shaken."* In the whole of the New Testament this is the only description of the *Parousia* as a "second coming."

The kingdom promised to the Israelites was a kingdom in the land that was made by God at creation, in the phenomenological realm of shakable things. And those who worshiped at the temple of Jerusalem hoped for a restoration of the shakable kingdom of David. What the Day will bring is "a kingdom that cannot be shaken." It is the kingdom that remains standing when all shakable kingdoms cease to exist. In other words, what remains when the phenomenological world is shaken out of existence is the hypostatic world which was there before the creation of the heavens and the earth in which humans live during the present age. It is not to be made, or made at the resurrection of Christ. The age to come consists of what has always been, and is destined "to remain." The future is not a return of the Garden of Eden which was made at creation. It is what remains when all that which was made at creation is shaken out of existence. The hypostatic world which we hope for, however, is already accessible to those who by faith hold firm their confession and draw near to their high priest in the hypostatic true tent.

The author's exhortation is for his readers to hold firm their hope as of first importance. Faith is what gives them knowledge and certainty of what they hope for. To fall away from their hope on account of the sufferings they are enduring at the hands of relatives and neighbors, or because they are tempted by the ways of the world that cover up the deceptions of sin, is to follow the example of Esau, who *"sold his birthright for a single meal,"* They should know that when Esau later with tears pleaded for a blessing from Jacob, he was rejected (Heb. 12:16-17). In the same way, if they were to "fall away" and offer sacrifices according to the Law of Moses, or display unchastity, they would have rejected the purifying power of Jesus' blood, and Jesus will not be sacrificed for a second time (Heb. 6:4-8). The need to avail oneself of the significance of the death and resurrection of Christ is determined by the fact that the sacrificial system according to the order of Aaron has become obsolete. Thus the hope that has informed all who are *"seeking a homeland"* (Heb. 11:14), according to the author, is sustained by a faith that gives hope its content in terms of a Stoic cosmology. This results in a quite unique apocalyptic trajectory.

The Synoptic Gospels

The gospels *According to Matthew, According to Mark* and *According to Luke* have been identified as the *synoptic* gospels because, as the Greek-derived word says, they "see together" (*syn* = together, *optic* = seeing). That is, they tell the story of Jesus mostly from the same angle. Since quite often the same words appear in all three, or in two of them, it was obvious that their relationship was based at the literary level. Thus, since the late eighteenth century efforts have been made to determine which of the three functioned as the source for the other two. Today, most scholars agree that the best way to understand their relationships is to see *According to Mark* as the basic source for the other two. It provided to them not only most of the information but also the basic structure of the story. After his baptism by John, Jesus' ministry took place in Galilee. He then journeyed to Jerusalem with a significant following. After his arrival on the city, before a week was over he was crucified just outside its walls.

This conclusion left open how to explain that in twenty-three sections the same material appears in *According to Matthew* and *According to Luke*, but is not found in *According to Mark*. After extensive examination of these sections trying to establish which of the two had been the source for the other, scholars have come to the conclusion that both of these gospels had a second common source which they used independently. The material in these sections consists only of Jesus' teachings; Jesus' other activities as well as his passion are not found in them. Thus, this second source used by *According to Matthew* and *According to Luke* is usually called the

Sayings Source. Since the efforts to understand how the synoptic gospels are related were conducted in the nineteenth century by German scholars, and in German the word for source is *Quelle,* The Sayings Source is also identified as *Q.* The postulation of the hypothetical Sayings Source, or *Q,* was based on the notion that, from an early stage in the development of the oral tradition, sayings of Jesus had been collected without any details as to the circumstances in which Jesus said them. Thus, the sayings found in this source appear in different contexts in the two gospels. Since the existence of the Sayings Source was a hypothetical explanation for the presence of the same sayings of Jesus with word by word agreement in *According to Matthew* and *According to Luke,* its existence was questioned by some. The discovery in 1947 of the *Gospel of Thomas,* among the manuscripts of the Khenoboskion Library at Nag Hammadi, in Egypt, however, proved that such collections of sayings were in existence already by the middle of the first century. Quite a few of the sayings in the *Gospel of Thomas* are also found in the Sayings Source and in *According to John.*

After the material in *According to Matthew* that comes from *According to Mark* and the material that comes from the Sayings Source had been identified, one fifth of its content remained unidentified as to its provenance. This material peculiar to *According to Matthew* is considered to have come to the author of the gospel from independent oral traditions known to him or from other written sources unavailable to us. That this material is found neither in *According to Mark* nor in the Sayings Source does not in any way prejudge its value. The same is true of the material found in *According to Luke* which does not come from the two sources known to us. In this case, the material that remains unaccounted is one third of the gospel. To look at the picture from a different perspective, *According to Matthew* has 1,068 verses and *According to Luke* has 1,149. *According to Mark* has 661 verses; 80% of them are found in *According to Matthew,* and 65% in *According to Luke.*

Taking into account the evidence just described, modern students of the synoptic gospels thought that they had been put

The End of the Scroll

together by compilers, or redactors who functioned as preservers of available traditions. In more recent years it has been recognized that this way of looking at the situation does not do justice to the intelligence and the originality of those who wrote them. Their authors have to be credited for having been able theologians in their own right. The author of *According to Luke,* a well-educated Hellenist, in his preface describes how he came to write his gospel. He distinguishes three stages in the transmission of the materials that he is using to tell Theophilus *"the truth concerning the things of which you have been informed."* According to him the oral tradition began with the *"eyewitnesses,"* and was carried on by *"ministers of the word."* From the oral reports available, some undertook to write down narratives *"of the things which have been accomplished among us."* Some of these written sources were available to the author of *According to Luke,* so he, *"having followed all things closely for some time past,"* had decided *"to write an orderly account for you, most excellent Theophilus"* (Lk. 1:1-4). This tells us that in order to write the gospel which we know now as *According to Luke,* its author had spent time studying written sources which were compiled from the oral preaching at local churches in different locations. These preachers, in turn, had told what they had heard from the eyewitnesses and their audiences. This description is amply confirmed by the results of the modern study of the synoptic gospels. Among the written narratives available to the authors of *According to Matthew* and *According to Luke,* we have been able to identify two: *According to Mark* and the Sayings Source, or *Q.*

From the preface of *According to Luke,* we also learn that in writing their gospels the authors organized the material according to their own agendas. In his account to Theophilus, the author says that he will write "an orderly account for you." The criteria he used to put his narrative "in order," however, are not specified. Since he was using written sources at his disposal, but not following their "order," it would seem that even though he was indebted to *According to Mark* for the overall basic structure he chose the order of the discrete episodes according to his own best judgment as to what had been Jesus' purpose while on earth. This is also true in the case of *According to Matthew*. That explains why now the same sayings, or anecdotes told in word for word agreement, do not appear in the same chronological order or similar circumstance in the synoptic gospels.

I conclude this introduction to the synoptic gospels by pointing out two things. The first is that it is universally agreed among scholars that all four gospels were written anonymously in locations that we identify, at best, by educated guesses. This means that the oral traditions that were available in different geographical areas had developed in ways that were relevant to the needs of the local congregations of believers. A tradition that becomes frozen in the past becomes irrelevant and forgettable. Only traditions that serve to energize the way into the future are alive and memorable. In the process of serving the needs of those living under different circumstances, oral traditions take up nuances that give them relevance. This means that the gospels were written to show how the story of Jesus illumined situations faced by particular Christian communities. Thus, many of the details in the stories found in the synoptic gospels are not the same, and the sequence of the events is not uniform. These differences, as well as our inability to identify the authors and the geographical areas where the gospels were written, do not in any way challenge their authenticity. The gospels reflect for us the living faith of early Christians who, under inspiration by the Spirit, wrote to communicate their faith in what God had done through Jesus Christ and in that way give guidance to others.

Later, when the four gospels now in the canon became disconnected from their original communities and began to be published together in manuscripts that circulated more broadly, the titles they now have were given to them in order to distinguish each among them, and facilitate the identification of quotations from them. The designation of *"According to"* two disciples and two early apostles, it must be understood, was introduced in the second century quite arbitrarily. Not much later their identities were given iconic representation by recourse to the faces of the four living creatures in the opening vision of *Ezekiel*, which also appear in *Revelation*: *According to Matthew*, the man (angel); *According to Mark*, the lion; *According to Luke*, the ox, and *According to John*, the eagle (Ez. 1:10; Rev. 4:7). To understand the synoptic gospels, it cannot be overlooked that they were written anonymously on the basis of oral traditions in different Christian communities that sought to understand themselves in the light of the life of Jesus.

The second thing I wish to point out is that recognizing the active participation of bearers of tradition, or tradents, and authors in the writing of the gospels is not in any way detrimental to their authority as inspired canonical writings. In his letter *To the Romans*, Paul asks, *"Do we, then, overthrow the law by this faith?"* He immediately answers, *"By no means! On the contrary, we uphold the law"* (Rom. 3:31). His argument is that while there is no excuse for trying to obtain salvation by obeying the Law, we need the Law (Torah=The Scriptures) to understand the Gospel. Taking the cue from Paul, I would ask, "Do we overthrow the synoptic gospels by recognizing their human authors and how they wrote them? By no means! On the contrary, we establish them as indispensable for our understanding of the Gospel." For Paul, the Gospel is not attached to the activities of Jesus' historical life; therefore, he safely ignored them. That the authors of what we now called "gospels" preached the Gospel by means of the stories of Jesus does not tie the Gospel to the details of Jesus' life on earth, either. Thinking that we establish the authority of these narratives by assigning their authorship to God, and insisting on their "objective, historical" reliability, demeans their authors to secretaries taking dictation, and ignores the limitations of all historical accounts. In fact, these artificial claims only serve to establish the insecurity and the lack of faith of their proponents. That Jesus was crucified in a Roman cross outside Jerusalem is something which historical reconstructions can deal with and come to positive conclusions. A historical account of the event, however, only establishes that he died because he was judged to be a seditious agitator. It does not establish the cosmic meaning of his death which faith proclaims. Righteousness by faith does not only inform our actions; it also informs our thinking and, as Paul insisted, salvation is by faith, not by accurate "historical" information.

    I conclude my introductory remarks making two clarifications. I am not concerned with Jesus as the person who walked the dusty roads of Galilee, Caesarea Philippi, the Decapolis, etc. and ended up crucified outside the walls of Jerusalem. I am concerned with the theology of each of the synoptic gospels. Deciding which of the different accounts of the same events in these gospels is the one most likely to describe what actually happened is not in my agenda. This is not a study of the "historical Jesus." It is a study of each of the synoptic gospels as theological reflections on the significance of the life, death and resurrection of Jesus for the understanding of how God is dealing with the world. It cannot be overlooked that these gospels were written between forty and seventy years after Jesus lived and died on this earth. Finally, I will point out that, for convenience sake, I will no longer make a distinction between the canonical title assigned to each of the canonical gospels and their authors. I will be referring to each gospel and its author by the traditional name given to its anonymous author without distinction.

THE GOSPEL OF MARK

Like the other gospels, the gospel of Mark was written using sources, but we have no way of tracing his sources. His sources may not have come from the same location and, therefore, may not have had the same line of tradition. This, however, does not place obstacles to the reading of the gospel. Mark gives us a most illuminating window to theological developments in the early Christian landscape. It is generally agreed that by the time Mark wrote he had at his disposal a collection of parables and accounts of healings and exorcisms. He also had an already existing short account of the Last Supper and a more detailed account of the trial and the crucifixion. It is also agreed that Mark was the one who decided the order in which to place the units of the oral traditions available to him.

As already stated, the oral traditions did not include references to time and place. This means that Mark also designed the general structure of his narrative. He concentrated Jesus' ministry in Galilee, with excursions into Gentile territories across the lake of Gennesaret, and north to Tyre, Sidon and Caesarea Philippi. Then he describes the journey to Jerusalem as an occasion to instruct his followers on the nature of discipleship by reference to the nature of his vocation, and culminates the story by connecting it to the temple in Jerusalem. In the description of the ministry in Galilee, Mark makes editorial summaries of Jesus' activity. It is in these summaries and in the details of the stories received from the tradition that one gets closer to Mark's theological vision.

Another aid to our understanding of his narrative is his way of making "sandwiches" with the stories. This literary device consists of starting a story, interrupting it with another story, and then finishing the story which had been interrupted. In the case of the journey to Jerusalem, in which he carries on a debate between two understandings of his vocation and points out the costs of discipleship, it begins with the story of the healing of a blind man at Bethsaida (Mk. 8:22-26) and concludes with the healing of a blind man at Jericho (Mk. 10:46-52). In this way it makes clear that the journey is to be read as the attempt to open the eyes of those who have a blurred understanding of Jesus' vocation and of discipleship. Similarly, the story of the beheading of John the Baptist (Mk. 6:14-29) is sandwiched by the sending out and the return of the disciples on their mission (Mk. 6:7-13, 30-31). The disciples of John, who buried him, are contrasted with the disciples of Jesus who continued his work of healings and exorcisms and failed to bury him. In general, it may be said that by means of this device Mark is giving the clue with which to interpret the larger story. Thus, for example, he recounts that going from Bethany to the temple Jesus was hungry and looked for figs on a fig tree near the road; finding none he cursed it. Then at the temple he expelled the money changers and the merchants. Coming back to the temple the next day, when he passed by the fig tree with his disciples, it was completely dried up, dead. The fig tree, of course, was a well known icon of Israel (Mk. 11:12-20), also found in *According to John*'s story of Nathanael (Jn. 1:47-48). By sandwiching the cleansing of the temple with the cursing of the fig tree Mark reveals that while, on account of his disruption of the commercial activities going on at the temple, the chief priests and the scribes decided "to destroy" him, Jesus had already accomplished the dismantling of Israel's universe on account of its barrenness.

At the very end of the nineteenth century, Wilhelm Wrede demonstrated that Mark had purposely brought into the narrative the notion that Jesus did not wish to be identified by others in public, least of all by demons about to be exorcised (Mk. 1:34, 43-44; 5:43; 7:36; 9:9), and that he used parables in order to be non-specific and enigmatic with the crowds (Mk. 4:11-12). On the other hand, with some consistency, he gave detailed explanations of what he had said or done publicly in private to his disciples (Mk. 7:33; 8:32; 13:3). Since Wrede, it has been understood that Mark's narrative is not concerned with historical accuracy but with a theological agenda. In my reading of Mark, therefore, I will try to decipher his agenda in reference to his apocalyptic theology.

MARK AS HEIR OF PAUL'S LEGACY

The study of Mark has demonstrated that in significant ways it is closely related to the apocalyptic theology of Paul. Chronologically and theologically, it is close to the letters of Paul. Chronologically, Paul wrote his letters between 49 and 62 C.E., and Mark was written around 70 C.E. As I have argued, *To the Hebrews* was written earlier than Mark. More significant, however, is Mark's theological closeness to Paul's letters. To start with, Mark is totally committed to the Gentile mission, and the non-requirement of obedience to the Mosaic laws for the believers in God's new access to life on account of Jesus' mission. Concerning the opening to the Gentiles, Mark recounts that in Tyre Jesus found more faith than in *"his own country"* (Mk. 6:1, 4-6). Tongue in cheek, Mark has Jesus reflect Jewish prejudices declaring that the food prepared for the children should not be given to the dogs. The Syrophenician woman then points out that dogs are happy to eat the crumbs that fall from the table where children eat. To this, Jesus now gives the punch line, *"For this saying you may go your way; the demon has left your daughter"* (Mk. 7:29). In this telling of the story, what is remarkable is the eagerness and the trust of the woman who actually received what she had come for. While in the country of the Gerasenes, unlike his common injunction to those who had been healed by him to tell nobody who had healed them or exorcised a demon from them, Jesus commands the man from whom he had exorcised a Legion of demons to tell everyone how he had been healed by him (Mk. 5:19-20). After healing a deaf/dumb in the Decapolis, he *"charged them to tell no one; but the more he charged them, the more zealous-*

ly they proclaimed it" (Mk. 7:36). A more open endorsement of the Gentile mission could not have been given, especially when it contrasts so starkly with the commands not to tell in Galilee and Judea (Mk. 1:25, 34, 44; 5:43; 8:26, 29; 9:9). It is noteworthy that while cleansing the temple, according to Mark, Jesus said *"My house shall be called a house of prayer for all the nations"* (Mk. 11:17). Both Matthew and Luke omit, for reasons of their own, "for all the nations." For Mark, like for Paul, the promise to Abraham included its benefits *"to all the families of the earth"* (Gen. 12:3).

In reference to matters of the Law, Mark specifically explains that Jesus declared *"all foods clean"* (Mk. 7:19), and that what defiles a person is not what they consume, which goes into their belly, but what they express, which comes out of their heart (Mk. 7:15-23). In reference to the Sabbath, Mark tells the contrived story of Jesus walking through a wheat field while his disciples were plucking, shelling and eating the grain. The Pharisees (who were following them through the field!) challenged Jesus for the conduct of his disciples. Their charge is not that they were all destroying somebody's precious crop, but that the disciples were doing the threshing of corn on the Sabbath. To this, Jesus answered that men and women were not created to keep the Sabbath, but the Sabbath was a gift for the benefit of humanity. He was, undoubtedly, thereby re-interpreting the function of the Sabbath. In the Law, a man who gathered wood on a Sabbath was put to death, thus demonstrating that the Sabbath is more important than a man's life. Jesus, to the contrary, declares that a person's need to eat is more important than the Sabbath. He then draws the ultimate conclusion: He can revise the commandment because He is Lord of the Sabbath (Mk. 2:23-28).

Another re-definition of a commandment in the Law is his abolition of the law of divorce. Since at the beginning God made them so that the male and the female *"are no longer two but one. What therefore God had joined together let no man* [Moses by his law of divorce] *put asunder"* (Mk. 10:4-9). Concerning divorce, Paul basically agrees, but gives an exemption: a Christian may consent to a divorce when an unbelieving spouse seeks it (1 Cor. 7:25).

The rationale given by Paul is that *"God has called us to peace."* I would think that the rationale for Mark's abolition of divorce is, like Paul's preference for being single, based on the understanding that *"the form of this world is passing away,"* and *"the appointed time has grown very short"* (1 Cor. 7:31, 29). That is, an apocalyptic horizon informs the account. In his endorsement of the Gentile mission (Mk. 13:10), and the relativizing of food and Sabbath laws (Rom. 10:4; 14:1-7), Mark is in line with Paul.

Also in close affinity with Paul is Mark's understanding that Christ has come to establish something which, even if related to traditional Jewish religion, is in its essence something new. Mark makes the point most explicitly by relating a challenge to Jesus for allowing his disciples not to fast, particularly since it is contrary of the behavior of the disciples of John the Baptist and of the Pharisees, who are the closest to his disciples since they share an apocalyptic symbolic universe (Mk. 2:18). According to Jesus, the future may bring a time for fasting. That time will be a *"tribulation as has not been from the beginning of the creation which God created until now, and never will be"* (Mk. 13:19). At the present, on the other hand, it is time for feasting as at a wedding. He had not come to patch an old piece of clothing. What he is bringing is "new wine," and new wine cannot be stored in old wine skins. *"New wine is for fresh skins."* If it were to be poured into old wine skins *"the wine will burst the skins, and the wine is lost, and so are the skins"* (Mk. 2:22). Paul understood Christianity as a new creation with new possibilities energized by the Spirit. Mark says the same thing with the metaphor of the new wine that is energized also from within by the Spirit and, therefore, cannot be contained by old cultic formulas.

A similar perspective informs the Pharisees' complaint that his disciples eat without first washing their hands. In an aside, the narrator informs his readers that all Jews wash their hands and follow closely all the traditions of the elders. Jesus answers this challenge by charging the Pharisees with being more concerned to obey their own traditions than with obeying God, even while pretending to be doing so: *"Well did Isaiah prophesy of you, hypocrites ... You leave the commandment of God, and hold fast the tradition of men"* (Mk. 7:1-8). He then charges them to have found the way to circumvent the commandment to honor father and mother.

Somewhat of a surprise is Mark's account of the conversation between Jesus and a scribe. Unlike the ones in the other two synoptics (Mt. 22:35; Lk. 10:25), here the scribe admires Jesus wisdom and comes forward not to test Jesus but with genuine interest. Mark couches the story as a Platonic dialogue in which, by means of questions and answers, a new level of understanding is reached. The scribe asks Jesus, *'Which commandment is the first of all?' "Jesus answered, 'The first is "Hear, O Israel: The Lord your God, the Lord is one; and you shall love the Lord your God with all your heart, and with all your soul, and with all your mind, and with all your strength." The second is this, "You shall love your neighbor as yourself." There is no other commandment greater than these."'* The scribe then restates Jesus' answer, gives his complete approval and draws the resulting logical conclusion: *"You are right, Teacher; to do what you just said is much more than all whole burnt offerings and sacrifices."* Now the narrator evaluates the scribe's answer, *"When Jesus saw that he answered wisely, he said to him, 'You are not far from the kingdom of God'"* (Mk. 12:28-34). In this case, as in Paul, love is the ultimate response to God and to one's neighbors. Also like Paul, Mark clearly shows his high esteem of the human intellect. Mark adds that love for God must also be "with all your mind," which the text being quoted (Dt. 6:5), does not contain, and describes the scribe's answer as "wise." His question is appropriate, and his answer is wise. He has identified God's will correctly by dismissing the function of the temple as already irrelevant, before its destruction by the Romans. Markan irony is in full view here.

Another connection between Paul and Mark is found in Mark's understanding that Jesus is not about comforting the righteous, but about calling sinners, and that what is demanded of sinners is faith. Mark's emphasis on faith as the *sine qua non* for a healthy life is in evidence throughout the text. Like Paul, he proclaims

"*Have faith in God*" (Mk. 11:22). I have already pointed out the contrast between the lack of faith in "his own country" (Mk. 6:6), and the amazing faith of the Syrophenician woman (Mk. 7:29). The paralytic brought to Jesus through a hole in the roof of a house was healed because of the faith of his porters (Mk. 2:5). To the disciples who fear drowning in the sea, Jesus' rebuke was the true to fact question, *"Have you no faith?"* (Mk. 4:40). The woman who had been losing blood for thirty eight years, was comforted by Jesus saying, "*Your faith has made you well*" (Mk. 5:34). When still far from his house Jairus received word that his daughter had died, and there was no longer need for Jesus to come to the house, Jesus said, *"Only believe"* (Mk. 5:36). To blind Bartimaeus, Jesus said, *"Go your way; your faith has made you well"* (Mk. 10:52). The most telling example is the cry of the father of the one who had been demon-possessed since childhood. The father had said to Jesus, *"If you can do anything, have pity on us and help us."* To this, Jesus reacted sharply, *"If you can! All things are possible to him who believes,"* and, of course, Jesus has faith in God; therefore, for him all things are possible. Now the father expresses what Mark seems to consider the sentiment every believer should express when praying: *"I believe; help my lack of faith!"* (Mk. 9:22-24, my translation). When afterward, privately, the disciples ask Jesus why they had not been able to cast out the demon, Jesus answers by explaining that in such cases what is necessary is prayer, the optimal expression of faith. In prayer conviction of its effectiveness is essential. As Paul explains it, faith involves full conviction (Rom. 14:5). Mark agrees, *"I tell you, whatever you ask in prayer, believe that you receive it, and you will"* (Mk. 11:24). This is why throughout the gospel Jesus seeks for solitude to pray, prays at Gethsemane and, more importantly, prays at the cross quoting Psalm 22.

In this connection it is well to notice that Mark does not consider doubt to be the opposite of faith, even when it may be mixed with faith. Faith makes all things possible. As Jesus said, it is not just very hard but actually impossible for humans by themselves to enter the kingdom of God. Hearing this, the disciples were *"exceedingly astonished, and said to him, 'Then who can be saved?' Jesus looked at them and said, 'With men it is impossible, but not with God; for all things are possible with God'"* (Mk. 10:26-27). What prevents God from accomplishing the possible is that in the fallen world humans live in fear of the world rather than faith in God. In Mark, fear is what prevents faith from blossoming (Mk. 4:40; 5:15, 36; 6:50; 9:6, 32; 10:32; 11:18, 32; 12:12; 16:8). At the temple which had been converted into a den of robbers by the priests, Jesus reminds them that God intended it to be a *"house of prayer for all the nations,"* assigning to it a universal function. When the priests and the scribes heard what he said, they *"sought a way to destroy him; for they feared him"* (Mk. 11:17-18). Here the house of prayer, the ultimate expression of faith, is contrasted with the lack of faith, the fear, of the chief priests and the scribes, the standard foils in the Markan narrative.

Defining Jesus' Mission

As already noticed, Mark, like Paul, does give value to the intellectual aspect of life (Mk. 12:30), and connects faith to understanding. The disciples frequently fail to understand what Jesus tells them or does because of their lack of faith. After Jesus had fed in Jewish territory a multitude of five thousand men plus women and children with five loaves of bread and two fishes, and the disciples had collected twelve baskets of left-overs (Mk. 6:35-44), and after he had fed in Gentile territory four thousand men plus women and children with seven loaves of bread, and the disciples had collected seven baskets of left-overs (Mk. 8:1-9), Jesus and the disciples find themselves crossing the Sea of Galilee to Dalmanutha, and the disciples are anxious because they have only one loaf of bread on board. They lament, *"We have no bread."* Knowing their preoccupation, Jesus asks them, *"Why do you discuss the fact that you have no bread? Do you not yet perceive or understand? Are your hearts hardened? Having eyes do you not see, and having ears do you not hear? And do you not remember?"* (Mk. 8:14-18). Then Jesus reminds them of the two feedings, and asks again, *"Do you not yet understand?"* Having a hardened heart and not remembering is another way of saying that they lack faith (Mk. 3:5; 6:52). To remember is to have internalized a past event and be energized by it; it is to understand theologically. To fully understand who Jesus is and what he is about, faith is of the essence. The feedings should have made them understand that bread can be produced in the desert. The impossible is possible. That does not mean, however, that he is the Messiah who will be able to feed an army and restore the fortunes of Israel. That is not his mission.

From there Jesus went to Bethsaida and gave sight to a blind man who after the first touch saw men, but they looked like trees walking. After a second touch he saw the men clearly (Mk. 8:24-25). He then went the farthest North into Gentile territory, to Caesarea Philippi, where he asks his disciples, *"Who do men say that I am?"* After responding that he is being identified as John the Baptist, Elijah or one of the prophets *redivivus*, Jesus asks them to identify him. Peter answers, *"You are the Christ"* (Mk. 8:27-29). Again, Jesus imposes silence on all of them about Peter's identification. Peter's confession brings about the necessity to give a true understanding of the significance of the feeding of the Jewish and the Gentile multitudes since *"they did not understand about the loaves, but their hearts were hardened"* (Mk. 6:52). Seeing the feedings as announcements of the coming Kingdom of God, and identifying Jesus as the Christ, was equivalent to the blind man of Bethsaida who saw objects that looked like trees walking. To see in Jesus the Christ, that is to say the Messiah is, according to Mark, to misunderstand, or not to understand at all. Messiah, or Son of David, are identifications that Mark explicitly rejects. At the temple, Jesus challenged his audience asking, *"How can the scribes say that the Christ is the son of David?"* He then quotes a Psalm in which *"David himself, inspired by the Holy Spirit, declared, 'The Lord said to my Lord, sit at my right hand,' … David himself calls him Lord; so how is he his son?"* (Mk. 12:35-37). Whether Jesus himself understood himself as Messiah is beyond our ability to determine. What is clear is that neither Paul nor Mark saw him as Messiah. Mark, however, brings out quite explicitly that both his disciples and the crowds identified him as the Messiah who would restore the fortunes of Israel. The Messianic aura surrounding the ministry of Jesus certainly was also seen by blind Bartimaeus (Mk. 10:45), by Pilate, who insists on identifying Jesus as "King of the Jews," apparently sarcastically (Mk. 15:2, 9, 12, 17-19, 26), and also sarcastically by the chief priests who called him the "King of Israel" (Mk. 15:32). Messiah, Son of David and King of the Jews, or of Israel, are synonyms. For Mark to see Jesus in these terms is to have a very blurred picture of Jesus, one that gives room to misunderstandings. To really see Jesus one must have better focus. It requires a second touch by Jesus.

The one story which would seem to make this interpretation of Mark unfounded is the account of the triumphal entry into Jerusalem. As Mark tells it, *"many spread the garments on the road, and others spread leafy branches which they had cut from the fields. And those who went before and those who followed cried out, Hosanna! Blessed is he who comes in the name of the Lord! Blessed is the kingdom of our father David that is coming! Hosanna in the highest!"* (Mk. 11:8-10). There is no question that as far as the crowd that entered Jerusalem with him, they were excited because the kingdom of their father David was coming. Does that mean that Jesus, contrary to what he had just said to his disciples, is coming as a ruler who is to exercise authority over the people (Mk. 10:42)? Is Mark agreeing that Jesus entered Jerusalem as the Messiah, the Son of David? This way of looking at the triumphal entry overlooks the way in which Mark introduces the story by demonstrating Jesus' knowledge of the minds of those around him. *"As he was approaching Jerusalem, he sent two unidentified disciples to fetch an untamed colt at the next village. He told them that, when the people expressed their disapproval of what they were doing, they should tell them that "the Lord has need of it and will send it back here immediately."* When the villagers heard that the Lord had need of it and that it would be brought

The End of the Scroll

back soon, *"they let them go."* When they brought the colt to Jesus, the two disciples placed their garments on it, and *"Jesus sat upon it"* (Mk. 11:1-7). It seems incredible that the future king of Israel would want to enter Jerusalem sitting on an untamed colt. The future king of Israel would want a well-trained horse accustomed to step brightly around people. The choice of an unusual, dangerous mount sets the arrival at Jerusalem in its proper context, setting Jesus apart from the excited crowd. The way the actual arrival is described confirms this interpretation: Jesus *"entered Jerusalem, and went into the temple; and when he had looked around at everything, as it was already late, he went out to Bethany"* (Mk. 11:11). Nothing happened that day. The people's excitement did not achieve a climax. The excitement faded into nothing; the people's expectations were a false alarm.

For Mark Jesus is the "Son of God," as he plainly states it in his preface (Mk. 1:1). Paul understood that Son of God was what Jesus became by the power of the Spirit at his resurrection from the dead (Rom. 1:4). Mark understood that Jesus became the adopted Son of God at his baptism, when the Spirit empowered him for his mission descending upon him as a dove. Anyone who has observed doves landing on the ground knows what Mark is describing, not the shape of the Spirit, but the manner of its descent. By means of their birth narratives, the other two synoptic gospels pushed back Jesus' being the Son of God to his conception, but Mark has no interest in Jesus before his baptism. He conceived Jesus to have been nothing more than a man fully empowered by the Spirit at his baptism to fulfill his vocation. Jesus is again identified as Son of God before a reduced circle of three disciples at the Mount of Transfiguration (Mk. 9:7), and is specifically declared to be such at the ultimate confession of Jesus' identity, placed by Mark on the lips of the Gentile Roman centurion at the foot of the cross: *"Truly this man was the Son of God"* (Mk. 15:39). It was not an unintended oversight on the part of Matthew to omit the word "man" when he copied the centurion's confession (Mt. 27:54).

According to Mark, separate from his identity as Son of God, Jesus' vocation is to be the Son of man. Son of God defines his empowerment, his dependence and his obedience. Son of man defines his vocation, his task. On the road to Jerusalem, three times Jesus defined his vocation, *"the Son of man must suffer many things, and be rejected by the elders and the chief priests and the scribes, and be killed, and after three days rise again. And he said this plainly"* only to his disciples (Mark. 8:31). Going incognito through Galilee, he taught his disciples, *"'The Son of man will be delivered into the hands of men, and they will kill him; and when he is killed, after three days he will rise. But they did not understand the saying, and they were afraid to ask him"* (Mk. 9:31-32). Finally, Mark describes Jesus' ministry in a pungent narrative: *"And they were on the road, going up to Jerusalem, and Jesus was walking ahead of them; and they were amazed, and those who followed were afraid. And taking the twelve again, he began to tell them what was to happen to him, saying, 'Behold we are going up to Jerusalem; and the Son of man will be delivered to the chief priests and the scribes and they will condemn him to death, and deliver him to the Gentiles; and they will mock him, and spit upon him, and scourge him, and kill him; and after three days he will rise'"* (Mk. 10:32-34). The journey to Jerusalem concludes with the saying that encapsulates the theology of Mark, *"For the Son of man also came not to be served but to serve, and to give his life as a ransom for many"* (Mk, 10:45). Jesus vocation, which is also the will of God, is for him to suffer and die in service to humanity. On account of this, among his disciples there will not be kings, rulers or princes, only servants (Mk. 10:42-44). In this way, Mark redefines the apocalyptic Son of man who will eventually come in the clouds, as in *Daniel*, by saying that he must suffer as a servant of humanity before God delivers to him the kingdom now in the hands of evil powers. In Mark's telling, during Jesus' ministry the disciples could not understand this on account of their fear, their lack of faith.

To be noticed is that Jesus defined himself as the Son of man as a correction on Peter's identification of him as the Messiah (Christ) (Mk. 8:29). The Messiah was the Son of David, the king who would destroy the enemies of Israel and restore the fortunes of Israel so that no nation would question from then on the power and the justice of the God of Israel. Mark rejects this job description and states that the job requires suffering and death before a glorious future could be achieved. It is not clear how Mark came to this understanding of Jesus' vocation. Usually it is thought that Mark has redefined Messiah by imposing on it the characteristics of the Suffering Servant of Isaiah (Is. 42:1-4; 49:1-6; 52:13-53:12). Thus, this understanding is commonly described as that of a Suffering Messiah. I am inclined to think that in this Mark is more likely taking his cue from Paul, than from Isaiah. Paul, as I have argued in the previous chapter, referred to Jesus Christ, but never used the word Christ in reference to the earthly Jesus, only in reference to the Risen Lord, the concrete object of faith. Paul has very little to say about the earthly Jesus. For him, Christ is Jesus' last name after his resurrection. As the Jew born of a woman under the Law, Jesus was to suffer and die. That was his vocation. Suffering, for Paul, was part and parcel of Jesus' mission, and part and parcel of the lives of those who have faith in what God did in his death and resurrection. Paul refers to Jesus Christ, the Lord, as the Son of God, and also to Christians as adopted sons of God, but he never uses the expression Son of man. Mark is the one who took Paul's understanding that Jesus Christ had to suffer and assigned to it the Danielic title of Son of man. While on earth, before he comes on the clouds, the Son of man was to suffer, die and be raised. This was Paul's understanding of the trajectory of the Son who was born of a woman under the Law (Gal. 4:4).

According to Mark, Jesus was empowered by the Spirit as the Son of God; he fulfilled his vocation, to die as a servant of humanity and be raised, as the Son of man. To understand him in any other way is not to understand him. Throughout their lives with him, his disciples failed to understand, particularly what *"the rising from the dead meant"* (Mk. 9:10). Faith is tested by the resurrection, which is the crucial ending to his vocation as the Son of man. It is the critical apocalyptic event that dispels all misunderstandings as to who

Jesus actually was. Repeatedly, as already noticed, Jesus imposed silence on anyone who knew who he was, but this demand had a time limit. A major scene in the story is the ascent to the mountain with Peter, John and James, at which time Jesus *"was transfigured before them, and his garments became glistening, intensely white, as no fuller on earth could bleach them,"* and *"a voice came out of the cloud, 'This is my beloved Son; listen to him.'"* This was a proleptic revelation of the risen Lord, but the three disciples who witnessed it saw it as confirmation that the time for the establishing of the kingdom had arrived. The presence of Elijah and Moses should have been a clear clue. Their expectations, no doubt, were misinformed. Mark makes it plain to the reader saying that, *"As they were coming down the mountain, he charged them to tell no one what they had seen, until the Son of man should have risen from the dead"* (Mk. 9:2-9). The resurrection of the Son of man, the one who *must* suffer, be rejected, be mocked and die puts an end to all misconceptions of Jesus as the Messiah, Son of David, King of the Jews who restores the fortunes of Israel. For Mark, there are two predetermined event in history. The first is the death of the Son of man rejected, despised, on a cross. The second is the hour of his coming as Son of man in the clouds with power and glory, which hour is fixed but known only by God, and none other (Mk. 13:32).

The narrative has pointed out that all things are possible to him who believes, and, of course, that all things are possible for God. Mark describes the events at Gethsemane saying that after having asked nine disciples *"Sit here while I pray,"* and having taken Peter, John and James a bit further and told them *"My soul is very sorrowful, even to death; remain here, and watch,"* Jesus then went a little further still and falling to the ground he prayed that, if it were possible, "the hour" might pass from him. Mark then quotes Jesus' prayer to the effect that he wished that God's will, rather than his, be done (Mk. 14:32-36). This places the whole ministry of Jesus as the Son of God in its true context. It was, no doubt, absolutely quite possible for God to have the hour pass from him. To be understood is that the expression "the hour" is the standard way of identifying the event that establishes the *raison d' etre* of a person's life. In John the expression is used throughout the gospel as a technical word that signals Jesus' glorification on the cross. Was it possible for God to find a different purpose for Jesus' life? Of course. But it was not God's will, and that is the only thing that counts, especially in an apocalyptic text where history is predetermined. God's will is that the Son of man suffer, die and be raised. This is what the disciples do not understand because of their fixation on a royal Messiah, and some of the Jews think that a resurrection is impossible. Mark takes up their lack of faith straight on.

MARK'S APOCALYPTIC MATRIX

Mark refers to the Sadducees only once, and it has to do with their contention that there is no resurrection. They came to Jesus with a trick question. According to the Law, a woman left a widow without a child must become the wife of her dead husband's nearest of kin. The Sadducees questioned Jesus with the hypothetical case of a widow who had been married to seven brothers who in turn died leaving her still without a child. The question was, *"In the resurrection whose wife will she be? For the seven had her as a wife."* Jesus' answer confirmed *Daniel*'s view that at the resurrection humans will be sexless angels. What is more important, however, is Jesus' counter-attack. *"Is not this why you are wrong, that you know neither the scriptures nor the power of God?"* (Mk. 12:18-25). This says that Mark considered that *Daniel* belonged in the scriptures (something which the Rabbis had not yet decided), and that what needs to be taken into account is not what is humanly possible, but what is possible for God. That necessitates an understanding of God's power, and that is what apocalyptic theology is all about. God has the power to do justice. Apocalyptic faith is based on the power of God to give life to the dead and thereby establish the rule of justice.

The apocalyptic matrix of Mark is not confined to his interest in the resurrection, and the discourse detailing the destruction of

Jerusalem. It characterizes the whole gospel. Casting the story in terms of the need to keep secret who Jesus really is until after his resurrection is the most obvious literary device of an apocalyptic text. Another clear indication is the prevalence of exorcisms. It seems that everywhere there were individuals possessed by demons. In the Markan summaries (Mk. 1:29-34, 39; 3:11-13; 6:13) and in the sending out of the disciples in their mission (Mk. 6:7, 13) exorcisms are prominent. That the divine and the human world were intertwined was a generally understood feature of the Hellenistic culture in which apocalyptic literature became popular. In his excellent critique of that culture, Petronius, the "arbiter of elegance" in Nero's court, described a world in which it was easier to meet a god than to meet a man walking down the street. Supernatural beings were everywhere (*Satyricon,* xvii). While Petronius sees divine incarnations everywhere in his polytheistic universe, Mark sees demons everywhere in his apocalyptic one. The multiple exorcisms reveal the human condition subjected to the dominion of demons.

As is well known, and as the instruction to sin no more given to those who had been healed explicitly points out, at the time every sickness was understood to be a punishment for sin. The punishment, however, was being inflicted directly by God, as the book of *Job* makes abundantly clear. As the Son of God, empowered to carry on God's will, Jesus as the Son of man has authority both to heal from sickness and to forgive the sins that caused it (Mk. 2:3-12). Exorcisms are not healings; they are something else altogether. They are manifestations of the power of evil over the lives of human beings. Exorcisms are staged enactments of an apocalyptic battle, a supernatural confrontation between good and evil. In the accounts of them, the demons assume to be in control and always take the initiative by identifying Jesus as "Son of God," and sarcastically asking, *"Have you come to destroy us?"* (Mk. 1:24). The answer, of course, is "Yes, that's what I am all about." Exorcisms are miniature versions of the apocalyptic universe.

The same horizon informs the stories of Jesus walking on the sea, or sleeping in a boat that is in danger of being swallowed by

The End of the Scroll

the sea. The body of water featured in this narrative is known as the Lake of Gennesaret. Mark is the one who, on account of his apocalyptic agenda, names it "the Sea of Galilee," to use it as the mythological symbol of the abyss from which comes all evil. In his narrative, Jesus crosses the sea several times demonstrating his power over the source of evil. With his characteristic irony, while in the middle of a storm in the sea, Mark has the disciples in desperation ask, *"Teacher, do you not care if we perish?"* (Mk. 4:38). The powers of evil bring about destruction and death, but the Son of God has been empowered to conquer evil. Thus, after Jesus had calmed the sea the disciples who still do not understand and have no faith, are amazed and say to one another, *"Who is this, that even the wind and the sea obey him?"* (Mk. 4:41). Jesus' action could only be understood by those who recognize that as the Son of God Jesus had been empowered by the Spirit with greater power than that of the forces of the underworld. In the account of his coming to the disciples walking on the sea in the middle of a storm, when he got into the boat with them *"the wind ceased"* (Mk. 6:51). The presence of the Son of God brings calm to those traveling in the realm of death. Power over a stormy sea and its strong winds, like power over the demons at exorcisms, were demonstrations that he did not come to fix an earthly political situation but to rescue the elect from, and put an end to, a creation fallen under the powers of sin and death.

The apocalyptic perspective of Mark is also in evidence in the way it elaborates on the saying about the significance of a lamp, which the other two synoptic gospels interpret differently (Mt. 5:15; Lk. 8:16). Mark has Jesus ask, *"Is a lamp brought in to be put under a bushel or under a bed, and not on a stand? For there is nothing hid, except to be made manifest; nor is anything secret, except to come to light. If any man has ears to hear, let him hear"* (Mk. 4:21-23). Mark considers his gospel to be the lamp that makes manifest what has been until then a secret to many. His purpose is to make possible to those who have ears to actually hear, something which even the disciples before the resurrection did not accomplish. In other words, his gospel is a revelation. His gospel is uncovering the real task Jesus performed while on earth, especially since he had insisted on keeping things hidden. The injunction to use one's ears is a typical apocalyptic call to pay attention when God's power and justice is being demonstrated.

Readers of Mark are taken aback learning that teaching in parables was Jesus' way of keeping the crowds uninformed. According to Mark, Jesus said to the disciples, *"To you has been given the secret of the kingdom of God, but for those outside everything is in parables; so that they may indeed see but not perceive, and may indeed hear but not understand"* (Mk. 4:11-12). At the end of the telling of the parables, the narrator says, *"he did not speak to them [the crowds] without a parable, but privately to his own disciples he explained everything"* (Mk. 4:34). Repeatedly, the gospel points out that the disciples also failed to understand Jesus' vocation before the resurrection. The parable of the sower, the parable of the earth that "produces of itself" and the parable of the mustard seed that "becomes the greatest of all shrubs" have to do with descriptions of the situation of Mark's community at later times (Mk. 4:3-30). The parable of the man who planted a vineyard and left for another country, told separately when Jesus had arrived to Jerusalem, is an announcement that the original keepers of the vineyard are to be *"destroyed"* and *"the vineyard will be given to others"* (Mk. 12:1-11). In other words, a confirmation that the Gentiles have become the heirs of the vineyard. These four are the only formal parables in Mark. It is remarkable that while Mark repeatedly says that Jesus taught the people and the people responded to the authority of his teaching (Mk. 1:21; 2:13:4:1; 6:2, 6, 34; 10:1; 14:49), he does not provide much of the teachings of Jesus. It is characteristic of apocalyptic texts to note that the secret being revealed does not reveal everything, and is only available to the few elect ones.

What has been described as the apocalyptic discourse of Jesus also places this gospel in its historical setting. It ties together the destruction of the temple and the coming of the *Danielic* Son of man in the clouds. Mark's Son of man, however, is not *Daniel's*.

His Son of man will come in power and glory with his angels soon. But he is not the representative of the holy ones [angels] of the Most High, or of the people of the holy ones of the Most High, who appears at the judgment where the Ancient of Day has opened the books (Dan. 7:10, 13, 18, 22). He is the one who *must* suffer, die and rise before he comes in the clouds with angels to establish God's kingdom (Mk. 8:38; 13:27).

The set up for the discourse takes place as Jesus and his disciples are leaving the temple and one of the disciples calls attention to *"the wonderful stones and the wonderful buildings."* To this, Jesus comments, *"Do you see these great buildings? There will not be left here one stone upon another, that will not be thrown down"* (Mk. 13:1-2). This "prediction" was said in public, but its significance was explained in private to four disciples on the Mount of Olives, following the Markan device of keeping things secret until the resurrection. The elaboration of the public prediction of the destruction of the temple given privately to only four disciples is another example of the apocalyptic device of *vaticinia ex eventu*. On account of it, it is possible to date the writing of Mark at the time when the Roman troops have already put siege to Jerusalem and the fall of the temple is imminent or has recently taken place. The Romans, led by Vespasian, came to put down the Jewish rebellion in 68 C.E. Their activities in Judea were interrupted by the death of emperor Nero. Vespasian left for Rome to secure his position of power. In the meantime "rumors of war" circulated freely. Two years went by between the initial landing of Roman troops and the eventual destruction of Jerusalem and its temple in 70 C.E. by Titus, Vespasian's son who had come to Judea with his father. The "predictions" of coming impersonators, wars and rumors of wars, the questioning of the allegiance of Christians to the Jewish state before councils and the beatings at synagogues while the gospel is preached to all nations and family units are being disrupted, all these "signs" fit the great disruptions of daily life during those fateful years. Accordingly, it is said that these things are not yet the end, they are *"the beginning of sufferings,"* and they need to be *"endured,"* the typical apocalyptic advice (Mk. 13:5-12).

A new situation is introduced with the apocalyptic warning *"let the reader understand."* It is a reference to the *"desolating sacrilege."* In other words, the Roman troops have desecrated the temple. At this juncture Christians are advised to flee from Judea and to pray that they will not have to do it in winter, which the Christians who were in Jerusalem at the time had wisely done, escaping to Pella in the Decapolis, and everyone knows that their flight took place in the summer of 70 C.E. Those days were a time of *"tribulation as has not been from the beginning of the creation which God created until now, and never will be."* Then Mark gives the clue as to the time of writing. *"If the Lord had not shortened the days, no human being would be saved; but for the sake of the elect, whom he chose, he shortened the days ... Take heed; I have told you all things beforehand"* (Mk.13:14-23). Noticeably, the verbs which up to that point had been in the future tense now have been shifted to the past tense.

Mark describes what will happen in the actual future in typical apocalyptic terms: the final death throes of the power of evil will engulf the earth in darkness, and the angels and the powers of evil that fill the space between heaven and earth will fall, described by Mark as *"the stars will be falling and the powers in the heavens will be shaken."* It is then that the Son of man will come in the clouds with great power and glory, and send his angels to gather the elect (Mk. 13:26-27). In this, Mark follows Paul's notion that the *Parousia* will take place after the authorities, dominions and powers of the air have been overcome (1 Cor. 15:24). The rest of the discourse advises all to "watch." According to Mark, that the coming of the Son of man is imminent is obvious on account of the fall of the temple, and for him the destruction of the temple is nothing other than the destruction of the established order in creation. In antiquity temples were not just important building for the conduct of worship. They were miniature representations of the cosmos. Jesus had said earlier, *"Truly, I say to you, there are some standing here who will not taste death before they see the kingdom of God come with power"* (Mk. 9:1), and now he says, *"Truly, I say to you, this generation will not pass away before all these things take place"* (Mk. 13:30). As a good apocalypticist, Mark writes for the benefit of his contemporaries. And to them, Mark says: *"He that is not against us is for us"* (Mk. 9:40). The apocalyptic vision sees humanity strictly divided.

In the apocalyptic discourse, the reader is informed about the destiny of the elect. They will be gathered from the four winds of the earth into the kingdom of God by the angels that accompany the Son of man who comes in the clouds. As we noticed in a previous chapter, Paul limits his interest in the resurrection to the elect. In *Daniel* the resurrection wakes those *"who sleep in the dust of the ground ... some to everlasting life, and some to shame and everlasting contempt"* (Dan. 12:2). Mark has a more developed vision of the place where the wicked are delivered to everlasting contempt. Visions of the underground where the evil ones end up had been developed by Hellenistic authors, and they soon became adopted in Christian scenarios of hell. Mark is the first one to describe it as a place of torments. Instructing his followers about the costs of discipleship, Jesus says, *"If your hand causes you to sin, cut it off; it is better for you to enter life maimed than with two hands go to hell, to the unquenchable fire. And if your foot causes you to sin, cut it off; it is better for you to enter life lame than with two feet to be thrown into hell. And if your eye causes you to sin, pluck it out; it is better for you to enter the kingdom of God with one eye that with two eyes to be thrown into hell, where their worm does not die, and the fire is not quenched. For every one [of those in hell] will be salted with fire"* (Mk. 9:43-49). The word translated "hell," in the original is the Hebrew word "Gehenna" written in Greek letters. That was the name of the valley where, according to tradition, Jews had offered sacrifices to Moloch before the exile. At the time of Christ it was the place where waste from the city was burned.

MARK'S AGENDA AND THE NARRATIVE'S END

Mark says that at the trial before the High Priest, who is not identified by name, some bore false witness against Jesus. Among the false accusation was, *"We heard him say, 'I will destroy the temple that is made with hands, and in three days I will build another, not made with hands.' Yet not even so did their testimony agree"* (Mk. 14:58-59). What the accusation claims is not found in the account of the cleansing of the temple in Mark. According to it, Jesus would not allow anyone to carry anything through the temple and said, instead, *"Is it not written, 'My house shall be called a house of prayer for all nations?' But you have made it a den of robbers"* (Mk. 11:16-17). It is, however, reported by John that at the cleansing the temple, when challenged by "the Jews" (John's standard foil) to give a sign demonstrating his authority over the temple, Jesus did say, *"Destroy this temple and in three days I will raise it up."* The narrator in John then explains that he was referring to the temple of his body, and ties the story to the post-resurrection experience of the disciples (Jn. 2:18-22). In John, however, the cleansing of the temple is unrelated to the trial and crucifixion, and the saying is a reference to the resurrection. In Mark the cleansing of the temple is what determines the decision of the chief priests and the scribes to kill Jesus, and the connection between Jesus' death and the temple is in full display. Thus, a traditional saying that is not included in the story of the cleansing is reported as an accusation at the trial before the High Priest. This reveals Mark's theological understanding of the saying by making a distinction between man-made and not man-made temples, something which the false witnesses in his story certainly would not have been able to make. Since it was a miniature representation of the fallen creation, the destruction of the temple was for Mark the ultimate indication that the *Parousia* had arrived.

In the trial before the High Priest the tipping point comes when answering the question, *"Are you the Christ, the Son of the Blessed?"* Jesus' answer is, *"I am"* (Mk. 14:61-62). The High Priest, of course, is quite wrong when he identifies the vocation of the Son of God as that of being the Messiah, the Christ. The High Priest, however, is right in identifying Jesus as the Son of God. Jesus' answer, *"I am,"* refers to the title Son of the Blessed, but not to the idea that his vocation is to be the Christ. He corrects the High Priest on that point by explaining his vocation as that of the Son of man. Having heard *"I am,"* the High Priest had what he needed, a cause for the sentence of death: blasphemy (Mk. 14:62-64). Apparently, he came to that conclusion on the understanding that *"I am"* is the name of Yahveh. In John, where there is no such thing as an apocalyptic secret to be revealed, Jesus himself openly identifies himself as *"I am,"* meaning *"equal to God,"* that is to say, *"God."* In Mark, however, by saying *"I am"* Jesus is identifying himself in reference to the second part of the question of the High Priest. He was the *"Son of the Blessed,"* the man empowered by God for a particular vocation. Thus, the sentence of death based on theological grounds, according to Mark, was misplaced.

The sentence of death pronounced by Pilate was based on everyone's understanding that he was the Christ, the Messiah, and as such one who was trying to bring to an end the Roman Empire's rule over Judea. Even his disciples fully shared this misunderstanding, demonstrated by Peter's rebuke to Jesus' description of his mission as the Son of man (Mk. 8:32), and the request of James and John to be given important positions in his coming kingdom (Mk. 10:35-37). Such understanding, of course, was based on mistaking him for the Christ. He did not come to destroy the Roman rule over Judea. He came to destroy the temple and the symbolic universe it represented, one in which demons had a free hand and the traditions of men had displaced the will of God (Mk. 7:5, 8, 13).

For Mark, the actual destruction of the temple by the Romans, which was taking place while he was writing, was anticlimactic. The real destruction of the temple took place when, at the time of Jesus' death on the cross, the curtain that separated the Holy from the Most Holy place, where atonement actually took place, was *"torn in two from top to bottom"* (Mk. 15:38). Mark does not wish to make the coming of the Son of man anticlimactic by descriptions of the Risen Lord. In his narrative the secret of the resurrection is at the core. It is what the disciples had a hard time to understand, but what must be believed (Mk. 1:14). In defense of the resurrection, against the Sadducees who did not believe in it, Jesus drew their attention to the story of Moses at the burning bush, where God identified himself saying, *"I am the God of your father, the God of Abraham, the God of Isaac, the God of Jacob"* (Ex. 3:6). Then he brought out the lesson: *"He is not God of the dead, but of the living; you [Sadducees] are quite wrong"* (Mk.12:26-27). As I pointed out in a previous chapter, the only place where the resurrection is affirmed in the Scriptures is in *Daniel*. Everyone knew that Abraham, Isaac and Jacob were dead by the time Moses stood before the burning bush. How could this identification on the part of Yahveh be taken to define him as the God of the living? The affirmation of the resurrection on the part of Mark was not based on history. It was based on faith, and that is what Mark is all about, just as Paul also was. Obviously, the Sadducees did not believe in the power of God.

At the cleansing of the temple in Mark, Jesus announced its destruction by telling the event in connection to the cursing and death of an unproductive fig tree. At the end of the apocalyptic discourse, after the reference to the coming of the Son of man in the clouds, Mark brings back a fig tree in a parable. *"From the fig tree learn its lesson: as soon as its branch becomes tender and puts forth its leaves, you know that summer is near. So also, when you see these things taking place, you know that he is near, at the very gates"* (Mk. 13:28-29). What happens with the fig tree is a clear parallel to what is happening before our eyes with the temple, says Mark. What is happening with the temple is a clear sign that the *Parousia* is here. As an event, the Roman destruction of the temple was anticlimactic; as a sign of the coming Son of man, it is as timely as it could possibly be.. To make the story reach its climax with the *Parousia*, Mark cuts the story short, abruptly, with the story of an empty tomb and women who lack faith.

The disturbing ending of Mark's narrative is quite in tune with his apocalyptic vision. Irony was not an unknown or useless tool in Mark's literary toolbox. The women who came to the tomb to anoint Jesus' body, were apparently unaware that he had already been anointed at the house of Simon the leper by a woman who came *"with an ointment of pure nard, very costly,"* in an alabaster jar which must have been also very costly. This unidentified woman broke the jar and poured the ointment on Jesus' head. The action indicates that she was anointing him as Messiah. The "indignant" reaction of *"some"* is that the ointment, that must have cost *"more than three hundred denarii,"* had been wasted, to say nothing of the alabaster jar. It is well to point out that the living wage of a soldier at the time was one denarius per day. As Jesus answered the High Priest question about being the Christ by referring to his vocation as the Son of man, he also re-interpreted the action of this woman. He said to those in the house, *"She has done a beautiful thing to me … She has done what she could; she has anointed my body beforehand for burying. And truly, I say to you, wherever the gospel is preached in the whole world, what she has done will be told in memory of her"* (Mk. 14:3-9).

In accordance with his vocation, the woman had anointed him before burial, as it was supposed to be. The time of his death, when he would no longer be with them, was already determined and approaching. Unknowingly, she had done something in accordance with God's will, and that is something to be remembered forever. This means that the women who discovered the empty tomb, due to their lack of faith, had attempted to carry out an irrelevancy. The angel who met them at the sepulcher told them, *"he is risen, he is not here; see the place where they laid him. But go, tell his disciples and Peter that he is going before you to Galilee; there you will see him, as he told you."* Having heard this, the women who had come on an ill-conceived errand to anoint one who had been anointed already became totally confused, revealing their lack of faith. The narrative ends saying, *"And they went out and fled from the tomb; for trembling and astonishment had come upon them; and they said nothing to any one, for they were afraid"* (Mk. 16:6-8). This is the highest of ironies. It is, however, the way of saying that the Gospel of the resurrection is believable because of its confirmation at the coming of the Son of man in the clouds which is at the gates, even if the disciples who were told that he would rise reacted with fear, *"and they all forsook him and fled"* (Mk. 14:50), and the women who saw the empty tomb and were told that he is risen reacted with fear rather than faith and *"fled from the tomb ... and said nothing to any one"* (Mk. 16:8). This ending of the gospel is the one supported by all the earliest manuscripts of Mark, and fits perfectly in its apocalyptic agenda.

Jesus was a man who at the cross prayed, *"'Eloi, Eloi, lama sabachthani?' Which means, 'My God, my God, why hast thou forsaken me?'"* (Mk. 15:34). It is important to understand that these are the first words of Psalm 22 and, as such, they are a way of bringing to mind the whole Psalm in prayer. Like all psalm of lament, it beginnings in a minor but suddenly shift to a major key that exalts the power and the triumph of God. The psalmist contrasts how in the past *"our fathers"* trusted in God and were not disappointed. He, however, is in need of help, but God is not answering his cries for help. His condition is terrible. Many bulls and dogs are round about him, so he pleads, *"Save me from the mouth of the lion, my afflicted soul from the horns of the wild oxen!"* Unaccountably, suddenly the mood changes, and the psalmist proclaims, *"From thee comes my praise in the great congregation .... All the ends of the earth shall remember and turn to the Lord; ... for dominion belongs to the Lord, and he rules over the nations. Yea, to him shall all the proud of the earth bow down; before him shall bow all who go down to the dust, and he who cannot keep himself alive. Posterity shall serve him; men shall tell of the Lord to the coming generation, and proclaim his deliverance to a people yet unborn, that he has wrought it."* Mark has chosen a perfect Psalm with which to express the meaning of the cross. Like the Psalmist, the Son of man who suffered and died despised and rejected, will sing the praises of God because, as the final words put it, God did bring about the deliverance of the people. As the people who witnessed Jesus' healing of the deaf and dumb in the Decapolis *"astonished beyond measure"* said, *"He has done all things well"* (Mk. 7:37). For Mark, the power and the justice of God has been revealed, they are no longer a well kept secret. As the Psalm says it, *"He Did It."*

The agenda of Mark is not just to correct a misunderstanding of Jesus' identity and mission, but to bring about a significant re-vision of the apocalyptic scenario. It is not a coincidence that the gospel lacks a reference to the last judgment, a major apocalyptic motif. The lamp that has been brought in to dispel the darkness, reveals that the words *"he will rise,"* the meaning of which the disciples failed to understand, refers to the Son of man's imminent coming in the clouds with power and glory and the angels who will gather the elect from the four corners of the earth. By then the world of the temple of Jerusalem and of the demons that have been infiltrating that world would have been destroyed, and it will be too late to do anything to improve one's chances at the judgment. The message of the gospel of Mark is: the time of trouble when remaining faithful with patient endurance was needed has passed. Now that the branch of the fig tree has become tender and is full of leaves the time to watch has arrived. Watch, watch, watch to be among those who are gathered into the kingdom of God (Mk. 13:33-37). The tomb where they laid him is empty, and his appearance in the clouds is imminent. This is what demonstrates the power and the justice of God. God does do all things well.

The Gospel of Matthew

To begin with, all the followers of Jesus, who gathered together after God raised him from the dead, were Jews, and there is no question that during his ministry Jesus had been an observant Jew. The resurrection of Jesus, however, had opened a totally new horizon before the disciples. The gospels make clear that none of the disciples expected the resurrection of Jesus after his crucifixion. According to Mark, the women who went to the tomb on Sunday morning early were going to embalm the corpse for permanent burial, unaware or undeterred by the symbolic embalming performed in the house of Simon the leper by another woman. The evidence in the gospels makes clear that after the crucifixion the disciples thought their expectations for the future with Jesus had been misplaced.

The need to come to terms with the resurrection caused the disciples to go back to the Scriptures in order to understand what was happening, and not all of them came to the same understanding, as the books of the New Testament testify. For Paul, it was the establishment of a new creation of life in the Spirit, in which humans could participate by joining Christ in his death and his resurrection at their baptism. For others, it meant that the death of Christ in the cross was the *real* sacrifice that actually cleanses from sins, something that the sacrifices performed at the temple in Jerusalem did not quite accomplish because they failed to cleanse the conscience, a psychological function unknown to the ancient Hebrews. For others, with a more apocalyptic worldview, the resurrection of Christ meant that the power of death to keep people in Hades had been broken. The key to the realm of the dead was now in the hand of the risen Christ. Some others drew other conclusions, like the notion that Jesus' death was the ransom paid to deliver humanity from slavery to the powers of sin and death. Early Christians held quite different understandings of the significance of *"the things which have been accomplished among us"* (Lk. 1:1).

Those holding these different views also differed in the way in which they conceived themselves in relation to Judaism. Thus, Paul insisted that he had not ceased being a Jew of the tribe of Benjamin, even though he had discarded his understanding of the Law as the agent of salvation. He insisted, and energetically argued, that the election of the Jews was *"irrevocable"* (Rom. 11:29), and that the Gentiles who were now benefiting from their election in Christ should in no way overlook this. They should be grateful and stand in awe praising God for having been grafted into the *"holy root"* of the elect of God (Rom. 11:17-20). Matthew, on the other hand, thinks that *"The kingdom of God will be taken away from you* [Israel] *and given to a nation producing the fruits of it"* (Mt. 21:43). As a result, Matthew says, *"your house* [Judaism] *is forsaken and desolate"* (Mt. 23:37). For Matthew, unlike for Mark, Jesus is the Messiah of the Jews, the son of David. The problem is that the Jews openly rejected him. At the trial, Pilate, sought a way to release him, *"he knew that it was out of envy that they had delivered him up"* (Mt. 27:18). So, following the custom to release a prisoner during the Passover feast, he asked the Jews whom he should release and they answered, *"Barabbas."* He then asked, *"What shall I do with Jesus who is called Christ?" They all said, 'Let him be crucified.' And he said,* "Why, what evil has he done?" Rather than to answer the question the crowd insisted, "Let him be crucified" (Mt. 27:21-23). When Pilate realized that if he fails to condemn Jesus the crowd, under the influence of its leaders, is going to become violent, he washed his hands and said, *"I am innocent of this man's blood."* To this *"all the people answered, 'His blood be on us and on our children'"* (Mt. 27:24-25). In this way Matthew explicitly assigns the responsibility for Jesus' death to the Jewish people, particularly to the Jewish leaders who have been manipulating the crowd at the trial. Paul, it may be recalled, did not consider the Jews responsible for Jesus' death, but the "rulers of this age," that is the principalities and powers of the air (1 Cor. 2:8). Matthew's notion that God had rejected Israel as a nation, complicates the way in which he views the relationship of God with Israel.

The first thing to be said about Matthew is that it is the New Testament document that most clearly reveals Jewish-Christianity. Other New Testament books reveal the existence of Jewish Christianity, a Christian branch that flowed, alongside what later became the mainstream, and became identified as the Ebionites. Matthew, however, is the one that is fully engaged in an internal defense of Christianity within the Judaism of the latter first century. While denying that as a people Israel was still the elect of God, Matthew needs to demonstrate that Christianity is the true heir of the religion that ceased to be at the destruction of the temple. To do this, he had to deny the claims of the Pharisees, the only other survivor of that cataclysm, that they were the legitimate heirs of the gifts God had prodigally entrusted to Israel.

Matthew, in opposition to the Pharisees, claimed that Christianity was the true heir. The gospel of John, for its part, reflects the animosity of those who are already outside Judaism and consider "the Jews" to be the enemy. The Jesus of John identifies the Law of Moses as "their law" (Jn. 8:17; 10:34, or "your" (18:31), or "their" law 19:7). In Matthew, Jesus assumes the validity of "the Law." Both the golden rule (Mt. 7:12) and the great commandment (Mt. 22:40) are closely related to the Law. The rich young ruler who asked what he needed to do to have eternal life was told by Jesus *"If you would enter life keep the commandments"* (Mt. 19 17), and the Pharisees, who tithed *"mint and dill and cummin"* as a demonstration of their strict observance of the commandments, were told that they should have been paying attention to *"the weightier matters of the law, justice and mercy and faith."* The punch line, however, points out that *"these you ought to have done, without neglecting the others"* (Mt. 23:23). That is, concern for justice, mercy and truth should not bring about neglecting the strict observance of the commandments.

That Matthew considers the teachings of Jesus to be an internalized reaffirmation of the Law of Moses is evident in the way he structured his gospel. Most modern students of the gospel think that Matthew took the teaching materials found in Mark and in the Sayings Source and edited it according to their content into five discourses. That this was done purposely is demonstrated by the ending of each one of the five discourses with the same formula, with minor variations: *"when Jesus finished these sayings"* (Mt. 7:28; 11:1; 13:53; 19:1; 26:1). The five discourses are: "The righteousness of the Kingdom," "Instructions for the Mission," "The Parables of the Kingdom," "The Solidarity of the Church" and "The Apocalyptic Discourse and the Judgment." It is obvious that in so doing Matthew was structuring his gospel with the pattern of the five books of Moses, that is to say the Law.

JESUS AS THE INTERPRETER OF THE LAW

Matthew, like Paul, is profoundly concerned with the function of Torah. But while Paul sees himself as a Christian no longer living "under the Law" because the Law is no longer where God's will to save humanity is revealed (Rom. 3:21), Matthew aims to establish the correct interpretation of the Law. It is certainly not that of the scribes and Pharisees, whom Jesus charges that *"for the sake of your tradition, you have made void the word of God"* (Mt. 15:6). Jesus calls their interpretations, or their teachings, their "leaven." Thus he warns his disciples, *"Take heed and beware of the leaven of the Pharisees and Sadducees"* (Mt. 16:6, 11-12). They should, on the other hand, take notice, remember and understand Jesus' "leaven," that is the teachings he has compiled in his five discourses. As he specifically states in the final apostolic commission, they are to go and *"make disciples of all nations ... teaching them to observe all that I have commanded you"* (Mt. 28:20). His "leaven" is his interpretation of the commandments. The bread cooked with this leaven is the bread that gives life. What is to be preserved in the Christian tradition, in contrast to the traditions of the scribes and Pharisees, is what *"I have commanded you."*

Students of Matthew have been debating whether Matthew sees Jesus' commandments as an alternative to the commandments in Torah, or as the distillation of the content of the commandments of Torah. I favor the notion that Matthew sees Jesus as the correct interpreter of the Law, rather than the one issuing a new law, that is, that he is a new Moses. This is an important point in reference to the apocalyptic theology of Matthew. At the final judgment the determining factor is a person's obedience to the teachings of Jesus, and the final judgment is central to Matthew.

Matthew's concern with the Law is featured at the beginning of the Sermon on the Mount, after the introductory beatitudes. The theme is introduced by offering three contrasting positions vis-a-vis the Law held within early Christianity. On the one hand, there were ultra conservatives who understood Christianity to be a right-wing branch of Judaism. They proclaimed that Jesus did not come *"to abolish the Law and the prophets,"* as some who had made Christianity a libertine ideology held. Their existence is confirmed by Paul, who condemned them. According to the radical conservatives, Jesus said, *"I have come not to abolish them but to fulfill them. For truly, I say to you, till heaven and earth pass away, not an iota, not a dot, will pass from the Law until all is accomplished"* (Mt. 5:18). According to this view the Law as written has validity as long as this age should last. The death of Christ had no effect on its unchangeable authority. It would seem that insisting on the binding force of the Law as written gives the Law total control over the lives of Christians, with no room for "ifs" and "buts." The opposite extreme view was held by those who thought that one should be aware of the relative importance of different laws. Thus, they held that it was permissible to relax unimportant parts of the Law and teach others so. Those who held this view granted that those who relax minor commandments *"shall be called least in the kingdom of heaven."* On the other hand, *"he who does them"* [the least of these commandments] *and teaches them shall be called great in the kingdom of heaven"* (Mt. 5:19). These Christians thought that one must exercise judgment over the commandments and distinguish those which are important from those which are less so. Still, according to this view all those who are in some way attached to the commandments will be in the kingdom of heaven. In the kingdom, however, there will be distinctions also, some will be "least" and some will be "great." Matthew, it is clear, rejects the views of both the ultra conservatives and the judges of the relative validity of individual commandments.

Matthew gives the Law its authority, but denies that insisting on a radically fundamentalist reading or on the freedom to assign relative values to different commandments is what Jesus taught. He offers a way out of the horns of the dilemma between these two extremes. The Law is to be obeyed as interpreted by Jesus, and his interpretation brings out the intentions of the giver of the Law. Thus, while he admits that the Law allows for divorce, he points out that *"from the beginning it was not so"* (Mt. 19:8). His proposal is, *"I tell you, unless your righteousness exceeds that of the scribes and the Pharisees, you will never enter the kingdom of heaven"* (Mt. 5:20). This immediately closes the door to the kingdom to some who are very concerned with obedience to the Law. He then elaborates on what the Higher Righteousness demands with a series of antitheses: *"You have heard that it was said to the men of old ... But I say to you"* (Mt. 5:21, 27, 31, 33, 38, 43). He characterizes the end result of practicing the righteousness that counts before God with the admonition, *"You, therefore, must be perfect, as your heavenly Father is perfect"* (Mt. 5:48). The perfection of the Father is evident in his love for all humanity without distinctions, and his lack of the need for a reward in order to do what his love demands (Mt. 5:43-47).

This outline of how to obey the will of God is further affirmed at the end of the second section of the Sermon of the Mount where traditional forms of piety, praying, fasting, giving alms, etc. are described: *"So, whatever you wish that men would do to you, do so to them; for this is the Law and the prophets"* (Mt. 7:12). To be noticed

The End of the Scroll

is that here the true life of piety is still described in reference to the Law and the prophets. That the Law and the prophets are guiding lights for Matthew is also brought out in his version of the Great Commandment. Matthew, in contrast to Mark, describes the scribe who asked Jesus about the Great Commandment as one seeking to test Jesus. This gives Matthew the opportunity to advance his own agenda: that is, to provide the key for the interpretation of the commandments. He reports that rather than to give the scribe a simple answer, he gave him two commandments of equal importance and then described their function, *"On these two commandments depend all the Law and the prophets"* (Mt. 22:36-40). In other words, Jesus wishes to have the Law and the prophets stand, but if the Law is not obeyed from the point of view of these two commandments, it fails to function properly; it does not stand. That is why the disciples at the end of the gospel are commissioned to teach *"all that I have commanded you,"* and not the Law and the prophets as commonly interpreted.

JESUS' TIME IS THE TIME OF FULFILLMENT

Rather than to be concerned to establish the difference between Jesus' identity and his vocation, as Mark's was, Matthew's concern is to recognize that the prophecies of the Scriptures were fulfilled in the life of Christ. Thus, Jesus does not only do things to fulfill the demands of righteousness in view of the future judgment. His life is the fulfillment of a predetermined historical course of action already announced by the prophets. This does not only establish the significance of what is taking place through him; it also serves to prove that the legitimate heirs to the riches of the Law and the prophets after the collapse of temple Judaism are the disciples of Jesus, not the Rabbis who are creating a new Judaism based on legal interpretations of the demands of the commandments. According to Matthew, the movement that centered around the life and teachings of Jesus was already visualized by the prophets who anticipated the details of Jesus' life. Throughout the Matthean narrative one reads the formula, *"all this took place to fulfill what the Lord had spoken by the prophet"* (Mt. 2:22; 26:56), or some other formulation of this idea. This formula appears eighteen times in Matthew. It makes absolutely clear that the life of Jesus and the movement that emerged from his life on earth were preordained by God. The emergent Christian church, not Rabbinic Judaism, is the rightful heir to the treasure found in the Scriptures. The claim that Christianity was the fulfillment of God's eternal design for history, of course, says more about the uses of history than about history itself. Within the apocalyptic perspective, however, it is always necessary to claim that history is predetermined by God's will in order to establish the credentials for announcing with certainty the future of history in apocalyptic language.

MATTHEW'S *APOLOGIA* FOR JEWISH SLANDERS

To return to Matthew's concern with life in Judaism and his debates with the scribes and Pharisees, as well as with the different opinions of fellow Christians, we shall now focus on the struggle developing between emergent institutional Christianity and the Pharisees who emerged as Rabbinic Judaism. Both sister faiths claimed to be the rightful heirs to the religion that had been centered on the temple of Jerusalem, of which they were the only two survivors from among the multiple forms of Judaism that had co-existed while the temple stood. Matthew is quite aware that Christianity is being denigrated by the slanderous accusations put forward by the scribes and the Pharisees of his time. Two of them are quite prominent and persisted for centuries. The Jews claimed that Jesus was the illegitimate son of a single woman, that is, a bastard. This charge is referred to indirectly in the gospel of John, where the Jews claim to be children of Abraham and Jesus challenges them by pointing out that children should be obedient to their father and do what he does. To this, the Jews reaffirm, *"Abraham is our father"* and counter-attack by saying, *"We were not born of fornication"* (Jn. 8:37-41). The implication is that Jesus was. That

Jesus was a bastard has remained a traditional description of Jesus among some Jews till today.

Matthew's response is couched in the story of Joseph's confusion when he discovered that Mary was pregnant, the intervention of an angel that explains what is going on, and Joseph's acceptance of what he had been told, so that *"he did as the angel of the Lord commanded him; he took his wife"* (Mt. 1:24). The counter-attack on this slander is couched in the genealogy, which like all ancient genealogies are artificial constructions with an agenda. Matthew breaks all precedents and includes five women in the genealogy. Mary is the last one mentioned in a list of Joseph's ancestors, even though she is not the descendant of those listed in the genealogy, and the text claims that Joseph was not the actual father of Jesus. Most surprising is not only the naming of the other four women, but also their reputations. Tamar played the harlot in order to seduce Judah. Rahab was a professional harlot in ancient Jericho. Ruth followed Naomi's instruction to slip into Boaz's bed during the afternoon nap, and Bathsheba, the wife of Uriah who became the mother of Solomon, in the early spring liked to bathe naked in the creek underneath a window of David's palace. If one were to accept the slander propagated by the Jews, Mary does not look particularly out of harmony with this line-up of the mothers of Israel. In this way Matthew suggests to the Jews that they better look at their own mothers before they make charges against the mother of Jesus. The only conceivable reason for starting the story with this unconventional and contorted genealogy is to advance the counter charge I am proposing. It is to be noticed also that the genealogy begins with Abraham, thus identifying Jesus as a Jew, but two of the women, Rahab and Ruth are foreigners. Tamar, the wife of Er the son of Judah, seems to have been also a foreigner. Judah's wife, Shua the mother of Er, is explicitly identified as a Canaanite, and Bathsheba was married to a Hittite when Solomon was conceived.

The second slander propagated by the Jews was that the tomb of Joseph of Arimathea was found empty because the disciples stole the body; therefore, there had been no such thing as a resurrection.

To answer this charge, Matthew tells that the Pharisees transgressed the Sabbath commandment and during the sacred hours of the Sabbath went to Pilate and reported that *"the impostor"* had said that *"after three days I will rise again."* Then, on account of their insecurity as to the real power at work in Jesus, the Pharisees asked Pilate, *"Order the sepulcher to be made secure until the third day, lest his disciples go and steal him away, and tell the people, 'He has risen from the dead,' and the last fraud will be worse than the first"* (Mt. 27:63-64). When the resurrection actually took place, according to Matthew, the Pharisees paid the guards to tell the people that the disciples stole the body while they were asleep (Mt. 28:11-15). It is significant that Paul, the first Christian whose writings we have, apparently ignored that there was an empty tomb in the vicinity of Jerusalem. Mark is the first to report an empty tomb, and closes his story of Jesus abruptly with it, thus emphasizing the expectation of the soon appearance of the Son of man in the clouds with power and glory. That the disciples had stolen the body was a charge that arose in response to the story of the empty tomb. That soldiers were placed to guard the tomb to prevent the stealing of the body, and that the guards admitted publicly to have been asleep while the robbery took place, is hard to imagine. This is Matthew's answer to the Jewish slander about the resurrection. If the criteria of contemporary academic history were to be applied to this story, it would be impossible to say that a first century Galilean who was crucified by Roman authorities outside Jerusalem under charges of sedition was buried in an identifiable grave. These responses given by Matthew to the attacks against the Christian story by emergent Rabbinic Judaism reflect the tensions existing between the two daughters who claimed to be the rightful heir of the mother's estate.

Besides the apologies for Jewish slanders, Matthew also feels the need to give a spin to the account of the baptism of Jesus for the remission of sins performed by John the Baptist after his affirmation that he was the Son of God on account of his miraculous birth. Mark considered Jesus to have been a man who became the adopted Son of God at his baptism. He saw no problem in his having been baptized. In the gospel of John, where Jesus is not just the result of a miraculous birth but of the incarnation of God, John the Baptist only identifies and endorses Jesus' mission. A baptism does not take place. Matthew did not feel that he could overlook what was known to have taken place; therefore, he takes a different tack. He says that John the Baptist did not wish to baptize Jesus on account of who he was, but relented and baptized him anyway after Jesus said, *"Let it be so now; for thus it is fitting for us to fulfill all righteousness"* (Mt. 3:15). For Matthew, the fulfillment of righteousness overrules all other considerations. It was in view of this consideration that John the Baptist baptized Jesus, not because of a need to repent from sins. The rationale for it given by Jesus is thoroughly Matthean. In the end, his baptism was just a formality. As the fulfillment of righteousness, his baptism was a public example for his followers. Matthew's concern with righteousness also causes him to qualify the beatitude found in the Sayings Source by writing, *"Blessed are those who hunger and thirst for righteousness"* (Mt. 5:6). For him the fulfillment of a higher righteousness is absolutely essential in view of the final judgment.

MATTHEW AND THE SOON APPEARANCE OF THE SON OF MAN

Writing while the Romans were fighting to put down the Jewish rebellion that included the destruction of the temple in Jerusalem and ended with the taking of the fortress of Massada (68-73 C.E.), Mark thought that the fall of the temple and the coming of the Son of man in the clouds were concurrent events. In his mind, the *Parousia* would take place momentarily. With this in mind, he ended his gospel with an absent Lord. It served to highlight the momentous significance of the soon appearance of the Son of man in the clouds. For Mark, to report post-resurrection appearances would make the *Parousia* anti-climactic. This perspective is evident in the way in which Mark phrases the dialogue between Jesus and his disciples as they were coming out of the temple and the disciples pointed out the beauty of the place. Jesus' reaction was to announce that in this beautiful place *"there will not be left ... one stone upon another, that will not be thrown down."* Later, on the Mount of Olives four disciples asked him privately, *"Tell us, when will this be, and what will be the sign when these things are all to be accomplished?"* (Mk. 13:2, 4). The descriptions that follow are Jesus' response to the specific question of when would the temple be destroyed. At the time Mark wrote, the temple is being or has recently been destroyed, but the Roman armies are still around. For him, the *Parousia* of the Lord is to take place in direct connection with the events being experienced by his contemporaries, thus he reports Jesus' words as referring to concurrent events.

Writing around the year 95 C.E., Matthew can no longer identify the *Parousia* with the destruction of the temple in 70 C.E. He, therefore, edits the story to fit his situation. Rather than four disciples in the Mount of Olives with Jesus, all twelve of them are there, and they asked two, rather than just one question, *"Tell us, when will this be, and what will be the sign of your coming and of the close of the age?"* (Mt. 24:3). Matthew distinguishes the destruction of the temple when no stone was left upon another from the "coming" of the Son of man and "the close of the age." He is quite aware that the Markan prediction that the coming of the Son of man would take place in connection with the destruction of the temple can no longer be affirmed.

While remaining close to the accounts in Mark, including the sayings that *"those standing here"* (Mt. 16:28) and *"this generation"* (Mt. 24:34) would see the coming of the Son of man, Matthew makes three important changes to the Markan scenario. One, he recognizes that there has been a delay. Two, he corrects the notion that Jesus is absent. Three, he changes the significance of the *Parousia* from the appearance of an absent Lord who will annul the significance of a Roman military victory to the appearance of the Son of man as Judge of all humankind. His coming is not attached to the destruction of the Jerusalem temple but to the Final Judgment, which, as noticed above, was not a major concern of Mark.

Faced with a delay in the coming of the Lord, Matthew finds a way to integrate it into the teachings of Jesus and to give it an important function. Matthew introduces parables that are unique to his account of the story. Three of them, in particular, are concerned with the delay: The parable of the gentleman who gives talents to his servants before leaving on a journey, the parable of the wicked and the wise servant and the parable of the ten virgins. The parable of the talents tells of a master who before departing gives different amounts of cash to three of his servants, *"to each according to his ability."* The story then says that *"after a long time the master of those servants came and settled accounts with them."* (Mt. 25:15, 19). As a whole, the parable deals with several important Matthean themes. For now, I will only point out that it specifies that the master was away for "a long time." This takes away the immediacy emphasized by Paul, the author of *To the Hebrews* and Mark.

The parable contrasting the faithful and wise servant from the wicked one tells that the master sets his servant *"over his household, to give them their food at the proper time."* When at his return the master finds his servant *"so doing,"* he sets him *"over all his possessions."* It may happen, however, that the servant *"says to himself, 'My master is delayed,' and begins to beat his fellow servants, and eats and drinks with the drunken."* When this servant least expects it, his master returns and punishes him, *"and puts him with the hypocrites; these men will weep and gnash their teeth"* (Mt. 24:45-51). In other words, the delay may become a temptation to fail to do what one was set up to do during the absence of the master. Matthew insists that the delay does not provide leisure time. It is taking place to give the disciples time to spread the gospel to all nations before the end comes. The servants have been left in charge of the household to feed everyone well.

Better known is the parable of the ten virgins. It does not consider the delay a temptation to abandon one's responsibilities; it highlights that since there may be a delay, preparations for it are in order. To be noticed is that all ten young women were invited, all ten had lights for the journey to the house where the wedding feast was to take place and all ten were virgins. Five of them were wise and took with them some extra oil for their lights. Five of them were foolish and did not think the bridegroom might be delayed; therefore, they did not take extra oil with them. Essential to the story is that *"the bridegroom was delayed, and they all slumbered and slept"* (Mt. 25:5). What distinguishes the wise from the foolish, is not that five were virgins and five only pretended to be, or that five had lights and five did not, or that some of them fell asleep and the others didn't. What distinguishes them is that five anticipated a delay and five did not. One can hardly imagine a more graphic demonstration that Matthew was writing in the midst of a delay, when extra oil is essential.

The first parable alluded to also brings out another Matthean concern about the delay, and that is the need to be engaged in producing benefits for the absent Lord no matter how many talents the Lord has entrusted an individual. Mark, expecting the coming to take place at any time now, asks his readers to watch, watch, watch (Mk. 13:32-37). Matthew asks his readers to keep busy and produce works of righteousness or, as the second parable puts it, to oversee well the household of the master. The servant who received one talent confesses, *"I was afraid, and I went and hid your talent in the ground. Here you have what is yours."* In other words, he did not quite understand the purpose for which the talent had been given. He never quite received a commission from the master and when he left, he continued to have a relationship with him based on fear rather than trust. That is totally unproductive. The master declares that servant *"wicked and slothful"* (Mt. 25:25-26). Matthew makes clear the purpose of the delay in his conclusion, *"Go therefore and make disciples of all nations, baptizing them in the name of the Father, and of the Son and of the Holy Spirit"* (Mt. 28:19). Paul understood that after the resurrection, the Risen Christ was busy bringing under subjection the principalities, powers, authorities and lords of the air that still opposed the will of God in the spheres between heaven and earth (1 Cor. 15:24-25). Matthew understands that

The End of the Scroll

the delay is caused by the need to make disciples of all nations and being responsible for their well-being.

Another indication that Matthew is aware that he can no longer identify the destruction of the temple with the *Parousia* is found in the way in which he transcribes the reference to God's shortening of the days of the coming tribulation for the sake of the elect. Answering the question of the disciples as to when would it be that there would not be left one stone upon another at the temple complex, Mark reports that when the people see *"the desolating sacrilege set up where it ought not to be (let the reader understand) ... those who are in Judea [should] flee to the mountains."* Those days will be days of tribulations like there never have been nor ever will be. *"And if the Lord had not shortened the days, no human being would be saved; but for the sake of the elect, whom he chose, he shortened the days"* (Mk. 13:14-20). In my reading of this passage in the previous section, I pointed out that Mark changes the verbs from the future to the past tense and thus pinpoints the time when the gospel of Mark was written. Building on this insight, I will point out what Matthew does with this passage from Mark which he quotes verbatim, only adding that the reference to the sacrilege comes from the prophet Daniel and that they should pray that their escape to the mountains besides not taking place in winter should also not take place on a Sabbath. Then Matthew copying Mark writes, *"And if those days had not been shortened, no human being would be saved; but for the sake of the elect those days will be shortened"* (Mt. 24:22). That is, while Mark reports that those days have already been shortened for the sake of the elect, Matthew foretells that those days will be shortened for the sake of the elect in the future, after the delay. Changing the tense of the verb makes a difference.

The delay of the coming of the Son of man, however, does not mean that the servants who have been commissioned to bring people into the kingdom of God have to do their work while the Lord is absent. Matthew makes clear that Mark's soon to appear absent Lord, is actually not absent at all. It is not necessary to wait until the close of the age for the Lord to be with his disciples. He is with them already at all times, he insists. The Lord is Emmanuel, God with us (Mt. 1:23). And as Jesus says both at his farewell commissioning, and at his instructions for the community. *"I am with you always," "where two or three are gathered in my name, there I am in the midst of them"* (Mt. 28:20; 18:20). The gathering of disciples, among which Jesus is present, is "the church," an institution that is identified only in Matthew among the gospels (Mt. 16:18; 18:17).

The delay of the *Parousia* is the time for the church to do its work. By the time Matthew wrote the community of disciples commissioned to make more disciples was already becoming an organization with established leaders. As Matthew specifically states, God has given men authority to forgive sins, much to the astonishment of the crowds (Mt. 9:8; 16:19; 18; 18). Other Christian documents of this time also show the beginnings of an institutionalized organization. Thus, for example, in the epistle *To the Ephesians* it is said that the household of God is *"built upon the foundation of the apostles and prophets, Christ Jesus himself being the cornerstone"* (Eph. 2:20). Matthew identifies Simon Peter as the rock on which the church is built, whether the rock is the disciple Peter, or Peter's confession, the statement makes clear that the church is to be built on something other than Christ himself. Evolving Christianity soon found out it needed recognizable leaders who operated within some kind of structure. When it was just a fledgling movement about the Risen Christ, Paul insisted that *"no other foundation can anyone lay than that which is laid, which is Jesus Christ"* (1 Cor. 3:11). Paul identifies local congregations as churches which are the product of, and are guided by the Holy Spirit, but by the end of the first century it became necessary to establish standards for the life of all the churches. This resulted in the establishment of channels through which the Holy Spirit could flow under ecclesiastical control. Thus Matthew has one of the five discourses in his gospel dedicated to how to conduct oneself as a church member, and how to keep the church on the path to perfection (Mt. 18). This had become necessary because "the bridegroom has been delayed."

The accommodation to the new circumstances was dictated by the apocalyptic vision of the coming judgment. Matthew's concern with the judgment serves to emphasize the need to live according to the demands of a higher righteousness as delineated by the interpretation of the Law according to its *"weightier matters."* For this, it was necessary to become *"a scribe who has been trained for the kingdom of heaven."* Such a scribe is not bound, like the Pharisaic scribes, to deal only with what is old, that is the written law. He is able to bring *"out of his treasure what is new and what is old"* (Mt. 13:52). In other words, the true disciple is one who recognizes the value of the old but applies it in the light of the new revelation in Jesus. And as said in what has been characterized as "a Johannine thunderbolt in the Matthean sky," unlike the heavy burdens put on people by the popular scribes, Jesus does not impose heavy demands. *"Come to me, all who labor and are heavy laden, and I will give you rest.... For my yoke is easy and my burden is light"* (Mt. 11:28, 30). The judge is demanding, but not oppressive. Jesus did not come to add burdens on those who are already loaded; he came to give rest to those carrying heavy burdens imposed by Rabbinic Judaism. His demand of a higher righteousness is not restrictive but liberating.

Since Jesus is already present in the church, the *Parousia* can no longer be considered to be what brings to the world an absent Lord. Matthew, therefore, changes the function of the coming of the Son of man from what makes possible to be with the Lord, as Paul would have it (1 Th. 4:17), or what brings to an end the time of *"tribulations as has not been from the beginning of the creation which God created until now, and never will be,"* as Mark will have it (Mk. 13:19). Even if Matthew actually quotes Mark's words (Mt. 24:21), for him the Son of man who comes in the clouds with myriad angels comes to judge the world and to assign the reward everyone will receive according to what they have done. All the many unique parables found in Matthew have to do with the judgment, even the parables which point out the delay are basically parables of judgment.

Significantly, Matthew emphasizes that the judgment will also distinguish the righteous and the wicked within the church. It is no longer the case that divine direct intervention in human affairs takes care of outsiders who cause trouble to the elect. Rather it is the case that insiders will also find themselves being judged and could end up confined to hell, where the fire never ceases and the worms never die. The Matthean church is a mixed church, where the righteous and the wicked live together. As Jesus states it, *"many are called, but few are chosen"* (Mt. 22:14). In Greek, the language in which Matthew was written, the word church is *ekklesia*. It is made up of two Greek words: *ek* meaning "out of," and *kalein* meaning "to call." Not all those who have been called out of "the world" into the church are "the elect," for the sake of whom the time of great tribulations will be shortened. The most astonishing evidence of the presence of outsiders inside the community is given in the final meeting of Jesus with his disciples at Galilee after the resurrection. The eleven disciples left after Judas had committed suicide *"went to Galilee, to the mountain to which Jesus had directed them. And when they saw him they worshiped him; but some doubted"* (Mt. 28:16-17). This is an astonishing outcome. Among the nucleus of the most intimate disciples who witnessed the resurrected Christ "some doubted." Undoubtedly, not all who are called are chosen.

That all those who have been called out of the multitude are not necessarily going to enter the kingdom of God is also brought out by adding an important observation to the command to flee from Jerusalem in a hurry when they see the desolating sacrilege set up at the temple. They are to leave immediately without trying to take with them something of value found in their house, or go to the house to pick up a mantel if one was out in the field working lightly dressed. To this Matthew adds, *"Then two men will be in the field; one is taken and one is left. Two women will be grinding at the mill; one is taken and one is left"* (Mt. 24:40-41). The idea is present also in the parable of the wheat and tares which points out that in the owner's field are found not only seeds planted by him, but also seeds planted by his enemy. The separation of the wheat from the weeds will have to wait until harvest time, when the weeds shall be burned and the wheat will be stored in the barn (Mt. 13:24-30).

Matthew describes the *Parousia* thusly: *"When the Son of man comes in his glory, and all the angels with him, then he will sit on this glorious throne. Before him will be gathered all the nations, and he will separate them one from another as a shepherd separates the sheep from the goats, and he will place the sheep at his right hand, but the goats at the left"* (Mt. 25:31-33). To be noticed is that in *Daniel* the one who sits on the throne and judges the nations is the Ancient of Days. The Son of man is the one who receives the benefit of the judgment done by the Ancient of Days. Paul, the witness to earliest Christianity, is always careful to establish that all the benefits received by those with faith come from God who did something extraordinary through Jesus Christ. In Mark and in *Revelation*, Paul's recognition of God as the ultimate source of goodness and arbiter of righteousness is maintained. It is notable that Matthew and John, the two gospels that have a strong animosity toward their contemporary Jews and heighten the divinity of Jesus, make him the judge of the world, John in a non-apocalyptic way and Matthew in a very apocalyptic way.

When the criteria on which the separation of the goats from the sheep are announced, it is a surprise to all those concerned. They are told that they had done or failed to do what they were unaware of having or not having done. The crucial test had been whether they had served or not served the needs of *"one of the least of these my brethren"* (Mt. 25:40, 45). The judgment is based on what Matthew has identified as the *"weightier matters of the Law, justice and mercy and faith."* These things do not take the place of observance of the more mundane commandments, however. He concludes his indictment of the Pharisees saying, *"These you ought to have done, without neglecting the others"* (Mt. 23:23). In other words, being ultra-careful about giving the tenth of one's earnings, as the Law demands, is also necessary. The distillation of the Law in the golden rule does not do away with the Law. It is what allows the Law to stand (Mt. 7:12), and exhibits the higher righteousness that culminates in perfection. The same point is made to the rich young man who came to Jesus asking what he needed to do to have eternal life. After informing Jesus that he had been a faithful observer of the commandments, he asked *"what do I still lack?"* Jesus' answer is another reference to that higher righteousness based on the weightier matters of the Law: use your possessions for the benefit of the least of these, the poor, and *"follow me"* (Mt. 19:16-21). In other words, keep observing all the commandments, but do it with the weightier matters of the Law in mind if you are to receive eternal life at the judgment. For Matthew, life in this age, whether in the church or out of the church, culminates at the judgment when the destiny of every human being will be determined. All the parables unique to Matthew bring out the ultimate significance of the judgment.

Throughout this presentation of the apocalyptic theology found in the Scriptures, my aim is to show that the apocalyptic literature of the Bible is concerned to demonstrate that God's retributive justice works. Even if in this world the righteous suffer and the wicked prosper, in the age to come every one will receive their just reward. Any attempt to demonstrate that justice works in God's world cannot but speak of a reward as the most effective way to prove it. The prominence of the reward is found throughout the synoptic gospels, especially in Matthew. In this gospel perfection, judgment and rewards are central motifs. Modern ethicists have criticized this aspect of the ethic of Jesus. It has been argued that modern humanistic ethics are superior to the ethic of Jesus as found in the gospels because they enjoin the doing of the good because it is the good, not because of a reward. The ethic of Jesus is inferior, it is argued, because it is based on self interest, the attainment of the reward. The difference between the modern humanist and the apocalypticists of all ages is that the latter are totally certain that they live in the world created by God. Most academic secular humanists either doubt or deny that God created the world or that he is involved in what happens in the world. This means that for the apocalypticists both good and evil are God's concerns. The teaching of Jesus found in the gospels gives assurance of a reward, but the reward is not necessarily a *sumum bonum*. It may turn out to be, in the language of the gospels, the fires of hell. The issue of rewards in the gospels is to be understood as absolutely essential to the agenda of all apocalyptic texts. They are concerned to demonstrate that retributive justice works, and consequences, rewards, are the evidence to show that. Apocalyptic authors are more concerned with advice for the conduct of life now than with the future.

Also to be noted in this connection is that in the elaboration of what the higher righteousness consists of, the perfection of the Father in heaven is revealed in that *"he makes his sun rise on the evil and on the good, and sends rain on the just and the unjust"* without expectations of a reward from them, and Christians who do whatever good things tax collectors and Gentiles also do have no reason to expect a reward for doing those things either (Mt. 5:45-47). The good rewards are only for those who do what a higher righteousness demands, a righteousness that exceeds that of the scribes, the Pharisees or the Gentiles. Recognizing this higher demand requires wisdom and perseverance because "the close of the age" may not take place this afternoon. Christians will be living in this age for a time longer than originally expected.

Finally, I will refer to Matthew's intensification of the apocalyptic significance of the resurrection. The resurrection, of course, is the essential element of the biblical apocalyptic universe. The difference between the apocalypticism of *Daniel* and that of the apocalyptic texts in the New Testament is that while for *Daniel* the resurrection is a hoped for future event, for the apocalyptic writers of the New Testament it is an already realized past event. As Paul would have it, the resurrection of Christ is the "first fruit" of the resurrection of the righteous (1 Cor. 15:23). He is not concerned with the resurrection of the wicked. Matthew and *Revelation*, which are more tied to the traditions of Israel, envision, like *Daniel*, the resurrection of some to eternal life and some to eternal death.

Concern for the delay of the *Parousia* causes Matthew to highlight the reality of the resurrection. Mark reports that resurrection was something that the Sadducees denied (Mk. 12:18), and the disciples of Jesus had difficulty understanding (Mk. 9:10). His whole apocalyptic vision, of course, is premised on the appearance in the Son of man who *"must suffer many things, and be rejected by the elders and the chief priests and the scribes, and be killed, and after three days rise again"* Mk. 8:31, cp. 9:31; 10:33-34). Mark also points out that when the disciples heard Jesus telling this, *"they did not understand the saying, and they were afraid to ask"* (Mk. 9:32). In other words they did not believe what Jesus had said. Matthew, on the other hand, repeatedly points out that the disciples did understand what Jesus was talking about (Mt. 13:51; 16:12; 17:12-13). Still, he admits that the resurrection did take the disciples by surprise, and that at the crucifixion none of the twelve disciples were present. Following Mark, he reports that all the disciples *"forsook him and fled"* (Mk. 14:50; Mt. 26:56). Only women who had followed him from Galilee to Jerusalem watched the crucifixion from a distance. Mary Magdalene and the other Mary (identified by Mark as the mother of James) also watched where Joseph of Arimathea buried him, and on Sunday morning *"went to see the sepulcher"* (Mt. 28:1) as a sign of mourning, not to anoint the body. This set of circumstances allows Matthew to report that there were witnesses to what happened at the crucifixion and at the resurrection, even while not necessarily giving a description of Jesus' exit from the tomb. The need for concrete details seems to have developed later, and the apocryphal *Gospel of Peter* satisfied it (Ev. Petr. 8-11).

Nothing gives a more clear demonstration of Matthew's dramatic heightening of the apocalyptic significance of the resurrection than the story of the resurrection of saints at the time of Jesus' crucifixion. This confirms that he had gained control of the key to Sheol. When Jesus expired on the cross, not only the curtain of the temple was ripped from top to bottom, but also *"the earth shook and the rocks were split; the tombs also were opened, and many bodies of the saints who had fallen asleep were raised, and coming out of the tombs after his resurrection they went into the holy city and appeared to many"* (Mt. 27:51-53). It is quite significant that the bodies of the saints were raised at the time of the earthquake that took place at his death

The End of the Scroll

on Friday. Whether they went out of the tombs and into the city at this time, or after the resurrection of Jesus on Sunday is not quite clear. Matthew leaves no room for doubt that both the earthquake and the resurrection of saints on Friday had witnesses. *"When the centurion and those who were with him, keeping watch over Jesus, saw the earthquake and what took place, they were filled with awe, and said, 'Truly this was the Son of God.' There were also many women there, looking on from afar"* (Mt. 27:54-55). That what they saw was not only an earthquake, but also what had taken place at the time, makes the whole Roman cohort witnesses to the resurrection of saints at the time. Besides, Matthew has not just the centurion, but all the members of the guard at the tomb confess that *"this was the Son of God."* Thus, Matthew modifies the Markan account in two ways, and both highlight the drama of the crucifixion as God's triumph over death. He has not only the centurion confessing that the crucified is the Son of God, but all the members of the guard, and he omits the Markan identification of the Son of God as "a man." Thus he has a group of Gentiles identifying Jesus according to his understanding of the divine origin of Jesus.

Besides, he has the Roman guard and many women witnessing the earthquake and the raising of saints who had fallen asleep. This represents a radical interpretation of the crucifixion as an apocalyptic event. The significance of the crucifixion, as said at the beginning, was interpreted differently among the early Christians. Matthew looks at the crucifixion and sees the conquering of Sheol and the anticipation of the resurrection of the righteous. Thus, given the predetermination of all historical events, he asserts the reality of the resurrection even before God raised Jesus from the dead. Paul knows a tradition that the Risen Christ *"appeared to more than five hundred brethren at one time."* Then he comments that *"most of whom are still alive, though some have fallen asleep"* (1 Cor. 15:6). Matthew knows a tradition that many of the saints who had died before the crucifixion were raised at that time and appeared to many in Jerusalem. These are powerful demonstration of Christianity as an apocalyptic movement based on the resurrection.

Then, with the guard of soldiers at the tomb, and the women who had come to see the sepulcher present, he tells that there was *"a great earthquake; for an angel of the Lord descended from heaven and came and rolled back the stone, and sat upon it. His appearance was like lightning, and his raiment white as snow. And for fear of him the guard trembled and became like dead men"* (Mt. 28:2-4). This time two women, Mary Magdalene and the other Mary, were there to witness the event also. The accounts of the two earthquakes and the two resurrections that took place during that Passover weekend allow Matthew to demonstrate most effectively what he considers to be the core of his gospel, even if in light of the Judgment he gives much emphasis to the need to obey the commandments of Jesus. God is the righteous God who raises the dead.

Matthew's need to make accommodations on account of the delay of the *Parousia* could be seen as a softening of his apocalyptic vision. That is not at all the case. It turns out that by shifting the focus from the main items in the apocalyptic agenda to other related matters he enlarges his apocalyptic horizon. As pointed out already, apocalypticism arose as an answer to the charge that the retributive justice of God was not working in God's world. Rather than to focus on the way in which God would at the end destroy all the powers of evil that have been operating freely in this world, Matthew emphasizes that the righteousness of God is fully operative in the life and teachings of Jesus. Jesus came to fulfill all righteousness and humans are expected to exhibit a higher righteousness than that which a pedestrian reading of the Law may produce. Those who pay attention to the weightier matters of the Law will receive their reward at their resurrection. God's retributive justice will be fully displayed at the end, when the Judgment will set apart the sheep from the goats.

The Gospel of Luke

The author of what in our Bibles is the third canonical gospel wrote two volumes which he dedicated to "most excellent Theophilus." The first is now known as the gospel *According to Luke*; the second as *The Acts of the Apostles*. As a consequence, the New Testament has more material written by this anonymous author than by any other writer. Like the author of Matthew, the author of Luke also used as sources Mark and the Sayings Source. Most students of the gospels think that the material from the Sayings Source is preserved closer to the original in Luke than in Matthew, thus when identifying individual sayings in this source the reference given is to their location in Luke. It is clear that all gospel writers incorporated the sayings and the stories of Jesus according to how they fitted into their own agendas. The oral traditions circulating among the first followers of Jesus kept alive sayings and anecdotes without circumstantial backgrounds. In the Sayings Source they were kept mostly without a reference to time, interlocutors or location. Thus, when recorded in Matthew or Luke, these are different.

When Mark wrote his gospel, he organized the material chronologically and geographically according to his theological agenda. Thus, while Matthew edited the sayings of Jesus he found in the Saying Source primarily in the five discourses that form the structure of his gospel, Luke has some of the sayings of Jesus now found in Matthew's Sermon on the Mount as the core of his Sermon on the Plain, but most of the sayings are found scattered in Jesus' long journey to Jerusalem. This tells us that while the contents of the Sermon on the Mount in Matthew are traditional, the structure of the sermon is Matthew's redaction of traditional material. In the same way, Luke edited the sources at his disposal according to his particular agenda. This means that a saying of Jesus may appear in all three of the synoptic gospels with some variations in its wording and in totally different contexts. Paying attention to how Luke edits and arranges the traditional materials at his disposal is, therefore, how one is able to identify Luke's theological agenda.

THE KEY TO LUKE'S STORY: IRONY

One third of Luke's content comes from sources other than Mark and the Sayings Source, a great proportion of it is found at the beginning, in the birth narrative, and at the end, in the post-resurrection appearances. This immediately calls attention to these two sections. Peculiar to the birth narrative is the way in which it interlocks the narrative of the birth of Jesus with that of John the Baptist, and makes the two babies close relatives by pointing out that Elizabeth is Mary's kinswoman (*syngenís*, Lk. 1:36). Both births are announced by an angel, both babies are duly circumcised, both are named by the angel who announces their birth and both are given testimonials predicting their vocation, causing many to rejoice. For their part, the post-resurrection appearances are characterized by their connection to the passion predictions and by their location in Jerusalem and its environs, rather than Galilee, as in Matthew. When Jesus was still with his disciples, he told them that the Son of man must be *"crucified, and on the third day rise"* (Lk. 24:7). The narrator then makes clear that when Jesus said that to the disciples *"they understood none of these things; this saying was hid from them, and they did not grasp what was said"* (Lk. 18:34). At the empty tomb, hearing the angel repeat Jesus' prediction, Mary Magdalene, Joanna and Mary the mother of James "remembered his words," and told to *"the eleven and to all the rest"* what they had learned at the tomb. The narrator then laments, *"but these words seemed to them an idle tale, and they did not believe them"* (Lk. 24:8-11).

Suddenly, the scene changes. Cleopas and a friend, who had gone to Jerusalem from Emmaus to celebrate Passover and had become attached to the events surrounding the trial and the crucifixion of Jesus, are joined by a stranger on their journey back home. As they engage in conversation with the stranger, they refer to what had taken place that weekend in Jerusalem and confess that *"we had hoped that he was the one to redeem Israel. Yes, and besides all this, it is now the third day since this happened."* They tell the stranger that some women who went to the tomb on Sunday did not find the body. They reported to the disciples having seen a vision of angels who said he was alive. Acting on this report, some disciples had gone to the tomb and did find it empty, *"but him they did not see"* (Lk. 24:21-24). To this the stranger reacts rather sharply, *"O foolish men, and slow of heart to believe all that the prophets have spoken."* Then the stranger, *"beginning with Moses and all the prophets, he interpreted to them in all the scriptures the things concerning himself,"* that is to say that *"it was necessary that the Christ should suffer these things and enter into his glory"* (Lk. 24:25-27).

The journey to Emmaus culminates when the two who expected Jesus to restore the fortunes of Israel invite the stranger to eat supper with them. *"When he was at table with them, he took the bread and blessed, and broke it, and gave it to them. And their eyes were open and they recognized him; and he vanished out of their sight"* (Lk. 24:30-31). It is no accident that Luke has the first post-resurrection appearance take place when bread is being blessed, broken and given to those at supper. Immediately, Cleopas and his companion rushed back to Jerusalem. When they arrive to where some disciples are still gathered, they tell the two from Emmaus, *"The Lord has risen indeed, and has appeared to Simon!"* No details of this sighting are given by the narrator. The two who had come from Emmaus then tell the disciples how *"he was known to them in the breaking of the bread"* (Lk. 24:34-35). This reference to the circumstances, the breaking of the bread, cannot be overlooked. Then *"Jesus himself stood among them,"* and the narrator comments, *"but they were startled and frightened, and supposed that they saw a spirit"* (Lk. 24:36-37). Realizing their confusion, Jesus calls their attention to his hands and feet, and asks them to touch him, but they are not convinced. *"They disbelieved for joy, and wondered."* Apparently, the appearance of one risen from the dead is unable to be convincing. Finally, Jesus proves he is not a spirit by eating some fish (Lk.24:41-43).

Luke ends his narrative telling what was absolutely necessary before the disciples could understand what Jesus was all about. *"Then he said to them, 'These are my words which I spoke to you, while I was still with you, that everything written about me in the Law of Moses and the prophets and the psalms must be fulfilled.' Then he opened their minds to understand the scriptures"* (Lk. 24:44-45). In other words, don't read the scriptures with your eyes fixed on apocalyptic descriptions of the restoration of Israel. What the scriptures say is all about me, the Christ who must suffer and enter into his glory. To be able to read the scriptures this new way, however, you must have your minds open. Luke is quite aware that no one understood Jesus' vocation prior to the resurrection. Rather than to have Jesus trying to make them understand during his time with the disciples, like Mark did, he links the story of Jesus to the life of John the Baptist from the very beginning. Both of them were prophets announced by the prophets of old, even though this was not understood. Throughout the narrative, on the other hand, Luke proves from scripture the expectations of a son of David who will restore the fortunes of Israel and give light to the nations, as the prophets of Israel had said. Only when readers come to the end of the story do they discover the irony that pervades the whole narrative.

In *Luke*, Jesus calls *"the multitudes," "You hypocrites."* Such a general strong accusation is rather surprising. It is also difficult to know what to make of it because it appears unconnected to a larger context. Taking into account the reason for the charge, however, makes it possible to understand its role. The incident begins with Jesus describing what the multitudes can do. *"When you see a cloud rising in the west, you say at once, 'A shower is coming'; and so it happens. And when you see the south wind blowing, you say, 'There will be scorching heat'; and it happens. You hypocrites! You know how to interpret the appearance of earth and sky; but why do you not know how to interpret the present time?"* (Lk. 12:54-56). Is this a loose outbreak of anger? Frustration? Pity? Not at all. It is a clear marker to what needs to be interpreted correctly: the present, the time of their divine visitation. To be noticed is that the charge is not stated as a fact, but as a question as to why. Not to be able to interpret it correctly is at the core of Luke irony. The reason why they cannot interpret it correctly is because they have a closed mind fixed on the restoration of the fortunes of Israel.

In his *Theology of Luke*, Joel B. Green argues that Luke is concerned with a socio-political reversal of fortunes. It is, indeed, true that Luke insists on the reversal of social and political fortunes, those who are now down will go up and those who are up will go down. He emphasizes the need to be clear about one's priorities, about concern with wealth and possessions (12:28-34). But to understand Luke on the basis of this theme is not enough. That the world is upside down is the coinage of irony. The reversal that Luke is concerned with is not just the reversal of the expectations of the rich, the mighty, the strong, the righteous, etc. Most significant is the reversal of the expectations of all the disciples of Jesus about his mission. It is through irony that Luke reveals the truth of the mission of Jesus. With a wrinkle in his cheek he tells the story of Jesus' life in line with everybody's expectations as the fulfillment of prophecies about the restoration of Israel, only to let the reader know that to interpret the scriptures correctly it is necessary to have the Risen Christ open one's mind. Rather than to see him as the Messiah who comes to defeat and conquer the enemies of Israel and to vindicate the power and justice of God, as in Mark, or as the Judge who demands obedience not only to the letter of the Law but also to the weightier matters of the Law, as in Matthew, Luke's Jesus comes *"to proclaim the acceptable year of the Lord"* (Lk. 4:19), *"to seek and to save the lost"* (Lk. 19:10). Thus, unlike the Jesus of Matthew who demands perfection (Mt. 5:48; 19:21), and sends his disciples to teach all nations *"to observe all that I have commanded you"* (Mt. 28:20), Luke's Jesus tells his disciples *"to preach in his name to all nations"* that *"repentance and forgiveness of sins"* are the order of the day (Lk. 24:47). He did not come with political objectives. He came as the agent of divine mercy. That the disciples expected a political upheaval is ridiculed by Luke saying that to fulfill the scripture that *"he was reckoned with transgressors"* it was necessary for them to buy a sword. This was in contrast to what he had told them when he sent them on their mission, when he told them to go *"with no purse or bag or sandals."* To the reader's surprise, he learns that in fact the disciples already had two swords (Lk. 22:35-38). Later, at the Mount of Olives, when the disciples see Judas coming with a crowd, they ask him, *"Lord, shall we strike with the sword?"* (Lk. 22:49). They are still thinking in terms of the restoration of the fortunes of Israel. Is the instruction to sell their purses and buy swords to be taken at face value? Is not this also part of the ironic narrative? Is not this a way of ridiculing the notion that a revolution is on the march, and a revolution needs swords?

Luke's Jesus specifically discourages looking for signs of the coming of the Son of man. *"The kingdom of God is not coming with signs to be observed; nor will they say, 'Lo, here it is" or 'There'"* (Lk. 17:20-21). Luke further warns, *"Take heed that you are not led astray; for many will come in my name, saying, 'I am he!' and 'The time is at hand!' Do not go after them. And when you hear of wars and rumors of wars, do not be terrified; for this must first take place, but the end will not be at once"* (Lk. 21:8-9). Luke is quite aware that the time of wars and rumors of wars, during the 6 years of the Jewish war, had long past. While on the journey to Jerusalem, knowing that *"they supposed that the kingdom of God was to appear immediately"* (apparently upon his arrival to the city which he would enter accompanied by a crowd proclaiming him the son of David), Jesus diffuses the expectations telling parables about the need to assume responsibility for the good use of the talents God bestows on people (Lk. 19:11). Throughout, Luke discourages expectations of the coming vindication of Israel.

That everyone's expectations, including those of his disciples, centered on the establishment of the kingdom of David as the manifestation of the kingdom of God is found beginning with the testimonials pronounced at Jesus' birth. Simeon, the *"righteous and devout man looking for the consolation of Israel,"* declares himself ready to die in peace because he had seen God's *"salvation"* which had been prepared *"for the glory of thy people Israel"* (Lk. 2:32). And the prophetess Anna, who did not depart from the temple, worshiping with fasting and prayer night and day, *"spoke of him to all who were looking for the redemption of Jerusalem"* (Lk. 2:38). It is quite amazing that Luke reports that after the post-resurrection appearances, and after Jesus had been appearing to them for forty days during which he spoke to them about the kingdom of God, the disciples asked him, *"Lord, will you at this time restore the kingdom to Israel?"* (Acts. 1:6). Ingrained expectations for a son of David who will restore the fortunes of Israel, first expressed by Jeremiah and Ezekiel, die hard.

The only way to understand this persistent interest in the restoration of the kingdom is to recognize that it is at the center of Luke's ironic twist. Other manifestations of his irony are quite evident in his parable of the rich man and Lazarus (Lk. 16:19-31). The parable tells the reversal of fortunes between a very rich man who enjoyed all the pleasures of life while alive and Lazarus, a beggar who sat at the door of the rich man's house hoping to get something to eat without success. Both of them died, and while Lazarus went immediately to rest in Abraham's bosom, the rich man ended up *"in Hades, being in torment."* While in agony, the rich man could see Lazarus comfortable in Abraham's bosom. In this situation the rich man appeals to Abraham to have Lazarus *"dip the end of his finger in water and cool my tongue."* The absurdity of the request is inescapable. Any one in that situation would have requested a strong shower of cold water, not two drops at the tip of a finger. Abraham's response is that in the next life everyone experiences a reversal of fortunes and that their destinations are final. There are no bridges over the chasm that separates Hades from Heaven.

Learning of the impossibility for Lazarus to come to him in Hades, the rich man asks Abraham to send Lazarus to tell his five brothers to live in such a way as to avoid ending up in his place of torment. Abraham's response is to remind him that his brothers have Moses and the prophets: *"Let them hear them."* The rich man now asks for something that will surely catch their attention, *"If someone goes to them from the dead, they will repent."* This calls for the punchline that establishes where Luke's final authority is found. *"If they do not hear Moses and the prophets, neither will they be convinced if someone should rise from the dead."* These words go to the heart of the situation of the disciples who, facing the risen Christ, were still not convinced. It is only by having one's mind open to read Moses and the prophets correctly that things become clear. The rich man and his five brothers had been reading Moses and the prophets with close minds. Still, it is only reading them that one may come to terms with the necessity for the Son of man to suffer, be killed, and rise on the third day. As the Christ, he did not come to be the one who would restore the fortunes of Israel, but the one who *"came to seek and to save the lost"* (Lk. 19:10) by opening their minds to understand God's ways.

The ultimate irony in Luke is that reading Moses and the prophets, everyone thinks Jesus has come to establish the kingdom of Israel as an independent nation. As noticed already this expectation is affirmed repeatedly. Luke's accounts of the triumphal entry, of the expulsion of those who sold things at the temple and his prediction that enemies would not leave one of the temple's stones upon another is very superficial. The three take a total of ten verses (Lk. 19:37-46). Later, within a different setting, he comes back to the destruction of the temple with material from Mark (Lk. 21:5-28). What is noticeable in the earlier short account is that only Luke has Jesus identified by the crowds as *"the King who comes in the name of the Lord"* (Lk. 19:38), and weeping over Jerusalem, Jesus laments saying *"Would that even today you knew the things that make for peace! But now they are hidden from your eyes"* (Lk. 19:42) because their minds were closed. Rather than to create an army with swords with which to fight a war for political independence, he came for peace. It is then that *"the chief priests and the scribes and the principal men of the people sought to destroy him"* (Lk. 19:47). He had not come to fulfill their dreams.

The popular expectation that Jesus will restore the fortunes of Israel is the basis for the charges made against him before Pilate: *"We found this man perverting our nation, and forbidding us to give tribute to Caesar, and saying that he himself is Christ a king"* (Lk. 23:2). It would seem that this accusation is sound, given the way the story had been told. From the Roman point of view this certainly was a very serious charge, and from what can be learned from all the gospels it is clear that Jesus was crucified as a seditious person. When Pilate asked Jesus, *"Are you the king of the Jews?"* his answer was, *"You have said so"* (Lk. 23:3). How could Pilate then tell the Jews who brought Jesus to him, *"I find no crime in this man"* (Lk. 23:4). When the Jews insist on his being guilty, Pilate finds out that Jesus is a Galilean. This gives him a way out of his predicament; he sends Jesus to Herod, the ruler over Galilee. Luke, with his ironic touch, says that Herod was glad to have the opportunity to meet him because he hoped to see him perform a miracle. Herod, however, finds Jesus uncooperative and sends him back ridiculing the supposed king by dressing him in *"gorgeous apparel."* Now Pilate confirms his earlier determination, endorsed by Herod's lack of action against Jesus: *"I did not find this man guilty of any of your charges against him ... Behold, nothing deserving death has been done by him"* (Lk. 23:14-15). So, the disciples and the crowds consider him the one who would save Israel from the oppression of Rome, but Pilate, the local personification of Rome, does not agree with them. The chief men of Israel who also hoped for the restoration of Israel as an independent nation, at the trial act as loyalists who wish to prevent a seditious pretender to disrupt Roman rule over Judea. Pilate, on the other hand, insists on finding Jesus not guilty of the charges against him. This is nothing other than another of the magnificent ironies permeating the gospel of Luke.

LUKE'S ANCHORS FOR HIS STORY

As already noticed, Luke gives Moses, the prophets and the Psalms the final authority for determining the will of God. Paul sees the Law as the tool used by the evil rulers of the spheres between heaven and earth to bring about the death of sinners and, therefore, as such reveals God's wrath (Gal. 3:19; Rom. 4:15). Matthew sees the Law as commandments that must be obeyed as interpreted by Jesus (Mt. 5:21-48; 28:20), Luke sees the ultimate authority of the scriptures *in toto* as an institution that reveals God's mercy and invites to repentance because God has already forgiven all sins. As such the scriptures provide an eternal invitation to repent. That, of course, is at the heart of the message of the prophets. As preachers of this message both John the Baptist and Jesus in Luke are depicted as prophets that announce what needs to be done now. Contrasting the way in which his message is being rejected with the way in which Jonah's message was accepted, Jesus declares, *"The men of Nineveh will arise at the judgment with this generation and condemn it; for they repented at the preaching of Jonah"* (Lk. 11:32).

In Luke's telling, John the Baptist is not presented as an apocalyptic preacher. To predict that the future will set in motion the ax that will cut down all trees that do not produce good fruit is part of the prophetic announcement of dire consequences resulting from present conduct (Mt. 3:10; Lk, 3:9). After this, according to Matthew, John the Baptist said that the one coming after him has a winnowing fork in his hand, and he will clear his threshing floor and gather his wheat in the granary, but the chaff he will burn with unquenchable fire (Mt. 3:12), thus pointing to his main concern, the final judgment. Luke, on the other hand, states that when the multitudes heard about the ax that will cut down unproductive trees, they began to ask, *"What then shall we do?"* In other words they sought ways to prevent that dire ax from falling on them. Here John is a prophet using the future to bring about repentance, just as the ancient prophets had done. He is a prophet of God's forgiveness and mercy. The angel who announced his birth proclaimed,

"He will turn many of the sons of Israel to the Lord their God, ... turn the hearts of the fathers to the children, and the disobedient to the wisdom of the just, to make ready for the Lord a people prepared" (Lk. 1:16-17). At his birth, his father, now healed from his dumbness, praises God saying, *"And you, child, will be called the prophet of the Most High; for you will go before the Lord to prepare his ways, to give knowledge of salvation to his people in the forgiveness of sins, through the tender mercy of our God, when the day shall dawn upon us from on high to give light to those in darkness and in the shadow of death, to guide our feet into the way of peace"* (Lk. 1:76-79). The mission of the prophet is to have the people "turn" from their evil ways. Forgiveness and peace are the soil on which human life can flourish. As already noticed, *"repentance and the forgiveness of sins"* is what the Risen Lord tells his disciples to preach to the world (Lk. 24:47). These are the means for saving the lost, and according to Luke this was already the message of John the Baptist. He came proclaiming God's forgiveness, the need for repentance and the peace that it provides.

For Luke, the most important thing to know is that God is merciful. This is repeated at every possible stage in the story. Luke, using the same traditional material Matthew used, rather than to emphasize the need of perfection at the judgment, brings out the need to be merciful and forgiving. Three instances are clear evidence of this. One is the culmination of the Matthean antitheses with the demand, *"You, therefore, must be perfect, as your heavenly Father is perfect"* (Mt. 5:48). Working with the same materials from the Saying Source, Luke comes to the conclusion that God *"is kind to the ungrateful and the selfish. Be merciful, even as your Father is merciful"* (Lk. 6:36). My second reference is to the parable of the fig tree. The details are somewhat different in each telling, but the main point is the same. In Mark and Matthew the parable is turned into a story. In Mark the story takes place over two days, and it says that when Jesus came looking for figs it was not the season for figs. Finding no figs, Jesus cursed the tree and the following day the tree was already dried up. This adds a twinkle that is difficult to interpret. It makes Jesus' expectation to find figs and the cursing of the tree out of season unreasonable (Mk. 11:12-25). In Matthew the cursing of the unproductive fig tree brings about the immediate withering of the tree (Mt. 21:18-19). In all three accounts the setup is that either Jesus, or the man who had planted the tree, came to the fig tree looking for figs and found none. In the Lukan account two things stand out. Rather than looking for figs out of season, the man who had planted the fig tree came looking for figs when the tree was already three years old. Finding none, he instructs the orchard keeper to cut the tree down. This seems quite reasonable. The keeper, however, changes the owner's mind. He tells him, *"Let it alone, sir, this year also, till I dig about it and put on manure. And if it bears fruit next year, well and good; but if not, you can cut it down"* (Lk. 13:6:9). This is a parable of how divine mercy works. Luke works within the prophetic horizon, where repentance and a change of behavior make for the expected future punishment to be rescinded. Besides, God's mercy will be expressed in more tender mercies to bring about a good outcome.

My third example is the parable of the king who prepared a feast for the wedding of his son and sent his servants to say to those who had been invited, *"Behold, I have made ready my dinner, my oxen and my fat calves are killed, and everything is ready; come to the marriage feast"* (Mt. 22:4). Both Matthew and Luke emphasize that the king's purpose to have a palace full of guests celebrating his son's wedding is to be realized, but they develop two quite different themes out of this basic set up. Matthew tells that the king sent out servants several times and those who had been invited dismissed, laughed at them and even killed some of them. The reaction of the king was swift. *"He sent his troops and destroyed those murderers and burned their city."* Then, he sent his servants yet another time telling them, *"Go therefore to the thoroughfares, and invite to the marriage feast as many as you find. As a result, the servants brought in "all whom they found, both bad and good; so the wedding hall was filled with guests"* (Mt. 22:7-10). Matthew goes on to point out that when the king came to the hall where the guests were dining he found one who did not belong there, something not surprising given that the servants had brought in *"both bad and good."* The parable affirms Matthew's theme that not all those who accept the invitation and find themselves enjoying the wedding feast will be successful when the king shows up at the judgment. So the parable ends with a Matthean apophthegm, *"Many are called but few are chosen"* (Mt. 22:14).

Luke places the parable in the context of advice to not use one's invitation to a feast to seek a place of honor, and when one is giving a feast not to invite one's friends who would feel obliged to return the favor. In such cases one should invite those who are unable to repay him (Lk. 14:13-14). All this was said when on a Sabbath Jesus had been invited *"to dine at the house of a ruler who belonged to the Pharisees"* (Lk. 14:1). One of those also enjoying the dinner heard Jesus' comments about whom to invite to a feast and said, *"Blessed is he who shall eat bread in the kingdom of God!"* (Lk. 14:15). Jesus' response is to tell the parable of the *"one who once gave a great banquet and invited many."* When the banquet was ready, the man sent his servants to tell those who had been invited to come to the feast. In this telling of the parable, those invited gave excuses and did not go to the feast. They had more urgent matters to attend to. When the servants returned and told their master the excuses given by those who had been invited. The master was "angry," but his reaction was totally different to the one reported in the Matthean telling of the parable. He tells his servants, *"Go out quickly to the streets and lanes of the city, and bring in the poor, and maimed and blind and lame."* Having accomplished their task, the servants come back and tell the master, *"'Sir, what you commanded has been done, and still there is room.' And the master said to the servants, 'Go out to the highways and hedges, and compel people to come in, that my house may be filled. For I tell you, none of those men who were invited shall taste my banquet'"* (Lk. 14:21-24). Thus, while Matthew uses the parable to teach that not all those who are invited appreciate the invitation, and among those who come to the feast, there are those who will also end up in unquenchable fire, Luke uses the parable to teach that the initial invitees did not appreciate the invitation and considered other things more important, but the one who had prepared the banquet brought in the dispossessed, the marginalized, and all those who appreciated the invitation. The intention of the master of the house will be accomplished. His house will be full of people celebrating.

While the parables peculiar to Matthew are concerned with the finality of the impending judgment, all the peculiar parables of Luke have to do with demonstrations of God's mercy, and how when these take place there is great joy, both in heaven and on earth. The story of Jesus in Mark takes place in turbulent times. The skies over Galilee and Judea are dark with black clouds and occasional flashes of lightning. The story in Matthew takes place in the midst of controversies about the way to obey God in order to be found righteous at the judgment. Matthew finds the solution in a Jesus who demands perfection in the literal and the spiritual subjection to the Law. Luke tells the story of Jesus in an atmosphere of joy. For him the time that Jesus spent on earth was the time of a divine "visitation" (Lk. 1:68; 7:16; 19:44). The presence of the divine among the people was transformative for all time. Through it, God is offering abundant forgiveness to all repentant sinners. He not only is ready to receive them into the kingdom, he is out actively looking for them and rejoicing when finding them. Typical of the Lukan parables are the three found in chapter 15: the lost coin, the lost son and the lost sheep. The lost were found and finding them caused a feast to celebrate the felicitous outcome.

Finally, I would explore the significant role played by the temple in the Lukan narrative. Luke wrote at a time when the temple had been destroyed by the Romans some twenty-five years earlier. This presented him with a great dilemma. On the one hand, the temple is the central axis for the divine/human communication. It not only is a miniature representation of the cosmic structure; it is also the sign of the people's dwelling under divine protection. On account of this, Luke needs it and uses it as what gives the Jesus movement antiquity and respectability. On the other hand, he has to admit that it has been destroyed. He explicitly links its destruction to the rejection of Jesus by the leading men of Israel. He tells them that their enemies will come *"and will not leave one stone upon another ... because you did not know the time of your visitation"* (Lk. 19:44). Like Matthew (23:37-38), Luke also has Jesus lament, *"O Jerusalem, Jerusalem, killing the prophets and stoning those who are sent to you! How often would I have gathered your children together as a hen gathers her brood under her wings, and you would not! Behold, your house is forsaken"* (Lk. 13:34-35). The prophet who has come with a message of forgiveness and repentance, of course, is himself. Their preoccupation to see the signs that announce the coming of the kingdom, have rendered them incapable of seeing what is happening in their midst. Their concentration to observe and interpret the signs of what the future will bring had prevented them from noticing what was taking place before their eyes. As said above, he charges everyone, *"When you see a cloud rising in the west, you say at once, 'a shower is coming;' and lo it happens. And when you see the south wind blowing, you say, 'there will be scorching heat;' and it happens. You hypocrites! You know how to interpret the appearance of earth and sky, but why do you not know how to interpret the present time?"* (Lk. 12:54-56). Their failure to recognize the time of the divine visitation that has opened up a new opportunity for a fruitful relationship with God is a demonstration of their failure to understand what is happening before their eyes.

Faced with the fact that the temple is central but the temple has been destroyed, Luke blames the Jews' failure to recognize the salvific function of Jesus for its destruction, but not in the condemnatory Matthean way. He only refers to it in passing. He needs the temple as a major element for his apology for the rise of The Way for the benefit of Theophilus, obviously a Roman citizen of some standing. It is important for Luke to tell Theophilus that the Jesus movement, and his followers in The Way, was not a phenomenon initiated by nobodies coming from nowhere. Its origins and its development took place in the temple of Jerusalem, one of the most recognized monuments of the contemporary world.

Its antiquity was well known and it gave the nascent Christian movement credibility. To impress a well stationed Roman citizen, Luke's narrative starts and finishes at the temple. Jesus is taken to the temple for the purification of Mary and the baby *"according to the Law of Moses"* (Lk. 2:22). He is lost having a good conversation, and making a deep impression of his wisdom, at the temple with the wise men of Israel when he was twelve years old (Lk. 2:46-47). Once he arrives to Jerusalem, he is found every day teaching at the temple (Lk. 19:47; 21:37). After their initial encounter with the Risen Lord, he went with the disciples as far as Bethany, and the disciples "returned to Jerusalem with great joy, and were found continually in the temple blessing God" (Lk. 24:52-53). After the ascension, Luke reports that *"all who believed were together and had all things in common ... day by day attending the temple together and breaking bread in their homes"* (Acts 2:44, 46). Peter and John went to the temple at the hour of prayer, the ninth hour (Acts 3:1). The Sadducees were jealous of the apostles who were performing many signs and wonders, so they arrested them all and put them in the common prison. At night, however, an angel of the Lord opened the prison door, brought them out and said to them, *"Go and stand in the temple and speak to the people all the words of this Life"* (Acts 5:17-20). Luke tells us that Paul, while in Europe, had determined to be in Jerusalem on the day of Pentecost, therefore he did not stop at Ephesus while on his way (Acts. 20:16). Then, when he had arrived to Jerusalem, he purified himself and *"went into the temple, to give notice when the days of purification would be fulfilled and the offering presented"* (Acts. 21:26). It is hard to imagine, knowing what we read in Paul's own letters about the temple and temple purification (2 Cor. 3:7, 10; 1 Cor. 5:7), that Paul was eager to celebrate a Jewish feast at the temple and purified himself, together with the men who had accompanied him to Jerusalem, in order to be able to participate in temple worship. This is another example of Luke's agenda to rehabilitate Paul into the main stream of Christianity, since during his lifetime he had been relegated to the fringes and had been maligned by the "pillars" in Jerusalem.

The End of the Scroll

Paul himself says that he went to Jerusalem, in spite of his better judgment to stay away due to the animosity of Christian leaders in Jerusalem. He went only because he felt obliged to deliver personally the money he had been collecting from the believers in Asia Minor and Greece (Rom. 16:25-29). Luke, apparently, knows nothing about the collection Paul took to Jerusalem for the relief of the poor in that city. Making Moses, the prophets, the Psalms and the temple the anchors of Christianity, however, was essential to Luke. In the process he also makes clear that all Roman officials had recognized Jesus and the apostles as good men who were falsely accused by Jews who opposed The Way as a legitimate heir to the treasure house of Israel. He ends the account of the *Acts of the Apostles* with Paul preaching the gospel unhindered, with perfect freedom at the capital of the empire.

Unlike Matthew who structured his gospel on the five discourses of Jesus, Luke structured both of his volumes on the same mold: childhood, mission on a journey, trial. In both the childhood is a demonstration of divine favor and ends with the baptism of the Spirit. In both, the mission is accomplished on a journey, on the way, and in both the trial brings about the rejection of the ones who were first invited and the opening of the gates for a new people. Thus, the childhood of Jesus and of the disciples after the resurrection is spent with demonstrations of wisdom. Jesus is baptized with the Spirit descending as a dove on him, and the disciples are baptized with the Spirit appearing as flames of fire on their heads. Jesus fulfills his mission traveling in Galilee and on the long journey to Jerusalem. The church fulfills her mission with Stephen establishing the roots of Christianity in the history of Israel, Philip on the road to Gaza, and Paul and his journeys in Gentile lands. The trial of Jesus results in the crucifixion of the one who has been declared not guilty by Pilate and is confessed "innocent" by the Roman centurion in charge of the crucifixion (Lk. 23:47). The trial of Paul is left open, because Luke sees the future as open to the mercies of a merciful God.

Luke follows Mark in his general structure of the narrative. In the process he keeps some of the Markan references to the *Parousia* of the Son of man (e.g., Lk. 12:40; 21:27). Among them, he has Jesus say that some of those standing around him will be alive at the coming of the Son of man (Lk. 9:27), and that *"this generation"* will not pass away before the end comes (Lk. 21:32). But Luke, like Matthew, is very much aware that there has been a delay (Lk. 12:45). It will last *"until the times of the Gentiles are fulfilled"* (Lk. 21:24), thus leaving the future open, even more so than in Matthew. Luke does not give the *Parousia* the dramatic role it plays in Mark; neither does he give a dramatic role to the resurrection as in Matthew. For him, both the *Parousia* and the resurrection of the just are seen in a distant horizon, not in the immediate future.

Luke gives to the story of Jesus a satisfactory ending with his additions to the post-resurrection appearances. Mark left the disciples fearful in a world without Jesus; all they had was an empty tomb. His return to earth would take place momentarily. Matthew has Jesus appear to the disciples and commission them to preach and baptize. He corrects the impression left by Mark that the disciples were left expecting the immediate return of an absent Jesus. The Matthean Jesus promises the disciples that where two or three of them are gathered in his name he will be there with them always. During the delay they are not being left "desolate," as Jesus promises in John (Jn. 14:18). Still, his presence will not be quite full until the delayed "closing of the age" as the judgment takes place (Mt. 28:20).

Luke provides closure to the "visitation" of Jesus on earth. He has Jesus stay around with the disciples for forty days after the resurrection, during which time he teaches them about the right way to conceive the kingdom of God and preach repentance and forgiveness. He further instructs them that he will *"send the promise of my father upon you,"* therefore they should stay in Jerusalem until they are *"baptized with the Holy Spirit."* After saying this to them, *"as they were looking on, he was lifted up, and a cloud took him out of their sight"* (Lk. 24:47-49; Acts. 1:3-4, 9). The forty days of instruction by, and the ascension of, the Risen Christ changes the dynamics of the relationship of the resurrection to the *Parousia*. Christ is now in heaven, and the disciples are going to be empowered by the Holy Spirit to carry on the preaching of repentance that was initiated by John the Baptists and Jesus, so that the joy that prevailed during Jesus' visitation may continue among women and men. Luke envisions The Way to continue to extend throughout the world.

Luke ends his second volume with Paul awaiting trial before Nero, where his prospects for success are encouraging given that in his narration every time Jesus or a follower of Jesus appears before a Roman official, consistently they are declared not guilty of the charges against them. Awaiting trial, in the company of Jews who live at Rome, Paul is empowered to preach freely, without interference from either the Jews (Acts 28:21) or the Roman authorities. Thus, in his second volume Luke gives a sketch of how the commission of Jesus to the disciples to wait for the power of the Spirit so as to be ready for a long journey taking the gospel from Jerusalem and all Judea to Samaria and to the end of the earth has been achieved (Acts. 1:8). For Luke, the empowerment of the Spirit, which directed every turn in the life of Jesus and every advancement of The Way to the capital of the empire (Lk. 1:80; 2:27, 40; 4:1, 14, 18; 11:13; 23:46; Acts 2:4; 7:59; 8:29; 11:28; 18:5, 25; 19:21; 20:22; 21:4) takes away from the *Parousia* much of its dramatic impact.

Luke felt bound to acknowledge the apocalyptic origins of the Jesus movement, but he also knew that he needed to provide the basis for a movement that would proclaim the mercy of God to a world bereft of an appreciation of God's involvement with the world he had brought into existence. Thus, he gives the church the commission to proclaim the prophetic message of the abundant supply of forgiveness available from a merciful God. This, of course, calls for a celebration, and Luke's gospel is nothing if not a feast in which *"all the people rejoiced at all the glorious things that were done by him"* (Lk. 13:17) and *"the whole multitude of the disciples began to rejoice and praise God with a loud voice for all the mighty works that they had seen"* (Lk.19:37). Rejoicing in the knowledge that God had visited his people, gave the Christian movement a new vision of their role in the world, and with Luke' two volumes as its main text, mainstream Christianity pushed forward more sure of itself in the Roman Empire. The apocalyptic dramatic end, while still within view, no longer occupied center stage. In this way, Luke deactivated the anxieties about the delay, and gave closure to the movement that had centered on the historical Jesus. In the process, he opened the gate to the future for a movement commissioned to bring joy to the world.

To the Thessalonians II

The author of *To the Thessalonians II* had a very discrete purpose for his letter, which he announces after a rather long introductory paragraph which in the original Greek is composed of only two sentences. He wished to make clear what is at stake with *"the coming of our Lord Jesus Christ and our assembling to meet him"* (2 Th. 2:1). Before launching his argument about the coming of the Lord, he follows rhetorical convention and praises his audience to gain their attention. He commends his readers *"because [their] faith is growing abundantly, and the love of every one of you for one another is increasing."* Their *"steadfastness and faith in all [their] persecutions and in the affliction which [they] are enduring"* is something that the author is proud to have been able to report in *"the churches of God"* (2 Th. 1:3-4).

The author, however, is concerned about their commitment to the traditional Truth they had learned from him. His diagnosis of what is happening among them is framed in traditional apocalyptic terms. Following the primary apocalyptic agenda, right at the beginning he assures his readers that *"the righteous judgment of God"* is working. Later he reassures them, *"But the Lord is faithful; he will strengthen you and guard you from evil"* (2 Th. 3:3). Their suffering is God's way of making them *"worthy of the kingdom of God"* (2 Th. 1:5). He tells them that *"God deems it just to repay with affliction those who afflict you, and to grant rest with us to you who are afflicted, when the Lord Jesus is revealed from heaven with his mighty angels in flaming fire, inflicting vengeance upon those who do not obey the gospel of our Lord Jesus"* (2 Th. 1:6-8). In sum, the introduction points out that, while their faith and love have been increasing, their suffering is to be understood apocalyptically. God is demonstrating his righteousness not only by making them worthy citizens of the kingdom but also by avenging their present suffering on those who now afflict them. In the process he places at center stage the crucial role of the day of the Lord.

When the Lord comes, *"on that day,"* those who do not obey the gospel *"shall suffer the punishment of eternal destruction and exclusion from the presence of the Lord and from the glory of his might."* On the other hand, *"on that day"* he will come *"to be glorified in his saints (holy ones = angels), and to be marveled at in all who have believed, because our testimony to you was believed"* (2 Th. 1:9-10). That God's purpose is already at work in the readers means that we can trust God to achieve his ultimate purpose, the revelation of his retributive justice *"on that day."* His readers are being called by God now so that they *"may fulfil every good resolve and work of faith by his power"* (2 Th. 1:11). Thus, in his introduction the author has foreshadowed the theme of his letter.

The author had become aware that some among the members of the Christian community in Thessalonica believe, and are acting on the basis of, the notion that *"the day of the Lord has come."* Exactly how they came to this understanding of the present the author, apparently, does not know. He speculates that it could have been taught them *"either by spirit, or by word, or by letter purporting to be from us"* (2 Th. 2:2). The three possibilities he considers provide a picture of how in the early years new ideas gained currency in Christian communities. One possibility could have been that a prophet among them had convinced others that the day of the Lord had arrived. Prophecy was a gift of the Spirit that a member of the community could display for the benefit of all. This was not at all "speaking in tongues," but what today would be described as preaching. Another possibility could have been that a recognized apostle had visited them and personally convinced them that the Lord had come. That is, they had come to this understanding by the "word" of a traveling apostle. Finally, the author considers the possibility that a person they recognized as authoritative had sent them a letter teaching that. Interestingly, the author tells them to dismiss whatever such letter taught them, even if the letter claimed to have been written by "us."

To the Thessalonians I claims being written by "Paul, Silvanus, and Timothy" (1 Th. 1:1), and throughout refers to being written by "us." The author of *To the Thessalonians II* follows the pattern used in the first letter by referring to the one writing the letter as "us" or "we." In one instance, however, he slips and writes *"Do you not remember that when I was still with you I told you this?"* (2 Th. 2:5). All other reference to the time when he had preached the gospel to them say "we" (2 Th. 2:15; 3:7-12). In his final effort to establish the authority of his letter by claiming it is written by Paul, Silvanus and Timothy, the author uses the first person singular and over-reaches by giving a bogus identifying sign. He writes: *"I, Paul, write this greeting with my own hand. This is the mark of every letter of mine"* (2 Th. 3:17). It would seem that this was his way of making clear that a letter lacking his signature and teaching that the Lord had already come could not possibly be one written by him. The problem is that not all authentic letters of Paul have his personal signature at the end, as the author claims to be the case. The author does copy phrases and rhetorical devices used by Paul, but certainly was not Paul. It may be noticed also that in *To the Corinthians II* Paul says that those who preached the gospel in Corinth were *"Silvanus and Timothy and I"* (2 Cor. 1:19). That the three worked as a team was, therefore, well known, and the pseudonymous author did his best to leave the impression that his letter had been written by this triumvirate. In the process he shows himself to be aware that others were also writing letters claiming the triumvirate as their author, and trying to distinguish his from them by given as a mark of authenticity something that some letters of Paul lack.

THE DAY OF THE LORD HAS NOT COME YET

When Paul wrote *To the Thessalonians I*, he made clear that he expected his readers, himself and his associates to be alive at the coming of the Lord. His purpose for writing was to point out that the death of some members of the community was not a cause for despair, and that returning to their former licentious lives would prevent them from being *"always with the Lord"* at the *Parousia* (1 Th. 4:13-17). Paul did consider that the apocalyptic day of the Lord had taken place at the death and the resurrection of Christ. His resurrection had established a new creation, and those who through baptism participated in his death and resurrection lived in "a new creation" (Rom. 6:5-7; 2 Cor. 5:17). This was a peculiar understanding of the Day of the Lord. It may have been the reason libertines came to think that at their baptism they had been resurrected with Christ and, therefore, were now free to live as they pleased. Arguing against their understanding that on account of their baptism they already had been raised with Christ and that, therefore, their life "in the flesh" was of no account, Paul insisted that the resurrection does not take place at baptism. The resurrection is going to affect "the dead" who were buried in bodies of flesh and will be raised in spirit bodies (1 Cor. 15:12-50). Baptism did not take them out of their bodies of flesh. As Christians they would be living both in the flesh and in the Spirit until their ultimate resurrection at the *Parousia*.

The ones being told by the author of *To the Thessalonians II* that the day of the Lord had not come yet had abandoned the normal responsibilities of those living on earth. They lived in *"idleness"* and *"having pleasure in unrighteousness"* because the day of the Lord had come (2 Th. 3:6; 2:12). Exactly how they drew the connection between the coming of the day of the Lord and their search for pleasure in unrighteousness the author does not say. It is quite possible that they were spiritual descendants of the Corinthian libertines. But the author's argument against their understanding of the present is quite different from Paul's argument against the Corinthian libertines. Paul argued that the resurrection deals with those who, like Christ, had been buried. He made a distinction between the prophetic announcements of The Day of the Lord, when God would intervene in history and reveal his righteousness, and the *Parousia* of Christ, when God would regain total control over his creation. The author of *To the Thessalonians II* argues that the day of the Lord, that is to say the *Parousia*, has not come yet because what needs to happen before "that day" has not yet happened.

The author builds his argument on an apocalyptic scenario that apparently had become adopted by those who, with the passage of time, came to constitute the Christian mainstream. Of course, at the time of Paul, there was no such thing as a Christian mainstream. Christianity was then characterized by its diversity. The apocalyptic trajectory considered the right one by the author, whether it was actually one agreed upon by all Christians at the time is doubtful, consists of a well marked sequence of events which he considers to be the truth that must be believed (2 Th. 2:10, 12). Paul, did not have a sequence of historical events that would anticipate the *Parousia* in mind, even though he was sure that "the appointed time has grown very short" (1 Cor. 7:29). It is impossible to imagine that he would consider any apocalyptic trajectory as the truth that must be believed (2 Th. 2:10-11).

According to the author of *To the Thessalonians II*, "*The mystery of lawlessness is already at work*" (2 Th. 2:7). Obviously, they were living at a time when lawlessness prevailed. That the author considers this to be a "mystery" only means that he sees himself and his readers to be the privileged elect ones who already know what is not known by the general public. We also know, the author claims, "*that the suffering which you are now experiencing is caused by the present prevalence of lawlessness. God, of course, is quite aware of what is going on.*" This means that those afflicting you now will "*suffer the punishment of eternal destruction ... when he comes on that day*" (2 Th. 1: 9-10). The freedom with which lawlessness now works is, as it were, under cover because "*he who now restrains it will do so until he is out of the way*" (2 Th. 2:7). In other words, the present prevalence of lawlessness is now a mystery because the power behind this lawlessness is at present unknown due to the activity of one "who now restrains" its revelation. This means that, rather than living now on the day of the Lord, as you are being told, we are living when "the one who now restrains" prevents people in general to identify the power that enables the free operation of lawlessness.

It will come a time, however, when the one who restrains will be taken out of the way. The *"man of lawlessness,"* the *"son of perdition"* will then *"be revealed"* (2 Th. 2:3). This will happen *"in his time"* (2 Th. 2:6), that is in God's predetermined time. The author does not make known, either expressly or metaphorically, the identity of the one who is now preventing the revelation (the *apokalypsis*) of the man of lawlessness who is responsible for the preponderance of lawlessness in the world. It is notable that he describes the revelation of the man of lawlessness with the word used for that of the Lord Jesus. Each of them will have an *apokalypsis,* and they will occur in rapid succession over a short period of time. The author, however, reminds his readers that they should remember *"that when I was still with you I told you this. And you know what is restraining him now"* (2 Th. 2:5-6). In other words, they know who is behind the prevailing lawlessness. Because the power behind the pervasive lawlessness is kept hidden by the one preventing its disclosure, it is impossible to counteract the active lawlessness all around. When he preached the gospel to them he told them about "the mystery" of lawlessness, that is, the identity of the power preventing the identification of the man of lawlessness. They are in possession of "the mystery." They know why lawlessness is now prevalent and difficult to explain. Since they know this, they should not believe anyone who says that the day of the Lord has come.

Besides not identifying in his letter "he who now restrains" the revelation of the man of lawlessness because they are already in on the mystery, the author does not make clear whether he considers "he who now restrains" to be an agent of God, or one in opposition to God. This is, however, a moot question when in the author's symbolic universe everything happens according to God's will. The one who restrains will be taken "out of the way" at God's appointed time. Thus, in the author's apocalyptic sequence of events, the present rule of lawlessness will culminate with the revelation of the man of lawlessness causing it, which will take place when the one preventing his revelation is removed. At his *apokalypsis*, the man of lawlessness will show himself fully, and the author gives an account of what he will do: *"he opposes and exalts himself against every so-called god or object of worship, so that he takes his seat in the temple of God, proclaiming himself to be God"* (2 Th. 2:4). The description is, obviously, paradigmatic. It is based on the description of Antiochus IV as one who *"shall do according to his will; he shall exalt himself and magnify himself above every god, and shall speak astonishing things against the God of gods"* (Dan. 11:36). That he shall establish himself in the temple is a way of saying that he will usurp for himself divine powers, as described in reference to the king of Tyre (Ezek. 28:1-10), the king of Babylon (Is. 14:4-20) and Nero (Syb. Or. 5:33). There is no doubt that he is a surrogate of Satan, here described by two Hebraic idioms used to describe either a person's main characteristic or what he is worthy of. When the restraining one is removed people will see the "man of lawlessness," meaning characterized by his disregard for the divine ordering of things according to the Law, and the "son of perdition," that is, worthy of perdition, or destruction.

For the author of this letter, that the man of lawlessness has not yet been revealed, and that his usurpation of divine powers and his opposition to all objects of worship has not yet taken place, is the obvious proof that the day of the Lord has not come yet. Therefore, he writes, *"Let no one deceive you in any way; for that day will not come, unless the rebellion comes first, and the man of lawlessness is revealed"* (2 Th. 2:3). Those saying that the day of the Lord has come are deceivers. He describes *"the coming of the lawless one by the activity of Satan will be with all power and with pretended signs and wonders, and with all wicked deceptions for those who are to perish, because they refused to love the truth and so be saved"* (2 Th. 2:9-10).

Here the man of lawlessness is described as a surrogate of Satan, but Satan is not otherwise a protagonist in the apocalyptic scenario. In *Revelation*, Satan as well as his surrogate are main protagonist identified with mythological identities as the dragon and the beast from the sea (Rev. 13:1-2, 14).

Like in all apocalyptic descriptions of Satan and his surrogates on earth, the lawless one works through deceptions carried on by *"pretended signs and wonders."* The deceptions, however, have been effective on those who, having at first accepted the truth, *"refuse to love the truth and so be saved."* They are the fulfillment of the prophecy that *"because wickedness is multiplied, most men's love will draw cold"* (Mt. 24:12). In other words, for some reason the love of the truth of some members of the Christian community at Thessalonica, that had been strong when it had been preached to them, has grown cold, and now *"they refuse to love the truth."* Since everything in the author's symbolic universe takes place according to God's will, he then explains, *"Therefore God sends upon them a strong delusion, to make them believe what is false"* (2 Th. 2:11). Apocalyptic authors are characterized by their very limited understanding of human will power.

When the man of lawlessness has been revealed, and as a surrogate of Satan he is deceiving people to believe that the day of the Lord has come, then, only then, will the *apokalypsis* of the Lord Jesus take place. The Lord will slay him with the breath of his mouth and destroy him by *"the epiphany of his Parousia"* (2 Th. 2:8, my translation). The public appearance of the Lord "on that day" will be the epiphany of a warrior. The author describes the *apokalypsis* of the Lord Jesus saying that *"when the Lord Jesus is revealed from heaven with his mighty angels in flaming fire, inflicting vengeance upon those who do not know God and upon those who do not obey the gospel of our Lord Jesus, they shall suffer the punishment of eternal destruction and exclusion from the presence of the Lord and from the glory of his might"* (2 Th. 1:7-9). On that day he *"will slay him (the lawless one) with the breath of his mouth and destroy him by his appearing* (epiphaneia) *and his coming* (parousia)*"* (2 Th. 2:8, the Greek original reads, "the epiphany of his public appearance). The description echoes Isaiah's vision of God's Day of Judgment. *"With righteousness he shall judge the poor, and decide with equity for the meek of the earth; and he shall smite the earth with the rod of his mouth, and with the breath of his lips he shall slay the wicked"* (Is. 11:4). Similar references to God's "flaming breath" are found in 4 Ezra 13:3, 8, 10-11; Pss. Sol. 17:23-24, 34. In this case, mythological beasts serve as models for the revelation of the Lord Jesus Christ.

Paul taught that after his resurrection Christ has been subjecting the powers of evil that have dominion over the world. When he has accomplished this task, he would present those under his dominion to God so that then everything is back under God's dominion. Once this was the case, the *Parousia* would take place. The author of *To the Thessalonians II* says that at the *Parousia* Christ will slay the man of lawlessness with his flaming breath. He does not tell what happens to Satan, the one whose power enabled the performance of pretended signs and wonders that deceive those whose love of the truth has grown cold. He ends his argument against those who hold that the day of the Lord has come telling his readers to *"stand firm and hold on to the traditions which you were taught by us, either by word of mouth or by letter"* (2 Th. 2:15). They are already those who *"God chose ... from the beginning to be saved through sanctification by the Spirit and belief in the truth"* (2 Th. 2:13). They should not, therefore, throw away their election by becoming *"quickly shaken in mind or excited"* by those who teach that the day of the Lord has come (2 Th. 2:2). Apocalyptic enthusiasm, the letter *To the Thessalonians II* reveals, took many shapes among the early Christians.

THE AUTHOR'S *COMMANDMENT*

Chapter 3 of *To the Thessalonians II* can be understood to be the introduction of a new topic by the author, or a fragment from a different letter that has been attached to the letter by the compiler of the Pauline correspondence at the beginning of the second century C.E. The reason for considering it a part of a different letter is that chapter 2 has a typical conclusion. *"Now may our Lord Jesus Christ himself, and God our Father, who loved us and gave us eternal comfort and good hope through grace, comfort your hearts and establish them in every good work and word"* (2 Th. 2:16). There is no doubt that this is a rather liturgical way to end a letter.

Chapter 3 begins with the typical introduction that asks for prayers on behalf of the author and offers a prayer on behalf of the audience. *"Pray for us, that the word of the Lord may speed on and triumph, as it did among you, and that we may be delivered from wicked and evil men; for not all have faith"* (2 Th. 3:1-2). *"May the Lord direct your hearts to the love of God and to the steadfastness of Christ"* (2 Th. 3:5, the original Greek reads *"the patient endurance of Christ"*). Besides, in chapter two the author says *"we beg you, brethren."* His tone reflects his desire to persuade rather than to impose. In chapter 3, on the other hand, he writes, *"we have confidence in the Lord about you, that you are doing and will do the things which we command"* (2 Th. 3:4). Here he is not persuading but demanding a specific course of action. He uses the expression "we command" four times in this short chapter.

Having considered the possibility that chapter 3 is a separate fragment, I think that the way in which the chapter starts, saying "finally," is the author's way of changing the subject from whether or not the day of the Lord has come to what should be the conduct of those who are still waiting for the day of the Lord. His affirmation *"but the Lord is faithful"* (2 Th. 3:3) is his way of connecting the content of his final words to the content of his main topic. Both his explanation of why the day of the Lord has not come yet and of the reason for having commanded that *"If anyone will not work, let him not eat"* (2 Th. 3:10) are based on the certainty that God's retributive justice works.

The chapter addresses what to do with those who, believing that the day of the Lord has come, have ceased from taking care of their needs by holding a job. The author has learned that *"some of [them]"* are *"living in idleness, mere busybodies, not doing any work"*

(2 Th. 3:11). Rather than being a way of demonstrating faith in the presence of the Lord among them, their conduct reveals their desire to take advantage of the goodwill of their fellow believers. The author considers this to be a way to have *"pleasure in unrighteousness."* Therefore, he writes, *"Now we command you, brethren, in the name of our Lord Jesus Christ, that you keep away from any brother who is living in idleness and not according to the tradition that you received from us"* (2 Th. 3:6). The tradition which the author upholds as the truth teaches that the coming of the Day of the Lord will not be soon, contrary to what Paul said in *To the Thessalonians I*. Christians will be on earth for some time still, at times experiencing sufferings which they must patiently endure. During this time, obviously, they need to work in order to provide for themselves and their families.

He reminds his readers that they *"know how you ought to imitate us; we were not idle when we were with you, we did not eat any one's bread without paying, but with toil and labor we worked night and day, that we might not burden any of you. It was not because we have not that right, but to give you in our conduct an example to imitate"* (2 Th. 3:7-8). Here he is referring quite literally to Paul's claim that as an apostle he had some privileges, such as the companionship of a wife and the supply of food and board but he did not take advantage of these rights, as other apostles considered by him illegitimate did (1 Cor. 9:3-12). To those living in idleness, the author commands *"to do their work in quietness and to earn their own living. Brethren, do not be weary in well-doing"* (2 Th. 3:12-13).

The strong terms with which he commands *"to keep away from any brother who is living in idleness"* is somewhat surprising after he had only begged them not to allow their minds to be shaken and become excited thinking that the day of the Lord had come. He reinforces his command writing, *"If anyone refuses to obey what we say in this letter, note that man, and have nothing to do with him, that he may be ashamed"* (2 Th. 3:14). Apparently this strong language is his way to show that love at times must be tough. He, however, qualifies his command saying, *"Do not look on him as an enemy, but warn him as a brother"* (2 Th. 3:15). He had earlier identified those living in idleness, from whom they were to keep away, as brothers.

The letter *To the Thessalonians II* reflects a Christianity that is beginning to conform the gospel to the Truth of a tradition. The author insists *"stand firm and hold to the traditions which you were taught by us"* (2 Th. 2:15). Those living in idleness are not acting *"in accord with the tradition that you received from us"* (2 Th. 3:6). He tells them that their faith will be effective at the day of the Lord *"because our testimony to you was believed"* (2 Th. 1:10). Three times he refers to what he taught them as the truth (2 Th. 2:10, 12, 13). The issue that became problematic at the end of the first century was the delay of the *Parousia*, as reflected in *According to Matthew, According to Luke, To the Hebrews* and *Second Peter*. The author of *To the Thessalonians II* apparently faced a different problem. Rather than having to account for a delay, he found himself needing to deny that the *Parousia* had already happened. Some, apparently, had found the way to solve the problem of the delay by claiming that the day of the Lord had come. There is no doubt that early Christianity was an apocalyptic movement, and efforts to get people excited about the *Parousia* when its' happening was not taking place were at times abused.

REVELATION

The book *Revelation* gets its name from the description given by its author in the introduction: *"The revelation of Jesus Christ, which God gave him to show to his servants what must soon take place; and he made it known by sending his angel to his servant John"* (Rev. 1:1). Since the Greek word used by the author is *apokalypsis*, some modern versions call the book *The Apocalypse*, and books that have a similar content are described as "apocalyptic." In our own time, the word has become a staple in popular culture and refers to stories of wars between cosmic forces of good and evil which, given our expanded understanding of the galactic world receive amazing pictorial power for the entertainment of the populace that has developed – oddly enough – a strong taste for cosmic warfare.

In its original use by the author of *Revelation*, *apokalypsis* means just what the English word says, the uncovering of something that had been covered, hidden, unknown. The revelation of what had been hidden has been made possible by a divine agent who revealed it to a chosen human agent. He is now in possession of a revealed "mystery," a piece of information that he will make available only to the chosen few, but will remain hidden to the public at large. The human agent of such important revelation feels that he must assure his readers that what he is writing has a divine origin; it is not something he has fabricated. As we saw in the case of the books of *Daniel* and *First Enoch*, their authors authenticated the divine origin of what they were revealing to the chosen few by claiming to be ancient worthies who, on account of their unusual divine connections, could tell what was the will of God. These ancient worthies had "predicted" the past up to the time when the author was giving advice as to what was expected of them in the present. That what an ancient worthy had "predicted" did take place guaranteed that what the author was predicting to his contemporaries about the immediate future would also take place. To explain how it happened that the ancient author's writing had not been known until now, the real author said that the ancient author had been told to seal the book, because it was not intended for his time (Dan. 12:4, 9).

What distinguishes the book of *Revelation* from other apocalyptic texts is that the author gives his real name with his present geographical location and does not authenticate his revelation by recourse to *vaticinia ex eventu*. He is John, the prophet, now on the isle of Patmos on account of his faithfulness to Jesus Christ (Rev. 1:9). What he is writing is true because he can trace its origin: it originated with God himself who gave it to Jesus Christ, who testifies to the divine origin. Christ has made known the information he received from God by sending his angel to his servant John, who is now, by writing the revelation down and sending it to the seven churches in Asia, bearing *"witness to the word of God and to the testimony of Jesus Christ."* For John, the testimony of Jesus is the key element in the transmission of the "mystery" from God to the elect in the seven churches. The angel and he himself were only servants of Christ. His testimony is what authenticates that God is the source of what he is now revealing. Christ's mediating "testimony" makes *vaticinia ex eventu* unnecessary.

The specific content of the revelation is *"what soon must take place"* (Rev. 1:1-2). John predicts for the benefit of his contemporaries what is going to take place soon, just as the authors of *First Enoch* and *Daniel* had done, but they pretended that their books had been written long ago and had been sealed until their time. Unlike the pseudonymous authors who were told to seal their books because what they reveal would happen later, John is told, *"Do not seal up the words of the prophecy of this book, for the time is near"* (Rev. 22:10).

The End of the Scroll 253

Among the early Christians, the author of *Revelation* was identified as John the theologian. This was to distinguish him from John the Elder (author of the letters), and John the disciple of Jesus, to whom the fourth gospel, written anonymously, was ascribed in the second century. I will identify him as John the prophet.

THE CONTENT AND GENRE OF REVELATION

The introduction tells us that John is writing about a divinely revealed mystery which he was told to communicate to the elect in seven churches. That is the hallmark of an apocalyptic book. On this basis, John's *Revelation* has been categorized not only as an apocalyptic book, but as the biblical apocalyptic book *par excellence*. On account of its apocalyptic character many early Christians did not considered it valuable, and did not include it in the list of books fit to be read at church services for the edification of the faithful. These lists were independently compiled by local bishops to guide the faithful in their territories. For some time it was not certain whether *Revelation* would be included in the list which became standard toward the end of the fourth century. Even after the Easter Letter of Athanasius (367 C.E.), which happened to list the twenty seven books now constituting the canon of the New Testament and which some modern authors consider to have been determinative, lists from other bishops did not include *Revelation*. Centuries later, Martin Luther wrote, *"my spirit cannot accommodate itself to this book. For me this is reason enough not to think highly of it: Christ is neither taught nor known in it"* (*Prefaces to the New Testament,* 1522 edition). On the other hand, throughout Christian history there have been times when apocalyptic enthusiasm was quite strong in different Christian groups, and for them *Revelation* became the canon within the canon.

With the passage of time it has become more and more obvious that what the book claimed would *"soon take place"* (Rev. 1:1; 22:6) has not yet happened. Apocalyptic enthusiasts, however, have not been deterred by this. They read the book using the hermeneutical key used by the writers of apocalyptic books. This key has two presuppositions:1) what the prophets wrote was written for "the time of the end," and 2) we are living in "the time of the end." What Daniel did primarily with *Ezekiel* and *Zechariah*, the Synoptic authors did with *Daniel*, the Covenanters of Qumran did with *Habakkuk*, John of Patmos did with *Ezekiel, Zechariah, First Enoch* and *Daniel* and the post-exilic chapters of *Isaiah*, Christian apocalyptic enthusiasts have repeatedly done through the centuries by interpreting *Daniel* and *Revelation* as allegories of history that culminate at their own time. According to them, it is for *our* generation that Christ says, *"Behold I am coming soon"* (Rev. 3:11; 16:15; 22:7, 12). These days reading *Daniel* and *Revelation* as allegories of historical events taking place in the present is very popular in many Christian communities.

Confronted with the alternatives of admitting that John's prediction of Christ's soon coming was not fulfilled, or recognizing that reading the book as if it were describing allegorically events in the distant future whose identification is capricious, new ways of reading the book have been proposed. According to one, the contents of the book do not reveal "what will soon take place." Pace Martin Luther, they reveal Jesus Christ. According to another, the revelation is about an ongoing "cosmic conflict." Those arguing that Christ is the subject of what is being revealed absolutize the first phrase in the book, "The revelation of Jesus Christ," and overlook what the rest of the introductory sentence says. As the text makes clear, "of Jesus Christ" refers to his agency in the transmission of God's message, not to the content of the revelation. Those arguing that the content of the revelation is the cosmic conflict of the ages between Christ and Satan overlook that throughout the book Christ is declared to have already conquered Satan. The Lamb, identified as the only one worthy to open the scroll with seven seals, is *"the Lion of the tribe of Judah, the Root of David, who has conquered"* (Rev. 5:5), and, as a result of his having conquered, he already sits with his father in his father's throne (Rev. 3:21). Besides, the first identification of Jesus Christ says that he is *"the faithful witness, the first born of the dead, and the ruler of kings on earth"* (Rev. 1:5). To leave no doubt about it, Christ identifies himself as *"the first and the last, and the living one; I died, and behold I am alive for evermore, and I have the keys of Death and Hades"* (Rev. 1:17-18). The one place where it is said that a *"war arose in heaven,"* the outcome is specifically stated: *"the dragon and his angels fought, but they were defeated"* (Rev. 12:7-8). In other words, John repeatedly affirms that Christ has already conquered Satan and rules over the cosmos, including Hades. A book that begins affirming and throughout specifies who was defeated and who rules over the cosmos cannot be about a cosmic conflict between Christ and Satan. The book does describe an ongoing drama, but it is not about a conflict whose outcome is already known.

Lately it has been argued that the book is not apocalyptic but prophetic. This view is primarily based on what is missing. As already noticed, it is unusual for the author of an apocalypse not to use a pseudonym, and to refrain from "predicting" past events. Besides, John wrote, *"Blessed is he who reads aloud the words of the prophecy, and blessed are those who hear, and who keep what is written therein"* (Rev. 1:3). Later, he is told *"to prophesy again"* (Rev. 10:11), and when at the end of the book Jesus speaks directly to those hearing the reading aloud of the book in the churches, he says, *"Behold I am coming soon. Blessed is he who keeps the words of the prophecy of this book"* (Rev. 22:7). Then he tells John, *"Do not seal up the words of the prophecy of this book, for the time is near"* (Rev. 22:10). The argument is that the author's characterization of the book as prophecy should be taken seriously.

I would add that, besides the characterization of the contents as prophecy, the first part of the book, containing the letters to the seven churches of Asia: Ephesus, Smyrna, Pergamum, Thyatira, Sardis, Philadelphia and Laodicea, is prophetic in nature. As I explained in the introduction, the prophets gave an account of what is going on, and predicted a disastrous outcome if the people continued on their present course. On the other hand, if they changed course, turned around, repented from their ways, God would bring about blessings as a reward. The message to the churches is, *"Those whom I love, I reprove and chasten, so be zealous and repent"* (Rev. 3:19). In other words, God is taking notice of what is going on and God's advice is to change course; repentance is in order. The predicted outcome of your present behavior is not fixed. The future is open. On the other hand, the letters also recognize that many are patiently enduring significant difficulties (Rev. 2:19, 25-26; 3:10), the typical apocalyptic situation.

Though the letters have specific things to say to each church, they were to be read in all of them. The letters report what the spirit says "to the churches" (Rev. 2:17); in that, they are prophetic. Besides, Jesus himself at the end of the book says, *"I Jesus have sent my angel to you with this testimony for the churches"* (Rev. 22:16). Thus linking the message to all the churches is valuable information to those reading the whole book. This means that Jesus' testimony authenticating the message coming from God serves to integrate the letters to the seven churches to the apocalyptic body of the book. Faithful servants of Jesus must keep this word of God in order to receive their just reward. This *"testimony of Jesus"* is what his servants must *"hold on"* to, and is specifically described as *"the spirit of prophecy"* (Rev. 19:10). It was agreed by all Christians that those who prophesy are moved by the authority of Jesus who acts through the Spirit. Therefore, identifying the authenticating testimony of Jesus with the spirit of prophecy now active among the readers also serves to identify the book as prophecy, and John at Patmos as one who was there *"on account of the word of God and the testimony of Jesus,"* and who *"in the Spirit"* received the revelation (Rev. 1:9-10). The advice to repent, which appears in the seven letters, is the typical prophetic advice. John justifies the final destruction of those who bear the mark of the beast by pointing out that, even after they had seen the punishment received by others, *"they did not repent"* (Rev. 9:20-21; 16:9,11). John lists the prophets as targeted victims of the anger of the dragon and the beast, as a result of which he finds himself now in Patmos. Since he is a prophet who *"was in the Spirit,"* what he wrote is a prophecy.

Prophecy, however, must be understood in the context of early Christianity, not in the way it is understood now. Anyone who spoke a word of the Lord at a community worship service was a prophet. Paul considered prophecy as a valued gift of the Spirit, certainly above speaking in tongues, since prophecy was for the edification of the faithful (1 Cor. 12:4-11). Prophecy was then what today would be designated as the inspired preaching that provides incentives for the faithful to live "according to the Spirit." As said in the introduction, the prophets of ancient Israel "spoke for" God; they did not "speak before" it happened. With the appearance of the apocalyptic imagination, and the need for an "apology" of the justice and the power of God based on the resurrection of the dead, predicting the future became a necessity. As a result, a predetermined understanding of history took the horizon, and ancient myths of creation were given new currency.

In antiquity, of course, no distinction was made between prophetic and apocalyptic texts. Distinguishing apocalyptic literature as a separate genre is a helpful classification for our own understanding of the books that are found in the Bible. But, as I explained in the Introduction, both prophetic and apocalyptic literature was written to give advice to the contemporaries of their authors. The criteria for distinguishing one from the other are heuristic tools for modern readers. As I also indicated earlier, there is no agreement among modern scholars as to which are the criteria with which to identify the genre. As my survey of the apocalyptic texts has been demonstrating, each one of these texts travels a peculiar trajectory in which the modern criteria for prophetic and apocalyptic are not always appropriate.

Considering Revelation's symbolic universe, one must also notice the way in which John nuances the doctrine of the Fall, which I have identified as a distinguishing mark of apocalypticism. In previous chapters we have noticed how different biblical authors give different accounts of the origin of evil within the world. Thinking in purely nationalistic terms, the prophets see the worship of the golden calf at Sinai as the sin that marked the people of Israel as a rebellious people. *First Enoch* sees the coming down of angels to marry the daughters of men as the entrance of sin in the world. Paul gives the Fall cosmic significance, and ties it to the sin of Adam and Eve in the garden. It brought about the subjugation of the whole of creation to the dominion of Satan. According to him, Satan is now the "god of this world." John, the prophet, sees Satan as a powerful actor in the drama of a sinful humanity. For him, however, Satan is not at all the "god of this world." In heaven, as with *Zechariah* and *Job*, he was the accuser of those who were considered righteous. In *Zechariah*, he accuses Josiah of being unworthy of the high priesthood (Zech. 3:1). In *Job*, he questions the motives of Job's goodness at the heavenly council. In *Revelation*, before he was thrown down from heaven, he was day and night accusing the martyrs before God (Rev. 12:10). That is the role of Satan in the Old Testament. As a Christian, John declares that Jesus conquered Satan because after having been dead he is now alive forevermore, and the martyrs in heaven *"have conquered him by the blood of the Lamb and by the word of their testimony"* (Rev. 12:11). Having been thrown down to earth, he sought to devour the male child about to be born from *"the woman clothed with the sun, with the moon under her feet, and on her head a crown of twelve stars"* (Rev. 12:1-2). At this he was unsuccessful; *"The child was caught up to God and to his throne"* (Rev. 12:5). Clearly, this refers to the incarnation, Christ's triumph over death and his enthronement in heaven. On earth, Satan's persecution of the woman also proved unsuccessful because she was given the means to escape to a safe place prepared for her by God (Rev. 12:6). It is at this junction that John writes, *"Now war arose in heaven. Michael and his angels fighting against the dragon; and the dragon and his angels fought, but they were defeated and there was no longer any place for them in heaven"* Rev. 12:7-8. The dragon who had been thrown down from heaven and had been defeated on earth, now with even greater anger, went after *"the rest of her offspring, on those who keep the commandments of God and bear testimony to Jesus"* (Rev. 12:17). The narration does not specify the outcome of this effort. Certainly, the saints who refused to worship the beast and its image suffered martyrdom (Rev. 13:2). They, however, are to be raised back to life in the first resurrection (Rev. 20:4-6). The conflict in *Revelation* is not a cosmic conflict. It cannot be because Satan has no longer any place in heaven. It is a struggle between a defeated dragon who uses surrogates, and men who must decide whom to worship. There is never a question as to who sits on the throne and reigns over the whole of creation. The drama in the book is about the struggle going on in the minds of those who are being asked to worship the beast and its image. The revelation of the mystery, the knowledge that Satan is a defeated warrior, should give the elect ammunition with which to conquer. In the process of depicting Satan as a defeated foe, the Fall in *Revelation* is not conceived as cosmic. It only allows Satan to use surrogates in his efforts to deceive the elect. His role is no longer that of an accuser in heaven, but that of a deceiver on earth.

The central icon in *Revelation* is the throne of God, John refers to it thirty seven times. And both Almighty God and the Lamb that was slain and lives forever sit upon it. That the one sitting on the throne is in total control of the universe is reflected in descriptions of the activities of agents of Satan on earth. The kings who worked for the beast and at first supported the harlot (Rev. 17:15, cp. 17:1) eventually changed their minds, turned against the harlot and destroyed her by devouring her flesh and burning her up with fire. They did this because *"God has put it into their hearts to carry out his purpose by being of one mind and giving over their royal power to the beast, until the words of God shall be fulfilled"* (Rev. 17:17). The destruction of the harlot by kings who had "committed fornication" with her (Rev. 17:2) is, in other words, divinely ordained. Describing the beast that rose out of the sea and received authority from the dragon, John says that it *"was given a mouth uttering haughty and blasphemous words, and was allowed to exercise authority for forty two months"* Rev. 13:5). Who gave and who allowed (the Greek original uses the same verb both times) is none other than God. Then John saw a second beast which rose out of the earth. It exercised all the authority of the first beast which rose out of the sea and has characteristics like those of the fourth beast in *Daniel* (7:7). John says that this beast works great signs, making even fire come down from heaven and giving "breath" [Greek, "spirit"] to the image of the beast, thus being able to deceive the inhabitants of the earth. The reason why this beast could do such great signs, however, was that "power was given to it" [Greek original]. That is, God "allowed" the performance of these great signs (Rev. 13:14, 15). It is evident that God is in full control of what happens on earth. John has adopted the view found in *Ezekiel*, where God is responsible for both good and evil. He can use "beasts" and "monsters" to accomplish his designs.

Different understandings of The Fall are reflected also in the way in which Paul and John the prophet view the role of the civil government. Paul sees the role of the civil government as an agency of God charged with the administration of justice in a fallen world (Rom. 13:1-5). It is well to remember that he wrote this when Nero was the Roman Emperor. John, on the other hand, sees the government, the Roman Empire (the beast and the harlot) and all its allies (the fornicating kings) as surrogates of Satan (the dragon) who is actively deceiving the saints to worship the beast and its image. As is the case with Paul (Rom 7), in *Revelation* the real conflict is an internal struggle in the experience of the elect who seek to do God's will.

Rather than being the "god of this world," Satan is identified as *"the great dragon ... that ancient serpent, who is called the Devil and Satan, the deceiver of the whole world"* (Rev. 12:9). When he appears again, an angel comes down to seize *"the dragon, that ancient serpent, who is the Devil and Satan"* who has nowhere to stand on account of his having been repeatedly defeated. The angel has no problem taking him and casting him into the bottomless pit and locking him in. He had come down from heaven with the key to the pit in his hand (Rev. 20:1-2). The angel who blew the fifth trumpet, the reader had been told, already had the key to the shaft of the bottomless pit, and when he opened it smoke came out as from a furnace (Rev. 9:1-3). In *Revelation* God is in control throughout the cosmos.

The narration about the dragon's inability to continue to accuse the martyrs in heaven, his failure to devour the male child at birth, his failure to harm the woman who was protected by God in the wilderness, and his desperate attempts *"to make war on the rest of her offspring,"* ends pointing out that the dragon *"stood on the sand of the sea"* (Rev. 12:17). This is in stark contrast to the mighty angel who came down from heaven *"wrapped in a cloud, with a rainbow over his head, and his face like the sun and his legs like pillars of fire."* This angel had *"a little scroll open in his hand,"* and stood with *"his right foot on the sea, and his left foot on the land"* (Rev. 10:1-2). In other words, this angel with characteristics resembling those of the Danielic Son of Man, has control over sea and land, the realm of evil and the realm of good. By contrast Satan stands on the sandy shore that is no man's land between the two realms. He has been left without a realm of his own ever since the male son of the woman clothed with the sun, with the moon under her feet, and on her head a crown of twelve stars, rather than being devoured by the dragon, was taken up to heaven to sit on the throne with his Father. In *Revelation*, Satan was an accuser in heaven, and since he was cast down from heaven he does not have a footing, neither on the sea nor on the land. He is a deceiver who has given power to the beast, but has been consigned to no man's land. This gives significant clarity to its notion of The Fall, and disproves any notion that *Revelation* is about a cosmic conflict.

According to Paul, since his resurrection the Risen Christ has been trying to subjugate the forces of evil that are loose in the heavenly places. Only after this has been accomplished, the *Parousia* can take place. Then, Christ will be the ruler of the universe, and he can present himself before God bringing with him everything under his control. In Paul's vision, a cosmic conflict is taking place from the time of Christ's resurrection until the *Parousia*, that is during the Age of Messiah. Only then will everything in creation be under God's control (1 Cor. 15:24-28). John, the prophet, has God and

Christ, after Christ's resurrection, already jointly sitting on the throne and in full control over everything that is. The Fall is not presented in reference to Satan's control over the world, as in Paul. It is expressed by pointing out the necessity for the establishment of the new heaven and the new earth after the final judgment of evil. John's apocalyptic universe does not have an Age of Messiah. It has a millennium.

Even though John depends on *Ezekiel's* vision of a Jerusalem in a purified land, he does not envision that the future will restore, or improve the existing creation. There is going to be a new heaven, a new earth and a new Jerusalem, in sum a totally new creation. After the millennium, the New Jerusalem will be on the new earth. This is a revision of Ezekiel's vision. In the new creation there will be neither a sun nor a moon. Writing after the Jerusalem temple had been destroyed by the Romans, he twice saw the temple in heaven open. In one occasion he saw inside *"the ark of his covenant"* (Rev. 11:19). The ark here serves to demonstrate God's faithfulness to the Covenant. In the other occasion, he saw *"the Faithful and True, who in righteousness judges and makes war"* riding a white horse (Rev. 19:11). This vision of the one who has conquered the dragon also serves to inspire confidence in God's power to vindicate the faithful. It is also most significant that in the new heaven and new earth, there will be no temple, no symbolic means of communication between heaven and earth. In the new creation God himself will be in direct communication with humanity. It is by his descriptions of the final results of God's power and justice that John gives his assessment of the Fall. He tacitly affirms that the existing fallen creation will be no more.

Taking into account the introduction of the book that calls it a revelation of what is soon to take place, even while not using standard apocalyptic devices, undoubtedly the book is indeed apocalyptic, but with significant prophetic touches. The description of what John writes as prophecy must be understood in terms of the early Christian understanding of the gift of prophecy. The appeals for repentance and the insistence that the universe is under the full control of God and the Lamb, only show that the apocalyptic imagination was never bound to the rules of a structured movement within Judaism or Christianity. The modern criteria used to distinguish prophetic and apocalyptic, as said already, are only heuristic devices.

As *Daniel* consists of two distinct types of materials which are used at the service of the author's agenda, *Revelation* consists of two types of material used to strengthen the author's agenda. In the case of *Daniel*, the court tales provide examples showing that those who remain faithful to God when facing death enjoy divine protection, and bring about the recognition of the God of Daniel and his three companions as the only true God. The author of *Daniel* wrote to his contemporaries who were facing martyrdom by refusing to offer a sacrifice to Zeus. He assured them that God protects and saves those who remain loyal to their covenant with God. John, the prophet, wrote to his contemporaries who were facing persecution and martyrdom by refusing to worship the beast and its image to assure them that if they conquer in their struggle with the dragon's surrogates, just as the Lamb conquered and now sits upon the throne with his Father who rules and judges the nations, they will sit in the throne of the Lamb and rule over the nations (Rev. 5:10). As I will detail below, the letters that John wrote to the seven churches in Asia are fully integrated into the apocalyptic descriptions of *"what soon is to take place."*

In the preface John is told, *"Now write what you see, what is and what is to take place hereafter"* (Rev. 1:19). What he is going to see is both what is now the case, and what is to be the case later. In the introduction to the messages to the seven churches, John greets them, *"Grace to you and peace from"* God, and from Jesus Christ *"who is coming soon"* (Rev. 1:4-8). Then John sets up the circumstances under which he received the message for the churches and the meaning of the symbols, "the mystery," (Rev. 1:9-20). This sets up the letters to the seven churches, which in format and content are prophetic, according to our modern classification. After the letters, John saw an open door in heaven and a voice said to him,

"Come up hither, and I will show you what must take place after this" (Rev. 4:1), that is, he has already seen what is going on now in the churches, now he will be shown what is going to happen after this. This sets up the apocalyptic section of the book with the ascent of a human being to be shown things as seen in heaven, a typical apocalyptic device. Of course, the apocalyptic section has to be connected to things that have already happened, specifically, the triumph of Christ over Death and Satan at the cross and resurrection, and the ongoing persecution of Christians who are being pressured to offer sacrifices to the emperor in order to be able to fully participate in the social and economic life of the empire. Thus, descriptions of the past and the present are needed to make sense of what is to take place hereafter, and that is what the apocalyptic chapters do.

In the final analysis, it turns out that the book is not really about what is to take place soon. The descriptions of the future are only needed to motivate resistance to the beast now. John's aim is to give comfort and warnings to those who are being tested and have to decide who they are going to worship. Descriptions of the future only serve to give guidance for how to live today. The central question ultimately is: Are you going to worship the image of the beast and receive its mark in your forehead, or are you going to worship the creator of heaven and earth? Are you going to be one of those who end up thrown into the lake of fire or one who is clothed in white robes, one of those *"who have come out of great tribulation, [who] have washed their robes and made them white in the blood of the Lamb"*? (Rev. 7:14). It is in the judgment, the punishment of those who deny the creator God and the vindication of those who worship the creator God, that the power and justice of *"the one sitting on the throne"* are revealed. And that, indeed, is the ultimate purpose of John's writing.

Throughout *Revelation* the throne is the dominant symbol, and God is most often identified as "the one sitting" on it, at times with the Lamb sitting with him (Rev. 4:2, 9, 10; 5:1, 7, 13; 6:16; 7:10, 15; 19:4; 20:11; 21:5). Their control over the whole of creation is never questioned. The struggle going on in *Revelation* is the

The End of the Scroll

internal struggle within the elect who must resist the deceptions of the beast and the false prophet and thereby conquer. If they conquer, their names will not be blotted out of the book of life. The letters to the seven churches in Asia are designed to motivate those who are to conquer over the temptations of the master Deceiver, just as the court tales in *Daniel* were designed to assure God's protection when facing martyrdom.

APOCALYPTIC FEATURES OF *REVELATION*

Given its two sections, letters to the seven churches and apocalyptic visions, which are distinguished by their content and their relation to the present and the future, it could be expected that the book would be not quite of one piece, with sections exhibiting opposing viewpoints. This is not the case. The book has been integrated by tying the end to the beginning while maintaining a consistent vocabulary, interrupting the narrative with scenes that set up or integrate what follows and announcing the same thing by giving different accounts of its arrival with different actors or circumstances. These features, however, sometimes make the reading of *Revelation* difficult.

The opening of the seven seals starts with the now-famous four horses of the apocalypse. What the riders on these horses bring is not earth shaking. The first one has a bow, which suggests that he is engaged in shooting the *"darts of the evil one."* It brings to mind the advice of the author of *To the Ephesians*, *"Above all taking the shield of faith, with which you can quench all the flaming darts of the evil one"* (Eph. 6:16). This rider did not have a crown of his own, but was given one and goes out *"conquering and to conquer"* (Rev. 6:2). That is, the first trumpet brings about the multiplying of temptations. The second rider initiates the proliferation of war, taking peace away from the earth (Rev. 6:3-4). The third rider, as a result of the many wars going on, empowers the black market, making the price of food exorbitant (Rev. 6:6). The fourth rider brings death by sword, famine, pestilence and wild beasts (Rev. 6:8).

After these four already well known evils appeared, there is a marked difference in what follows. When the Lamb opens the fifth seal a dialogue is going on between *"the souls of those who had been slain for the word of God and for the witness they had borne"* and someone who, having heard their complaint, advises them *"to rest a little longer, until the number of their fellow servants and their brethren should be complete, who were to be killed as they themselves had been."* The souls of the martyrs had been asking an existential question: *"How long before thou wilt judge and avenge our blood on those who dwell upon the earth?"* (Rev. 6:9-11). This is the typical apocalyptic question, and it receives a typically apocalyptic answer: Have patient endurance; hold on; wait. Everything must take place according to the will of God as it was predetermined from the beginning. The number of those who are to be martyred has not yet been reached. The apocalyptic perspective claims to reveal the future hidden in a locked box.

When the Lamb opens the sixth seal, things that seem to be fixed in nature become unhinged. The sun, the moon, the stars, the sky, the mountains, the islands are dislodged, become unrecognizable or vanish. All the mighty men on earth then seek a place to hide *"from the face of him who is seated on the throne, and from the wrath of the Lamb; for the great day of their wrath has come"* (Rev. 6:16). This unsettling description of the divine wrath as displayed in creation is a proleptic interruption which, in turn, is followed by another interruption that envisions not the future of those who now enjoy power and prosperity, but the future of those whose souls are under the altar in heaven asking for justice, including those who had not yet been martyred. The number of those to be martyred will be 144,000 who will be sealed with the seal of God (Rev. 7:1-4).

Besides these martyrs, John is also shown *"a great multitude which no man could number, from every nation, from all tribes and peoples and tongues standing before the throne and before the Lamb."* They sing with loud voices, *"Salvation belongs to our God who sits upon the throne, and to the Lamb!"* (Rev. 7:9-10). These interruptions, before the opening of dramatic seals, are characteristic of the author of *Revelation*. Important balancing scenes anticipate the opening of the seventh seal. When opened, it consists of *"silence in heaven for about half an hour"* (Rev. 8:1). Exactly what this silence indicates is difficult to determine. Does it indicate that the mystery is being revealed? That the future will bring salvation to those who have washed their robes in the blood of the Lamb? Or, is it just an attention-getting device?

What follows is the appearance of seven angels standing before God who receive seven trumpets which are to be blown in sequence. Before this could be done, however, an angel with a censer came to the altar and mingled much incense with the prayers of the saints. The intensification of the power of prayer at this point is ominous. Then, this angel placed fire from the altar on the censer and threw it on the earth. As a result, *"there were peals of thunder, loud noises, flashes of lightning, and an earthquake"* (Rev. 8:2-5). This sequence of events is the introduction to the blowing of the seven trumpets which, like the seals, are divided into the first four which bring about unexpected phenomena in different areas of the planet and the last three which are characterized as *"Woe, woe, woe to those who dwell on the earth"* (Rev. 8:13). The first trumpet brings out locusts with the tails of scorpions which can sting and hurt human beings. They have come out of the bottomless pit (Rev. 9:1-11). The sixth trumpet opens the door to the armies East of the Euphrates river who come into the Roman empire with horses whose heads *"were like lion's heads, and fire and smoke and sulfur issued from their mouths ... For the power of the horses is in their mouths and in their tails; their tails are like serpents with heads, and by means of them they wound."* In other words, these horses are weaponized both in the front and in the rear. The destructive power of the locusts, however, did not cause the survivors to give up *"worshiping demons and idols of gold and silver and bronze and stone and wood, which cannot either see or hear or walk; nor did they repent of their murders or their sorceries or their immorality or their thefts"* (Rev. 9:13-21). Revelation's cardinal sin is idolatry.

John deploys again an interruption with tangential scenes before finishing the sequence of the seven trumpets, or the three woes. These scenes balance the accounts and link the sequences of sevens. A mighty angel appears *"wrapped in a cloud, with a rainbow over his head, and his face was like the face of the sun, and his legs like pillars of fire. He had a little scroll open in his hand. And he set his right foot on the sea, and his left foot on the land"* (Rev. 10:1-2). This mighty angel, who seems to be a stand-in for the Son of man, is in control of good and evil and has an open scroll in his hand. As one who has control over sea and land, he is a stand-in for the Lamb, but rather than being the only one who could open a sealed scroll he has in his hand a scroll already open. This angel swore *"by him who lives for ever and ever, who created heaven and what is in it, the earth and what is in it, and the sea and what is in it, that there should be no more delay, but that in the days of the trumpet call to be sounded by the seventh angel, the mystery of God, as he announced to his servants the prophets, should be fulfilled."* (Rev. 10:6-7). The confirmation that the future determined by God will be fulfilled without further delays reflects awareness that by the end of the first century many were wondering about a delay. The assurance that there will be no further delays is confirmed by the announcement that the martyrdom of two witnesses must happen first, but, as it turns out the two witnesses have been martyred already. The warning against idolatry is thus reinforced by the notion that martyrdom is preferable.

Loud voices in heaven exclaim, *"The kingdom of the world has become the kingdom of our Lord and of his Christ, and he shall reign for ever and ever"* (Rev. 11:15). This heavenly anticipation of the final triumph is then qualified. God's two witnesses must suffer martyrdom before this can happen. As noticed in the previous chapter, this is a feature of *To the Thessalonians II*, but here it is being used to reaffirm the immediacy of the Lord's kingdom. The two witnesses are identified as *"the two olive trees and the two lampstands which stand before the Lord of the earth"* (Rev. 11:4). By their own prophesying, the two witnesses *"have power to shut the sky, that no rain may fall ... and they have power over the waters to turn them into blood, and to smite the earth with every plague, as often as they desire."* Thus, they were *"a torment to those who dwell on the earth,"* and, as a consequence, they were killed by the beast. Their *"dead bodies,"* John is told, *"will lie in the street of the great city which is allegorically* (Greek: *pneumatikos,* spiritually) *called Sodom and Egypt, where their Lord was crucified"* (Rev. 11:6-8). The description of these witnesses may suggest references to Elijah and Moses in terms of their powers, but their unceremonious death in the city where Jesus had been crucified does not support these identifications. John continually demonstrates his freedom to use images from the Scriptures to describe recent or current events. That Jerusalem, now in possession by the Romans who had destroyed the temple, is called Sodom and Egypt, two traditional location of evildoers, gives further light to the role of the Roman empire in the mind of John. I am calling attention to this passage, however, to document John's writing technique of alternating his descriptions of the future with culminating scenes of worship to the creator God because the time had finally arrived for him to apply his great power. The martyrdom of the two witness, which John's contemporaries could no doubt identify, function as *vaticinia ex eventu,* and serves to confirm the imminent final judgment. While the nations raged, his *"wrath came, and the time for the dead to be judged, for rewarding [his] servants, the prophets and saints, and those who fear [his] name, both small and great, and for destroying the destroyers of the earth"* (Rev. 11:18). By the swearing of the mighty angel standing on land and sea that there would be no more delays to the fulfillment of God's designs announced by the prophets and interjecting the ministry of the two witnesses, John is integrating apocalyptic descriptions of the present with the preface's announcement of Jesus' soon coming. At the same time, he demonstrates being aware that among his contemporaries some admit that something is delaying the soon coming of the son of Man in the clouds, as the author of *According to Matthew,* and the authors of *Second Peter* and *Jude* corroborate. Besides, he highlights the necessity to worship only the Creator God whose justice will be vindicated, the core theme of his prophecy.

The presentation of a scene of triumph before a scene of existential struggle is found also when the Lamb, and the 144,000 *"who had his name and his Father's name written on their foreheads,"* appear on Mount Zion. They are playing their harps and singing a new song before the throne, the four living creatures and the twenty four elders. No one else could sing their song because they are the ones who follow the Lamb most closely and are "spotless" (Rev. 14:1-5). How they got from Mount Zion to a place before the throne in heaven is not said. Let us just remember that in the apocalyptic perspective heaven and earth are mutually permeable. The appearance of the 144,000 serves to counterbalance the appearance of the three angels who announce that the hour of judgment has arrived and describe what will happen *"to anyone who worships the beast and its image, and receives a mark on his forehead or on his hand."* They *"shall be tormented with fire and brimstone in the presence of the holy angels and in the presence of the Lamb ... they have no rest, day or night, these worshipers of the beast and its image"* (Rev. 14:9-11). John then warns his readers, *"Here is a call for the endurance of the saints."* In other words, the message of the three angels is to motivate loyalty on the part of the "called and chosen" contemporaries of John. He gives the same advice to those hearing the reading of his book after telling them that the beast *"was allowed to make war on the saints and to conquer them,"* because this was predetermined by God's will. As a consequence, all those *"whose name has not been written before the foundation of the world in the book of life of the Lamb that was slain"* will worship the beast. To this piece of information, John adds the warnings, *"If anyone has an ear, let him hear,"* and *"Here is a call for the endurance and faith of the saints"* (Rev. 13:9-10). That the names found in the Book of Life were written before the foundation of the world clearly reveals John's totally deterministic view of history. Apocalyptic determinism is necessitated by the apocalyptic agenda: to encourage perseverance under extreme circumstances only carries weight when the future is already determined. As said in the letters to the churches. *"I am coming soon; hold fast what you have"* (Rev. 3:11); *"hold fast what*

The End of the Scroll 271

you have, until I come" (Rev. 2:25); *"be faithful unto death"* (Rev. 2:10). The notion also informs the answer to the plea for vengeance by the martyrs under the altar. That they will have to wait in their present condition until the already determined number of martyrs is achieved is acceptable only to those holding a predetermined view of history.

Something similar to the account of the message of the three angels with trumpets in chapter fourteen happens in chapter fifteen. Before the unleashing of the *"seven plagues, which are the last, for with them the wrath of God is ended,"* John sees *"what appeared to be a sea of glass mingled with fire, and those who had conquered the beast and its image and the number of its name, standing beside the sea of glass with harps of God in their hands. And they sing the song of Moses, the servant of God, and the song of the Lamb"* (Rev. 15:1-3). Repeatedly John prefaces horrific scenes of divine wrath and vengeance with scenes that demonstrate God's divine purpose to bring about justice. These scenes serve to encourage John's contemporaries who are facing martyrdom at the hands of Roman officials. They are enforcing worship of the genius of the emperor as a sign of allegiance that entitles to full participation in the social and economic life of the empire.

Another one of John's literary devices is well known to good teachers: repetition. Three times he has an angel come down from heaven announcing the fall of Babylon. The first one says, *"Fallen, fallen is Babylon the great, she who made all nations drink the wine of her impure passions"* (Rev. 14:8). The second gives more details about the angel and about Babylon. *"I saw another angel coming down from heaven having great authority; and the earth was made bright with his splendor. And he called out with a mighty voice, 'Fallen, fallen is Babylon the great! It has become a dwelling place of demons, a haunt of every foul spirit, a haunt of every foul and hateful bird; for all nations have drunk the wine of her impure passions, and the kings of the earth have committed fornication with her, and the merchants of the earth have grown rich with the wealth of her wantonness'"* (Rev. 18:1-3). Idolatry and harlotry are twins in the message of the Old

Testament prophets. The third time he gives a visual description of the Fall: *"Then a mighty angel took up a stone like a great millstone and threw it into the sea, saying, "So shall Babylon the great city be thrown down with violence, and shall be found no more; and the sound of harpers and minstrels, of flute players and trumpeters, shall be heard in thee no more; and a craftsman of any craft shall be found in thee no more; and the sound of the millstone shall be heard in thee no more; and the light of a lamp shall shine in thee no more; and the voice of bridegroom and bride shall be heard in thee no more; for thy merchants were the great men of the earth, and all nations were deceived by thy sorcery. And in her was found the blood of prophets and of saints, and of all who have been slain on earth"* (Rev. 18:21-24). This leaves no doubt as to who is the culprit for the evil engulfing the life of John and his contemporaries: it is "Babylon."

Babylon is also described by an angel as a *"great harlot who is seated upon many waters, with whom the kings of the earth have committed fornication, and with the wine of whose fornication the dwellers on earth have become drunk"* (Rev. 17:1-2). When John actually looks at her, he saw *"a woman sitting on a scarlet beast which was full of blasphemous names, and it had seven heads and ten horns. The woman was arrayed in purple and scarlet, and bedecked with gold and jewels and pearls, holding in her hand a golden cup full of abominations and the impurities of her fornication, and on her forehead was written a name of mystery: 'Babylon the great, mother of harlots and of earth's abominations.' And I saw the woman, drunk with the blood of the saints and the blood of the martyrs of Jesus"* (Rev. 17:3-6). Elaborating on the importance of the scene, John writes that the beast's *"seven heads are seven hills on which the woman is seated"* (Rev. 17:9). Thus the woman who was first seated on many waters, and later is said to be seated on a scarlet beast ends up identified as seated on seven hills. The "mystery" of the woman whose name is 'Babylon the great' is none other than Rome, the city built on seven hills, represented by the seven heads of the scarlet beast on which she sits. That the name given is a "mystery" is a clue to its allegorical function as a cover for Rome.

The seven heads, however, *"are also seven kings, five of whom have fallen, one is, the other is yet to come, and when he comes he must remain only a little while"* (Rev. 17:10). Prior to this description of the seven heads of the beast, John was told that the scarlet beast that he saw *"was, and is not, and is to ascend from the bottomless pit and go to perdition; and the dwellers on earth whose names have not been written in the book of life from the foundation of the word, will marvel to behold the beast, because it was and is not and is to come"* (Rev. 17:8). The fifth emperor of Rome was Nero. According to Tacitus, Nero set fire to Rome and then charged the Christians with arson. Tacitus knows that they were being used as scapegoats for Nero's crime. He goes on to say that they were also charged with *"hatred of the human race,"* and that not only those who confessed being Christian, but *"an immense multitude was convicted."* They suffered all kinds of humiliations and death (*Annals*, xv. 44. 2-8).

This first persecution and death of Christians at the hands of a Roman emperor does not meet the description of the martyrdom suffered by those who died for their allegiance to the one sitting on the throne and the Lamb. Nero's use of Christians as scapegoats was limited to those in Rome; it was not an empire-wide event. Tacitus makes clear that they had been used for political advantage by a hateful emperor. After Nero's death there was a struggle among several pretenders to the throne. Three of them, Galba, Otho and Vitelius reigned for a few months each within the space of a year. It would appear that John overlooks the precarious reigns of these three weak emperors. In 69 C.E. Vespasian was installed, and he retained the throne until 79 C.E. John's identification of Vespasian as the king who "now is," and of his son Titus as "the other [who] has not yet come, and when he comes he must remain only a little while" are *vaticinia ex eventu*. In fact, Titus ruled only for a little over a year (79-81 C.E.). John then goes back to the beast that "was and is not," which caused those whose names are not written in the book of life to marvel at it to which he had referred. *"As for the beast that was and is not, it is an eighth but it belongs to the seven, and it goes to perdition"* (Rev. 17:11). This beast, or eighth king, is

Domitian (81-96 C.E.), who is actually the emperor at the time when John was at Patmos on account of his witness to Christ at the time of writing, and who from a Christian perspective was a maleficent re-incarnation of Nero coming out of the pit. When John introduces this alignment of the Roman emperors with the warning *"This calls for a mind with wisdom"* (Rev. 17:9), he is revealing his use of *vaticinia ex eventu*, and "predicting" that Domitian, who is an evil reincarnation of Nero, would "go to perdition." In the process, he fits the emperors of Rome into a schema of seven, while recognizing that Domitian is the eighth.. It was during Domitian's reign that worship of the genius of the emperor became coercive in some regions within the empire, even if it was not yet an empire-wide official policy but a spasmodic occurrence. The cult of the emperor did not arise to satisfy his high view of himself, but as a means to promote social cohesion and security for the aristocratic elites in the provinces. The following description of the ten horns as ten future kings who would be conquered by the Lamb (Rev. 17:13-14), unlike what preceded, is an actual prediction which, like the prediction that no human activity was going to go on at Rome after the soon coming hour of its judgment (Rev. 18:21-23), did not take place.

The scarlet beast with the seven heads and ten horns that *"was, and is not and is to come,"* it would seem, is none other than the dragon who was the accuser of the martyrs in heaven and, when cast down to earth, made war on earth against the other offspring of the woman clothed with the sun, but they defeated him. So, now he is not. He is, however, to *"ascend from the bottomless pit and go to perdition"* (Rev. 17:8). John tells his audience later that an angel came down from heaven *"holding in his hand the key to the bottomless pit and a chain. And he seized the dragon ... and bound him for a thousand years, and threw him into the pit, and shut it and sealed it over him"* (Rev. 20:1-30). *"And when the thousand years are ended, Satan will be loosed from his prison and will come out to deceive the nations"* (Rev. 20:7-8). Then, when Gog and Magog and a great multitude under the leadership of the dragon, recently

The End of the Scroll

released from the bottomless pit, attack the city of the redeemed, *"fire came down from heaven and consumed them, and the devil who had deceived them was thrown into the lake of fire and brimstone"* (Rev. 20:9-10). This account of the trajectory of *"the dragon, that ancient serpent, who is the Devil and Satan"* fits well with the description of the scarlet beast who *"was, is not, and is to ascend from the bottomless pit and go to perdition."* The accounts of the fall of Babylon not only exhibit John's use of repetition. They also show that he had at his disposal different sources with different details that he wove together. Thus, not only is the fall of Babylon told three times; the judgment of the harlot is told twice (Rev. 17:17; and 18:6, 17, 18, 19, 20).

Similarly, there are several descriptions of the destruction of the wicked. The first tells the defeat and capture of the beast by the Faithful and True who in righteousness judges and makes war (Rev. 19:11). Riding a white horse he leads his army. *"The beast and the kings of the earth with their armies gathered to make war against him who sits upon the horse and against his army. And the beast was captured, and with it the false prophet who in its presence had worked the signs by which he deceived those who had received the mark of the beast and those who worshiped its image. These two were thrown alive into the lake of fire that burns with brimstone. And the rest were slain by the sword of him who sits upon the horse, the sword that issues from his mouth"* (Rev. 19:19-21). Those killed by the sword, who were not thrown into the lake of fire, became the meal on which the birds which had been invited to *"the great supper of God"* now gorged themselves (Rev. 19:17, 21).

The false prophet that is thrown into the lake of fire with the beast is a new protagonist. It is not clear why he appears at this junction. His appearance here is somewhat of a surprise, but he serves to elaborate the prevalent description of the dragon, and his surrogate, the beast, as masters of deception. As noticed earlier, the one who had been an accuser in heaven, and attempted to make war in heaven was defeated. Once cast down to earth, as one without power standing on the sandy shore without a realm of his own, he became a deceiver. The only weapon left to those without power is deception. He now used surrogates, the beast and the false prophet. These descriptions of the defeated Satan corroborate the initial announcement of one of the twenty four elders to John, *"the Lion of the tribe of Judah, the Root of David, has conquered"* (Rev. 5:5).

The final destiny of the multitude of the wicked is taken up with significant elaborations in the following chapter. First, John describes the activity of the dragon which is again deceiving the inhabitants of the earth after his thousand-year captivity in the bottomless pit. He deceives the nations from the four corners of the earth, Gog, Magog and others, to gather for battle against the saints in "the beloved city." Their campaign is terminated by fire coming down from heaven and consuming them. Now the devil, who had deceived Gog, Magog and others to join him in battle against the saints, is thrown into the lake of fire and brimstone where the beast and the false prophet already were. There they *"will be tormented day and night for ever and ever"* (Rev. 20:7-10). That the wicked who die eschatologically will be tormented through eternity is a prominent feature of the apocalyptic description of God's retributive justice as vengeance. The millennium only serves to have the wicked die the second death, rather than have them die biologically and eschatologically at the same time, as is the case in Paul's view. This is a demonstration of sadistic vengeance that only makes sense in a culture in which everyone enjoyed going to amphitheaters to see human beings fighting wild predators from the animal kingdom.

Then John describes a judgment scene where all *"the dead, great and small,"* stand before the one who sits on a great white throne. Books were opened, *"and the dead were judged by what was written in the books, by what they had done."* Besides the books of record, the book of life was also opened, and *"if any one's name was not written in the Book of Life, he was thrown into the lake of fire"* (Rev. 20:11-15). Were all those whose carcasses had been eaten by birds at "the great supper of God" included among those who are now being judged before the throne and then thrown into the lake

The End of the Scroll 277

of fire? These different versions of the same event clearly argue for a writing process in which different sources were put together, or different earlier version of a scene were edited for the final version that has come down to us. Different descriptions of the judgment, the destruction of the wicked, the need to have the name written in the book of life and the mortal mistake of worshiping the beast and its image, most likely are the result of a writing process in which previous apocalyptic texts and several sources were woven together.

That John recycled many images from the Old Testament is clear. What in Ezekiel was Gog from the land of Magog (Ezek. 38:1) becomes Gog and Magog, two warring peoples. That beasts are destroyed and burned with fire, and that the judgment is done by searching open books are details from the judgment scene in Daniel (Dan. 7:10, 11). The examples are easy to find:

- The redeemed receive a new name (Rev. 2:17 / Is. 62:2)
- Balaam is the prototype of the false prophet (Rev. 2:14 / Num. 22-24; 31:16)
- Ruling with a rod of iron that results in broken pottery (Rev. 2:27 / Ps. 2:9)
- A new name for Jerusalem (Rev. 3:12 / Ezek. 48:35)
- Horses with riders (Rev. 6:1 / Ezek. 1:1-17; 6:1-8)
- Purification by martyrdom (Rev. 14:1, 5 / Dan. 11:33-35; 12:10)
- Seal on the forehead (Rev. 7:3 / Ezek. 9:4)
- Asking to hide in the crags of rocks (Rev. 6:12 / Is. 2:10; Hos. 10:8)
- Martyrs pleading for justice (Rev. 6:10 / 1 En. 9:3)
- Eating a scroll (Rev. 10:8-10 / Ezek. 2:8 – 3:3)
- Satan as an accuser in heaven (Rev. 12:10 / Job 1:10-11; Zech. 3:1)
- Measuring the temple (Rev. 11:1 / Ezek. 40:3 – 42:20; Zech. 2:1-5)
- The ark of the covenant (Rev. 11:19 / 1 Kg. 8:1-6)
- Michael (Rev. 12:7 / Dan. 10:13, 21:12:1)
- Rescued by an eagle (Rev. 12:14 / Ex. 19:4)

- Wine of God's anger (Rev. 14:10 / Jer. 25:15-16)
- Song of Moses (Rev. 15:3 / Ex. 15:1-18; Ps. 145:17)
- Kings against Jerusalem (Rev. 16:14 / Zech. 14:1-3)
- Placing the devil in a pit and sealing it until the judgment (Rev. 20:3 / 1 En. 10-11)
- Birds gorging on dead bodies (Rev. 19:21 / Ezek. 39:18-20)
- A city as a whore (Rev. 17:1-18 / Ezek. 16:15)
- Babylon as a golden cup with wine (Rev. 17:4 / Jer. 51:7)
- Lament over Babylon/Rome (Rev. 18:1-24 / Ezek. 26-27; Jer. 51)
- A call to come out of her (Rev. 18:4 / Jer. 50:8; 51:45)
- Satan as a deceiver (Rev. 19:20 / Dan.11:30-33)
- Garments stained with blood at a wine press (Rev. 19:3 / Is. 63:1-3)
- Abaddon the angel of destruction (Rev. 9:11 / Job 28:22; Ps. 15:11; 27:20)
- Jerusalem restored (Rev. 21:2 / Zech. 14:8-10)
- Eating the fruit of the tree of life after the judgment (Rev. 22:7 / 1 En. 25:3-5)
- If any one adds or takes away from what is written (Rev. 22:18-19 / Deut. 4:2; 12:32)

Recycling and giving new functions to Old Testament images is a characteristic of the apocalyptic genre fully in evidence in John's writing.

INTERNAL COHESION AND MESSAGE

Another prominent feature of the structure of Revelation is the way in which John, who obviously was working with diverse sources and uses both prophetic and apocalyptic perspectives, was nevertheless able to integrate the text into a whole. This is not only evident in the sections that we have examined in terms of thematic interruptions and repetitions. It is particularly noticeable in the way in which the message to the seven churches announces themes and details that appear later in the book, especially in the descriptions of the new heaven and the new earth. To each of the churches he who is *"the first and the last, and the living one,"* and identifies himself saying, *"I died, and behold I am alive for evermore, and I have the keys of Death and Hades"* (Rev. 1:17-18), tells what will be the reward of those who follow his advice and conquer. These promises are fulfilled at the final scenes.

To the church at Ephesus he says, *"To him who conquers I will grant to eat of the tree of life, which is in the paradise of God"* (Rev. 2:7). The description of the new earth, on which the holy city of Jerusalem has descended from heaven, says that *"on either side of the river"* John saw *"the tree of life with its twelve kinds of fruit, yielding its fruit each month; and the leaves of the tree were for the healing of the nations"* (Rev. 22:2). After this description, John pronounces, *"Blessed are those who wash their robes, that they may have the right to the tree of life"* (Rev. 22:14). Before closing, he issues a warning to those who will be handling the book he has written, *"If any one takes away from the words of the book of this prophecy, God will take away his share in the tree of life and in the holy city which are described in this book"* (Rev. 22:19).

To the church at Smyrna, Christ promises, *"He who conquers shall not be hurt by the second death"* (Rev. 2:11). As such the promise is not quite intelligible. The reader must come to the end of the narrative to learn that the second death is the one suffered by anyone whose name is not found in the book of life (Rev. 20:14-15). They are *"the cowardly, the faithless, the polluted, ... the murderers, fornicators, sorcerers, idolaters and ... liars; their lot shall be in the lake of fire that burns with fire and brimstone, which is the second death"* (Rev. 21:8).

To the church at Pergamum Christ promises, *"To him who conquers I will give some of the hidden manna, and I will give him a white stone, with a new name written on the stone which no one knows except him who receives it"* (Rev. 2:17). Pointing out that the throne of God and of the Lamb shall be in the New Jerusalem that has descended to earth, John says that *"his servants shall worship him; they shall see his face, and his name shall be on their foreheads"*

(Rev. 22:3-4). What Moses could not see (Ex. 33:20), the servants of God who worship him in the New Jerusalem shall see, and they will have God's name on their foreheads.

To the church at Thyatira Christ says, *"He who conquers, and who keeps my works until the end, I will give him power over the nations, and he shall rule them with a rod of iron, ... even as I myself have received power from my Father; and I will give him the morning star"* (Rev. 2:26-28). Christ, the male child who was to be born of the woman clothed with the sun (Rev. 12:52), and who is the Faithful and True, whose name is The Word of God, who rides the white horse and captured the beast and the kings with their armies, is the one who will rule the nations with a rod of iron (Rev. 19:15). Then, as Jesus concludes his personal address to the readers of John's book, he says, *"I Jesus have sent my angel to you with this testimony for the churches. I am the offspring of David, the bright morning star"* (Rev. 22:16). Thus, what is promised to the conquerors at Thyatira is that they, like Jesus, will rule over the nations and have the morning star, the messenger of the light of day.

To the church at Sardis Christ promised, *"He who conquers shall be clad thus in white garments; and I will not blot his name out of the book of life"* (Rev. 3:5). That the redeemed are dressed in white garments that have been washed with the blood of the Lamb is said more than once (Rev. 6:11; 7:9, 13; 19:14). The book of life also becomes a prominent factor in the determination of the fate of women and men. It is imperative to have one's name written in it (Rev. 17:8; 20:12; 21:27), and those who remain faithful are promised that their names, which were written in the book of life before the foundation of the word, will not be blotted out. It is only when the whole of John's book has been read that the promises given to the conquerors at the beginning can be understood.

To the church at Philadelphia Christ says, *"He who conquers, I will make him a pillar in the temple of my God; never shall he go out of it, and I will write on him the name of my God, and the name of the city of my God, the New Jerusalem which comes down from God out of heaven, and my own new name"* (Rev. 3:12). It would seem that the intention is to promise something similar to not having one's name blotted out from the book of life. In this case, however, there is a problem with the metaphor of a pillar in the temple of God. It turns out that when the New Jerusalem comes down from heaven, there is no temple in it (Rev. 21:22), Apparently, while the New Jerusalem is in heaven, and the Jerusalem on earth is described allegorically as Sodom and Egypt (Rev. 11:8), being a pillar firmly integrated to the temple's structure is a way of assuring conquerors of their standing before God. Once the New Jerusalem has descended on earth, something else must fill the role: the name of God, of the city and of Christ himself written on the forehead serves the purpose. In the description of the redeemed, as we noticed, only the name of God is written. That conquerors are given more than one promise most likely is due to the need to integrate different sources used in the composition. Still, the linkage of the promises in the letter to the final scenes is evident.

To the church of Laodicea Christ promises, *"He who conquers, I will grant him to sit with me on my throne, as I myself conquered and sat down with my Father on his throne"* (Rev. 3:21). That Christ, the Lamb that was slain and lives for evermore, sits with his father on his throne is clear from reference to *"the throne of God and of the Lamb"* (Rev. 22:1, 3). This promise explains the promise that conquerors will rule with a rod of iron, just as Christ does. They will rule because they sit in Christ's throne. It cannot be overlooked that all seven promises to the churches are to those "who conquer" just as the Lamb had conquered. Those who come out victorious are those who are not deceived by the lies of the Devil, who is a deceiver and a liar. The struggle with which *Revelation* is concerned is the struggle that the contemporaries of the author are engaged in. It is a struggle against the promise of prosperity and security by worshiping the genius of the emperor of Rome. This promise of earthly security and prosperity, of course, is considered by John to be a deception and a lie. These promises also make evident that while the author considers that Christ has conquered the dragon, it is not yet established who among the members of the churches will conquer. Those who fail to conquer will have their names blotted out of the Book of Life (Rev. 3:5). Thus all the promises are given to encourage perseverance and faithfulness so as to conquer. The Lamb who was slain and lives forever had conquered the dragon, cast it out of heaven, and keeps it now in no-man's land. It is also established that the martyrs in heaven who constitute the 144,000 have conquered. What is in the balance, not yet clearly settled, is who among the followers of the Lamb now living on the earth will conquer in the struggle taking place between the beast and the saints. Thus, while the names of the redeemed were written in the book of life before the foundation of the world, the promise that their names will not be blotted out of the book of life is given only to those who overcome in the struggle taking place now on earth. What is going on is not a cosmic conflict, but a very earthly spiritual struggle.

John is without doubt a Christian prophet. His book reveals, however, that culturally he is very much a Jew. His models were Hebrew prophets. He patterns himself after Moses, considered at the time to have been the greatest of all the Hebrew prophets. Moses told the Israelites not to add or to subtract any word from what he was commanding to every one of them, *"that you may live, and go in and take possession of the land which the Lord, the God of your fathers, gives you"* (Deut. 4:1-2; 12:32). John tells the churches in Asia, *"I warn everyone who hears the words of the prophecy of this book: if any one adds to them, God will add to him the plagues described in this book, and if any one takes away from the words of the book of this prophecy, God will take away his share in the tree of life and in the holy city, which are described in this book"* (Rev. 22:18-19). He introduced his book in the manner of Ezekiel, placing himself in time and place and having received instructions as to what he is to do. Ezekiel wrote, *"In the twenty-fifth year of our exile, at the beginning of the year, on the tenth day of the month, in the fourteenth year after the city was conquered, on that very day, the hand of the Lord was upon me, and brought me in the visions of God into the land of Israel, and set me down upon a very high mountain, on which was a structure like a city opposite me."* There, a man *"whose appearance was like bronze"* said to him, *"Son of man, look with your eyes, and hear with your ears, and set your mind upon all that I shall show you, ... declare all that you see to the house of Israel"* (Ezek. 40:1-4). Similarly, John the prophet writes, *"I John, your brother, who share with you in Jesus the tribulation and the kingdom and the patient endurance, was on the island called Patmos on account of the word of God and the testimony of Jesus. I was in the Spirit on the Lord's day, and I heard behind me a loud voice like a trumpet saying, 'Write what you see in a book and sent it to the seven churches'"* (Rev. 1:9-11). He not only recycled images from the Old Testament. He also followed the pattern established by the prophets, not Christian models.

John shows himself attached to Judaism when he considers that saints in the churches of Asia should be true Jews. He identifies some members of the churches at Smyrna and Philadelphia as dispensers of slanders, liars, who say that they are Jews and are not (Rev. 2:9; 3:9). Apparently, for John good Christians are real Jews. They are faithful keepers of the commandments of God (Rev. 12:17; 14:12). Once he became a Christian, Paul thought that his life as a commandment-keeper Pharisee had been a waste (Phil. 3:7), and insisted that Christians do not live under the Law (Rom. 6:14; 7:5-6). The Jews, of course, are distinguishable because they do live under the Law (1 Cor. 9:20; Gal. 4:4).

John reflects his ties to Judaism also when he describes the New Jerusalem that descends from heaven after the millennium. The city has a great, high wall with twelve gates, ... and on the gates the names of the twelve tribes of the sons of Israel were inscribed. Besides the twelve gates, the wall of the city had twelve foundations, *"and on them the twelve names of the twelve apostles of the Lamb"* (Rev. 21:12-14) were inscribed. In this case the twelve sons of Jacob/Israel are balanced by the twelve disciples of Jesus. It would seem, therefore, that when he says that the one sitting on the throne has twenty four elders as acolytes who offer praises and sing hymns worshiping God and the Lamb, John has in mind the sum of the twelve sons of Jacob and the twelve disciples of Jesus.

The pair of twelves serve to establish a strong continuity between Judaism and Christianity.

It is somewhat unexpected to learn that the 144,000 who received the seal of God on their foreheads are identified as belonging to the twelve tribes of the sons of Israel. Their number is due to the fact that twelve thousand have been sealed from each of the twelve tribes. John emphasizes its significance by listing the twelve tribes individually by name and giving the number of those sealed in each one. This is particularly surprising because, as I said above, it would appear that the 144,000 are the martyrs already in heaven. Immediately following their sealing, John saw *"a great multitude which no man could number, from every nation, from all tribes and peoples and tongues, standing before the throne and before the Lamb, clothed in white robes, with palm branches in their hands, and crying out with a loud voice, 'Salvation belongs to our God who sits upon the throne, and to the Lamb!'"* (Rev. 7:2-10). The setting apart of a group identified as members of the tribes of the sons of Israel and distinguishing them from those in a multitude with members of tribes from other nations is difficult to comprehend, if one does not recognize John's allegiance to Judaism. In this way he establishes continuity between the Jewish martyrs under Antiochus IV and the Christian martyrs that come from both among both Jews and Gentiles, including those who may become martyrs in the future on account of their non-participation in the cult of the emperor and who, therefore, are not yet sealed.

That his cosmology remains basically Jewish is evident by having the conquerors over the dragon and its surrogates, the beast and its image, *"those who are written in the Lamb's book of life"* (Rev. 21:27), living in the New Jerusalem settled down on earth forever and ever more. For John, the ultimate human home is on earth, not in heaven, as the Hellenistic cosmology that informs the gospel writers and Paul would have it. For Paul bliss is to be achieved when the saints are taken up to *"always be with the Lord"* (1 Th. 4:17). For John, bliss is to be achieved when the called and chosen live in the New Jerusalem, *"prepared as a bride adorned for her husband"*

(Rev. 21:2), in a new heaven and a new earth, in a cosmos without sun, moon or sea, and a city without a temple here on earth (Rev. 21:1, 22-23). Then a great voice from the throne will say, *"Behold, the dwelling of God is with men. He will dwell with them, and they shall be his people, and God himself will be with them"* (Rev. 21; 3) There *"the Lord God will be their light and they shall reign for ever and ever"* (Rev. 22:5). This description of life in the New Jerusalem is the apocalyptic version of the prophetic vision of life in a restored, not a new, Jerusalem. In the prophetic vision, God is the one who descends and dwell with men at their home on earth (Is. 2:1-4; Mic. 4:1-4). Like in the vision found in both Isaiah and Micah which includes the kings of the nations coming to Jerusalem for wisdom, in Revelation the glory of God is the light of the new heaven and a new earth, and the lamp is the Lamb, and *"by its light shall the nations walk; and the kings of the earth shall bring their glory to it"* (Rev. 21:24). That is, John recycles the prophetic vision of Jerusalem as the capital of the world that attracts the kings of the nations to live in the light that emanates from God's presence on earth. Obviously, in such a cosmos there is no need for a temple.

Also indicative of John's Jewish culture is the way in which he reveals the "mystery" for the identification of the beast by means of a number. *"This calls for wisdom: let him who has understanding reckon the number of the beast, for it is a human number, its number is six hundred and sixty six"* (Rev. 13:18). Whereas in other instances he warns, *"This calls for patient endurance,"* and describes difficult times to come, here John warns that in this case wisdom and understanding are necessary to determine the identification of the beast by means of the number six hundred and sixty six. The most likely interpretation of the number is arrived by realizing that the number is to be read in Hebrew rather than Greek letters. Written in Hebrew, the letters in "Nero Caesar" sum up to six hundred and sixty six. This, again, tells us about the cultural setting of John and his sources. At that time many expected that after the turbulent times brought about by the fighting for his succession, Nero would return to power redivivus. The description of *"the beast that was and is not, it is an eighth but it belongs to the seven"* (Rev. 17:11) is a clue to the myth about Nero's return to power. As I suggested above, on the basis of the myth, Christians identified Domitian as another Nero.

What Revelation presents as "the gospel" is that the day of the wrath of God is near. The final judgment is upon us. Its announcement is the book's leitmotiv. Already the letters make sure the saints understand the consequences of failing to conquer. The sixth trumpet compels those facing death confessing, *"...the great day of the wrath (of him who is seated on the throne, and the wrath of the Lamb) has come, and who can stand before it?"* (Rev. 6:17). When the seventh angel blew his trumpet, the twenty four elders who sit on thrones, say to God, *"The nations raged, but thy wrath came, and the time for the dead to be judged, for rewarding thy servants ... and for destroying the destroyers of the earth"* (Rev. 11:18). The first of the three angels who proclaims *"an eternal gospel"* announces, *"Fear God and give him glory, for the hour of his judgment has come"* (Rev. 14:7). The seven last plagues are described as bringing with them the culmination of the wrath of God (Rev. 15:1, cp. 16:1). When the seventh angel pours his bowl into the air, a voice from the throne in the temple declares, *"It is done"* (Rev. 16:17). What happened was that *"the great city was split into three parts, and the cities of the nations fell, and God remembered great Babylon, to make her drain the cup of the fury of his wrath"* (Rev. 16:19). The judgment of Babylon is then described in detail in chapter 18, where first a voice from heaven announces that God will *"repay her double for her deeds, and mix a double draught for her in the cup she mixed,"* then the kings of the earth, the merchants and all shipmasters and sailors will lament that *"in one hour she has been laid waste."* What God had done, however, gives way to the exclamation, *"Rejoice over her, O heaven, O saints and apostles and prophets, for God has given judgment for you against her"* (Rev. 18:20). The triumph of God's power and justice brings about the casting of the wicked in the bottomless pit where they will be tormented forever to avenge the sufferings of the righteous saints. That God' judgment displays his wrath by casting all those who fail to worship him into an everlasting fire where they will suffer forever and ever is not a very appealing "gospel" outside an apocalyptic horizon. It is difficult to share in the joy to which the apostles and prophets are called by a divine voice that displays the herd mentality that finds satisfaction in revenge. This "gospel" can only be understood when one considers that John did not write to tell his readers to do whatever was necessary to have their names in the Book of Life. He wrote to them warning them not to do what would cause the blotting of their names from the Book of Life (Rev. 3:5). He did not write to evangelize pagans, but to warn the elect whose names had been written in the Book of Life even before the foundation of the world (Rev. 17:8).

Revelation is concerned with the temptation to abandon the worship of God when the social and economic conditions of life in the world make it necessary to pay homage to the beast and its image. Satan is actively trying to deceive women and men as they decide who is to be worshiped. I repeat, this is the central issue of the book. *Ezekiel* argues that, contrary to what the exiles are claiming, God is just, and that, contrary to what the neighboring nations are saying, God is all-powerful. *Daniel* argues that God can be trusted to rescue those who face martyrdom; therefore, they should refuse to worship Zeus. *Revelation* emphasizes the need to keep worshiping God because the wrath of God will sadistically avenge their present sufferings caused by their refusal to worship the beast and its image.

The many hymns that give the book a poetic tone to counterbalance the obscene descriptions of torture brought about by God's vengeance serve to drive the theme home. In *Daniel* there is a specific attack on the Jewish way of life when the continual burnt offerings were stopped and the abomination that makes desolate was set up at the temple of Jerusalem, the altar having been transformed as an altar to Zeus. Three different series of events culminate with the setting up of this outrageous act (Dan. 8:11; 9:27; 11:31). They created the conditions that put pressure on the faithful to offer sacrifices to Zeus. In *Revelation* there are several references to the critical role played by the beast and its image as objects of worship (Rev. 13:4, 12; 14:9; 19:20; 20:4). To "conquer" is to refuse to worship the beast and its image in spite of the powerful efforts to deceive the saints put forth by the beast and the false prophet. Those who conquered the beast and its image *"and the number of its name"* are the ones standing beside what appeared to be a sea of glass mingled with fire.

The central question of the book is, who is worthy of your worship? The role of the twenty four elders and the four living creatures who surround the throne is to impress on the readers and hearers of the book the need to worship the Creator God. John was shown *"those who had conquered the beast and its image and the number of its name, standing beside the sea of glass with harps of God in their hands. And they sing the song of Moses, the servant of God, and the song of the Lamb"* (Rev. 15:2-4). They worship the one *"who made heaven and earth, the sea and the fountains of water."*

Revelation is the only New Testament book in which the Hebrew word of praise "Hallelujah" is found. It must have been natural for John to praise God using this Hebrew word. Its presence calls attention to the ultimate advice given by John: *"Worship God"* (Rev. 22:9). John says he heard *"what seemed to be the mighty voice of a great multitude in heaven, crying, 'Hallelujah! Salvation and glory and power belong to our God, for his judgments are true and just; he has judged the great harlot who corrupted the earth with her fornication, and has avenged on her the blood of his servants,' Once more they cried, 'Hallelujah! The smoke from her goes up for ever and ever'"* (Rev. 19:2-3). Then the twenty four elders and the four living creatures worshiped the one sitting on the throne and said, *"Amen, Hallelujah!"* (Rev. 19:4). Finally, he hears *"the voice of a great multitude, like the sound of many waters and like the sound of mighty thunder peals, crying, "Hallelujah! For the Lord our God the Almighty reigns"* (Rev. 19:6). The four Hallelujahs make clear what the whole book is about. It is to establish that God's judgments are true and just. He has taken away the great harlot, imperial Rome, and avenged the blood of those martyred for their decision to keep the commandments of God. The theme of the book is to affirm that God's retributive justice will ultimately be revealed with a vengeance, and all creation will sing God's praises. That God's praises are cast in the language of inhuman revenge reveals the different sensibilities of different historical times.

Revelation deals with a perennial question for which no one has yet found an answer. In fact, with the passage of time giving a compelling answer has become even more difficult because in the West the concept of freedom has become a major contributor to our understanding of human responsibility. The issue left unanswered by *Revelation* is how to understand the relationship between God's sovereignty and human ethical responsibility. *Revelation* does not face up to the question, but sets up God's predetermined control over history side by side with the need for the elect to avoid having their names erased from the book of life by resisting the deceptions of the beast and the false prophet. The book offers a compelling argument for the elect to remain faithful and worship the Creator God within the limits of its Jewish-Christian culture where human freedom is not a primary concern. Its editing of traditional materials may not have produced a cogent narrative sequence. Still, its effort to defend the power and justice of God for Christians living at the end of the first century is quite impressive by its display of a fertile imagination and singularity of purpose. As a witness to the faith of John in trying circumstances, who may be better thought of as the final editor of the book, it is quite remarkable. To read it as a chart with which to find the meaning of historical events in the twenty-first century, or in any previous century, is a travesty of its message. The book does not hide but reveal God's purposes to uphold his justice. Those promoting themselves as endowed with the key to unlock mysteries supposedly hiding in the book dispense an ideology which deceptively allows them to claim power for themselves.

First Peter, Jude, and Second Peter

Together with *James* and *First, Second* and *Third John*, *First* and *Second Peter* and *Jude* are called the General Epistles of the New Testament. They are distinguished from the epistles of Paul and the Pastoral Epistles in that, rather than to being named after their recipients, they are named after their presumed authors. In this chapter I intend to analyze only the three in the title because they trace discrete apocalyptic trajectories that emphasize the unavoidable final judgment which will establish God's retributive justice.

It is generally agreed that these three letters were written anonymously by authors who used a pseudonym. Why they chose to use the names of Peter and Jude has been an unresolved puzzle. The author of *Second Peter* claims to have been the author of *First Peter* (2 Pet. 3:1), but this is most unlikely. It is obvious, however, that *Jude* and *Second Peter* are literately related. The relationship between them has been studied carefully over the years and scholars have arrived at a consensus that *Jude* was written first and the author of *Second Peter* expanded on it according to his own agenda. It is also the majority opinion among scholars that several factors inform the conclusion that *First* and *Second Peter* were not written by the same author, including matters of style and content; most significantly, while *First Peter* is the work of an author with a very good command of Greek, the author of *Second Peter*'s writes in a provincial Greek, described as Asiatic. Besides, while *First Peter* was written toward the end of the first century, that is in the last years of Domitian's principate, *Second Peter* was written toward the end of the first quarter of the second century. Like *To the Thessalonians II* and *Jude*, it refers to the gospel as the faith or the truth, an intellectual commodity that the author claims to have become standard. All three letters take for granted that, after the lives of the original apostles, the church is now under human authorities who are to be recognized by the faithful. This clearly places these letters at a time when Christianity was becoming an ecclesiastical entity.

First Peter is unique in that it was sent to the churches in Pontus, Galatia, Cappadocia, Asia and Bithynia. That is, it was a circular letter to churches in the Roman provinces in northwestern Asia Minor. Coming south from Pontus to Galatia and Cappadocia, west to Asia and back north to Bithynia the carrier of the letter would have completed a rather large circle. From his own letters and from *Acts of the Apostles* we know that Paul traveled and founded churches in Galatia and Asia. It would seem, then, that Pontus, Cappadocia and Bithynia were evangelized by apostles sent from Jerusalem, where Peter and James were the leaders. Since the author of *Jude* identifies himself as *"Jude, a servant of Jesus Christ and brother of James"* (Jude 1), the choice of the pseudonyms may be accounted for as an appeal to the founders of these churches. In this connection, it must be noticed that the author of *Second Peter* tells his readers that his advice to *"be zealous to be found in him* [Jesus Christ] *without spot or blemish and at peace"* at the judgment is one that *"our beloved brother Paul wrote to you according to the wisdom given him, speaking of this as he does in all his letters"* (2 Pet. 3:14-16). This suggests that by the beginning of the second century the letters of Paul, which had been written between 50 and 62 C.E., had already been collected and were circulating as a corpus among these churches. By this time the oral traditions, and their compilations into narratives of what Luke calls *"the things that have been accomplished among us"* (Lk. 1:1), had also reached a large geographical area. Since these letters evidence access to these materials, they must have been written about the time when Christians had began to codify a standard "Faith." Whether "the faith"

The End of the Scroll   293

formulated in these letters was the standard in other regions which a rapidly-expanding Christianity also had reached is another matter.

As noticed in a previous chapter, these three letters knew and considered *First Enoch* authoritative. The author of *Jude* further identifies the author of this text as an antediluvian from the seventh generation after Adam (Jude 14). All three refer specifically to what The *Book of the Watchers* says about the angels who came down to have children with the daughters of men before the flood, and give a contemporary application to what Enoch "prophesied." As shown in the preceding chapter, the author of *Revelation* also used material from The *Book of the Watchers* (Rev. 6:10 / 1 En. 9:3; Rev. 22:7 / 1 En. 25:3-5) in his account of "what soon must take place." That *First Enoch* was written by the seventh direct descendant of Adam is, of course, unbelievable. It would mean that, if the story of the flood were to be given also historical reliability, besides preserving his own family and samples of all existing animals in the ark, Noah also saved a copy of the book of *First Enoch*. That *First Enoch* was well known and considered authoritative by the early Christians, the apocalyptic authors of the New Testament among them, is, however, unquestionable.

FIRST PETER

This circular letter sent from Rome ("Babylon," 1 Pet. 5:13) to Christians living in Northwestern Asia Minor aims to alert its audience that "completion" of their sufferings is required of those who expect their faith and hope to find fulfillment in the glory that is now Christ's (1 Pet. 5:9). In the introduction, the author describes what God has done for them and ends stating, *"in this you rejoice"* (1 Pet. 1:6). He then affirms that *"now for a little while you may have to suffer various trials"* (1 Pet. 1:6), and recapitulates his message stating, *"Beloved, do not be surprised at the fiery ordeal which comes upon you, ... but rejoice in so far as you share Christ's sufferings"* (1 Pet. 4:12-13). The body of the letter deals with the reason, the conditions, the required behavior and the consequences of their suffering because *"the end of all things is at hand"* (1 Pet. 4:7). The author's agenda is to tell his readers that they must not only rejoice on account of what God has done for them in Christ, but must rejoice also in their sufferings before they will share in the glory in store for them. The opening salutation already establishes the main theme. They have been chosen *"for obedience to Jesus Christ and for sprinkling with his blood"* (1 Pet. 1:2). The metaphor says it best. Having been elected for salvation involves expectations of obedience to the will of God and participation in the sufferings of Christ.

It is clear that the Christians being addressed were Gentiles who had been living according to *"the futile ways inherited from [their] fathers,"* also described as *"the passions of your former ignorance"* or *"wild profligacy," "living in licentiousness, passions, drunkenness, revels, carousing, and lawless idolatry"* (1 Pet. 1:18, 14; 4:4, 3). The author (whether he was a Jew or a Gentile makes no difference) includes himself as the beneficiary of what God has done *"through the resurrection of Jesus Christ from the dead."* By God's mercy *"we have been born anew to a living hope, ... and to an inheritance which is imperishable, undefiled, and unfading, kept in heaven for you, who by God's power are guarded through faith for a salvation ready to be revealed in the last time"* (1 Pet. 1:3-5). Since as *"newborn babes"* (1 Pet. 2:2) they live by hope in the salvation at present kept in heaven, but to be revealed *"in the last time,"* while living on earth they are *"chosen sojourners of the Dispersion"* (1 Pet. 1:3, my translation), *"temporary residents and sojourners"* (1 Pet. 2:11, my translation) who must conduct themselves faithfully throughout their time as strangers in a foreign land knowing that they are guarded by God's power (1 Pet. 1:17). In other words, their election can be annulled by their disobedience when the sprinkling of Jesus blood on them arrives in the form of "various trials." As newborn babes, however, they are meant to grow into salvation. This should be well within their reach because they have already *"tasted the kindness of the Lord."* This is a most felicitous use of language. The Greek word etymologically refers to the taking of food, and refers back to their longing for spiritual milk that will facilitate their growth in Christ (1 Pet. 2:2). The rich flavor of that milk should remind them of a joyful experience and allow them to rejoice in their suffering.

The author of *First Peter* demonstrates that he had excellent writing skills in Greek. This has been one of the primary reasons supporting the denial that Peter, a most likely poorly-educated fisherman from Galilee, wrote this letter. Those wishing to defend the authorship of Peter, the disciple of Jesus, offer as explanation that the letter was written by Silvanus (1 Pet. 5:12). According to this reasoning, Peter told him the basic thoughts he wanted to convey, and Silvanus produced a beautifully written letter in Greek for Peter. This of course is explaining two knowns, the excellent Greek of the letter and the actual background of Peter, by an unknown, the writing skills of Silvanus. What the author of the letter actually says is that Silvanus is the authorized carrier of the letter to the churches listed at the beginning.

In connection with the good Greek and literary talents of the author already noticed in reference to his use of metaphors and the fine distinctions that he makes, I would also single out his notion that the elect who will enjoy "eternal glory in Christ" must have a "clear conscience" (Greek original, *agathe* = good conscience, 1 Pet. 3:16, 21). As noticed in a previous chapter, this testifies to a development in the ethical vocabulary taking place at the time. In its first appearances, the word conscience, in Greek *syneidesin* (*syn* = *together with*, *oida* = to know), described a condemnatory function of the mind. Paul used the word with that meaning when he argued that both the Jews who are condemned by the Law of Moses and the Gentiles who are condemned by their conscience stand on equal terms before the judgment of God (Rom. 2:15-16). By saying that Christians should have a "good conscience" the author is using the word with a positive meaning, expanding on the use found in *To the Hebrews*. There the issue was that the blood of Christ could "perfect" or "purify" the conscience (Heb. 9:9, 14). Here the conscience is conceived as capable of confirming one's good behavior. In this case, after having suffered for a little while, their conscience will confirm their obedience, and *"the God of all grace, who has called you to his eternal glory in Christ, will himself restore, establish, and strengthen you"* (1 Pet. 5:10). This means that you are no longer a newborn baby but have grown in the faith as a result of your suffering. That is why "whoever has suffered in the flesh has ceased from sin" (1 Pet. 4:1).

The symbolic universe of *First Peter* is one in which the earth is a place where women and men live in darkness (1 Pet. 2:9), and *"the devil prowls around like a roaring lion, seeking some to devour"* (1 Pet. 5:8). Christ, on the other hand, is said to have *"died for sins once for all"* (1 Pet. 3:18), and after having been raised by God *"has gone into heaven and is at the right hand of God, with angels, authorities and powers subject to him"* (1 Pet. 3:22). Like in *Revelation,* in *First Peter* the angels and the rulers of the spheres between heaven and earth have been conquered and are at present already subjected to God's power. Paul, on the other hand, thinks that at present Christ is not seated at the right hand of God, but engaged in subjecting the rulers of the spheres. The author of *To the Hebrews*, for his part, affirms that Christ is officiating as High Priest while seated in the throne with his father, not subjecting powers of the air.

In *Revelation* the dragon, who had been defeated and cast out of heaven and now stands in the sands that separate the earth and the sea (Rev. 12:17), has given power to the beast from the land, and the horns of the beast are now persecuting the people of God (Rev. 13:2). In *First Peter,* on the other hand, the devil himself, like a roaring lion, is loose on the earth and is trying to destroy the faith of the people of God who are *"a chosen race, a royal priesthood, a holy nation, God's own people"* (1 Pet. 2:9). This means that unlike the author of *Revelation*, who sees the Roman empire as the surrogate of the devil which is bent on destroying God's people (Rev. 17:11-14), the author of *First Peter,* like Paul (Rom. 13:7), considers the civil authorities worthy of respect. He writes: *"Be subject for the Lord's sake to every human institution, whether it be to the emperor as supreme, or to governors as sent by him to punish those who do wrong and praise those who do right…. Live as free men, yet without using your freedom as a pretext for evil; but live as servants of God. Honor all men. Love the brotherhood. Fear God. Honor the emperor"* (1 Pet. 2:13-17). This gives to the darkness of the world in which Satan roams loose a significant check. In this symbolic universe, God and Christ still rule, and the emperor together with all civil governors occupy legitimate places of authority in the hierarchy of earthly life. At the moment, the Devil is not quite in control.

In *Revelation* the outcome of the "war in heaven" is already known; The Lamb and the martyrs have conquered (Rev. 12:7-8, 11); the ultimate destruction of the powers of Evil at the end of the millennium is an anticlimactic demonstration of sadistic vengeance (Rev. 17:13-14; 19:11, 16). Now the saints find themselves in a struggle with the surrogates of the dragon who are forcing them to worship the beast and its image. In *First Peter* the war is not a cosmic war either. Here the author writes, *"Beloved, I beseech you as aliens and exiles to abstain from the passions of the flesh that wage war against your soul"* (1 Pet. 2:11). From the rest of the advice given to his audience it would seem that the author understands that the passions of the flesh are aroused by the devil who like a roaring lion is seeking to destroy as many of the elect as possible. Clearly the war that is going on, like in *Revelation*, is a spiritual struggle inside individuals. It is in this connection that the author points out that they must live "in fear" while sojourning in a foreign land because God "judges each one impartially according to his deeds" (1 Cor. 1:17). This is what apocalyptic theology is about.

The author of *First Peter* agrees with Paul (Rom. 12:2) that Christians should use their minds and be guided by their desire to do the will of God (1 Pet. 4:2), rather than by their passions or by the Law of Moses. Since Paul wrote his letter *To the Romans* to Christians who were mostly Jews, he says that the passions of the flesh are aroused by the Law of Moses (Rom. 7:5), rather than by the wiles of the devil, as the author of *First Peter* seems to indicate. Paul understood that the Law "was ordained by angels" (the rulers of the spheres between heaven and earth), was given "through an intermediary" (Moses, Gal. 3:19), and operates in the world where

Satan is god (2 Cor. 4:4) as an agent of God's wrath (Rom. 4:15). For Paul the obedience of Christians was "obedience of faith." It is not quite clear how does the author of *First Peter* understand the role of the law of Moses in the lives of Christians who are bound to "obedience to the truth."

Like all apocalyptic texts, *First Peter* inhabits a symbolic universe where historical existence has been predetermined since before the foundation of the world. The addressees are identified as *"the exiles … chosen and destined by God the Father"* (1 Pet. 1:1-2). The Greek original says that *"Peter an apostle of Jesus Christ"* is writing *"to the chosen sojourners in the diaspora … according to the prognosin* (foreknowledge, previous determination) *of God the Father."* Concerning the sufferings and the glory of Christ, the author writes, *"He was destined (proegnosmenou) before the foundation of the world but was made manifest at the end of the times for your sake"* (1 Pet. 1:20). According to the apocalyptic perspective, what was predetermined before the foundation of the world is being revealed *"at the end time"* (1 Pet. 1:5, 20). If, as time comes to its end you find yourself suffering on account of your doing right, it is not something happening to you by chance or because the devil has been after you like a roaring lion. It is happening because it was God's will (1 Pet. 3:17). In this universe, God's retributive justice is not evident to those who lack faith, but as Paul said, *"we know that in everything God works for good with those who love him, who are called according to his purpose"* (Rom. 8:28). The universe of the author of *First Peter* is not one in which Satan is the god of this world. He is a loose enemy seeking to destroy the faithful only because it fits God's purpose.

This point of view is further elucidated by the way in which the author makes reference to the prophets of old who were, according to him, eager to find out about the salvation which is *"ready to be revealed"* at the time of the end. The recipients of the letter should therefore rejoice not only because they know what the prophets wished to know about their salvation, but also because *"God's power"* is guarding them for it *"through faith"* (1 Pet. 1:5). Through the prophets, the Spirit of Christ predicted the significance of the sufferings and the subsequent glory of Christ. It was revealed to them, however, that by their prophesying they were *"serving not themselves but you, in the things that have now been announced to you by those who preached the good news to you through the Holy Spirit"* (1 Pet. 1:10-12). In this way what was determined before the foundation of the world has come to be revealed to the Christians living at the time of the end by the Spirit of Christ and by the Holy Spirit. A similar perspective informs the letters of Paul. He reminds the Corinthians that the Israelites who saw God performing miracles on their behalf, crossing the sea, covered by a cloud during the day and drinking water from the Rock that was Christ, died in the wilderness because of their idolatry and immorality. He then draws the purpose of the recording of these events. Those things happened, but *"they were written for our instruction, upon whom the end of the ages has come"* (1 Cor. 10:11). What the author is telling is based on what prophets wrote about which was intended for those living *"at the end of the ages."* The prophets wrote for our time, and what they said is fully endorsed by the Spirit. The apocalyptic perspective depends on recognizing that what was written in antiquity was not written for the benefit of the contemporaries of the authors but of those living at the end of time. Antiquity and the endorsement of the Holy Spirit, of course, also give authority to what was written.

What is peculiar to *First Peter* is that what is being revealed is not the sequence of events that *"must soon take place."* The revelation concerns God's power to guard *"through faith"* those whom he has elected to rejoice in *"this salvation,"* which is uniquely linked to what God did in Jesus Christ. Thus, the author informs his readers, *"Through him you have confidence in God, who raised him from the dead and gave him glory, so that your faith and hope are in God"* (1 Pet. 1:21). In other words, just as God took notice of the obedience and the sufferings of Christ and rewarded him with glory at his right hand, you may be confident that God will also do the same for you if you *"purify you souls by your obedience to the truth"* (1 Pet. 1:22). Everything is the work of God who guards you through faith and purifies you through sufferings. As a result you have a *"living hope"* (1 Pet. 1:3, 20).

Given the prominent place given to suffering both in the case of Christ and in the lives of Christians who must follow in his steps, it is necessary to pay attention to the role played by suffering in "this salvation." As said already, while they are strangers in a foreign land God is guarding the elect "through faith." Faith, however, is something that, like hope, is expressed by "obedience." Their faith is to be tested by the "various trials" which they may have to suffer in a little while, which should not surprise them. The author thinks of suffering as analogous to the process used to establish the worth of gold. It is not just any stuff that is put in the fire to find out its value. That is done only with gold nuggets. So the Christians are going to be put to the test of various trials because they are elected and destined for salvation; there is gold in them. Gold is tested by fire, and the faith of Christians is tested by trials which are designed by God (1 Pet. 1:7). The author compares how those destined to an imperishable, undefiled and unfading inheritance are purified by suffering to how gold nuggets of undefined value are purified by fire. The purification process takes out a multitude of sins accumulated before their having been born as babies in Christ. Thus, the author exhorts, *"Having purified your souls by your obedience to the truth for a sincere love of the brethren, love one another earnestly from the heart"* (1 Pet. 1:22), and later adds, *"Above all hold unfailing your love for one another, since love covers a multitude of sins"* (1 Pet. 4:8). Like Paul, the author of *First Peter* holds the trinity of faith, hope and love to be what constitutes a Christian life.

First Peter, most likely, was written toward the end of the reign of Domitian, 81-96 C.E. At that time there was no official imperial policy that tied worship of the emperor to a loyalty oath to Rome. This only came to be the case much later, under Emperor Decius in the third century. Nero's use of Christians as scapegoats for the fire of Rome, 65 C.E., was a purely local event (Tacitus, *Annales*, xv. 44). The correspondence between Pliny the Younger and Emperor Trajan, 112-115 C.E., confirms that there was no official policy on the matter at the time, and Pliny makes clear that as far as he is concerned Christians were politically and morally harmless (*Epistles*, x. 96). Historians have come to the conclusion that the persecutions of Christians in the provinces were brought about by local elites who were concerned with maintaining the social fabric of the Roman Empire. They wished to preserve cultural continuity and their privileged status. As a result, persecutions of Christians and of other minorities were unofficial, spontaneous and transitory. They seem to have been the type of harassment that traditional elites carry out against those whom they perceive as threats to the *status quo*.

The author of *Daniel* is motivated by the need to encourage his contemporaries not to become discouraged and feel abandoned by God by the taking away of *"the continual burnt offering, the transgression that makes desolate, and the giving over of the sanctuary and host to be trampled underfoot"* (Dan. 8:13). His concern is with what Antiochus IV is doing by discontinuing the offerings to Yahveh at the altar of the temple in Jerusalem and instituting the use of the altar for offerings to Zeus in 167 B.C.E. The author of *According to Mark* takes over the language of *Daniel* and refers it to the impending destruction of the temple and the fall of Jerusalem by the army of Titus in 70 C.E. (Mk. 13:14). John, the prophet, writing at the end of the first century warns his contemporaries that offering a sacrifice to the genius of the emperor will prevent a person's name from being found in the Book of Life (Rev. 20:15). The authors of *According to Matthew* and of *According to Luke*, also writing toward the end of the first century, are concerned with the delay of the *Parousia* and provide guidance for life on earth.

By contrast, the author of *First Peter* does not provide a context for the sufferings experienced by his readers.

The sufferings referred to by the author of *First Peter* seem to have been caused by unofficial harassment. The author refers to them hypothetically *"so that in case they speak against you as wrongdoers, they may see your good deeds and glorify God on the day of visitation"* (1 Pet. 2:12). He asks a rhetorical question, *"Who is there to harm you if you are zealous for what is right?"* If retributive justice and God's will were visible to everyone, the answer, of course, would be "none." The author then explains that if they were to suffer doing right *"you will be blessed. Have no fear of them, nor be troubled."* (1 Pet. 3:13-14). Suffering for righteousness' sake takes place within the preordained divine plan. His advice is, *"Keep your conscience clear* ["good," as opposed to bad], *so that, when you are abused, those who revile your good behavior in Christ may be put to shame"* (1 Pet. 3:16). Suffering may happen both for doing right and for doing wrong. If it should happen to be God's will that you suffer for doing right, that is better than the alternative (1 Pet. 3:17). In his concluding recapitulation, the author again reaffirms his view, *"If you are reproached for the name of Christ, you are blessed, because the spirit of glory and of God rests upon you."* Then he exhorts, *"let none of you suffer as a murderer, or a thief, or a wrongdoer, or a mischief-maker; yet if one suffers as a Christian, let him not be ashamed, but under that name let him glorify God"* (1 Pet. 4:14-16). Suffering for doing right is God's will to purify the elect.

That they may be reviled, accused before magistrates, reproached, abused by their non-Christian fellow citizens in the Roman Empire, according to the author, could be explained in reference to two causes, one earthly, historical and one heavenly, spiritual. Both are intertwined and are in evidence depending on one's point of reference. One was that their neighbors resent the fact that they no longer participate in the activities which they had happily carried out with them before. *"They are surprised that you do not now join them in the same wild profligacy, and they abuse you"* (1 Pet. 4:4). According to Tacitus, the Christians who were charged with setting the city of Rome on fire were also charged with *odium humani generis*, hatred of the human race (*Annales*, xv. 44). Non-participation in the life style of the rest of society was interpreted as revealing a sense of superiority, of disdain for all others. Their conduct was considered a disruption of the social fabric that could result in unrest and social dislocations. The harassment of Christians by neighbors who accused them before magistrates aimed to prevent those outcomes.

The other cause for the sufferings of Christians was that *"the time has come for judgment to begin with the household of God; and if it begins with us, what will be the end of those who do not obey the gospel of God?"* (1 Pet. 4:17). Notice that the gospel is not to be understood, but to be obeyed. That is what the judgment will take into consideration. The impending suffering is required for your purification so that you may be approved at the judgment which is to begin with us, the household of God. The present, therefore, is charged with apocalyptic urgency.

The suffering to be experienced by the recipients of the letter, as already noticed, is closely tied to the sufferings of Christ. He is the one who *"died for sins once for all, the righteous for the unrighteous, that he might bring us to God"* (1 Pet. 3:18). They are being called to suffer *"because Christ also suffered for you, leaving you an example, that you should follow in his steps"* (1 Pet. 2:21). In this letter, the life of Christ is compressed to the passion and the ensuing ultimate glory. *"The sufferings of Christ and the subsequent glory"* (1 Pet. 1:11) established the pattern of what is going to be the future of those who remain *"obedient to the truth"* (1 Pet. 1:22). His suffering had been prophesied by those who inquired in antiquity *"about this salvation"* (1 Pet. 1:10). It was revealed to them that their prophecies were not for the benefit of their contemporaries, but for the benefit of those living at the end of time, that is the author's audience. They had received *"the good news"* through the Holy Spirit sent from heaven (1 Pet. 1:11-12). What the prophets of old *"indicated by the Spirit of Christ within them"* was that the sufferings of Christ were to culminate in subsequent glory. That the prophets foretold this for the benefit of the recipients of the letter means that their future is to follow this pattern. Exactly how the pattern is to become effective in the life of each one of the strangers and sojourners in the diaspora of life on this earth is something that the future will tell. This is what the angels are eager to find out (1 Pet. 1:12). How will it turn out for the newborn babes who are growing to become the heirs to an imperishable salvation? Will they come out of the various trials that will test their faith, during which God' power will be guarding them, with a good conscience?

The readers are told that the purification of their faith through fiery trials will *"redound to praise and glory and honor at the revelation of Jesus Christ."* They have not seen him, but they love him and they believe in him; therefore, they *"rejoice with unutterable and exalted joy."* Then the author announces, *"...as the outcome of your faith you obtain the salvation of your souls"* (1 Pet. 1:7-9). In other words, salvation depends on a faith in what God has done through Jesus Christ that, like gold, has been purified by fire. This means that the impartial judgment of God examines the genuineness of the faith in each individual. Given this premise, the author finds it necessary to give the dead the opportunity to exercise faith in what God did through Jesus Christ. To do this he refers to the account in The *Book of the Watchers* about the angels who had sons with the daughters of men, based on Genesis 6:2-4. According to the account the sons born from such unnatural sexual encounters were giants who brought about havoc on earth. God therefore did away with both the angels and the giants and confined them to a prison in the nether world where they are being kept until the judgment (1 En. 10-11).

To fulfill his mission as a defender of God's justice, the author of *First Peter* adds another element to the Enochic elaboration of the story in Genesis: *"Christ also died for sins once for all, ... being put to death in the flesh but made alive in the spirit; in which he went and preached to the spirits in prison, who formerly did not obey, when God's patience waited in the days of Noah, during the building of the ark"* (1 Pet. 3:18-20). Then, referring to those who still engage in the wild profligacy in which his readers also had been involved in the past, the author affirms that *"they will have to give an account to him who is ready to judge the living and the dead"* (1 Pet. 4:5). This gives him the basis for having said that Christ went to preach to the spirits in prison: *"For this is why the gospel was preached even to the dead, that though judged in the flesh like men, they might live in the spirit like God"* (1 Pet. 4:6). The realization that the judgment involves both the living and the dead makes it necessary that the dead be given the opportunity to exercise faith in the God that raised Jesus Christ from the dead, and thus be approved at the judgment. It was to fulfill this requirement that, according to the author of *First Peter*, Christ went to preach to the spirits in prison, the fallen angels and their progeny who had been cast to the pit to await the judgment. Years later, taking into account this text, Christians included in their confessions of faith, "he descended into Hell."

First Peter's description of Christ's descent to the pit to preach to the dead is based on Paul's understanding that those who are raised from the dead live in spirit bodies (1 Cor. 15:44), which is the body of the risen Christ. Thus the author distinguishes the death of Christ in a body of flesh from the life of the risen Christ in a spirit body, and the judgment of the dead on account of what they did in a body of flesh from the life they may have in a spirit body like God's, if they believed the gospel that was preached to them while dead. *First Peter* exhibits an anthropology that makes it possible for the dead in Hades to hear the gospel being preached to them, and to respond to the gospel with faith. This anthropology was introduced by the *Book of the Watchers'* understanding of the soul as an independent entity that survives the death of the body. *First Peter* twice refers to salvation as what is experienced by the soul apart from the body (1 Pet. 1:9; 4:19).

My reading of *First Peter* does not agree that the letter encourages its audience to fit into the fabric of the empire by living in accord with the standards of their society. As primary support for this point of view is offered the presence of a household code. These codes were the means by which a *pater familias* established order within the household on a hierarchical basis. At the top were the emperor and his governors (1 Pet. 2:13-14). Servants are to be submissive to their masters (1 Pet. 2:18-20), and wives to their husbands (1 Pet. 3:1-6). Unlike other household codes, this one reminds husbands to bestow *"honor on the woman as the weaker sex, since you are joint heirs of the grace of life"* (1 Pet. 3:7), thus giving it a Christian touch. The author then adds a code of conduct that applies to everyone: *"all of you have unity of spirit, sympathy, love of the brethren, a tender heart and a humble mind. Do not return evil for evil or reviling for reviling; but on the contrary bless, for to this you have been called, that you may obtain a blessing"* (1 Pet. 3:8-9).

There is no question that the author of this letter, like Paul (1 Cor. 11:3), lives in a hierarchically structured society and does not think that the function of the Gospel is to bring about revolutionary changes. Like Paul, he advises honor and respect for all governing authorities. The advice given to Zerubbabel by Zechariah (Zech. 3:6), *"Not by might, nor by power, but by my Spirit, says the Lord of hosts."* was followed by all biblical apocalypticists. The household code of the author of *First Peter* does not indicate that he was advising his readers to accommodate themselves to the norms of their society. On the contrary, he makes clear that because they have been called *"out of darkness into his marvelous light"* they who at one time were *"no people"* now are *"God's people"* (1 Pet. 2:9-10). As a result they are strangers in a foreign land and therefore are a counter cultural force that produces a negative reaction within their society and forces them to have to give *"an account"* for their hope (1 Pet. 3:15). As noticed above, their non-accommodation to the norms of the surrounding culture is what causes their having to suffer the harassment brought about by their neighbors. Given the tone in which the whole letter is written as an account of the function of suffering, it cannot be argued that the letter teaches accommodation to the prevailing social culture. It is clear that for the author theology trumps sociology. That he lives in a hierarchical symbolic universe, however, is clear.

It is somewhat ironic that *First Peter* should be considered a call to be integrated into the surrounding social structure. It is also ironic that the author should have chosen Peter as his pseudonym. According to Paul, Peter and he had a strong confrontation at Antioch, at which time Paul called Peter a hypocrite to his face in front of everyone at a communal meal (Gal. 2:11-16). It happens that this letter is more informed by the theology of Paul than some of the letters written by authors who used his name as their pseudonym. That faith is demonstrated by obedience, that sufferings are inevitable by those who participate in the passion and the glory of Christ, that the mind of newborns is capable to identify the will of God, that the Gospel is power for the obedience of faith, not information, that the resurrection body is a spirit body, that as free persons Christians are servants of God, that civil authorities are the servants of God, that Christians live in a struggle with the passions of the flesh, that the Christian is a citizen of heaven, that history is predetermined, these are all hallmarks of Paul's theology. If *First Peter* is quite often not seen as an apocalyptic text it is because its apocalypticism, like Paul's, is concerned with the final triumph of God in the glory of those whom he has chosen, rather than with descriptions of how God is going to avenge all the wrongs done to his people. Facing life at a particular time under particular circumstances, the author of *First Peter* advised his readers, *"So, all those who suffer according to God's will, let them commit themselves to doing good before a Faithful Creator"* (1 Pet. 4:19, my translation). This is the apocalyptic gospel in a nutshell.

JUDE

This very impassioned and short letter *"to those who are called, beloved in God the Father and kept for Jesus Christ"* (Jude, 1) takes up a theme held in tension in apocalyptic texts. All apocalyptic texts in the Bible presuppose that history is predetermined and that everyone will have to stand before God at the judgment. They do not see that these two presuppositions are in tension with each other. This may be due to a limited understanding of human freedom. Only Paul, who may have been the one with the best education, noticed the tension and considers an objection: *"You will say to me then, 'Why does he still find fault? For who can resist his will?'"* (Rom. 9:19). Since he has a strong sense of the freedom of those "in Christ" (Gal. 5:1), he does see the problem, but the sovereignty of God wins the day, *"For God has consigned all men to disobedience, that he may have mercy upon all"* (Rom. 11:32). Still, he admits that human disobedience can trump God's mercy. Thus, the tension remains.

The author of *Jude* feels duty bound to remind his readers, *"though you were once for all fully informed"* already (Jude, 5), that their being the elect who are loved by God and kept for Christ does not mean that they cannot end up *"undergoing a punishment of eternal fire"* (Jude, 7), just as was the case with unrighteous people who were among the elect in the past. This is basic to Paul, the author of *To the Hebrews* and the author of *First Peter*. Given the limitations of their cultural intellectual horizon, these authors do not develop an argument to show how God's will and human freedom interact. The author of Jude just hammers in with unrelenting force that history shows that those who once had been saved by God could later be destroyed by God on account of their disobedience. Therefore, he confesses that *"being very eager to write to you of our common salvation, I found it necessary to write appealing to you to contend for the faith which was once for all delivered to the saints"* (Jude, 3). In other words, don't think that having been elected guarantees your salvation. The point was also made by the author of *According to Matthew*: *"For many are called, but few are chosen"* (Mt. 22:14). He closes his letter reminding them, "build yourselves up in your most holy faith" (Jude, 20). Like the author of *To the Thessalonians II*, the author emphasizes that salvation depends on remaining in the traditional faith delivered to them, and argues against the deceptions of pseudo-Christians who could lead them astray and, thus, annul their election.

The author of *Jude is* concerned with the rise of some among the elect who are perverting the faith. His readers are not facing sufferings brought about by their relatives, their neighbors or by the civil authorities. They are having to contend with some who, having been admitted into their Christian community, are now bringing divisions among them. They are *"ungodly persons who pervert the grace of our God into licentiousness and deny our only Master and Lord, Jesus Christ."* They, of course, will be judged and destroyed by

God. As a matter of fact, they *"long ago were designated for this condemnation"* (Jude, 4). As in all apocalyptic texts, what bring about trials to the faithful, be they the civil authorities, the neighbors, their relatives, their passions, the dragon, or fellow Christians, are part of God's predetermined course of events.

Further descriptions of the ones who distort the faith say that *"these men in their dreamings defile the flesh, reject authority, and revile the glorious ones"* .... *"Woe to them! For they walk in the way of Cain, and abandon themselves for the sake of gain to Balaam's error, and perish in Korah's rebellion"* (Jude, 8, 11). The author knows well the elaborations of the stories of those who stood in the way of Israel's progress according to God's designs. Cain had become a symbol of lust and self-indulgence; Balaam represented greed and covetousness, and Korah was the prototype of those who lead a revolt against legitimate leaders. All three confirm that those who reject authority and seek selfish gain end up severely punished. How those who pervert the faith were reviling "the glorious ones," that is the angels, is not specified.

After referring to the activities of proverbial evil-doers, the author refers to the celebration of the Lord's Supper in their community. The men who are perverting the faith, he points out, *"are blemishes on your love feasts, as they boldly carouse together, looking after themselves; waterless clouds, carried along by winds; fruitless trees in late autumn, twice dead, uprooted; wild waves of the sea, casting up the foam of their own shame; wandering stars for whom the nether gloom of darkness has been reserved for ever"* (Jude, 12-13). As if these rhetorical flourishes with concrete charges were not enough, the author adds, *"These are grumblers, malcontents, following their own passions, loud-mouthed boasters, flattering people to gain advantage"* (Jude, 16). The real problem is that they pretend to be Christians and take part in the communal love feasts. That the love feasts were abused by members of the community who took care of themselves, so that while some were hungry others were drunk, was already the case at the Corinthian church at the time of Paul (1 Cor. 11:21). The author of *Jude* does not give a theological basis for condemning such behavior, like Paul does. He just wants to make sure that other members of the community do not join these rebellious, self-indulgent carousers who once were counted among the elect but are destined to *"the nether gloom of darkness."* The images of waterless clouds, sea waves that throw up foam and stars that end up in darkness seem to be based in Prov. 25:14; Is. 57:20 and Is. 14:12-15. The reference to fruitless trees may be an allusion to the fig tree in the gospel story of Jesus' visit to the temple (Mk. 11:13, 20).

The men who had been admitted into their Christian community and lived among the elect, were now disturbing and dividing the community. Their condemnation by God was sure. What the recipients of the letter should fully understand was that the same would be their end if they allowed these men to pervert their faith. The author supports this conclusion with two examples. The first brings into focus the fate of the angels who *"did not keep their own position but left their proper dwelling."* They are the angels who on their own left heaven in order to marry daughters of men (Gen. 6:4). They are now being *"kept by him [God] in nether gloom until the judgment of the great day"* (Jude, 6), as reported by the Book of the Watchers (1 En. 6-10; 18:14-16; 21: -7). The readers should also remember what happened to Sodom and Gomorrah and the surrounding cities. People in those cities were *"acting immorally and indulging in unnatural lust,"* which is what those about whom the author warns his audience against are doing. As a result they *"serve as an example by undergoing a punishment of eternal fire"* (Jude, 7).

The author then contrasts the evil doers who pervert the gospel with the archangel Michael. According to a Jewish legend, likely found in *The Assumption of Moses*, when Moses died the devil accused Moses of having been a murderer. On that account, he was not to be given burial. Facing the devil, Michael did not engage himself in an argument with him. According to the story in Exodus, Moses had killed an Egyptian who had been beating a Hebrew slave and hid him on the sand (Ex. 2:11-12). Building on the Jewish *haggadah*, the author of *Jude* points out that, rather than to *"presume to pronounce a reviling judgment"* upon the devil, Michael said, *"The Lord rebuke you"* (Jude, 9). This is in sharp contrast to those who disturb the community of Christians being addressed by the author. They have no qualms in passing judgment and reviling *"whatever they do not understand, and by those things which they know by instinct as irrational animals, they are destroyed"* (Jude, 10). Clearly, this author places a premium on the rational capacities that should guide the lives of Christians. Ignorance, superstition, prejudices and irrationality are not the Christian way to uphold the gospel, but these are the tools used by those destroying the community he is addressing. Their use of them should be a clear sign that they are false prophets.

As the last argument to strengthen the faith of his readers, the author reminds them that *"Enoch in the seventh generation from Adam prophesied"* concerning the men dividing their community. He quotes *First Enoch*: *"Behold, the Lord came with his holy myriads, to execute judgment on all, and to convict all the ungodly of all their deeds of ungodliness which they have committed in such an ungodly way, and of all the harsh things which ungodly sinners have spoken against him [God]"* (1 En. 1:9). Apparently, in the author's horizon, *First Enoch*, a book that according to him was written by an ancestor of Noah, is the source of all later references to the necessity for all humanity to appear before the judgment. As a result, those who act contrary to God's will and speak against God's ways will be convicted and punished severely. That the author thought that to quote *First Enoch* was the best way to drive his message home and to impress on his readers the need to take the final judgment with all seriousness testifies to the important role played by this book among the early Christians.

Finally, the author says, *"you must remember, beloved, the predictions of the apostles of our Lord Jesus Christ; they said to you, 'In the last time there will be scoffers, following their own ungodly passions.' It is these who set up divisions, worldly people, devoid of the Spirit"* (Jude, 17-18). The exact quotation is not found in the canonical gospels. It may have come down to the author through the oral tradition. Similar injunctions are, *"Take heed that no one leads you* astray" or *"False Christs and false prophets will arise and show signs and wonders, to lead astray, if possible, the elect"* (Mk. 13:5, 22). The concern of the author is for his readers not to be led astray by what he identifies as "scoffers," and in *According to Mark* are identified as "false prophets." His point is that the appearance of scoffers, or false prophets, had been prophesied by the apostles for the benefit of those living at the time of the end. They are part of the divine design. The attention of the readers, however, should not be on the predetermined appearance of scoffers. Their presence, however, is a sign of the end of time. The readers are told specifically what should guide their conduct: *"you, beloved, build yourselves up on your most holy faith; pray in the Holy Spirit; keep yourselves in the love of God; wait for the mercy of our Lord Jesus Christ unto eternal life"* (Jude 20-21). Thus, while fully aware of the significance of the final judgment, they should remain focused on the salvation to be enjoyed by those who keep themselves in the love of God.

Toward those who are perverting the gospel of Jesus Christ and those who are tempted to adopt their way of life, they should have two different approaches. They should convince and snatch out of the fire those who are undecided, those *"who doubt."* With the others, the scoffers, they should *"have mercy with fear."* They should not even get close to them, *"hating even the garment spotted by their flesh"* (Jude 22-23). To have mercy with fear is to pity them while keeping a safe distance from them, since they are taboo, and what touches them becomes "spotted." The right thing to do is to let them go their own way, and let God take care of them at the judgment. Within the horizon of the author the presence of destroyers of the faith is a clear sign that the time of the end has arrived; given this context, the apocalyptic judgment and God's ability to punish severely the ungodly are the two things to take most seriously into account. One's conduct should be guided by the most holy faith with the help of the Holy Spirit. While trying to snatch out of the fire those who seem unaware of the seriousness of the choice before them, they should not concern themselves with

The End of the Scroll

those who promote a perverted gospel that denies the effectiveness of God's retributive justice and devalues God's grace.

The author of *Jude* does not consider the promoters of a perverted gospel to be surrogates of Satan. He does not envision a war between the forces of good and evil, neither in the heavens nor inside human beings. While he envisions salvation as eternal life on account of Christ's mercy, he does not refer to a new heaven and a new earth in which justice prevails. Since he does not consider that his readers are experiencing sufferings, he does not advise patient endurance, the typical apocalyptic virtue. His short missive, however, is fully apocalyptic. His concern is to remind his readers that retributive justice works. God's final judgment overrules God's grace. Their having been elected does not guarantee salvation. And since he and his audience are living at the end of time, the imminence of the judgment places a premium on the need to remain true to *"the faith once for all delivered to the saints"* (Jude 3).

The letter ends with a doxology worthy of a well-trained liturgist. It has been a favorite of preachers who use it to conclude their sermons. As such, it tells something important about the educational level of the author, which the letter as a whole also supports. As an author he demonstrates possession of an extensive vocabulary, and writes with spontaneous fluidity and vigor.

SECOND PETER

As noticed in the introduction to this chapter, *Second Peter* is the last of the letters being analyzed here, and among the New Testament books it is the last to have been written. Its author recycles all the contents of *Jude* in his text, and knows the existence of *First Peter* and the letters of Paul. He considers essential the preservation of the established apostolic faith, which he characterizes as "most holy," and confirms its undiminished relevance to post-apostolic Christianity. He defends the truth of prophecy, or the word of God, as scripture, the depository of the most holy faith. Thus, he reflects a Christianity that has become a self-conscious institution that preserves the apostolic tradition. Therefore, his letter is to be dated sometime in the first half of the second century. Its publication, using the name of the leader of the apostles as its pseudonym, took place at the time when several texts appeared under Peter's name: *The Apocalypse of Peter* (c. 135, considered canonical in the Muratorian Canon), *The Preaching of Peter* (early second century), *The Gospel of Peter* (c. 190), *Acts of Peter* (c. 175). Some of these were among the Nag Hammadi MSS found in Egypt. The author of the popular *The Apocalypse of Peter* used *Second Peter*.

Even though it reproduces with slight deviations the contents of *Jude*, it has the basic structure of a well-known literary type: a testament. In these texts, a prominent leader, aware of his soon departure from this world, gives a summary of his message and a warning against coming dangers to be faced by his followers once he is dead. The primary example is the book of *Deuteronomy*, where Moses repeats the Law and tells the Israelites about the dangers they will face once they have entered the Promise Land. Another classic of the genre is *The Testament of the Twelve Patriarchs*, where the twelve sons of Jacob advise and warn their descendants. In the New Testament, the farewell speeches of Jesus (Jn. 13-17), the sermon of Paul at Ephesus (Acts 20:17-28) and the pseudonymous second letter to Timothy are examples of "testaments." It is because of this feature of the text that in *Second Peter* the activity of those who pervert the gospel and lead licentious lives, which in *Jude* is said to be taking place at the time of writing, is presented as what will take place in the near future, after the author's death. To counteract the activity of these false prophets, the author reminds his audience of what the gospel is about (2 Pet. 1:12; 3:1).

The opening paragraph sets the substance of the gospel that had been preached to them in a nutshell. The author reminds his readers that God's power has given them all *"knowledge of him who called us to his own glory and excellence."* Knowledge of Christ means knowledge of the *"precious and very great promises"* which are at the core of *"all things that pertain to life and godliness."* The purpose for the granting to both the author and his audience these rich promises is to make it possible for them to *"escape from the corruption that is in the world because of passion, and become partakers of the divine nature"* (2 Pet. 1:3-4). In this account, knowledge of the promises of Christ is what the preaching of the gospel provides. According to the author, his audience has this knowledge and is *"established in the truth that* [they] *have"* (2 Pet. 1:12). He is writing to them to *"arouse* [their] *sincere mind"* (2 Pet. 3:1), so that they may not be *"carried away with the error of lawless men and lose* [their] *own stability"* (2 Pet. 3:17, the Greek word *sterigmos* has the idea of being firm, stable in what they have in mind). Thus, he closes the letter advising, *"Grow in the grace and knowledge of our Lord and Savior Jesus Christ"* (2 Pet. 3:18). In the opening paragraph he repeats the word knowledge four times. The notion that the gospel is knowledge of promises which must be kept firmly in mind gives to the Christianity of the author a strong Hellenistic flavor.

Also in this context is the concrete advice given by the author as to how to achieve the goal of becoming *"partakers of the divine nature."* He introduces his method by recognizing that it will require *"every effort"* to follow his prescription. It was commonplace for the mystery cults to prescribe ascetic practices in connection with reaching higher levels of being. The road to becoming *"without spot or blemish and at peace"* (2 Pet. 3:14), according to the author, is *"to supplement your faith with virtue, and virtue with knowledge, and knowledge with self-control, and self-control with steadfastness, and steadfastness with godliness, and godliness with brotherly affection, and brotherly affection with love"* (2 Pet. 1:5-7). This ladder of ascent to perfection parallels the stages of initiation to the ultimate mystery typical of the Eastern religions that became popular in the Roman Empire after the Punic wars. Even some emperors were initiates in several of them at the same time. It may be that the author is providing this ladder of ascent as an alternative to the one being promoted by the "lawless men" among them. The author's reason for demanding this course of action is that *"if these things are yours and abound, they keep you from being ineffective and unfruitful in the knowledge of our Lord and Savior Jesus Christ"* (2 Pet. 1:8). In other words, this ladder of ascent does not culminate in knowledge of a "mystery," but in knowledge of the Lord Jesus Christ, which is the key to life and godliness.

The author identifies what they had come to know about Jesus Christ as *"the power and coming of our Lord Jesus Christ"* (2 Pet. 1:16). He does not specifically describe in what way Christ demonstrated his power. He does not refer to his earthly activities or to the passion. He does say that anyone who lacks the elements in the ladder of ascent he endorses *"is blind and shortsighted and has forgotten that he was cleansed from his old sins"* (2 Pet. 1:9), and that Christians have been bought by their Master (2 Pet. 2:1). These may be references to the power of Christ as the Savior who cleanses from sins and owns his followers. The coming, on the other hand, is undoubtedly the substance of the precious and great promise. He refers back to it, after he had dealt with the errors of the *"lawless men"* among them, by advising his audience to be found living holy and godly lives, *"waiting for and hastening the coming of the day of God"* (2 Pet. 3:12). What they must keep firmly in mind is the promise of the coming of the Lord Jesus Christ.

To reaffirm the promised coming of Christ, the author, recalls Peter's experience at the Mount of Transfiguration. It serves to establish the divine origin of what the prophets proclaimed, and the wisdom found in the letters of Paul. Identifying himself as Peter, the author claims to have heard the heavenly voice declaring, *"This is my beloved Son, with whom I am well pleased,"* (2 Pet. 1:16-18). To be noticed is that he makes clear that the experience at the mountain was not just a private experience of his. He says, *"we heard this voice"* and *"we were with him in the holy mountain."* The reference is to the account of the scene in the synoptic gospels in which three disciples were present. That is, the power and the coming is certified by the apostles, not just Peter alone.

Besides the testimony of eyewitnesses, there is the *"prophetic word"* which is like *"a lamp shining in a dark place."* The prophets also announced the power and coming of the Lord. When they spoke, they did not speak driven by a subjective impulse. They were *"men moved by the Holy Spirit* [who] *spoke from God"* (2 Pet. 1:21). Moreover, Paul, who apparently the author considers neither an apostle nor a prophet, *"wrote to you according to the wisdom given him, speaking of this as he does in all his letters."* He then warns his readers that *"the ignorant and unstable twist to their own destruction"* what Paul wrote, *"as they do the other scriptures"* (2 Pet. 3:15-16). Having the evidence of apostles who were eyewitness, of prophets and of Paul, the author affirms, *"we did not follow cleverly devised myths when we made known to you the power and the coming of our Lord Jesus Christ"* (2 Pet. 1:16). The promise of his coming is firmly established and so should be the mind of the elect.

False prophets rose among the people at the time of the prophets, the apostles announced that false prophets would arise, and Paul had to deal with false interpreters of his words who twisted what he said. So too *"...there will be false teachers among you who will secretly bring destructive heresies, even denying the Master who bought them, bringing upon themselves swift destruction"* (2 Pet. 2:1). This introduces a description of the lawless men who pervert the gospel which is based on the text of *Jude*.

The parallels between these two texts are plain to see. I will point out the most apparent. The false teachers disown their Master and Lord, Jesus Christ, and on account of their dissolute practices, their condemnation has already been sealed (Jude 4 / 2 Pet. 2:1). The angels who left their heavenly dwelling are consigned to utter darkness until the judgment (Jude 6 / 2 Pet. 2:4). Sodom and Gomorrah are an object lesson (Jude 7 / 2 Pet. 2:6). The pseudo-Christians are defiled by lusts, flout authority and insult heavenly beings (Jude 8 / 2 Pet. 2:10). Angels do not engage in arguments; they defer to God's judgment (Jude 9 / 2 Pet. 2:11). Those who pervert the gospel operate on instinct like irrational beasts and judge what they do not understand (Jude 10 / 2 Pet. 2:12). They profane the love feasts with their selfish indulgences (Jude 12 / 2 Pet. 2:13). Like Balaam, they are greedy for money (Jude 11 / 2 Pet. 2:15). They are clouds without water, mist that is blown away (Jude 12 / 2 Pet. 2:17). They are reserved for the most utter darkness (Jude 13 / 2 Pet. 2:17). They spout bombast and follow their lusts (Jude 16 / 2 Pet. 2:18).

Scholars have spent serious efforts to explain these common elements in both texts and have come to the conclusion that the author of *Second Peter* took up the descriptions from *Jude*, rather than the reverse. This conclusion is based on several factors. Prominent among them is the way in which the common material is used. In *Second Peter* the harsh language of *Jude* is softened and references to what would become apocryphal texts are reduced. The author does not refer to the legend about Moses' burial and does not identify Enoch as the seventh from Adam. Arguing on the basis of a parallel situation in the case of the synoptic gospels, where *According to Mark*, the shortest, is expanded by the authors of *According to Matthew* and *According to Luke*, it follows that *Jude* was expanded, and applied to his specific concern with the delay of the *Parousia* by the author of *Second Peter*. In terms of style, *Second Peter* is somewhat uneven, with rapid mood changes, and sometimes unintelligible on account of structural disconnects and the use of flamboyant terms. The author uses 25 words which are not found in any other New Testament book, and 32 which are found neither in the New Testament nor in the Greek version of the Old Testament, the Septuagint. The presence of 57 unusual words and flamboyant descriptions have been used as evidence of a "baroque" style. Its Greek belongs to the Asiatic style used by writers of Asia Minor, rather than the Attic style used in Greece. The end result of these analyses of the Greek in *Second Peter* argues against its author being also the one who wrote *First Peter*. The latter exhibits some of the best Greek style found in the New Testament.

The characteristics given to the pseudo-Christians by the author of *Second Peter*'s use of those found in *Jude*, are somewhat paradigmatic. Thus, the portrait is that of the standard profile of a heretic. Even though the details produce a prototype, they do allow the identification of some features: these men operate within the community, and they promote a form of "Christian freedom" already practiced in Corinth at the time of Paul (1 Cor. 5:11). To use the phrase made popular by Dietrich Bonhoeffer, they promoted a "cheap grace" (*The Cost of Discipleship, passim*), that is a denial of the gospel. According to it, God's grace allows for all types of behavior to Christians who are free from the Law. *Jude* refers specifically to the abuse of God's grace (Jude 4), and *Second Peter* to their false understanding of freedom in Christ (2 Pet. 2:19). They seem to be descendants of the antinomian libertines with whom Paul had to deal at Corinth (1 Cor. 6:9-13; 10:23-24).

Given the characteristics of those disturbing and dividing the community, both authors remind their readers that the appearance of such evil people among them had been predicted (Jude 17 / 2 Pet. 3:1). While in *Jude* the prediction was made by the prophets, *Second Peter* ascribes it to the apostles of Jesus Christ. These predictions, of course, were for "the last days" (Jude 18 / 2 Pet. 3:3). Identifying exactly what would be the concern of the false teacher that would appear at the end of time, the author of *Second Peter* reveals his agenda: to counteract those who deny the promised *Parousia*. *Jude* says that the apostles announced that *"in the last time there will be scoffers, following their own ungodly passions,"* and then identifies those who fulfill this prediction with those among them who *"set up divisions, worldly people, devoid of the Spirit"* (Jude 18-19). *Second Peter* says that *"scoffers will come in the last days with scoffing, following their own passions and saying, 'Where is the promise of his coming? For ever since the fathers fell asleep, all things have continued as they were from the beginning of creation"* (2 Pet. 3:3-4).

The report of what the scoffers say reveals the unique perspective, and concrete agenda, of the author of *Second Peter*. Like the author of *Jude*, the author of *Second Peter* refers to licentious conduct in general terms and to disruptions and carousing in their love feasts, but neither of them gives specificity to that charge. In *Second Peter*, however, the mocking of those who still expect the *Parousia* by those who pervert the Faith is given specificity, and the author feels obliged to give counter arguments in order to defend *"the truth which you have"* (2 Pet. 1:12). The argument presented by the scoffers is that the promise of the Second Coming of Christ, affirmed by the Christian tradition, has proven unfounded. Almost one hundred years after the passion of Christ, it cannot be affirmed that he would come *soon* to redeem the faithful. The author quotes the scoffers saying, *"Where is the promise of his coming?"* Nothing has changed, nothing significant has happened since the promise was given to the disciples. The non-fulfillment of the promise, according to the scoffers, supported the notion that Christians are free to live their lives as they please, putting into practice their freedom by living licentiously. This interpretation of the situation, according to the author, reviles *"the way of truth"* (2 Pet. 2:2). Since the author's agenda was to re-affirm the promise of the *Parousia*, it becomes clear why he chose to cast his message as the testament of Peter. Doing this he was giving a new, creative version to the apocalyptic device of *vaticinia ex eventu*. That the appearance of such scoffers had been predicted by Peter gives authority to his counter arguments.

The diagnosis of the situation advanced by the false teachers is actually correct. The *Parousia* has not taken place and things continue to be the same since the fathers fell asleep. It often happens, however, that an accurate diagnosis is followed by an erroneous prescription as the solution to the problem. The long delay, the author points out, does not mean that licentious freedom is now in order. Rather, it should be understood to mean that one's dependence on God for a life worthy to be rewarded with participation in the divine nature is more urgent than ever. To defend God's power and faithfulness to promises, the author, like Paul, resorts to the way in which the Wise men of Israel explained their inability to account for the injustices taking place in God's world: *"God is in heaven, and you upon earth"* (Ec. 5:2).

Arguing that God had not failed to keep his promise to the Jews, Paul realized that his efforts did not quite succeed. Frustrated by his inability to build a convincing argument, he threw his arms up in the air and confessed, *"O the depth of the riches and wisdom and knowledge of God! How unsearchable are his judgments and how inscrutable his ways!"* (Rom. 11:33). The author of *Second*

Peter does the same by reminding his readers that God does not count time depending on the solar cycles. His time table runs on his own terms. He reminds his readers, *"... do not ignore this one fact, beloved, that with the Lord one day is as a thousand years, and a thousand years as one day"* (2 Pet. 3:8). In other words, God's time is not human time. The explanation is based on a Psalm that starts contrasting the everlasting being of God with the ephemeral life of humans. Pointing this out, it says, *"For a thousand years in thy sight are but yesterday when it is past"* (Ps. 90:4). Given the radical difference between the being of God and the temporal existence of humans, the psalmist goes on to request that just as God in his wrath exposes the iniquities of humans he should also make known to them his favor on *"the work of* [their] *hands"* (Ps. 90:17). In other words, Psalm 90 recognizes the difference between the heavenly and the earthly realities, and pleads for God to recognize the good as well as the evil in humans. *Second Peter* agrees. It affirms that that is exactly what God does while being in a totally different realm of being.

Not only do the scoffers forget that God dwells in a different reality. They also, *"deliberately ignore this fact; that by the word of God heavens existed long ago, and an earth formed out of water and by means of water, through which the world that then existed was deluged with water and perished. By the same word the heaven and earth that now exist have been stored up for fire, being kept until the day of judgment and destruction of ungodly men"* (2 Pet. 3:5-7).

That the world that existed prior to the flood, which was created by the word of God, was destroyed by water, and that the world that has been in existence since the flood will be destroyed, according to God's word also, by fire, is something which the scoffers know, but deliberately ignore. Of all men, they should be the ones who are cognizant of their future destruction by fire. The author returns to this theme pointing out that *"the day of the Lord will come like a thief."* This undoubtedly will catch the scoffers by surprise. When it comes, *"...the heavens will pass away with a loud noise, and the elements will be dissolved with fire, and the earth and the works that are upon it will be burned up"* (2 Pet. 3:10). What the author emphasizes is the ultimate destruction by fire of both what is in the heavens and what is upon the earth. In the heavens, *"the elements will be melted by fire"* as the heavens themselves are *"dissolved."* The elements, of course, are the rulers of the spheres, the principalities, the powers, the rulers of this present darkness, the spiritual hosts of wickedness in the heavenly places, as identified by the author of *To the Ephesians* (6:12), who wrote just a few years before the writing of *Second Peter*. But, as the heavens and their inhabitants are dissolved by fire, so also the earth and its "works" will be burned up, accomplishing the destruction of its inhabitants, "ungodly men."

The author of *Second Peter* is not only concerned to argue that God is faithful to his promise of the *Parousia*. His agenda is also to establish that God has the power to make retributive justice work. His aim is to have the elect keep alive in their *"sincere minds"* (2 Pet. 3:1) that the word of God that created a world from water and destroyed it by water, will destroy the present world by fire when the Lord comes like a thief in the night. On this basis, the author makes his final appeal: *"Since all these things are thus to be dissolved, what sort of persons ought you to be in lives of holiness and godliness"* (2 Pet. 3:11). He insists, *"According to his promise we wait for new heavens and a new earth in which righteousness dwells"* (2 Pet. 3:13). What motivates the Christian is the knowledge that the power and the coming of the Lord Jesus Christ will destroy the present heaven and earth with fire and bring about a new heaven and a new earth. God's justice will triumph.

Second Peter is a cogent reaffirmation of the *Parousia* that will dissolve the present creation by fire and bring about a new creation *"in which righteousness dwells."* In this way the conclusion recalls what the introduction claims to be the substance of *"the truth that you have"* (2 Pet. 1:12). What is at stake is *"the righteousness of our God and Savior Jesus Christ"* (2 Pet. 1:1). The scoffers who deny the truth of the promise are denying the righteousness of God, the very essence of what apocalypticism is committed to uphold.

The End of the Scroll

Ever since the Jews went through some radical changes in their experience as a nation during and after the exile in Babylon, there have been those who have adopted apocalyptic ways for expressing their faith in the biblical God who created the world. As argued in the Introduction, they were particularly concerned to affirm that, contrary to what experience says, God's control of the world was not in jeopardy. Their God was the only true, Almighty God. To affirm their faith in the creator, the apocalypticists expanded their horizon into heaven and showed the way in which what is going on in the world is seen from a divine perspective. Looking at their experience from a human perspective the present was tragic and provided no reasons for expectations of a brighter future. Having received a revelation from God, the apocalypticists were able to communicate to the elect few the "mystery" of what God had in mind for the future as a way to encourage the right way to conduct themselves in the present.

Since the foundation for their faith in God was the evidence provided by creation and by their providential existence as the people of God in the world, their vision of the future was cast in the language of the creation stories that were well known to their contemporaries. In the beginning, the time before time, in *urzeit*, God defeated the forces of chaos in the deep waters engulfed by prevailing darkness. God began to create by causing Light to defeat darkness. The wind (Spirit) of God had to calm down the deep ocean. In other creation myth, Marduk had to defeat Tiamat, or Bell had to defeat Rahab. Reality is not confined to what takes place within a narrow human horizon. Human life takes place on a cosmic plane, not just an earthly one. This required the use of language that conveyed that human existence transcends the world of the senses. Apocalypticism adopted the language of myths, that is, a language that was understood to refer to cosmic realities beyond the reach of human limitations. The symbolic language of apocalyptic texts was not primarily used for its ability to deal with what cannot be described with certainly in human terms, or because it had aesthetic, poetic value. It was used because the future announced by the apocalypticists, unlike the future envisioned by the prophets, was not the future of a nation but the future of the cosmos that had fallen under the power of primordial evil forces.

Genesis states that when God *"was sorry that he had made man on the earth, and it grieved him to his heart,"* he said *"'I will blot out man ... for I am sorry that I have made them.' But Noah found favor in the eyes of the Lord"* (Gen. 6:6-8). According to the story, God did not destroy the earth and all that he had created. The corruption that had become entrenched in the world was destroyed by water, but Noah and his family, the legitimate descendants of Adam and Eve, were preserved and continued to live on the earth God had created. The apocalypticists took this story and applied it to their vision of the future. They, however, had to make an adjustment because they conceived the present situation as even more dire than the one at the time of the flood. The situation then, according to the apocalypticists, had been brought about by the angels who had impregnated women who then gave birth to a race of giants. The situation now is that men who have become surrogates to primordial evil forces are killing those who wish to remain loyal and worship the only true God. This time, rather than water, God will use fire and utterly destroy the world and create a new one, which can best be described in terms of the creation of the original one. When the end of history is described, end time becomes (returns to) primeval time, *Endzeit wird Urzeit*, as the Germans who first analyzed the apocalyptic visions of the future in the nineteenth century phrased it.

The identification of apocalypticism with descriptions of how the present cosmos that was brought out of chaos by God at creation is to be destroyed, and a new cosmos is to be brought in to take its place, has resulted in the identification of apocalypticism with cosmic battles between Good and Evil. Through the centuries of Christian history, apocalyptic enthusiasts have conceived their time as the time of the end and have interpreted the ancient stories found in the Bible as descriptions of their own time, since they were written in scrolls that were sealed until the time of the end. It is the privileged role of chosen individuals to have the key which gives access to the secrets kept in the symbolic descriptions of the events the ancient apocalypticists described in the scrolls they were ordered to seal. Repeatedly Christian preachers and scholars have claimed to be the ones who can open the sealed scroll left by biblical authors and reveal *"what must soon take place"* (Rev. 1:1), only to be proven misguided by the course of history.

All apocalyptic texts, as I have demonstrated, recycled earlier biblical stories and symbols and gave them new functions in their accounts of how the story of human life on earth will come to its end. This pattern has been repeated by Christians through the centuries. Among the many outstanding examples is found the impact of Giordano Bruno in Renaissance Rome, who was burned at the stake on *Campo di fiori* for his identification of the church as a surrogate of Satan. Another notable apocalyptic revival took over the political discourse of Restoration England. The days and dates mentioned in the biblical texts were understood to be code for recent or imagined historical events. The University of Cambridge in the seventeenth century had a strong tradition of scholarship in biblical prophecy particularly interested in establishing when and how the Catholic Church had became a surrogate of Satan, and to help alert the public of the imminent downfall of the papal Antichrist. One of those deeply involved in the promulgation of this tradition was Isaac Newton, the great mathematician who could certainly deal with the numbers found in *Daniel* and *Revelation*. He was a devout, but also a very intellectually independent Christian, who was more concerned with the recovery of true Christianity from the travesty into which both the Catholic Church and the Church of England had perverted it than with his mathematical and physical inquiries. The fear that the Protestant English throne of King Charles II would be occupied by his Catholic brother James prompted extensive efforts in the interpretation of the symbols used by apocalyptic authors to find the way in which God would prevent such outcome. In the course of Christian applications of apocalyptic texts, every interpreter, of course, comes up with his own apocalyptic trajectory to the End. All apocalyptic interpreters recycle earlier apocalyptic interpretations of biblical texts which may or may not have been apocalyptic themselves.

The apocalyptic enthusiasm that swept New England in what has been described as the Second Great Awakening with exalted millenarian expectations at the beginning of the nineteenth century was a transplant of Restoration England fears of a Catholic in the throne. The beginnings of the large immigration of Catholics from Ireland gave rise to fears of a Catholic invasion that would change the character of the nation founded by Puritan pilgrims who had sought to escape from the impositions of established churches. When the preaching of John Wesley gave to the Christianity of the Church of England and the Puritans a new emphasis on the role of experience, and prescribed ways to improve one's experience and enjoy life in the Spirit, apocalyptic concerns were given a prominent role in the process. Then, when John Wesley and George Whitefield transplanted Methodism to America and the Great Awakening blanketed the former British colonies with revivals and paroxysms of the Spirit, apocalyptic enthusiasm also took roots in America.

In the 1830s, William Miller, a Vermont farmer, came up with the date for the Second Coming of Christ; it was to take place in October 1843. When that did not happen, he rechecked his calculations and came up with a more precise date, October 22, 1844. He and his followers made a big impact on most of New England, even making inroads into New York City, where most of the recent immigrant arrivals lived in squalid conditions, and, like all immigrants, worked under oppressive disadvantages. Some of the followers of William Miller eventually formed the Seventh-day Adventist Church. They reaffirmed the correctness of the date, but transferred what occurred on that date to a heavenly sanctuary, something beyond experiential confirmation. Like Isaac Newton, the new apocalyptic enthusiasm in America also found traditional Christianity in need of reformation. Newton had declared that besides the prevention of a Catholic becoming king of England it was necessary to identify Athanasius, the fourth century Church Father, as the one who perverted Christianity by introducing the notion that Christ was of the same divine nature as the Father, a point of view that two centuries later resulted in the doctrine of the Trinity. Seventh-day Adventists, besides declaring the Papacy the Antichrist, also claimed that all Christian churches had apostatized from true Christianity when the church under the leadership of a Pope had declare Sunday to be the Christian Sabbath and Protestant churches followed the papal decree. The founders of the church also followed Isaac Newton by declaring themselves against the Trinity; they did, however, uphold the identity of the Father and the Son. The Jehovah's Witnesses, who devised an apocalyptic trajectory of their own, not only denied the Trinity but also that the divine being who became incarnated as Jesus was of the same nature as the Father. Lately, evangelicals of the United States have been exercising significant political power in the foreign policy of their country by dictating what must be done with the State of Israel on the basis of their own peculiar apocalyptic interpretations. It used to be that apocalyptic enthusiasts were concerned only with the purification of the faithful by the rejection of doctrinal or ethical errors advanced by perverters of the Faith. These days they are breaking new ground by exercising political power to "hasten" the coming of the Lord by bringing about the condition in which, according to their interpretation of the apocalyptic "predictions," Jerusalem is to be found for the *Parousia* to take place. Some of those who promote these apocalyptic scenarios pose as experts on the history and politics of all the Islamic nations in the Middle East and assure their audiences that what is about to take place within them will precipitate a Third World War that will be the harbinger of the Second Coming of Christ.

The repeated attempts to read apocalyptic texts as allegorical descriptions of the course of history to the present, no doubt, have had an effect on the credibility of those who continue to recycle apocalyptic language to identify the time of the end with their own time. In our time the very powerful apocalyptic references to tours of the confines of the universe in reference to the elimination of evil powers have been dressed with modern technological advances and have become the coin of the realm of an entertainment industry that finds customers eager to escape from the prevalence of injustice and real wars. No one is expected to think that what they are reading or watching deals with historical realities. The appeal is to the emotions, but no action is expected of those who are entertained for an hour or two by an imaginary ride in the back seat of the airships of those who triumph over the cosmic forces of Evil. Satan who had a long career as the mastermind of Evil has also become the subject of satire. C. S. Lewis' *The Screwtape Letters*, which certainly have a heavy dose of irony, have now been made into a satiric stage drama. After its premier performance, *The Washington Post* declared that now *"the devil is an equal-opportunity entertainer."* The creative adaptation of apocalyptic scenarios to provide world-wide audiences escape routes from the world in which they live has transferred the language of apocalyptic from the realm of ethics to the realm of entertainment. Distractions from reality in imaginary supersonic aircraft have become more congenial than calls to prepare ones self to face the final judgment of a God who seeks vengeance on evil doers. Preachers claiming to have a monopoly on the interpretation of apocalyptic monsters, time-frames and diabolic armies have become an irrelevant side show.

It is not a coincidence that the popularity of apocalyptic stories as entertainment came after the detonation of atomic bombs over Hiroshima and Nagasaki. Until August 6, 1945, only God had the power to destroy the present world and put an end to history. That had been the basic premise of apocalypticism. God had the power to create the world, and God has the power to destroy the present fallen world and create a new one. Already during the Second World War, Dietrich Bonhoeffer declared that humans had become adults; he was referring to the fact that it was not necessary to bring in Satan to understand what evil does. The Hitler dictatorship was a revelation of pure evil to the degree that, he thought, justified its termination by the assassination of the Fuhrer. According to Bonhoeffer, humans are no longer adolescents in need of supervision.

Not only have human beings become adults in terms of their secular symbolic universe but, with atomic power now in their hands, they can determine the future of the world; they can bring God's creation to an end. The destruction of creation is no longer only in God's hands, as one of those involved in the construction of the atomic bomb pointed out citing a Japanese text. This alone makes necessary the formulation of a new theology for a whole new symbolic universe, a new cosmology. The future is now in unreliable and untrustworthy human hands. This new reality in our experience makes it absolutely necessary to reconsider how we express our faith in the creator God we worship. Theology is not made in heaven. It is the work of human beings who try to understand their own existence in relationship to God and the world he created. The new realities of our world call upon us to rethink the apocalyptic theology of the early Christians.

Besides the radical demands imposed by the human acquisition of power to destroy God's creation, the advances in our knowledge of how the cosmos in which we live works makes it impossible for us to do theology according to the ways in which biblical authors conceived of themselves, their world, and how God is related to both. Thus, for example, until recently it was universally agreed that the cosmos is a fixed structure. Nature is ruled by laws which are irrevocable, like "the laws of the Medes and the Persians." Trying to understand nature was trying to understand its laws. It is now clear that "the laws of nature" are actually human constructs, heuristic tools useful for the understanding of nature; they are not laws of nature but humanly conceived paradigms. Nothing in nature was fixed "at creation." Creation is not something that took place in the beginning, in *Urzeit*. Creation is continuously going on; it is a process where new things take place, and what already exists experiences mutations. Apocalypticism, on the other hand, presupposes that history was determined "before the foundation of the world," and that everything takes place at the time appointed. According to it, God has already fixed not only the date when the end will come but also every event in between.

This static understanding of creation is no longer credible. Humans have taken pictures of black holes in which new worlds are being created. The universe has no spatial limits and is continuously expanding. The Mariner probes launched in the 1960s to explore Mercury, Venus and Mars have shown that Venus and Mars had at one time great amounts of water. About four billion years ago they were bombarded by asteroids that left large craters on their surfaces. At that time, Mars not only had large lakes or seas, but also rivers that indicate that rain was a regular event. In fact, the largest waterfall in the solar system was on Mars. This means that Mars had at one time all the conditions that make life possible, and the plans for landing a human being on Mars in 2030 are designed to establish whether at one time there actually had been life in Mars.

In January 2006, NASA launched, by an Atlas V rocket from Cape Canaveral, the small spacecraft *New Horizons*. At a speed of 36,400 miles per hour, it was the fastest ever man-made object to leave Earth. Its mission was to explore beyond the solar system. The spacecraft is about the size and shape of a grand piano and weighs about one thousand pounds. In 2015 this spacecraft flew by Pluto, 3.2 billion miles from Earth, at a speed of 32,000 miles per hour taking the first sharp images of this icy blab of methane frost which takes 248 years to complete its extremely elliptical orbit. In 1930 Pluto had been identified as the planet farthest away from the sun. *New Horizons* showed that Pluto is not a planet. It is a "dwarf planet," a new distinction assigned to objects which meet only two of the three criteria established for planets. It is found in the Kuiper Belt, a zone of the solar system densely cluttered with cosmic debris that extends from the orbit of Neptune to fifty five times the distance from the sun to Earth. Not too long ago this region was thought to be empty space, but is now known to contain over eighty thousand objects of similar size to Pluto, besides an infinite number of smaller ones.

On January 1, 2019, *New Horizons* flew by a small object in the Kuiper Belt whose orbit scientists on earth had been able to trace and identified as 2014 MU69, also known as Ultima Thule. This made it possible for them to guide the spacecraft to it. Flying by Ultimate Thule, *New Horizons* proved that the solar planetary system that was formed about 4.6 billion years ago is made of planets formed by pebble accretion. At first the accumulation of debris on a pebble took place rather slowly. Once one had achieved enough mass to have gravitational force, it expanded rapidly and eventually by the balance of gravitational forces fell on an orbit around the sun. The signal sent by *New Horizons* while flying by Ultimate Thule, sent from four billion miles away, took six hours to reach earth. It revealed that it was formed at the beginning of the formation of the solar system. *New Horizons* has enough atomic fuel extracted from the radioactive decay of plutonium to last into the 2030s, making it possible for it to flyby past other objects in the Kuiper Belt. These explorations are changing the way in which we understand the universe in which human life takes place, and this new understanding cannot but call for a new way of expressing our faith in the God we worship as the creator of the universe.

All this means that the notion that God had fixed things in the whole universe at the beginning can no longer be held. Studies of our home planet Earth make the point even more apparent. It has been know for some time already that the tectonic plates on the surface of Earth are in constant motion. Maps of Earth millions of years back show continents that were at one time together and have been separating from each other over time. The abundance of seashells found on the surface of a high plateau demonstrate that what is now the surface of the land was once the floor of the ocean. Exploration of ice cores in the polar caps shows that at one time both polar regions were covered with luxuriant forests that sustained a great variety of fauna. These discoveries have brought about a new understanding of how life on earth is totally interdependent within ecological systems that are in a constant process of readjustments. Many variables are at work in the way things in nature and among human beings take place. In our universe many things are possible; therefore, things are unpredictable. If in doubt, pay attention to forecasters of the weather who think they know the laws of nature, or predictions about future political events by political pundits who think that history repeats itself. In our experience the key assumption for the formulation of apocalyptic scenarios, that history is pre-determined, has been removed.

Not only the advances in science and technology have changed our cosmology, our current understanding of ourselves has also changed our symbolic universe. Most significantly the collapse of the philosophy of the "chain of being," which conceived the being of everything in creation as fixed within a hierarchical structure, has given way to a new understanding of human freedom. According to the apostle Paul, humans are either slaves of sin or slaves of obedience (Rom. 6:16). Apocalypticists, as noticed in the previous chapters, for the most part saw no need to explain how everything had been predetermined by God and humans were to be punished for their disobedience because their view of human freedom was quite limited. In our days, feminists are having a hard time establishing their participation in the freedom of all human beings because, according to the chain of being, females are below males, and biblical authors wrote in terms of a symbolic universe which included the chain of being. Apocalypticists brought into the picture how things look from the divine perspective within their symbolic universe. Their aim was to emphasize the need to know that God's justice manifests itself as wrath and glory, so that human actions have ultimate consequences. The Protestant Reformers held fast to the notion of divine predestination, especially John Calvin. Martin Luther defended the freedom of Christians who live by the power of the life of Christ, but argued against Desiderius Erasmus' notion of the freedom of the will. He upheld the bondage of the will to divine foreknowledge. For him, the freedom of the Christian was entirely a gift of God's grace. For their part, Christian apocalyptic texts in the Bible refer to God's grace as primarily evident in their election even before the foundation of the world which, however, could be annulled by a recipient's idolatry. The apocalypticists conceived the Fall as having done major damage to God's creation. It affected humanity in particular to a greater degree than that envisioned by the prophets. It is within the horizon of the Fall that the apocalypticist understood the contours of human freedom. In our times, freedom and equal civil rights for all human beings is universally presupposed, even if its application is fragile. There is no ontological chain of being classifying individuals within a hierarchical cosmic structure. That in some quarters humanity is classified in racist and gender strata does not contradict that the notion that all human beings are equally endowed with freedom is the new norm. The statement drafted by the founders of the United States reflects the view of deists who were establishing the rights of citizens of an emerging political state. They wrote, *"All men are endowed by their Creator with the right to life, liberty and the pursuit of happiness."* Liberty as a political right granted by the state was a major development of the notion of freedom, even when conceived as a divine endowment of a god who does not interfere in human affairs. That statement does not actually affirm that liberty is essential to human nature, however, which is what western culture affirms today.

Post-modern humanity does not find relevant a gospel expressed in a totally foreign symbolic universe. Least of all the prediction of what must soon take place which has been predicted by members of previous generations *ad infinitum* without ever having taken place. Such preachers, whether they stand on a box in the public square or have command of a television station, are worthy only of being ridiculed in cartoons. Their apocalyptic scenarios only provide materials to the entertainment industry. Preachers who find eager listeners among those living in sections of the world where they feel trapped in miserable social, economic and political situations seem to think that their success confirms their apocalyptic interpretations of the present. That they have found eager listeners only shows that apocalyptic descriptions provide needed release from the frustrations of life in a world where justice and peace do not prevail even in republics with democratic constitutions. Their predictions of imminent deliverance from the tragic situation in which their listeners find themselves are going to join the multitude of such predictions offered by their predecessors. Offering apocalyptic trajectories for escape from the present rather than providing guidance for how to live well in the present is a misuse of the apocalyptic agenda. It does not differ much from what the entertainment industry does with apocalyptic scenarios.

This means that the apocalyptic texts in the Bible must be read for what they actually told audiences who found them relevant and, therefore, kept them for future generations. Obviously, they did not discard them when their predictions of what would happen soon did not take place, as certainly they would have done if they had thought that this was their main purpose. Any attempt to come to terms with their message must begin with the recognition that they propose different apocalyptic trajectories for different historical situations, while openly acknowledging that none of their predictions have been confirmed by their occurrence. This can only mean that their descriptions of the future were not their main concern, even if they claimed to have a revelation of what must soon take place. In fact, their different visions of the future shed a great deal of light on the different circumstances in which the authors and their audiences found themselves. The described future was conditioned by the threats being faced in the present.

The first prophet to give a description of the future, Ezekiel, was in exile in Babylon having to defend his trust in God while his contemporaries complained that God was unjustly punishing them and the neighboring nations were ridiculing the god of Israel as weak, incapable of preventing their exile. His answer was to announce that the exile would last only forty years and that when they were back in their land the neighboring nations would rise under the leadership of Gog of the land of Magog and attempt to take over their land. God would then show his power by totally destroying all the nations that now judge him to be a weak god. God would show his justice, however, by selecting who would enter the Promised Land. Not all those who would become free to leave Babylon at the end of the exile, or to leave Assyria after they were taken captives at the fall of Samaria, would enter the restored land. Only those individuals who remained loyal to the Covenant would live in the Promised Land.

Not too many years after, Zechariah, living in Jerusalem under Persian rule, finds it necessary to argue against dreams of an independent nation under the rule of a Messiah. Rather than being led by a king, as the people expected, they were going to be led by a High Priest in a restored temple. Their security in a hostile world would not come from walls that prevented attacks on Jerusalem and a warrior king on a white horse. Their future security would be guaranteed by their Almighty God. Jerusalem would continue to be a city without walls as a manifestation of God's providence. In the tradition of the prophets, Ezekiel and Zechariah envisioned the establishment of God's justice and power as a national restoration to political independence in the earthly Promised Land.

With *First Enoch*, a clear expansion of the horizon has taken place. The Book of the Watchers introduced angels as the ones responsible for what was going wrong in the earth. They not only defiled themselves by marrying women; they also brought in the arts of metallurgy and pharmacopeia. Most tragically, they corrupted God's creation by the introduction of a race of giants. They were responsible for the degradation of the human condition. The introduction of divine agents into the human drama expanded the geography of the universe to regions beyond human perception. Within this symbolic universe the author of the Book of the Watchers finds answers to the existential questions asked by those who live under foreign oppressors. Why do people rebel against God? Why do the righteous suffer? Where does evil come from? How can this be going on in God's world? To answer these questions, the author explores the possibility for God's justice becoming effective in the realm of the dead.

The author of *Daniel* demands that those who are tempted to worship other gods, and suffer the consequences from the power of human beings who exalt themselves pretending to be gods, refrain from idolatry. He justifies his demand by reaching down to the realm of the dead explored by the author of *First Enoch*. Those who have died and are asleep will be raised from death. This is a most significant expansion of the apocalyptic horizon into the land of darkness and doom. Those who refrain from idolatry, if they die on account of their faithfulness to God, will be raised from their graves to become shining stars. Those who worship other gods will rise to shame and everlasting contempt. In other words, one's life on earth must be lived in a way that is conscious that death is not the ultimate consequence of one's actions. The final judgment will determine the consequences of one's life on earth. Eternal life may be in glory or in shame. In *Daniel*, as in *Ezekiel* and *Zechariah*, the verdict does not apply to a nation but to individuals. The consequences of each individual's life will be revealed in an afterlife. The author of *Daniel* crossed the most important threshold in the development of apocalyptic thought. God's justice cannot be seen when looked at from within life in this fallen world. It must be looked at from within an expanded horizon that includes life after death.

The apostle of Jesus Christ, Paul of Tarsus, gave to the apocalyptic symbolic universe two radical features. He did not think that the problem of sin, already explored in *First Enoch*, was a Jewish problem caused by the rebellion of the people at Sinai, or that it was just a human problem caused by the emergence of a race of giants among men and women. It was a problem caused by Adam and Eve and their expulsion from the garden God had created for them. Death entered the world as the result of disobedience and they were blocked from access to the tree of life. Thus for Paul, sin and death are twins that rule the fallen world. He, however, distinguished biological death from the death that entered the world with the entrance of sin. Biological death is inconsequential. While in prison facing the possibility of death, he stated that whether or not he died executed by the Roman authorities made no difference to him (Phil. 1:20-21). For those who live in Christ, biological death has no ultimate significance because the Law no longer has power to condemn them (Rom. 8:1). The death that resulted from sin, eschatological death, however, has ultimate significance for those who do not live in Christ. In this way, Paul expanded the notion of the resurrection, first expressed in *Daniel*, by making the resurrection of Christ, a past event, the determining factor in the resurrection of human beings. Only those who crucify themselves with Christ will be raised. To all others, their biological death is also their eschatological death.

Paul also changed the apocalyptic notion of the day of the Lord. He maintained with all apocalypticists that on that day God intervenes in history in a radical way, destroying what exists and creating something new. But rather than to project that day into the future, Paul understood that God's radical intervention in history had taken place at the crucifixion and the resurrection of Jesus Christ. Jesus' crucifixion put an end to the reign of eschatological death because though he was sinless he had been put to death by the rulers of the spheres, the acolytes of the Devil. The resurrection of Christ in a spirit body was not the resuscitation of Jesus. It was the foundation of a new creation of life in the Spirit. In sum, the fallen creation's bondage to sin and death had been broken and humanity can now, on account of the grace demonstrated by God at the Christ Event, live free from sin and death in the Spirit that raised Christ. Paul is the only biblical apocalyptic author who does not see Christ sitting at the right hand of God having already conquered Satan, the Devil and all the angels who rebelled with him. He realizes that as long as humanity remains subject to biological death God's ultimate purpose has not been achieved. Therefore, he envisions that during the time between his resurrection and his *Parousia* Christ is *"destroying every rule and every authority and power. For he must reign until he has put all his enemies under his feet."* He does not envision the resurrection of some to shame and everlasting contempt. He does not say a word describing a succession of events, or how the enemies of God are going to be destroyed. His only description of the *Parousia* says that "the dead in Christ" will ascend to be with the Lord ahead of the those living in Christ at the time. In the process he has made a distinction between the day of the Lord and the *Parousia*, which he characterizes as the day of Christ. Paul's apocalyptic vision is based on his transferring of the day of the Lord from the end of history to the end of the power of the Law, or of anyone's conscience to condemn sinners to eschatological death.

The author of *To the Hebrews* is very much aware that he is living in the time of the end, but his symbolic universe is somewhat unique because it depends on a Stoic understanding of reality. His concern is to prevent followers of Christ from reverting to the Jewish sacrificial system in search of forgiveness from their sins. He, therefore, offers a detailed demonstration of the limitations of that system and of the superiority of the forgiveness offered by the sacrifice of Christ. After his resurrection from death on a cross, Christ now functions as High Priest in the true sanctuary in the hypostatic, heavenly realm. He is the real High Priest who actually is able to forgive sins, but also to clear the conscience of guilt. His apocalyptic scenario does not bring about the creation of a new world. In agreement with the cosmology of the Stoics, it brings about the removal of the present phenomenological world so that the preexisting, primary, hypostatic, material world may take its place. His is a very different apocalyptic trajectory, adding yet another one to the many streams of apocalyptic scenarios.

The author of the gospel of Mark understands that God's intervention in history took place in a most significant way in the life of Jesus, not just in his crucifixion and resurrection, as Paul had it. At his baptism by John for the remission of sins, Jesus had become the adopted Son of God, and during his life he had revealed the power of God by exorcising demons and subjecting the forces of evil by the power of his word. Mark's two stories of Jesus calming a storm in the Sea of Galilee are further evidence of Jesus apocalyptic presence. Writing at the time when the Romans had been in Palestine putting down the Jewish rebellion that brought about the destruction of the temple, Mark superimposes the *Parousia* onto the destruction of the temple. In his apocalyptic trajectory the two are simultaneous events.

Matthew, writing twenty years later is quite aware that the expectations of Mark have proven premature, and adjusts things to the obvious delay that is taking place. His way of doing it is by having Jesus warn his listeners not to become confused or distracted by the delay. Matthew's Jesus assures his disciples that his coming departure will not result in a temporary absence. He is going to be with them always as they go to all the world baptizing people for the remission of sins and teaching them to attain to perfection by keeping Jesus' exposition of the will of God. The end, in Matthew's symbolic universe, has been pushed further back into the future. In the meantime, Jesus is going to be with them at all times while they advance the goals of the kingdom of God.

Of all New Testament authors, the author of Luke and Acts is probably the one with the highest social position and best education. He wrote two volumes for the benefit of Theophilus, whom he addresses as *"most excellent,"* a distinction only given to someone with social and political standing. Aware that in the estimation of his audience, the crucifixion placed Jesus' reputation in jeopardy by dishonoring him, Luke with a deftly ironic touch consistently describes the Roman authorities as supportive of, or attracted to Jesus and his followers. He characterizes the Jewish leaders as the ones who falsely accuse him and brought about the crucifixion of an innocent man. They are the disturbers of the peace, the ones who should be charged with sedition against Rome. Jesus' "kingdom" is not of this world. As a peaceful spiritual reality it is already present among his followers as they remain together to express love for their neighbors and acts of mercy for the benefit of the dispossessed. Jesus not only appeared in his own physical body to the disciples to confirm his resurrection, but also spent forty days teaching them prior to his ascension to heaven before their very eyes. The promised descent of the Holy Spirit upon his disciples empowered them to bring about reconciliation between God and humanity on account of God's abundant and anticipatory forgiveness. Luke's vision of the future is one in which the *Parousia* has been pushed even further back in the horizon. Thus, he took away all drama from the *Parousia,* even if he could not discard *in toto* the apocalyptic features of the synoptic tradition.

The author of *To the Thessalonians II* engages in an argument against those who, apparently, had failed to understand Paul's distinction between the Day of the Lord and the *Parousia*. Christians who had been nursed within an apocalyptic community, but were living at the end of the first century, no doubt, were quite aware of the delay of the *Parousia*. It would seem that some in Thessalonica had decided that the best way to answer the question of the delay was to affirm that the *Parousia* had already taken place, thus absolutizing one of the two poles in Paul's conception of God's intervention in history. To combat the notion that the *Parousia* had already happened, the author of *To the Thessalonians II* points out that before the *Parousia* can take place a series of events must take place, according to a traditional apocalyptic trajectory which he considers to be the true one, the one affirmed by what he considered the faith of the elect. It would seem, however, that he is more interested in condemning the way of life adopted by those holding that the *Parousia* had already taken place that he is in describing what must happen before it can take place. The trajectory he describes in broad outline conforms with traditional expectations of increased sufferings.

Unlike Paul, who describes the time between the resurrection, the Day of the Lord, and the *Parousia* as the time when Christ is engaged in a cosmic struggle with his enemies, John, the author of *Revelation,* understands that the cosmic forces of evil have been defeated; Christ is sitting on the throne with his Father, and human surrogates of the Devil are trying to derail the faithful worshipers of the creator God. He describes a scenario which assures his readers that God will avenge their sufferings on the Dragon, the beast from the sea, the beast from the land with seven horns and ten heads, and all the evil surrogates of the Dragon. They will be raised also at the end, and will think that it is within their power to undo God's future for the elect. In fact, they will be raised only to be burned with fire throughout eternity. Earlier in the book, the author describes how all the women and men who worship the beast and its image are killed; then God called upon all the birds of prey to come and gorge themselves on their corpses. This is a sadistic apocalyptic trajectory that can only provoke repulsion today. The apocalyptic identification of the gospel with the final judgment and God's vengeance is not at all good news, gospel.

With the passage of time, Christians in different regions of the empire experienced different difficulties. Some faced persecutions at the hands of neighbors who resented their unwillingness to join them in the activities in which previously they had participated with them; some suffered injustice from relatives who disinherited them. Others confronted the appeal of a different understanding of what the Gospel was about, or thought that the emergence of an official structure of authority within the community was uncalled for and a denial of the power of the Spirit. The delay of the *Parousia*, of course, was even more troublesome with the passage of time. The General Epistles I have examined address these situations from the perspective of those in authority claiming to be written by Peter and Jude, the brother of James. The author of *First Peter* justifies the suffering being experienced by Christians on account of their faithfulness to Christ as a means of purification, similar to what is done to gold nuggets. Their suffering happens in the pattern established by the suffering of Christ; according to it, suffering flowers into glory. He assures his readers that their suffering is actually a sign that the time of the end is here.

The author of *Jude* finds himself arguing against some of the members of the community who are bringing about divisions by challenging the authority of its leaders. His agenda is to emphasize

God's willingness and ability to punish those who disobey their leaders. There is no lack of examples of God's punishment of those who had been elected to salvation, but become rebellious. God's final judgment overrules God's grace. The author of *Second Peter* recycles the contents of *Jude* to argue against those in the community who are denying the promise of the *Parousia*. The delay was having its effects. The scoffers of those who still believed in a *soon* coming affirmed that since they were still living in the same world, their expectations of a new age were unfounded. The author deploys the arguments he found in *Jude* against the scoffers, and rationalizes the delay by giving it a purpose and pointing out that the human way of counting time is not God's way. He ends his defense of the soon coming of the *Parousia*, pointing out why he is writing to them. It is to emphasize that the soon coming calls for a life of holiness and godliness now.

This quick review of the apocalyptic texts I have analyzed shows that their authors were not at all concerned with predicting the future. Their predictions were adapted to the demands of the circumstances in which they lived. The apocalyptic scenarios were props for the main item in their agenda which, contrary to what apocalyptic enthusiasts claim, was not to predict how history would end. On those terms, apocalyptic texts have lost all credibility. The reason they wrote, their objective, their goal, their end was to encourage faithfulness to God's will in their conduct, and to warn against turning away from the path they had taken when they accepted God's grace and became heirs to the promised life in the kingdom of justice and peace.

As predictors of coming events, apocalyptic scrolls have been recycled over and over again to the point of having become fodder for ridicule and entertainment. That they continue to be used for that purpose does not legitimatize such use. The expectations resulting from such adulterations are usually short lived and sometimes tragic. The deaths of the followers of Jim Jones in Guyana, the events at the Branch Davidian compound just outside of Waco, TX, some twenty-five years ago, and the suffering and dying taking

The End of the Scroll

place in the Middle East, to a large degree, due to the inability of the president of the United States to be a creditable mediator of a peace agreement between the Palestinian Authority and the State of Israel on account of the political power of evangelical Christians who hold a particular apocalyptic trajectory, are powerful reminders of what can result from the application of apocalyptic scenarios by misguided believers. Those who claim to have the key that unlocks the secrets of the scroll give to its symbolic language whatever meaning fits their own limited imaginations. The results produced by extreme apocalyptic messianic hopes should be cautionary tales to those who continue to arbitrarily match ancient descriptions of contemporary events in mythological symbols to events in the twenty-first century, as if they were reading an allegory. To many, of course, they are reason enough for dismissing apocalyptic texts all together. The Jews did that when they established the canon of Tanakh in the second century C.E., after the fiascos of two wars with Rome fueled by apocalyptic dreams. Many Christians have done that by just ignoring and forgetting them.

My purpose in writing this book has been to examine these texts to find out what their authors thought they were doing when they felt the need to write them. My survey reveals that their objective, the end they were pursuing, was to give guidance for living in the present under chaotic, confusing circumstances which put in doubt God's control of the world he had created. Their aim was not to give information about the future, but to give guidance for the present. They appealed to the imagination and used the symbolic language of ancient myths because they knew that the conduct of life is not guided by rules and commands but by the power of emotions that are energized by the imagination more than by reason alone. Given the way in which humans experience life in this world, reason alone can never demonstrate God's justice as the controlling power over his world. The complexities of existence can best be illuminated imaginatively. Factual prose that appeals to logic does not reach the limits of the mind's conceptual range. To communicate a sense of being secure in a confusing world so as to energize and guide the way one lives a language that appeals to the imagination is indispensable.

The apocalypticists understood that the crisis of human existence in a world where injustice and violence prevail was more dire than that conceived by the prophets of Israel. This crisis could not be solved by the tools used by God described by the prophets: locusts, drought, famine, foreign armies, etc. This crisis required a direct, personal intervention that resulted not just in the restoration of the Jews as a nation, but the restoration of the ultimate purpose of God at creation. Therefore, the only language up to the task of describing God's personal involvement in the solution of a cosmic crisis was the language of the ancient creation myths which was alive and meaningful in the minds of their contemporaries, but is incongruous to many today. That language described God's direct intervention to bring about the termination of chaos and the creation of cosmos. Our understanding of the cosmos is one informed by the explorations taking place on account of sciences that are making possible new amazing technologies, and deepening our understanding of social, economic and psychological forces at work in the lives of human beings. The language used by those who worship the Creator God today must reflect the contemporary understanding of the universe and the human situation in it. It must be able to transcend the limits of what historical and scientific descriptions are able to depict and establish the power and the justice of God not only by what a believer says, but also by how believers conduct their lives in society.

The irony of the modern quest for what is ultimately real is that as natural phenomena are stripped of what scientists and philosophers designate as the superficial world of appearances in which humanity lives, they present as real colorless, soundless, impalpable, skeletal, basic structures, and they communicate their discoveries in scientific terms. The symbols of scientific language are meaningful among scientists, but are not meaningful to the public at large; they are not present in the language of the imagination that informs daily life. I have argued that the apocalyptic language that uses ancient myths of creation that have lost meaningfulness, to a large degree as technology based on scientific discoveries has allowed the exploration of the cosmos and the course of history has brought about a deeper understanding of how human beings function as whole persons endowed with freedom. Pointing out that the language of mathematics and the sciences that have facilitated the modern understanding of ourselves in the world is irrelevant to the way in which people act on a daily basis does not take away my respect and gratitude for the advances in both the physical and the human sciences. Philosophers who have attempted to uphold God's justice, just as the ancient apocalypticists also attempted, by using logic have not been convincing to those who understand them and are totally irrelevant to those who do not. To recognize that the language of mathematics, of pure logic, does not provide guidance for the conduct of life is to accept its limitations; it does nothing to the effectiveness of mathematics and logic within their intellectual horizons. To live confidently in the present the imagination must work with the certainty, the security that faith in God's justice and hope based in God's ultimate sovereignty provide. But the language of faith cannot be the language of ancient creation myths taken as if they were historical accounts or cryptic descriptions of future events. The end sought by the writers of apocalyptic scrolls was the affirmation of God's power and justice which only faith can envision and actualize in behavior and worship.

To understand the message of the Christian Gospel it is essential to take seriously the goal, the end sought by those who used apocalyptic language. They were men and women of faith who lived in different symbolic universes. We can admire their creativity in the recycling of mythical creatures as apocalyptic symbols, but we must recognize that, taken as divine predictions of future history, they cannot communicate faith in the creator God in our time. It is a gross mistake, however, to think that we can dismiss their texts and understand what Christianity is about. What is necessary is to recognize that those who used this language were not concerned to describe what would actually take place in the future.

No one writing about the past in antiquity pretended to be doing that; therefore, much less did those who "predicted" the future by retelling the past. They were concerned with giving purpose and meaning to their lives in a very confusing present that offered little hope for the future. Their excursions into the future were meant to emphasize the need to appropriate both the past and the future for guidance in the present. The diverse trajectories of future events described by apocalyptic writers reveal that knowledge of the future was not what prompted them to write. Their aim was to insist that, in spite of all present evidence to the contrary, God's sovereignty is to be taken seriously. Therefore, we need to live now as women and men who believe in the God who created the world and behave according to his will. As the saying goes, acts speak louder than words. The Gospel announces that God is fully involved with the world and is graciously providing for both the physical and the spiritual needs of his people. The good life must be in accord with God's love for the world. Believers live as lovers of God because he loved them first (Rom. 5:5).

Those of us in the twenty-first century who are heirs of the faith of Abraham and believe the God who created heaven and earth find ourselves having to radically change our understanding of creation on account of the scientific and technological advances which have allowed us to explore its wonders. Our increased knowledge of the cosmos and of our interior lives, as such, does not provide guidance for living meaningful and fulfilling lives in the present. For that we need not only to understand the past; we need also to have a compelling vision of the future. For those of us who believe that the significant past was the intervention of God in the death and the resurrection of Christ, the only significant future is the future of Christ, that is, his resurrection as the establishment of a new creation. This is something that only faith can grasp. Faith grasps God as creator both of the world and of our future. Christ's resurrection gave him a future with God on account of the faith he demonstrated facing an undeserved death. As a result of his faith, he lives forever with God. That is the future that we believe will be for those who live believing in the God who raised Christ from the dead and hoping that God will also give them life with him. It is with this vision of the past and the future that Christians find meaning and guidance for life in the present. Today's Christians experience or are witnesses to all sorts of injustices. This makes the apocalyptic agenda always relevant, but not as a description of the future. Its message is to affirm faith in God when experience does not support it. Faith always transcends the evidence.

Paul radically revised the apocalyptic vision and identified the crucifixion and the resurrection of Christ as the Day of the Lord. By those events God had brought to an end the reign of sin and death and created new life in the Spirit. It was by the power of the Spirit that raised Christ from the dead that now Christians live empowered and guided by the Spirit. This is a very powerful Gospel with which to live the present. Paul understood that the final judgment was a reality all humans were to face, but he did not place it as the most prominent feature on the horizon. The future was God's promise of full life in the Spirit based on the resurrection of Christ. His radical redirection of the apocalyptic imagination to a past Christ Event and a future with Christ is a model for those who believe in the God who created the world and is bound to fulfill the purpose for which he created it.

For Paul, baptism is not just a rite of passage; it is an event that is stamped into memory and illumines the imagination so that those who are baptized live crucified with Christ and are given life by the power of the Spirit who raised Christ from the dead. They now live in Christ even while still living in the fleshly body of a fallen creation. As part of the new creation they are no longer under the Law that imposes eschatological death on transgressors. They live empowered and guided by the Spirit that not only now illumines their imagination to see their future in Christ but will give them also a spirit body at the *Parousia*. This is the future that empowers those in Christ to live as members of the body of Christ.

Paul's hope for life with Christ was not an escape from the present life in the world. He was not a mystic who sought solitude away from the maddening crowds. He lived fully engaged with the present world in which diversity and conflicts were found everywhere. As he confessed, *"For though I am free from all men, I have made myself a slave to all, ... To the Jews I became a Jew ...; to those under the law I became as one under the law — though not being myself under the law ... To those outside the law I became as one outside the law — not being without law toward God but under the law of Christ ... To the weak I became weak ... I have become all things to all men, that I might by all means save some. I do it all for the sake of the gospel"* (1 Cor. 9:19-23). Paul's apocalyptic Gospel forces him to face the present with all its challenges fully engaged with his fellow human beings. That is what Paul understood to be the significance of Christ's apocalyptic crucifixion and resurrection, and what those who at their baptism participate in and receive the benefits of Christ's death and resurrection must now live for. They must actualize the love of God for the world by the way they live in society. Just as Christ revealed the love of God for the world when he by faith went to an unmerited death in fulfillment of God's will, so also those who live by faith in God's past action in Christ's death and resurrection and hope in a future with Christ, reveal God's love by manifesting their faith and hope in their daily lives. They use their imagination under the guidance of the Spirit to determine the way in which to live according to God's will in the present, while still living in a body of flesh by the power and under the guidance of the Spirit, that is, the law of Christ. *Apocalypsis* means revelation. What the Gospel reveals is the power of God to give life to those who are dead now in bodies of flesh, so that they may live as manifestations of the power and the justice of God.

These days the apocalyptic imagination is flourishing on account of the insecurity and the fear in which people in different social and political situations live. Security has always been a primary need; in our time it has become an obsession. The populist political rhetoric filling the airways in most countries provides an escape similar to that of cosmic battles or apocalyptic preaching on the screens. What is needed is a theological construct based on the end pursued by those who wrote the scrolls in apocalyptic language. The Gospel of justice and peace provides security by affirming the sovereignty of God. In our time what is needed is to allow the imagination to see that God loves the world he created, even if sometimes it is difficult to experience it. Our further understanding of human freedom must inform our theological constructs of the present, not historical allegorizations of apocalyptic texts as divine predictions that exhibit theological immaturity in descriptions of bodies eaten by untold maggots and torments in never-ending fires. The language of faith that appeals to the imagination is quite intelligible to reasonable people who understand its function; probably more so than logical arguments that reason alone produces as explanations of the sovereignty and the righteousness of God. The biblical apocalypticists expressed their faith with the language that envisioned the universal sovereignty of their God to their contemporaries. Those who wish to affirm the sovereignty and justice of God today must use language that upholds God in a way that is meaningful today. Faith in the God who creates must be expressed. The language with which to express it is the language of love for neighbors and enemies, which is always being created by the experiences of those who live by faith and hope. When faith and hope are expressed in actions that demonstrate one's interest in the Other, the language reveals that Christians know themselves loved by God, and their God is eager to prodigally pour his love on sinners.

MORE BIBLICAL THEOLOGY FROM HEROLD WEISS

When Weiss walks you through the Gospel of John, the maze turns to amazement. You will discover another world with all the favorable conditions for a better life.
Dr. Abraham Terian
St. Nersess Armenian Seminary

This text will inspire pastors, professors, seminarians, and educated laypersons.
– Bruce Epperly, PhD, author of *Experiencing God in Suffering: A Journey with Job*, *Philippians: A Participatory Study Guide*, and *Process Theology: Embracing Adventure with God*

www.ingramcontent.com/pod-product-compliance
Lightning Source LLC
Chambersburg PA
CBHW021141160426
43194CB00007B/645